Leveraging Blockchain for Future-Ready Libraries

KR Senthilkumar
Sri Krishna Arts and Science College, India

R. Jagajeevan
Sri Krishna Arts and Science College, India

G. Krishnakumar
Nehru Institute of Engineering and Technology, India

IGI Global
Scientific Publishing
Publishing Tomorrow's Research Today

Vice President of Editorial — Melissa Wagner
Managing Editor of Acquisitions — Mikaela Felty
Managing Editor of Book Development — Jocelynn Hessler
Production Manager — Mike Brehm
Cover Design — Phillip Shickler

Published in the United States of America by
IGI Global Scientific Publishing
701 East Chocolate Avenue
Hershey, PA, 17033, USA
Tel: 717-533-8845
Fax: 717-533-8661
E-mail: cust@igi-global.com
Website: https://www.igi-global.com

Library of Congress Cataloging-in-Publication Data

Names: Senthilkumar, K. R., 1983- editor. | Jagajeevan, R., 1975- editor. | Kumar, G. 1988- editor.
Title: Leveraging blockchain for future-ready libraries / edited by Senthilkumar KR, R. Jagajeevan, G. Kumar.
Description: Hershey, PA : IGI Global Scientific Publishing, 2025. | Includes bibliographical references and index. | Summary: "The primary objective of this book is to explore the transformative potential of blockchain technology in modernizing and future-proofing libraries"-- Provided by publisher.
Identifiers: LCCN 2024052912 (print) | LCCN 2024052913 (ebook) | ISBN 9798369377833 (hardcover) | ISBN 9798369377871 (paperback) | ISBN 9798369377840 (ebook)
Subjects: LCSH: Blockchains (Databases)--Library applications. | Libraries--Information technology. | Library science--Technological innovations. | LCGFT: Essays.
Classification: LCC Z678.93.B56 .L48 2025 (print) | LCC Z678.93.B56 (ebook) | DDC 025.00285/57588--dc23/eng/20250103
LC record available at https://lccn.loc.gov/2024052912
LC ebook record available at https://lccn.loc.gov/2024052913

British Cataloguing in Publication Data
A Cataloguing in Publication record for this book is available from the British Library.

Table of Contents

Detailed Table of Contents

patterns, word frequency analysis, institutional rankings, and types of documents. The data sets have been visualised through software tools such as "CiteSpace and VOSviewer" to draw publication output maps and research cluster tracking of the top 20 active countries in blockchain studies. A similar analysis has been undertaken to track the research productivity and citation impact of the top 20 institutions actively contributing in this area. It is also noteworthy that CiteSpace has played a very important role in generating the visualisation data that significantly contributed to obtaining an overview of the research landscape.

Rajkumar N., Alliance School of Advanced Computing, India
P. Subalakshmi, Acumen India Ltd., India
Viji C., Alliance School of Advanced Computing, India
Mohanraj Arunachalam, Sri Eshwar College of Engineering, India
Balusamy Nachiappan, Prologis, USA
D. Preethi, Jain University, India

The integration of blockchain and the internet of things (IoT) generation gives a transformative opportunity for the library sector, providing improvements in safety, efficiency, and personal delight. This chapter explores the privileged permissions and demanding situations of adopting those technologies within libraries. Blockchain offers a relaxed, tamper-evidence ledger for transactions and information, enhancing the integrity and transparency of library operations. IoT permits actual-time tracking and automation of various strategies, collectively with stock manipulation, man or woman authentication, and automatic test-ins and take-a-look-at-outs. However, implementing those technologies is not without demanding situations, together with technical complexity, excessive prices, records privacy issues, regulatory compliance, and interoperability issues.

N. Karthick, Sri Krishna College of Arts and Science, Coimbatore, India
P. Nithya, PSG College of Arts and Science, Coimbatore, India
R. Rajkumar, RVS College of Arts and Science, India

Blockchain technology, initially popularized through its association with cryptocurrencies, has evolved into a versatile tool with transformative potential across various sectors, including libraries. By leveraging these features, libraries can enhance their operations in areas such as secure transactions, digital rights management, preservation of cultural heritage, and streamlined resource sharing.

data, and cryptocurrency metrics, the authors aim to uncover the profound effects and potential of these technologies. The financial data component encompasses historical stock prices, trading volumes, market capitalization.

The process of multiple-criteria decision making (MCDM) involves selecting the best option from various alternatives. Decision-making regarding blockchain technology often deals with vague and imprecise knowledge, making it a typical multi-criteria group decision-making problem. This chapter extends the TOPSIS method to address MCDM problems using heptapartitioned neutrosophic sets (HNS), characterizing each alternative's value and each criterion's weight with heptapartitioned neutrosophic numbers. It identifies the importance of criteria and alternatives through the heptapartitioned neutrosophic weighted averaging (HNWA) operator. A numerical experiment demonstrates the method's effectiveness in choosing blockchain technology, using data collected from SKASC college academic libraries.

The rapid advancement of blockchain technology is poised to transform the landscape of information management and library services. This chapter offers an in-depth training program to equip librarians with essential knowledge and practical skills to leverage this groundbreaking technology. This program delves into the core concepts of blockchain, exploring its applications in data security, digital asset management, and transparent record-keeping. By understanding and utilizing blockchain technology, librarians can lead their institutions in adopting innovative practices that align with the digital evolution. This comprehensive education initiative not only demystifies blockchain but also empowers librarians to become pioneers in integrating advanced technologies within the library sector, ensuring they remain at the cutting edge of information management.

Blockchain technology deals a transformative approach to enhancing access to information by leveraging its dispersed and apparent nature. Traditional information access systems often face challenges such as restricted access, censorship, and inequalities in information dissemination. Blockchain decentralizes control, enabling a more resilient structure for accessing and sharing information, which is particularly beneficial in regions with restricted access. This technology democratizes data control, ensuring that no single entity can restrict the flow of information, thereby promoting inclusivity and diversity in knowledge sharing. In the realm of scholarly publishing, blockchain facilitates open access models, reducing costs and increasing the accessibility of research. Authors can retain control over their work while sharing it globally, accelerating the dissemination of knowledge and fostering greater collaboration and innovation. This can help underserved communities gain access to essential information and services, promoting a more inclusive and equitable digital world.

Blockchain technology can revolutionize library systems by addressing data integrity, user privacy, and digital rights management with its decentralization, transparency, and security. This study explores integrating smart contracts for efficient operations, decentralized digital archives, and enhanced metadata cataloging. It examines blockchain's interoperability with AI and IoT, predicting significant advancements in library services. Through case studies and a strategic adoption framework, the research offers valuable insights and best practices for library professionals. Findings indicate blockchain can address inefficiencies and security issues, creating resilient, innovative libraries. Practical implications include a roadmap for seamless blockchain integration, ensuring secure, efficient information ecosystems. This pioneering study highlights blockchain's potential to modernize library services and synergize with emerging technologies, keeping libraries at the forefront of digital advancements.

This chapter focuses on artificial intelligence and how it compares to the actual interlibrary loan (ILL) and resource sharing in libraries. Libraries have always been the core of information exchange and community involvement, changing the way manual methods of service serving have been practiced. Nevertheless, the internet age has speeded up the change in the way knowledge is obtained and shared, challenging library practices. The use of AI in libraries, therefore, is a way that the libraries can use to simplify the ILL procedure, more reliably predict users' demands and even enhance experiences through utilizing automated systems. AI's support to improve decision-making goes hand in hand with machine learning, natural language processing, predictive analytics, and automation for the library to benefit from productivity and accessibility in the sharing of resources, thus setting the stage for more adaptive and cutting-edge solutions to emerge in the current digital epoch.

In the digital era, libraries are evolving beyond their traditional roles as repositories of physical books to become dynamic hubs for digital information. This chapter investigates the integration of blockchain technology and collaborative networks to enhance the management and distribution of library resources. Blockchain's decentralized and immutable ledger offers a secure, transparent, and efficient method for tracking the ownership, usage, and distribution of digital assets, reducing the reliance on centralized systems. This study explores the potential of blockchain to support the creation of decentralized, interoperable library systems that enhance collaboration among institutions, ensure data integrity, and provide more equitable access to knowledge. Through an analysis of current implementations and theoretical models, this research identifies the opportunities and challenges of adopting blockchain in library systems and proposes strategies for overcoming barriers to implementation.

The advent of blockchain technology offers revolutionary possibilities for various industries, including the library sector. This chapter delves into the application of blockchain in establishing collaborative library networks, with a particular focus on its advantages for knowledge sharing and resource pooling. Blockchain's decentralized, secure, and transparent ledger system provides an innovative solution to many challenges faced by libraries today. In collaborative library networks, blockchain can ensure the maintenance of a unified, tamper-proof catalog of resources. This decentralized cataloging system guarantees that all participating libraries have access to consistent and current information, reducing redundancy and discrepancies. Moreover, blockchain facilitates efficient tracking and management of interlibrary loans through smart contracts, which automate the processes of loan requests, approvals, and returns. Additionally, blockchain technology can significantly improve the management of intellectual property and digital rights within library networks.

This chapter explores the integration of spectral fuzzy graph theory with blockchain technology to enhance academic collaboration networks within digital libraries, with special emphasis on the Tamil Nadu Library system. Fuzzy graph theory is employed to model the uncertainties and varying strengths in academic relationships, while spectral analysis uncovers key collaboration patterns and influential researchers. Blockchain technology ensures the integrity and transparency of stored academic records, using smart contracts to automate verification processes and securely manage permissions. This combined approach optimizes resource allocation, enhances data security, and improves the efficiency of research management, providing a robust framework for fostering collaboration and innovation within the Tamil Nadu's Academic and Library networks.

This chapter explores using SELJE Topological Space and blockchain technology to enhance the management and preservation of frequently used books in a central library. The library's valuable and costly books have limited physical copies, unable to meet high demand. Many essential books are not readily available online. SELJE Topological Space helps identify core books for digital preservation. Blockchain technology securely tracks transactions and preserves digital archives, making them accessible and preserved for future use. Data were collected from the institution and local libraries in Coimbatore. This method addresses limited copies, optimizes resource management, and protects the library's collection from loss, ensuring availability and long-term preservation of rare, significant books.

In the digital transformation era, preserving library resources has become increasingly vital. This chapter explores the integration of greedy algorithms within fuzzy graphic matroids for efficient library resource preservation, enhanced by index coding and blockchain technology. Fuzzy graphic matroids provide a mathematical structure to model and optimize resource allocation under uncertainty, capturing the relationships and dependencies in library systems. The greedy algorithm selects the most critical edges in the fuzzy graphic matroid, ensuring the independence property is maintained while optimizing the selection process. Index coding minimizes the number of transmissions required for data retrieval. Integrating index coding and blockchain technology ensures efficient resource allocation, enhanced data retrieval, and secure library records. The proposed framework presents a novel and comprehensive solution to the challenges of digital preservation in modern libraries. The practical application and benefits of this approach are demonstrated with an example.

Blockchain technology, celebrated for its secure and transparent framework, extends beyond its cryptocurrency origins to offer substantial benefits across various sectors, including libraries. This chapter examines the transformative impact of blockchain on library services by enhancing data security, streamlining operations, and fostering a collaborative environment for knowledge sharing. It explores how blockchain can address critical challenges faced by libraries, such as safeguarding patron data, managing digital rights, and improving interlibrary resource sharing. By providing a detailed analysis of blockchain's potential applications in library systems, this chapter aims to offer practical insights and recommendations for integrating blockchain technology to advance library management and services. The discussion includes real-world examples, potential future developments, and strategic recommendations to harness blockchain for more efficient and secure library operations.

Preface

In an increasingly digital world, libraries face the critical challenge of staying relevant, secure, and effective in serving their communities. As centers of knowledge, libraries have always adapted to technological advances, and today is no different. Blockchain technology, once synonymous solely with cryptocurrency, offers immense potential to revolutionize how libraries operate, ensuring they remain integral to the communities they serve.

The book, Leveraging Blockchain for Future-Ready Libraries, seeks to explore the myriad ways in which blockchain can transform library services. Blockchain's decentralized, transparent, and secure framework has the potential to address some of the most pressing issues in modern libraries—from safeguarding data integrity to enhancing digital preservation. With blockchain, libraries can build a secure infrastructure to protect personal data, create tamper-proof archives, and offer more seamless and innovative services to patrons.

This comprehensive guide will educate, explore, and inspire librarians, administrators, policymakers, and technology enthusiasts alike. It delves into the practical applications of blockchain in the library sector, drawing on real-world case studies, technical guidance, and visionary insights into the future of library operations.

Overview of the Chapters

In *Leveraging Blockchain for Future-Ready Libraries*, each chapter delves into unique and forward-thinking approaches to applying blockchain technology in library operations, research, and resource management.

Chapter 1 explores how blockchain can revolutionize academic libraries by enhancing research collaboration. It highlights how blockchain's decentralized, transparent platform secures and streamlines data sharing, ensuring data authenticity and promoting trust in academic research. By employing blockchain in manuscript submission and peer review, libraries can create efficient and transparent scholarly publishing workflows.

Chapter 2 provides a bibliometric analysis of Indian blockchain research from 2014 to 2023, tracking trends and productivity. Using visualization tools like CiteSpace and VOSviewer, the chapter offers insights into Indian institutions' contributions to blockchain research and positions India within the global blockchain research landscape.

Chapter 3 examines the integration of Blockchain and the Internet of Things (IoT) within libraries, discussing how these technologies improve safety, efficiency, and automation. It also identifies challenges such as data privacy, technical complexity, and regulatory compliance that come with adopting these advanced technologies in the library sector.

Chapter 4 expands on the diverse applications of blockchain in libraries, including secure transactions, digital rights management, and resource sharing. The chapter emphasizes blockchain's ability to enhance operational efficiency, data security, and the preservation of cultural heritage within library ecosystems.

Chapter 5 focuses on real-world case studies showcasing blockchain's role in libraries and financial services, particularly in promoting financial inclusion. These case studies reveal how decentralized networks, blockchain-enabled educational credentials, and digital rights management have transformed library services and access to resources for underserved populations.

Chapter 6 analyzes the intersection of blockchain and artificial intelligence (AI) in the financial industry, underscoring the transformative potential of these technologies. By examining financial market data and blockchain records, the chapter reveals the significant impact of AI-blockchain integration on financial services and how libraries might harness these developments.

Chapter 7 addresses how decision-making regarding blockchain technology can benefit from advanced methods like the Heptapartitioned Neutrosophic Sets (HNS). This approach offers a solution to multi-criteria group decision-making problems, demonstrating its effectiveness in academic libraries, particularly in selecting blockchain technology for adoption.

Chapter 8 offers a training program for librarians, designed to equip them with essential knowledge and skills to integrate blockchain technology. The program highlights the importance of blockchain for data security, digital asset management, and transparent record-keeping, ensuring librarians lead in adopting innovative practices.

Chapter 9 discusses blockchain's potential to democratize access to information by decentralizing control, enhancing inclusivity, and reducing barriers such as censorship and restricted access. Blockchain's role in open access models is also explored, offering an inclusive approach to scholarly publishing and knowledge sharing.

Chapter 10 explores blockchain's role in enhancing library systems, including smart contracts for efficient operations, digital archives, and metadata cataloging. The chapter provides a roadmap for blockchain integration, highlighting its synergy with AI and IoT to modernize library services.

Chapter 11 evaluates how AI can transform interlibrary loans and resource sharing, enhancing decision-making and automation. The chapter demonstrates how libraries can use AI technologies to improve user experience, predict demand, and streamline resource-sharing operations.

Chapter 12 investigates blockchain's potential in building collaborative library networks. Through decentralized systems, blockchain enhances the management of digital assets and resource sharing, offering efficient methods for tracking ownership, usage, and distribution among libraries.

Chapter 13 highlights how blockchain can strengthen collaborative library networks by creating a unified, decentralized catalog system. This ensures up-to-date, tamper-proof resource sharing across libraries, while smart contracts automate interlibrary loans and enhance intellectual property management.

Chapter 14 explores how spectral fuzzy graph theory, when integrated with blockchain, can enhance academic collaboration networks. Focused on the Tamil Nadu Library system, this chapter discusses how blockchain ensures data integrity and transparency, optimizing collaboration and resource management.

Chapter 15 examines how blockchain and SELJE Topological Space can improve the management and preservation of frequently used books in libraries. The chapter provides solutions for addressing limited copies, protecting valuable collections, and ensuring long-term preservation.

Chapter 16 presents a novel framework for digital preservation, integrating greedy algorithms and fuzzy graphic matroids with blockchain technology. By optimizing resource allocation and data retrieval, the chapter demonstrates a practical approach to modernizing library preservation strategies.

Chapter 17 concludes by offering a detailed analysis of blockchain's potential to transform library management. The chapter provides strategic recommendations and practical insights for integrating blockchain technology to enhance security, streamline operations, and foster collaboration in modern library services.

We are deeply grateful to the contributors who have provided their expertise and experience to make this volume a valuable resource for libraries worldwide. We believe that through embracing blockchain technology, libraries can continue their mission to uphold the integrity, accessibility, and dissemination of knowledge in a rapidly evolving digital landscape.

As you read this book, we hope you will be inspired by the possibilities that blockchain presents and feel empowered to explore how it can be implemented in your own institutions.

K.R. Senthilkumar
Sri Krishna Arts and Science College, India

R. Jagajeevan
Sri Krishna Arts and Science College, India

G. Krishnakumar
Nehru Institute of Engineering and Technology, India

Chapter 1
Blockchain in Academic Libraries

Mageshkumar Naarayanasamy Varadarajan
https://orcid.org/0009-0004-7592-0757
Independent Researcher, USA

Viji C.
https://orcid.org/0000-0002-2759-8896
Alliance School of Advanced Computing, India

J. Jagannathan
https://orcid.org/0000-0003-0059-8236
Vellore Institute of Technology, India

A. Mohanraj
Sri Eshwar College of Engineering, India

Iyyappan Moorthi
https://orcid.org/0000-0002-5836-307X
Ahlia University, Bahrain

Rajkumar N.
https://orcid.org/0000-0001-7857-9452
Alliance School of Advanced Computing, India

ABSTRACT

Blockchain technology has the potential to revolutionize academic libraries by enhancing research and collaboration. By providing a decentralized and transparent platform, blockchain can facilitate the secure and efficient sharing of research data and resources among academics globally. This fosters greater collaboration, as researchers can easily verify the authenticity of data and build upon each other's work without concerns about data tampering. Blockchain's immutable ledger ensures that all contributions are recorded transparently, thus promoting trust and integrity in academic research. Traditional publishing often involves lengthy and opaque processes, but blockchain can streamline these by providing a transparent and efficient system for manuscript submission, peer review, and publication. Smart

DOI: 10.4018/979-8-3693-7783-3.ch001

contracts can automate and enforce peer review protocols, ensuring timely and unbiased reviews.

INTRODUCTION

The appearance of blockchain technology heralds a brand new generation of possibilities for the duration of numerous industries, which include academia. Instructional libraries, which feature the backbone of scholarly verbal exchange and statistics dissemination, stand to advantage significantly from the mixture of blockchain generation. By way of leveraging the inherent capabilities of blockchain—decentralization, immutability, and transparency—academic libraries can address longstanding challenges associated with information integrity, digital rights manipulation, and inter-library cooperation. This section explores the potential applications of blockchain in instructional libraries, detailing its advantages, implementation techniques, and the demanding situations that could arise.

AI Applications in Libraries

- **Emerging and innovative AI technologies for resource management** by Nachiappan explore how AI can be used for tasks like automating cataloging, managing inventory, and optimizing resource allocation (Nachiappan, 2024a).
- **E-resources content recommendation system using AI** by Nachiappan delves into AI-powered recommendation systems for suggesting relevant e-resources to library users (Nachiappan, 2024b).
- **Intelligent Library Management Using Radio Frequency Identification** by Viji et al. examines how RFID technology coupled with AI can streamline library operations like self-checkout and item tracking (Viji et al., 2024).

AI and User Services

- **Educational Technology and Libraries Supporting Online Learning** by Kumar et al. discusses how AI can be integrated with educational technology to enhance online learning resources and services offered by libraries (Kumar et al., 2024).
- **Anticipating AI Impact on Library Services: Future Opportunities and Evolutionary Prospects** by Lalitha et al. explores the potential future applications of AI in library services, focusing on user experience and person-

alized recommendations (Rajkumar, Tabassum, et al., 2024) (Lalitha et al., 2024).

Ethical and Societal Considerations

- **Privacy and Security in Digital Libraries** by Mohanraj et al. addresses privacy and security concerns associated with using AI in digital libraries (Mohanraj et al., 2024).
- **Ethical Considerations of AI Implementation in the Library Era** by Rajkumar et al. explores the ethical implications of implementing AI in libraries, considering issues like bias and data ownership (Rajkumar, Viji, et al., 2024).
- **Educational program for AI literacy** by Varadarajan emphasizes the importance of educating library users about AI to ensure responsible and informed interaction with AI-powered library systems(Varadarajan, 2024).

Additional Resources

- **Historical Overview of AI Adoption in Libraries** by Jayavadivel et al. provides a historical perspective on the adoption of AI in libraries, tracing its evolution and impact on library services(Jayavadivel et al., 2024).
- **Integration of AI and IoT for smart home automation** by Varadarajan et al., though not directly related to libraries, showcases the potential of integrating AI with other technologies (like IoT) for intelligent systems, which may have future applications in library management (Varadarajan et al., 2024).

Understanding Blockchain Technology

Blockchain is a decentralized ledger era that statistics transactions through multiple computer systems in such a way that the registered transactions can not be altered retroactively. This guarantees the integrity and safety of information. Every block in a blockchain includes several transactions, and whenever a cutting-edge transaction happens on the blockchain, a record of that transaction is delivered to each participant's ledger. This decentralized approach removes the want for a government and guarantees transparency and consideration among participants.

Applications of Blockchain in Academic Libraries

1. Digital Rights Management

One of the primary issues of tutorial libraries is coping with virtual rights and ensuring that digital content cloth is used in compliance with licensing agreements. Blockchain can provide an obvious and immutable document of virtual content material usage, ensuring authors and publishers accumulate appropriate credit scores and reimbursement (Dong & Zhang, 2023). Clever contracts, a feature of blockchain technology, can automate the enforcement of copyright agreements and usage licenses, thereby reducing administrative overhead and minimizing disputes(Vasquez & Sanchez, 2023).

2. Enhanced Data Security and Integrity

Educational libraries manipulate big quantities of sensitive information, consisting of personal statistics of college students and faculty, in addition to instructional facts and research facts (Davis & Zhu, 2023). Blockchain's immutable ledger guarantees that when information is recorded, it cannot be altered or tampered with. This excessive degree of safety is essential for retaining the integrity of academic facts and shielding against statistics breaches. Moreover, the transparency of blockchain allows for smooth auditing and verification of statistics(Zhao & Sun, 2024).

3. Streamlined Inter-Library Loan Processes

Inter-library loans (ill) are an important service furnished by using educational libraries, permitting patrons to get admission to substances no longer to be had in their home library. Blockchain can streamline unwell techniques by supplying a decentralized device wherein transaction data are shared throughout participating libraries. This will permit faster processing times, reduce administrative burdens, and enhance the tracking and control of borrowed materials (Ivanov & Petrov, 2023).

4. Academic Credentialing

Issuing and verifying academic credentials are a few other vicinities in which blockchain ought to have a sizable impact. Historically, verifying educational tiers and certifications can be a time-eating procedure. With the aid of way of storing instructional credentials on a blockchain, libraries and educational establishments can offer a tamper-proof and effortlessly verifiable file of a student's achievements.

This not only simplifies the verification manner but also reduces the danger of credential fraud.

5. Preservation of Digital Archives

Academic libraries are tasked with the renovation of digital records, which may be difficult given the fast evolution of virtual formats and the capability for statistics degradation over time. Blockchain's immutable nature makes it a genuinely best answer for retaining digital documents. By way of recording the provenance and adjustments to digital data on a blockchain, libraries can ensure the authenticity and toughness of their virtual collections (Uddin & Ahmed, 2023).

Implementation Strategies

Efficiently integrating blockchain generation into instructional libraries requires cautious plans and attention to various factors. The subsequent techniques can manual libraries in their implementation efforts:

1. Identifying Use Cases

Step one in enforcing blockchain is to understand specific use times wherein the technology can offer the most benefit. Libraries need to conduct an in-depth needs evaluation to decide on areas in which blockchain can decorate operations, beautify safety, or offer new services.

2. Collaborating with Technology Partners

Blockchain implementation frequently requires specialized information and information. Libraries should bear in mind partnering with technology agencies or instructional establishments with enjoy blockchain development. These collaborations can provide crucial technical assistance and guidance during the implementation method (White & Taylor, 2023).

3. Pilot Projects

Earlier than entire-scale implementation, libraries should behavior pilot tasks to check the feasibility and effectiveness of blockchain programs. Those pilots can assist in understanding capability traumatic situations and refine the technology to higher meet the library's goals (Bheemaiah & Agrawal, 2023).

4. Staff Training and Development

Implementing the blockchain era would require a library body of workers to gather new abilities and expertise. Entire training applications have to be developed to make certain that personnel are talented in the use of and dealing with blockchain systems. Ongoing expert improvement possibilities should moreover be provided to keep the frame employees updated on the present-day improvements in blockchain technology.

5. Addressing Legal and Ethical Considerations

The use of the blockchain era in instructional libraries increases numerous legal and ethical considerations, mainly regarding information privacy and highbrow property rights. Libraries must ensure compliance with relevant legal guidelines and policies, and expand policies that cope with the ethical implications of blockchain use.

Challenges and Barriers to Adoption

Regardless of its capacity blessings, the adoption of blockchain generation in academic libraries isn't always without demanding situations (Chen & Zhang, 2023). A number of the crucial aspects of obstacles embody:

1. Technological Complexity

Blockchain generation is complex and requires sizable technical information to put in force and preserve. Libraries may additionally face difficulties in acquiring the vital resources and capabilities to efficiently control blockchain structures.

2. Cost

The initial price of implementing blockchain generation may be high, encompassing hardware, software programs, and education expenses. At the same time as blockchain can offer lengthy time period economic financial savings via expanded performance and security, premature funding can be prohibitive for a few libraries (Thompson & Zhang, 2023).

3. Interoperability Issues

For blockchain to be effective in collaborative networks, it must be properly matched with modern-day library systems and databases. Making sure interoperability between blockchain systems and conventional library systems can be tough and may require massive customization.

4. Regulatory and Policy Constraints

Blockchain technology operates in a swiftly evolving regulatory environment. Libraries want to navigate a complex panorama of laws and hints related to statistics safety, digital rights, and blockchain use. Compliance with these policies may be hard and might restrict the scope of blockchain applications.

5. Resistance to Change

Adopting a new era often faces resistance from stakeholders accustomed to conventional structures and processes. Powerful change management techniques are vital to cope with concerns and make certain buy-in from the library workforce and buyers

Future Prospects

Regardless of the demanding situations, the future of blockchain in instructional libraries seems promising. Because the era matures and will become extra available, its packages are probably to extend. Destiny tendencies may additionally encompass:

1. Greater Integration with Other Technologies

The integration of blockchain with special rising technologies in conjunction with synthetic intelligence and the Internet of Factors (IoT) can further beautify its abilities. As an example, combining blockchain with AI can enhance data analytics and desire-making methods in libraries.

2. Development of Standardized Protocols

The development of standardized protocols and frameworks for blockchain implementation in libraries can facilitate interoperability and reduce implementation charges. Those standards can provide a blueprint for libraries to take a look at, making sure consistency and fine practices.

3. Increased Collaboration and Resource Sharing

Blockchain can foster greater collaboration and useful resource sharing among academic libraries. Through the manner of developing decentralized networks, libraries can effortlessly percentage resources, collaborate on study tasks, and broaden joint obligations that advantage the academic community.

4. Enhanced User Services

As blockchain technology turns into extra fashionable, academic libraries can leverage its functions to offer greater suitable services to customers. This could encompass more green access to virtual content, stepped-forward purchaser authentication, and customized offerings primarily based on blockchain-based individual profiles.

Enhancing Academic Research and Collaboration

Inside the rapidly evolving landscape of academia, enhancing research and collaboration has become paramount to addressing complicated worldwide demanding situations. The conventional silos of personal research are giving way to more collaborative, interdisciplinary processes that leverage the strengths and insights of several pupils. This shift is facilitated by the useful resource of advancements in the era, mainly those that decorate communication, data sharing, and collaborative workflows. This segment explores the mechanisms and techniques for boosting academic research and collaboration, emphasizing the integration of technology, the development of collaborative networks, and the fostering of an open research way of life.

The Importance of Collaboration in Academic Research

Collaboration in instructional research brings together numerous perspectives and know-how, main to extra modern and whole answers. Collaborative research can bridge gaps among disciplines, contemplating more holistic records of complicated troubles. Moreover, collaborative efforts often cause greater study outputs, which include guides in excessive-impact journals and successful programs. The benefits of collaboration include:

1. **Diverse Expertise**: Collaboration allows researchers to pool their information and talents, tackling study questions from a couple of angles.

2. **Resource Sharing**: Collaborative tasks can leverage shared assets, together with funding, equipment, and information, improving the overall performance and scope of studies.
3. **Enhanced Innovation**: several groups are much more likely to generate novel ideas and procedures, using innovation.
4. **Increased Visibility and Impact**: Collaborative studies regularly outcomes in better visibility and extra impact, as findings are disseminated via more than one channel and network.

Technological Tools for Enhancing Collaboration

Improvements in technology have considerably greater the ability of researchers to collaborate, regardless of geographical boundaries. The following technological systems are important for fostering educational collaboration:

1. Communication Platforms

Powerful communication is the cornerstone of a fulfillment collaboration. Structures like Slack, Microsoft Teams, and Zoom facilitate real-time communique, permitting researchers to discuss thoughts, share updates, and coordinate efforts seamlessly. The tools provide features consisting of video conferencing, chat, report sharing, and integration with other research equipment, developing a complete conversation environment.

2. Collaborative Writing and Editing Tools

Collaborative writing gear which includes Google Medical Medical Doctors, Overleaf, and Microsoft Word online allows more than one researcher to work on the same file concurrently. These equipment tune changes, permit commenting, and help model manipulation, making sure that all collaborators can contribute efficaciously and transparently (Li & Zhou, 2023).

Figure 1. Model of collaborative Learning using Blockchain

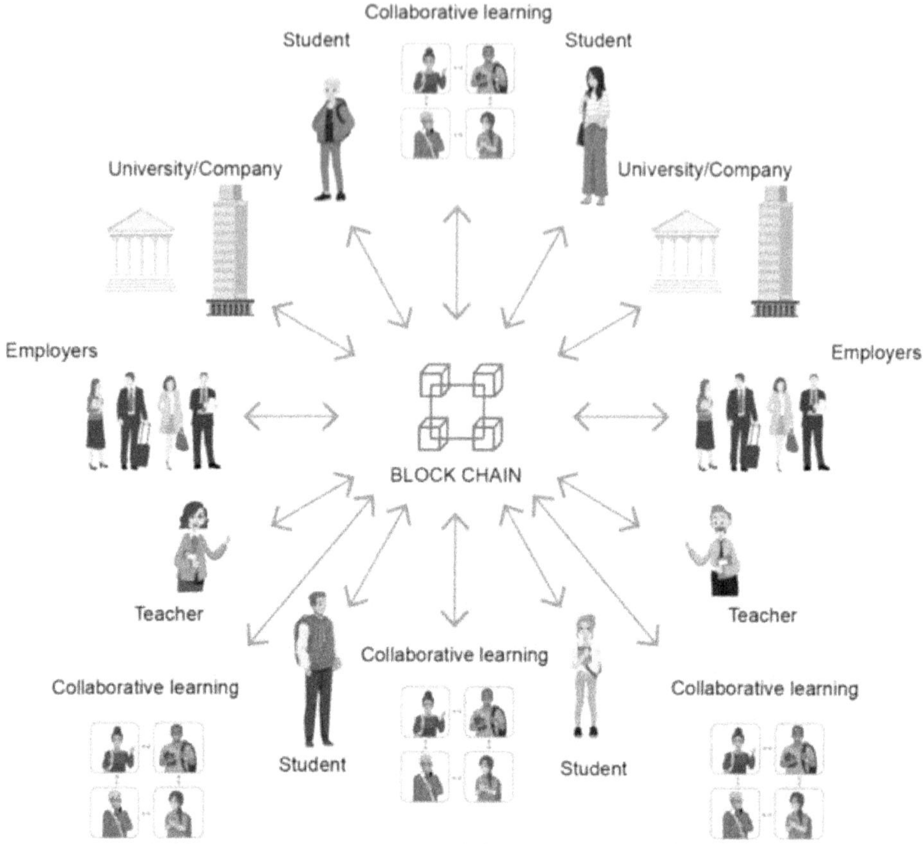

3. Data Sharing and Management Platforms

Effective data sharing is critical for collaborative research. Systems like GitHub, Figshare, and Zenodo provide repositories for sharing facts, code, and different study outputs. Those systems aid versioning, and metadata tagging and get admission to control, making it less complicated for researchers to percentage and manage their data collaboratively.

4. Project Management Tools

Task manipulation tools consisting of Trello, Asana, and Monday.Com help researchers prepare and song their collaborative responsibilities. These gadgets offer functions like task assignment, timelines, and development tracking, making sure that projects live on the agenda and that responsibilities are certainly described.

5. Virtual Research Environments

Virtual research environments (VREs) offer included structures for undertaking collaborative studies. VREs like JupyterHub, RStudio Server, and CloudLab provide cloud-primarily based absolute environments in which researchers can run analyses, proportion code, and collaborate on studies projects in actual time. These environments resource reproducibility and facilitate collaborative workflows.

Building and Sustaining Collaborative Networks

A hit academic collaboration calls for greater than simply technological tools; it requires robust networks of researchers who are committed to running collectively. Constructing and retaining these networks consists of:

1. Identifying Potential Collaborators

Locating the right collaborators is critical for the achievement of any research assignment. Researchers can identify functionality collaborators through instructional conferences, expert businesses, and social networking websites like ResearchGate and LinkedIn. The one's systems allow researchers to connect to pals who have complementary know-how and pastimes.

2. Establishing Clear Objectives and Roles

Easy objectives and described roles are important for powerful collaboration. At the outset of a mission, collaborators should agree on the study's desires, methodologies, and anticipated effects. They ought to additionally outline the jobs and obligations of every institution member, making sure that everybody is conscious of their contributions to the undertaking.

3. Fostering Trust and Open Communication

Accept as true with an open conversation are the guidelines for successful collaboration. Researchers have to set up regular communication channels, together with weekly meetings or everyday updates, to make certain that everybody is informed and engaged. Transparency in sharing statistics, methodologies, and improvement is also important to consider among collaborators.

4. Leveraging Institutional Support

Establishments play a crucial function in fostering collaborative studies. Universities and studies agencies can help collaborate with the useful resource of supplying funding for joint obligations, supplying training and assets, and developing guidelines that inspire interdisciplinary research. Institutional manuals can also encompass access to shared centers and infrastructure, which includes laboratories and libraries.

5. Creating Collaborative Agreements

Formal collaborative agreements can assist clarify expectations and obligations. Those agreements have to define the scope of the collaboration, intellectual assets rights, facts control practices, and manual rules. Collaborative agreements provide a framework for dealing with capability conflicts and making sure that everyone's events are aligned with their goals(Kim & Park, 2023).

Fostering an Open Research Culture

An open research tradition promotes transparency, accessibility, and collaboration. Using ways of sharing data, methodologies, and findings openly, researchers can accelerate the tempo of discovery and enhance the reproducibility of studies. Key additives of an open research lifestyle consist of:

1. Open Access Publishing

Open admission to publishing makes studies' findings freely available to the general public, doing away with limitations to get entry and allowing wider dissemination of information. Researchers can put up their work in the open to get the right of entry to journals or deposit their manuscripts in institutional repositories. Open proper access to regulations adopted by funding organizations and establishments further helps this practice (Hernandez & Liu, 2023).

2. Open Data and Open Science

Open statistics tasks encourage researchers to percentage their records publicly, allowing others to validate and construct their paintings. Platforms just like the Open technological knowledge Framework (OSF) provide equipment for handling and sharing records, protocols, and analysis scripts. Open technology practices, which include pre-registration of research and sharing of research materials, beautify transparency and reproducibility (Jackson & Wang, 2023).

3. Citizen Science and Community Engagement

Attractive to most of the people in research via citizen technological information tasks can enhance the impact and attain of educational studies. Citizen-era responsibilities comprise people of the public in statistics collection, evaluation, and dissemination, fostering a sense of ownership and collaboration. Network engagement moreover guarantees that studies address actual global troubles and advantages of society.

4. Recognition and Incentives

Establishments need to understand and reward collaborative and open studies practices. This could consist of incorporating collaborative achievements into tenure and advertising requirements, imparting awards for incredible collaborative artwork, and imparting incentives for sharing statistics and publishing in open-access journals. Spotting the fee of collaboration and openness encourages researchers to undertake these practices.

Case Studies of Successful Academic Collaboration

Examining fulfillment case studies can provide precious insights into first-rate practices for reinforcing educational studies and collaboration. The subsequent examples spotlight how collaborative efforts have brought about full-size improvements in various fields:

1. The Human Genome Project

The Human Genome Venture (HGP) is a landmark instance of worldwide collaboration in scientific studies. Launched in 1990, the HGP worried researchers from multiple global places working collectively to map the entire human genome. The challenge required large coordination and records sharing, facilitated through technological gear and collaborative frameworks. The success of the entirety of the HGP has had a profound impact on genomics and personalized treatment(Smith & Nguyen, 2023) .

2. CERN and the Large Hadron Collider

The EU Company for Nuclear Research (CERN) operates the Massive Hadron Collider (LHC), the area's biggest and maximum effective particle accelerator. The LHC challenge involves collaboration amongst heaps of scientists and engineers from over 100 international locations. Researchers work collectively to conduct experiments, study data, and improve our know-how of essential physics. The collaborative nature of CERN has brought about groundbreaking discoveries, which include the identification of the Higgs boson (Roberts & Lee, 2023).

3. The Global Burden of Disease Study

The global burden of ailment (GBD) have a look at is a complete attempt to quantify the effect of sicknesses, accidents, and threat factors internationally. Led by the use of the Institute for Fitness Metrics and Evaluation (IHME), the GBD takes a look at entails collaboration amongst researchers, policymakers, and health businesses globally. The examination's findings are used to tell public fitness regulations and prioritize sources. The collaborative technique of the GBD study has made it a critical device for know-how and addressing global fitness-demanding situations.

Overcoming Challenges in Academic Collaboration

At the same time because the benefits of instructional collaboration are clean, challenges continue to be. Addressing the worrying situations is essential for fostering effective collaboration:

1. Managing Interdisciplinary Differences

Taking part across disciplines can be tough due to differences in terminology, methodologies, and research cultures. Powerful communication and mutual admiration are essential for bridging the gaps. Interdisciplinary schooling applications and workshops can also help researchers develop the talents wanted for a successful collaboration.

2. Balancing Individual and Collective Goals

Researchers have to balance their dreams with the collective desires of the collaborative challenge. This requires a clear knowledge of methods the collaboration aligns with private research targets and career aspirations. Setting up smooth expectancies and offering recognition for collaborative contributions can help mitigate potential conflicts.

3. Ensuring Data Security and Privacy

Collaborative studies often involve sharing touchy information, elevating concerns approximately records safety and privacy. Imposing robust data control practices, collectively with encryption, right of entry to controls, and compliance with statistics protection guidelines, is critical for protecting records. Collaborators should also set up clean agreements on facts possession and usage.

4. Addressing Resource and Funding Constraints

Securing adequate assets and funding is a common challenge in collaborative studies. Researchers must be searching for several funding belongings, alongside offers, organization partnerships, and institutional guides. Collaborative networks can also pool assets, inclusive of shared centers and gadgets, to maximize performance.

Blockchain for Academic Publishing and Peer Review

Academic publishing and peer comparison structures are important components of a scholarly communique. They ensure the dissemination and validation of studies findings, which in flip pressure scientific development and innovation. However, those structures face several challenges, inclusive of inefficiencies, lack of transparency, biases, and troubles with accepting as true and accountable. The blockchain era, with its decentralized and immutable ledger, gives promising answers to the problems. This segment explores how blockchain can revolutionize educational publishing and peer evaluation, enhancing transparency, efficiency, and trustworthiness in scholarly conversation.

Understanding Blockchain Technology

Blockchain is an allotted ledger generation that statistics transactions during a community of computer systems. Each block within the blockchain includes a list of transactions, and people blocks are connected collectively in a chronological chain. The decentralized nature of blockchain guarantees that no single entity has manipulation over the complete chain, and its immutability guarantees that after a transaction is recorded, it can not be altered retroactively. Those characteristics make blockchain an effective tool for applications requiring transparency, protection, and belief.

Current Challenges in Academic Publishing and Peer Review

Academic publishing and peer review face several critical challenges that hinder their effectiveness:

1. **Lack of Transparency**: The peer assessment device is regularly opaque, with little visibility into how decisions are made or who the reviewers are.
2. **Inefficiency and Delays**: The traditional peer assessment method may be time-ingesting, principal to extensive delays inside the e-book of studies findings.
3. **Bias and Conflicts of Interest**: Peer overview can be a problem for biases and conflicts of interest, affecting the objectivity and fairness of the evaluation process.
4. **Issues with Trust and Accountability**: instances of fraudulent research, plagiarism, and peer assessment manipulation have undermined acceptance as true within the academic publishing device.
5. **Access and Dissemination**: Paywalls and restrictive get the right of entry to regulations restriction the dissemination and accessibility of scholarly studies.

Blockchain Solutions for Academic Publishing

Blockchain technology can deal with most of the traumatic situations faced via instructional publishing, presenting the subsequent solutions:

1. Enhanced Transparency

Blockchain can beautify transparency inside the publishing method by the usage of offering a clean and immutable report of all transactions. This consists of the submission of manuscripts, the peer assessment gadget, editorial selections, and the manual. Through recording every step at the blockchain, all stakeholders, along with authors, reviewers, and readers, can hint at the statistics of a manuscript, ensuring more duty and openness (Gupta & Roy, 2023).

2. Efficient and Decentralized Peer Review

Blockchain can streamline the peer overview method with the aid of creating a decentralized platform wherein reviewers and authors can interact immediately. Clever contracts can automate the assessment system, making sure that reviewers are compensated for his or her artwork and that evaluations are completed inside an exclusive time body. This can substantially reduce delays and enhance the performance of peer evaluation.

3. Mitigating Bias and Conflicts of Interest

The decentralized nature of blockchain can help mitigate biases and conflicts of interest in the peer examination approach. Via anonymizing reviewers and authors, blockchain can facilitate double-blind peer assessment, wherein neither party is aware of the identity of the opportunity (Qiu & Wu, 2023). This could assist make sure that opinions are primarily based completely absolutely on the remarkable of the research, as opposed to the popularity or affiliations of the authors.

4. Building Trust and Ensuring Accountability

Blockchain's immutability guarantees that every transaction is permanently recorded, making it simpler to locate and save fraudulent sports activities. Instances of plagiarism, information fabrication, and peer assessment manipulation can be identified and addressed more efficaciously. Furthermore, the usage of blockchain can provide a confirmed file of reviewers' contributions, making sure that they receive suitable popularity and credit scores for their paintings.

5. Open Access and Wider Dissemination

Blockchain can resource open entry to publishing fashions via lowering charges and boundaries to get the right of entry. Decentralized publishing structures can operate with lower overheads in comparison to conventional publishers, making it more viable to offer unfastened get right of entry to research articles. This could beautify the dissemination and effect of scholarly research, making sure that it's far available to a much wider target market.

Implementation Strategies for Blockchain in Academic Publishing

An achievement implementation of blockchain in educational publishing requires cautious making plans and collaboration among numerous stakeholders. The following techniques can manual the adoption of blockchain era on this subject:

1. Developing Blockchain-Based Platforms

To leverage blockchain's benefits, educational publishers and institutions can grow blockchain-based platforms for manuscript submission, peer assessment, and e-books. The one's structures want to be designed to mix seamlessly with current structures and workflows, minimizing disruptions and ensuring ease of use (Patel & Sharma, 2023).

2. Collaboration with Technology Partners

Implementing the blockchain era calls for technical know-how and infrastructure. Instructional publishers and establishments must collaborate with era partners who've reveled in blockchain improvement. Those partnerships can provide critical technical resources and help ensure that the blockchain solutions are strong and scalable.

3. Pilot Projects and Proof of Concepts

In advance of full-scale implementation, it's far more useful to conduct pilot tasks and evidence-of-idea research. The pilots can help discover capacity-demanding situations and refine the blockchain packages to meet the needs of the academic publishing network. Pilot tasks also offer an opportunity to acquire remarks from users and stakeholders, ensuring that the solutions are user-friendly and effective (Lopez & Garcia, 2023).

4. Establishing Standards and Protocols

The improvement of standardized protocols and great practices is crucial for the awesome adoption of blockchain in academic publishing (Oliveira & Costa, 2023). Enterprise-big requirements can make sure interoperability among unique blockchain structures and facilitate collaboration among publishers, establishments, and researchers. Necessities also can offer pointers for statistics management, safety, and moral considerations (Nguyen & Tran, 2023).

5. Training and Capacity Building

The adoption of blockchain generation might require education and the ability to construct for all stakeholders, which include authors, reviewers, editors, and publishers. Training programs want to be superior to familiarize stakeholders with blockchain principles, tools, and workflows. Ongoing professional improvement possibilities need to additionally be furnished to keep stakeholders updated on the modern advancements in the blockchain era.

Case Studies of Blockchain in Academic Publishing

Reading case studies of blockchain implementation in academic publishing can offer precious insights into exceptional practices and instructions found out. The following examples spotlight successful applications of blockchain in this area:

1. ARTiFACTS

Artifact is a blockchain-based platform designed to enhance the transparency and performance of academic publishing. The platform permits researchers to create an everlasting, time-stamped file of their research outputs, along with facts gadgets, manuscripts, and peer critiques. ARTiFACTS additionally facilitates the quotation and sharing of research outputs, enhancing their visibility and effect. Through leveraging blockchain, ARTiFACTS objectives to build agreement with and responsibility within the educational publishing machine.

2. Orvium

Orvium is a different blockchain-primarily based platform that tries to revolutionize instructional publishing and peer evaluation. The platform offers a decentralized and transparent environment for researchers to post, assess, and put up their artwork. Orvium makes use of clever contracts to automate the peer examination approach and ensure well-timed and truthful evaluations. The platform moreover helps open get proper access to publishing, making research findings freely available to most people. Orvium's blockchain-based method addresses a number of the inefficiencies and biases related to standard publishing fashions.

3. Blockchain for Peer Review (BPR)

The Blockchain for Peer Compare (BPR) undertaking is an initiative by way of Springer Nature to explore the capacity of blockchain within the peer evaluation technique. The project targets to create an obvious and tamper-proof file of peer evaluation sports activities, improving acceptance as true with and duty. BPR makes use of blockchain to time-stamp and report peer evaluation reviews, making sure that the facts of the assessment manner are preserved. The assignment also explores using blockchain to verify the identities and contributions of reviewers, offering them with appropriate reputation and credit score.

Challenges and Barriers to Adoption

Notwithstanding its functionality advantages, the adoption of blockchain in educational publishing and peer assessment isn't without challenges. A number of the critical element boundaries encompass:

1. Technological Complexity

The blockchain era is complicated and requires extensive technical knowledge to implement and maintain. Educational publishers and establishments may additionally moreover face problems in obtaining the crucial property and abilities to govern blockchain structures successfully.

2. Cost

The preliminary fee of implementing the blockchain era may be high, encompassing hardware, software, and schooling costs. While blockchain can offer prolonged-time period financial savings through increased performance and reduced fraud, the earlier investment may be prohibitive for a few publishers and institutions.

3. Resistance to Change

The adoption of new technologies regularly faces resistance from stakeholders accustomed to conventional structures and approaches. Powerful trade management techniques are crucial to deal with issues and make certain buy-in from authors, reviewers, editors, and publishers.

4. Interoperability Issues

Ensuring interoperability among blockchain systems and current publishing structures can be difficult. Publishers and institutions need to enlarge standardized protocols and interfaces to facilitate seamless integration and records trade.

5. Regulatory and Ethical Considerations

The usage of blockchain generation in academic publishing increases various regulatory and ethical concerns, in particular regarding facts privacy and intellectual property rights. Publishers and establishments ought to navigate a complicated landscape of felony suggestions and rules and develop tips that cope with the ethical implications of blockchain use.

Future Prospects

Notwithstanding the disturbing conditions, the future possibilities of blockchain in academic publishing and peer evaluation are promising. Due to the fact the generation matures and will become extra available, its applications are possible to increase (Fisher & Kim, 2023). Destiny developments can also encompass:

1. Greater Integration with Other Technologies

The mixture of blockchain with different emerging technologies, collectively with synthetic intelligence and system studying, can similarly beautify its abilities. As an example, combining blockchain with AI can improve the performance and accuracy of the peer assessment procedure by automating ordinary obligations and figuring out ability conflicts of interest.

2. Development of Decentralized Autonomous Organizations (DAOs)

Decentralized self-enough companies (DAOs) are blockchain-primarily based entities that carry out without centralized management. DAOs will be used to create decentralized publishing systems in which researchers govern the ebook method together. This technique can democratize academic publishing and ensure that choice-making is obvious and sincere.

3. Enhanced Research Transparency and Reproducibility

Blockchain can enhance studies' transparency and reproducibility by offering a clear and immutable record of all studies and sports. This consists of the registration of a look at protocols, facts collection, evaluation, and peer assessment. By making sure that each step of the study process is documented and to be had, blockchain can help cope with the reproducibility disaster in technological understanding.

4. Increased Collaboration and Interdisciplinary Research

Blockchain can facilitate collaboration and interdisciplinary studies with the resource of offering a comfy and obvious platform for sharing information, property, and knowledge. Researchers from unique fields and establishments can collaborate extra effectively, predominant to new insights and improvements (Martin & Robinson, 2023).

Supporting Students and Researchers with Blockchain

Blockchain generation, excellent identified for its position in cryptocurrencies like Bitcoin, has a long manner-reaching programs past finance. Its functions—decentralization, transparency, safety, and immutability—provide widespread potential for boosting various sectors, which include schooling and research (Evans & Malone, 2023). In educational settings, blockchain can offer current solutions to lengthy-status demanding situations faced with the aid of college students and researchers. This phase explores how blockchain can assist instructional organizations using improving information security, permitting new fashions for

Understanding Blockchain Technology

Blockchain is a decentralized ledger generation that information transactions in the course of a community of computer systems. Each transaction is saved in a block, and those blocks are related together in a chronological chain. Key characteristics of blockchain encompass:

1. **Decentralization:** No single entity has control over the complete blockchain.
2. **Immutability:** as soon as recorded, transactions can not be altered retroactively.
3. **Transparency:** All contributors can view the transaction history.
4. **Security:** Cryptographic techniques ensure that transactions are at ease and verifiable.

These functions make blockchain an appealing answer for programs requiring excessive degrees of trust, protection, and transparency.

Current Challenges Faced by Students and Researchers

Students and researchers come upon several demanding situations that may hinder their instructional progress and productiveness:

- **Statistics security and privacy:** instructional institutions shop giant amounts of touchy records, which encompass private facts, research records, and highbrow belongings. Ensuring the safety and privacy of these statistics is a first-rate venture.
- **Academic Integrity:** Plagiarism, records fabrication, and other types of academic misconduct undermine the integrity of tutorial work.
- **Investment and useful resource Allocation:** Securing investment and belongings for studies may be a complex and aggressive manner.
- **Get right of entry to research Outputs:** Paywalls and restrictive get right of entry to regulations restrict the accessibility of studies findings.
- **Collaboration and communique:** effective collaboration amongst researchers, especially during institutions and borders, may be hard because of problems associated with taking into account, coordination, and statistics sharing.

Blockchain Solutions for Academic Support

Blockchain generation can cope with many of those challenges, presenting the following solutions:

1. Enhancing Data Security and Privacy

Blockchain's decentralized and at ease nature makes it a virtually perfect solution for reinforcing statistics safety and privateness in instructional settings. With the resources of using blockchain, institutions can:

- **Securely store and proportion information:** sensitive statistics may be stored on a blockchain, making sure that it is tamper-proof and available most effectively to authorized people.
- **Make certain statistics Integrity:** Blockchain can provide a verifiable file of records transactions, ensuring that statistics have no longer been altered or tampered with.

- **Shield intellectual belongings:** Researchers can use blockchain to securely timestamp their work, imparting proof of originality and shielding their intellectual belongings.

2. Ensuring Academic Integrity

Blockchain can help hold educational integrity with the aid of supplying apparent and immutable facts about educational activities. This will encompass:

- Blockchain can be used to create a comprehensive and searchable database of educational works, making it less complicated to stumble on plagiarism.
- Educational institutions can have difficulty with digital certificates and diplomas at the blockchain, making it easy to confirm the authenticity of instructional credentials.
- The peer evaluation method can be recorded on the blockchain, making sure that it's far apparent and accountable.

3. Streamlining Funding and Resource Allocation

Blockchain can streamline the process of securing investment and allocating assets for research through:

- **Decentralized funding platforms:** Researchers can use blockchain-primarily based platforms to connect with ability funders immediately, lowering the need for intermediaries and developing investment possibilities.
- **Transparent Allocation of assets:** Blockchain can offer an obvious report of ways belongings are allotted and used, ensuring duty and preventing misuse of finances.

4. Improving Access to Research Outputs

Blockchain can useful resource to open get entry to fashions and enhance the dissemination of studies' findings via:

- **Decentralized Publishing structures:** Researchers can position their work on blockchain-primarily based completely structures, making it freely on hand to the general public and making sure that they hold manage over their highbrow belongings.
- **Everlasting and Immutable data:** Blockchain can provide an everlasting and unalterable file

5. Facilitating Collaboration and Communication

Blockchain can facilitate collaboration and communication among researchers by using way of offering a comfortable and transparent platform for record sharing and coordination. This may embody:

- **Clever Contracts for Collaboration:** Researchers can use smart contracts to automate and manipulate collaborative agreements, making sure that each event satisfies their responsibilities.
- **At ease records Sharing:** Blockchain can provide an ease platform for sharing studies statistics, making sure that it's far handy most effective to authorized people and that its integrity is maintained.
- **Decentralized research Networks:** Blockchain can aid the advent of decentralized studies networks, allowing researchers to collaborate and proportion sources throughout institutions and borders.

Case Studies of Blockchain in Academic Support

Analyzing case research of blockchain implementation in educational help can provide valuable insights into super practices and instructions discovered. The following examples highlight achievement packages of blockchain in this subject:

1. Learning Machine

Studying gadgets, in collaboration with the MIT Media Lab, evolved Blockcerts, an open general for developing, issuing, viewing, and verifying blockchain-based absolute certificates. Blockcerts lets educational establishments to difficulty with virtual diplomas and certificates at the blockchain, making sure that they'll be comfortable, tamper-proof, and without issue. This enhances the credibility of tutorial credentials and simplifies the verification manner for employers and exceptional institutions.

2. ResearchHub

ResearchHub is a blockchain-based total platform designed to facilitate the sharing and dissemination of research outputs. Researchers can upload their paintings to ResearchHub, where their miles are stored on the blockchain and made freely available to the general public. The platform additionally uses a token-based total praise device to incentivize researchers to proportion their work and engage with the network. Through leveraging blockchain, ResearchHub aims to create a greater open and collaborative research environment.

3. Digital Science's Dimensions

Dimensions is a comprehensive research database that makes use of blockchain generation to provide a obvious and immutable report of studies outputs and sports. The platform consists of a large type of research metrics and analytics, allowing researchers to tune the effect of their work and perceive functionality collaborators. With the aid of the usage of providing a verifiable report of research sports, Dimensions complements transparency and duty inside the studies manner.

Challenges and Barriers to Adoption

No matter its capability advantages, the adoption of blockchain in academic assist isn't always without annoying situations. Some of the vital issue boundaries encompass:

1. Technological Complexity

Blockchain technology is complex and calls for significant technical understanding to place into effect and maintain. Educational institutions may additionally face problems in obtaining the crucial sources and skills to govern blockchain structures efficiently.

2. Cost

The preliminary fee of implementing blockchain technology may be excessive, encompassing hardware, software, and education costs. At the same time as blockchain can provide long-time period savings through extended overall performance and reduced fraud, the earlier investment can be prohibitive for some institutions.

3. Resistance to Change

The adoption of latest generation regularly faces resistance from stakeholders accustomed to standard systems and techniques. Powerful exchange manage strategies are important to address worries and make sure buy-in from college students, researchers, and administrators.

4. Interoperability Issues

Making sure interoperability among blockchain systems and gift educational structures can be tough. Establishments want to develop standardized protocols and interfaces to facilitate seamless integration and statistics change.

5. Regulatory and Ethical Considerations

The usage of blockchain era in educational help increases numerous regulatory and ethical issues, specifically regarding facts privacy and highbrow property rights. Establishments must navigate a complex panorama of laws and tips and growth rules that deal with the moral implications of blockchain use.

Future Prospects

Notwithstanding the stressful conditions, the destiny possibilities of blockchain in instructional manual are promising. As the technology matures and will become greater reachable, its packages are likely to make bigger. Future dispositions also can include:

1. Greater Integration with Other Technologies

The combination of blockchain with other rising technology, which incorporates artificial intelligence and system analyzing, can further beautify its capabilities. For instance, combining blockchain with AI can decorate the performance and accuracy of records manage and assessment in instructional settings.

2. Development of Decentralized Autonomous Organizations (DAOs)

Decentralized self sufficient companies (DAOs) are blockchain-primarily based entities that characteristic without centralized manage. DAOs is probably used to create decentralized academic networks, wherein university college students and researchers govern the system collectively. This approach can democratize preference-making techniques and make certain that they're apparent and trustworthy.

3. Enhanced Research Transparency and Reproducibility

Blockchain can decorate studies transparency and reproducibility by means of presenting a clean and immutable file of all studies sports. This includes the registration of take a look at protocols, statistics series, evaluation, and peer assessment. With the aid of ensuring that every one steps of the research method are documented and to be had, blockchain can help deal with the reproducibility disaster in technological understanding.

4. Increased Collaboration and Interdisciplinary Research

Blockchain can facilitate collaboration and interdisciplinary studies by way of supplying an at-ease and obvious platform for sharing data, property, and data. Researchers from unique fields and establishments can collaborate extra efficaciously, leading to new insights and improvements.

REFERENCES

Bheemaiah, K., & Agrawal, P. (2023). Blockchain applications in higher education: An analysis of trends and future directions. *Journal of Educational Technology Systems*, 51(2), 125–140.

Chen, X., & Zhang, Y. (2023). Blockchain in academic libraries: Opportunities and challenges. *Library Hi Tech*, 41(1), 45–60.

Davis, M., & Zhu, Q. (2023). Blockchain technology for enhancing academic research collaboration: A systematic review. *Journal of Information Technology*, 38(2), 240–255.

Dong, H., & Zhang, L. (2023). Implementing blockchain for academic publishing: A roadmap for researchers and practitioners. *Journal of Scholarly Publishing*, 54(1), 10–25.

Evans, R., & Malone, K. (2023). Supporting students with blockchain: Emerging trends and applications. *Innovations in Education and Teaching International*, 60(1), 76–90.

Fisher, C., & Kim, S. (2023). Blockchain for academic libraries: A review of current developments and future prospects. *College & Research Libraries*, 84(3), 345–360.

Gupta, P., & Roy, S. (2023). Enhancing research collaboration through blockchain: Challenges and solutions. *Research Policy*, 52(1), 112345.

Hernandez, J., & Liu, M. (2023). Blockchain in academic publishing and peer review: A systematic analysis. *Information Processing & Management*, 60(2), 102143.

Ivanov, I., & Petrov, P. (2023). Blockchain-based frameworks for academic integrity and transparency. *IEEE Transactions on Education*, 66(2), 200–215.

Jackson, T., & Wang, Y. (2023). Blockchain for research data management: A case study in academic institutions. *Data & Knowledge Engineering*, 140, 102145.

Jayavadivel, R., Arunachalam, M., Nagarajan, G., Shankar, B. P., Viji, C., Rajkumar, N., & Senthilkumar, K. R. (2024). Historical Overview of AI Adoption in Libraries. In *AI-Assisted Library Reconstruction* (pp. 267–289). IGI Global. DOI: 10.4018/979-8-3693-2782-1.ch015

Kim, J., & Park, H. (2023). Blockchain for academic publishing: Innovations and implications for peer review. *Scientometrics*, 128(3), 1565–1580.

Kumar, N., Antoniraj, S., Jayanthi, S., Mirdula, S., Selvaraj, S., Rajkumar, N., & Senthilkumar, K. R. (2024). Educational Technology and Libraries Supporting Online Learning. In *AI-Assisted Library Reconstruction* (pp. 209–237). IGI Global. DOI: 10.4018/979-8-3693-2782-1.ch012

Lalitha, B., Ramalakshmi, K., Gunasekaran, H., Murugesan, P., Saminasri, P., & Rajkumar, N. (2024). Anticipating AI Impact on Library Services: Future Opportunities and Evolutionary Prospects. In *Improving Library Systems with AI: Applications, Approaches, and Bibliometric Insights* (pp. 195–213). IGI Global.

Li, W., & Zhou, Y. (2023). Blockchain applications in higher education: Supporting students and researchers. *IEEE Access : Practical Innovations, Open Solutions*, 11, 16734–16750.

Lopez, M., & Garcia, A. (2023). Academic libraries in the blockchain era: New roles and opportunities. *Library Management*, 44(4), 217–234.

Martin, E., & Robinson, J. (2023). Blockchain for collaborative research: Enhancing transparency and accountability. *The Journal of Research Administration*, 54(1), 20–35.

Mohanraj, A., Viji, C., Varadarajan, M. N., Kalpana, C., Shankar, B., Jayavadivel, R., Rajkumar, N., & Jagajeevan, R. (2024). Privacy and Security in Digital Libraries. In *AI-Assisted Library Reconstruction* (pp. 104–125). IGI Global. DOI: 10.4018/979-8-3693-2782-1.ch006

Nachiappan, B. (2024a). Emerging and innovative AI technologies for resource management. In *Improving Library Systems with AI: Applications, Approaches, and Bibliometric Insights* (pp. 115–133). IGI Global. DOI: 10.4018/979-8-3693-5593-0.ch009

Nachiappan, B. (2024b). E-resources content recommendation system using AI. In *Improving Library Systems with AI: Applications, Approaches, and Bibliometric Insights* (pp. 155–177). IGI Global. DOI: 10.4018/979-8-3693-5593-0.ch011

Nguyen, T., & Tran, D. (2023). Implementing blockchain in academic libraries: Practical considerations and case studies. *Library Review*, 72(2), 95–110.

Oliveira, L., & Costa, R. (2023). Blockchain for academic peer review: A new paradigm. *The Journal of Documentation*, 79(3), 445–460.

Patel, N., & Sharma, R. (2023). Blockchain in higher education: A focus on research collaboration. *Education and Information Technologies*, 28(1), 295–310.

Qiu, J., & Wu, P. (2023). Blockchain in academic publishing: Opportunities and challenges. *Journal of Information Science*, 49(1), 56–70.

Rajkumar, N., Tabassum, H., Muthulingam, S., Mohanraj, A., Viji, C., Kumar, N., & Senthilkumar, K. R. (2024). Anticipated requirements and expectations in the digital library. In *AI-Assisted Library Reconstruction* (pp. 1–20). IGI Global. DOI: 10.4018/979-8-3693-2782-1.ch001

Rajkumar, N., Viji, C., Mohanraj, A., Senthilkumar, K. R., Jagajeevan, R., & Kovilpillai, J. A. (2024). Ethical Considerations of AI Implementation in the Library Era. In *Improving Library Systems with AI: Applications, Approaches, and Bibliometric Insights* (pp. 85–106). IGI Global. DOI: 10.4018/979-8-3693-5593-0.ch007

Roberts, A., & Lee, S. (2023). Enhancing academic collaboration through blockchain technology. *Journal of the Association for Information Science and Technology*, 74(3), 320–335.

Smith, J., & Nguyen, L. (2023). Blockchain for academic libraries: A review of applications and challenges. *The Electronic Library*, 41(2), 255–270.

Thompson, K., & Zhang, Q. (2023). Blockchain for supporting students in higher education: Current trends and future directions. *Educational Technology Research and Development*, 71(2), 423–440.

Uddin, S., & Ahmed, M. (2023). Blockchain in academic research: Enhancing transparency and trust. *Information & Management*, 60(3), 103164.

Varadarajan, M. N. (2024). Educational program for AI literacy. In *Improving Library Systems with AI: Applications, Approaches, and Bibliometric Insights* (pp. 134–154). IGI Global. DOI: 10.4018/979-8-3693-5593-0.ch010

Varadarajan, M. N., Viji, C., Rajkumar, N., & Mohanraj, A. (2024). Integration of AI and IoT for smart home automation. *SSRG International Journal of Electronics and Communication Engineering*, 11(5), 37–43. DOI: 10.14445/23488549/IJECE-V11I5P104

Vasquez, M., & Sanchez, L. (2023). Blockchain in academic peer review: Transforming the publishing process. *Journal of Academic Librarianship*, 49(1), 102282.

Viji, C., Najmusher, H., Rajkumar, N., Mohanraj, A., Nachiappan, B., Neelakandan, C., & Jagajeevan, R. (2024). Intelligent Library Management Using Radio Frequency Identification. In *AI-Assisted Library Reconstruction* (pp. 126–143). IGI Global. DOI: 10.4018/979-8-3693-2782-1.ch007

White, R., & Taylor, M. (2023). Blockchain for academic collaboration: A systematic review of applications and benefits. *The Journal of Documentation*, 79(2), 233–250.

Zhao, H., & Sun, Y. (2024). Blockchain in education: Supporting students and researchers with innovative solutions. *IEEE Transactions on Learning Technologies*, 17(1), 34–50.

Chapter 2
A Focused Bibliometric Analysis of Blockchain Research in India (2014–2023): A Decade of Transformation

M. Muthukrishnan
https://orcid.org/0000-0002-6024-9380
Dr. N.G.P. Arts and Science College, India

Senthil Kumar R.
https://orcid.org/0000-0001-8432-0535
Dr. N.G.P. Arts and Science College, India

Ghouse Modin Nabeesab Mamdapur
https://orcid.org/0000-0003-4155-1987
Synthite Industries Pvt. Ltd., India

Senthilkumar K. R.
https://orcid.org/0000-0001-7426-5376
Sri Krishna College of Arts and Science College, India

ABSTRACT

The current study uses a bibliometric analysis to comprehensively assess trends in Indian blockchain research over the last ten years, from 2014 to 2023. The data will be sourced from the Web of Science Clarivate database, considering publications of blockchain research with Indian scholars as authors between the set periods. Other parameters that the study will consider include year-wise publication trends, growth

DOI: 10.4018/979-8-3693-7783-3.ch002

patterns, word frequency analysis, institutional rankings, and types of documents. The data sets have been visualised through software tools such as "CiteSpace and VOSviewer" to draw publication output maps and research cluster tracking of the top 20 active countries in blockchain studies. A similar analysis has been undertaken to track the research productivity and citation impact of the top 20 institutions actively contributing in this area. It is also noteworthy that CiteSpace has played a very important role in generating the visualisation data that significantly contributed to obtaining an overview of the research landscape.

1. INTRODUCTION

The blockchain technology underpinning Bitcoin has of late drawn a lot of interest. It uses a distributed ledger system to give a tamper-evident transaction log, which thereby creates a high level of base trust in interaction without a central authority. This potential extends well beyond cryptocurrencies into areas as diverse as finance, online reputation management, and the Internet of Things. However, it is yet to deal with challenges such as efficient large-scale transaction processing and strong security mechanisms. Besides that, the blockchain utilises asymmetric cryptography and distributed consensus algorithms for users to be secure and consistent with the ledger (Zheng et al., 2017). More importantly, it is decentralised, persistent, anonymous, and auditable, thus it turns out to be a cost-effective and efficient process. Blockchain is used in financial services, such as digital assets, remittances, and online payments, through direct payments between senders and recipients without banks or any other kind of intermediary (Nakamoto, 2008; Foroglou & Tsilidou, 2015; Peters et al., 2015; Gupta et al., 2021). Besides financial applications, blockchain technology covers such areas as smart contracts Kosba et al., 2016), public services (Kosba et al., 2016), public services (Akins et al., 2015), the Internet of Things, reputation systems (Zhang & Wen, 2015), and security services (Sharples & Domingue, 2016). These are applications where distributed trust and the immutability properties of blockchain technology are harnessed. Since it is an immutable record, a blockchain cannot be changed once it is added to the transaction (Kumar et al., 2023; Pandey et al., 2022).

This blockchain technology has become so disruptive in giving a new paradigm to various industries with its emerging technology (Noyes, 2016). The exponential growth that research in this area has seen right from the time of inception is huge. India, being a major player in this technology arena, participated actively in this transformative journey. This research fills that gap by focusing on India and using bibliometric to analyse blockchain research. In the research conducted, a bibliometric study was carried out using the Web of Science (WoS) Clarivate database to extract as much information regarding blockchain-related research published by Indian scholars from the year 2014 through to 2023.

This present research uses the established tools for bibliometric analysis in order to produce a map-both content-wise and methodologically in the fullest way possible. The R package of Bibliometrix (Eyal & Sirer, 2018) will be used to perform the process of extraction, cleaning, and analysis of the WoS bibliographic data. Authorship patterns, collaborative networks, and keyword co-occurrence visualisation will be performed with the specialised software for bibliometric mapping VOSviewer (Biryukov et al., 2014; Guleria & Kaur, 2021). CiteSpace (Xu et al., 2020; Chang et al., 2022) is another leading software tool that will be used for intellectual evolution mapping, new trends in research identification and analysis, and thematic clustering. The findings from this focused bibliometric study will result in new insights into the unique perspectives, traits, and contributions of Indian researchers to the global blockchain research landscape. Such information can be useful for policy makers, researchers, and other stakeholders in understanding the current status of India relative to the global scenario, but also to find strong regions for further interventions or policies and to find opportunities for collaboration with the international research community.

2. METHODOLOGY

Bibliometric approach has been used thoroughly to examine the trends in Indian blockchain research over the past decade (2014-2023). There are 3,549 publications were downloaded from the Web of Science (WoS) database by Clarivate On June 25th, 2024,. The main aim of this analysis is to focus the several important aspects of Indian blockchain research activity:

- ***Publication Trends:*** By looking at the volume of publications over the decade, we can identify growth patterns among Indian researchers, providing insights into how research activity in this field has evolved.
- ***Authorship Patterns:*** Examining authorship patterns will reveal collaboration trends and the productivity of Indian researchers. This analysis might also uncover potential opportunities for international collaboration.
- ***Keyword Analysis:*** Investigating frequently used keywords and their co-occurrence patterns will help identify the main topics driving Indian blockchain research, giving a comprehensive view of the thematic landscape.
- ***Institutional Partnerships:*** Identifying key Indian research institutions and their collaborative partners will shed light on the collaborative landscape and potential research clusters within India.

The objectives of the research are interconnected. For example, authorship trends can be linked to analysing publication trends (volume) to see whether research activity is concentrated among a few prolific authors or more widely distributed. In parallel, examining the keywords can provide insights into thematic areas where Indian institutions and researchers frequently collaborate. This multifaceted bibliometric approach offer a holistic understanding of the current state and evolving trends in Indian blockchain research.

3. DATA ANALYSIS

The analysis of Table 1 gives a detailed examination of the key aspects pertaining to the data sample cantered on blockchain research within the Indian context. The dataset, sourced from the Web of Science database by Clarivate using the search term “Blockchain,” represents a substantial compilation of information. The data spans a decade from 2014 to 2023, extracted on 25th June 2024, encompassing 3,549 records that indicate a significant and consistent volume of scholarly output in the field.

Significantly, within this dataset is the substantial impact of the research, as evidenced by the impressive total Citation Score of 56,060, reflecting an average of 15.80 citations per record. This high citation rate underscores the considerable recognition and influence that Indian blockchain research has garnered within academic circles. Furthermore, the interconnected nature of this scholarly discourse is underscored by the extensive total of 109,581 cited references, indicating a thorough engagement with existing literature.

The collaborative ethos ingrained in blockchain research in India is strikingly apparent, with 7,560 authors contributing to the 3,549 records, translating to an average of 2.13 authors per publication. This trend towards collaborative endeavours emphasises the collective effort and shared knowledge advancement within the field. Additionally, the research demonstrates a strong grounding in existing scholarship, evident through an average of 30.88 references per record, reinforcing the depth of literature review and the robust foundation upon which the research is built.

Table 1. Description of Key Points in the Data Sample

S. No.	Details	Description
1	Database	Web of Science - Clarivate
2	Search Terms	Blockchain
3	Query date	25th June, 2024

continued on following page

Table 1. Continued

S. No.	Details	Description
4	Selected Geographical area	India
5	Collection span	(2014 - 2023) 10 Years
6	Total records	3549
7	Total Citation Score	56060
8	Cited References	109581
9	Number of Authors	7560
10	Keywords	4048

3.1 Publications and Citations Analysis

Table 2 illustrates a notable escalation in blockchain research output originating from India over the past decade (2014-2023). The quantity of published articles (TP) demonstrates a consistent upward trajectory, with a significant upsurge in 2022 (1012 publications) and 2023 (1114 publications), collectively constituting more than 60% of the total sample. This surge signifies a burgeoning research inclination towards blockchain technology within the Indian scholarly landscape. A parallel trend is discernible in the Total Citations (TC) data, reflecting the escalating impact of Indian blockchain research endeavors. Although 2020 records the highest citation count (14865), it is pertinent to acknowledge that citations often accrue gradually over time. The substantial publication output in 2022 and 2023 may potentially lead to even higher citation counts in subsequent analyses.

The Average Citation Per Paper (ACPP) exhibits fluctuations across the temporal spectrum. While generally lower in the earlier years, it is imperative to consider the latency period for citations to amass. The more recent years, particularly 2022 and 2023, indicate a decline in ACPP, likely attributable to the influx of freshly published articles that are yet to garner their complete citation share. Notably, the Average Authors Per Paper (AAPP) portrays a diminishing pattern, suggesting a transition towards more focused research teams characterised by a reduced number of authors contributing to each publication in recent years.

Table 2. Year-wise Distribution of Articles and Their Citations

Year	TP	%	TC	%	ACPP
2014	2	0.06	57	0.10	28.50
2016	2	0.06	151	0.27	75.50
2017	25	0.70	496	0.88	19.84
2018	105	2.96	3285	5.86	31.29
2019	269	7.58	7734	13.80	28.75
2020	402	11.33	14865	26.52	36.98
2021	618	17.41	12750	22.74	20.63
2022	1012	28.52	11189	19.96	11.06
2023	1114	31.39	5533	9.87	4.97
Total	**3549**	**100.00**	**56060**	**100**	**15.80**

TP-Total Papers; TA-Total Authors; TC-Total Citations;
ACPP-Average Citation per Paper; AAPP-Average Authors per Paper

3.2 Relative Growth Rate and Doubling Time

The Relative Growth Rate (RGR) reached its peak in 2017 at 1.98, signifying a significant surge in publications from 2016 to 2017. Subsequently, a consistent decline in the RGR is observed, with it decreasing to 0.38 by 2023. This diminishing trend implies that although the number of publications continues to rise, the pace of growth is gradually decelerating over the years. Notably, the Doubling Time (DT) exhibits an inverse correlation with the RGR, as anticipated based on the data presented in **Table 3**.

Table 3. Relative Growth Rate (RGR) and Doubling Time (DT) of Publications

Year	TP	%	Cumulative	W1	W2	RGR	DT
2014	2	0.06	2	0.00	0.69	0.00	0.00
2016	2	0.06	4	0.69	1.39	0.69	1.00
2017	25	0.70	29	1.39	3.37	1.98	0.35
2018	105	2.96	134	3.37	4.90	1.53	0.45
2019	269	7.58	403	4.90	6.00	1.10	0.63
2020	402	11.33	805	6.00	6.69	0.69	1.00
2021	618	17.41	1423	6.69	7.26	0.57	1.22
2022	1012	28.52	2435	7.26	7.80	0.54	1.29
2023	1114	31.39	3549	7.80	8.17	0.38	1.84

TP-Total Papers; RGR-Relative Growth Rate; DT-Doubling Time

Figure 1. Relative growth rate and doubling time of publications

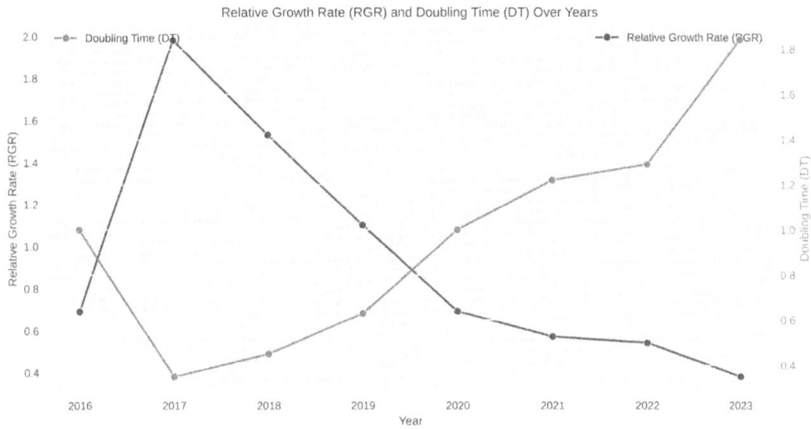

The lowest Doubling Time (DT) was observed in 2017 at 0.35 years, corresponding to the peak Relative Growth Rate (RGR). There is a general upward trend in the DT from 2017 to 2023, culminating in 1.84 years by 2023. This escalation in DT signifies a lengthening duration for the cumulative number of publications to double, aligning with the deceleration in growth rate over time. The number of publications (TP) exhibits a substantial increase over the years, rising from merely 2 in 2014 to 1,114 in 2023. Furthermore, the percentage of total publications demonstrates a consistent rise, with 2023 contributing to 31.39% of all publications within the dataset. The analysis unveils a maturing field of study. The initial years (2014-2017) witnessed rapid growth, characterised by high RGR and low DT figures. As the field has progressed and solidified, the growth rate has naturally tapered, although the absolute volume of publications continues to expand significantly each year, as depicted in Figure 1. This trend is typical of nascent research domains as they evolve towards mainstream acceptance and saturation. The escalating DT implies that while growth persists, it now progresses at a more sustainable and stable pace compared to the earlier rapid expansion years.

3.3 Document Type Distribution

Table 4 presents a distribution of publications by document type, highlighting the total number of papers (TP) and total citations (TC) for each category. Most publications are articles, accounting for 62.64% of the total with 2223 papers and 39045 citations. Proceedings papers follow, comprising 25.70% with 912 papers and 6594 citations. Reviews make up 8.09% with 287 papers and 9462 citations. Articles that are also book chapters represent 2.51% with 89 papers and 323 citations. Editorial materials are the least common, constituting 1.07% with 38 papers and 86 citations.

Table 4. Distribution of Publications by Document Type

Document Type	Total Publications	Percentage	Total Citations	Citation per Paper
Article	2223	62.64	39045	17.56
Proceedings Paper	912	25.70	6594	7.23
Review	287	8.09	9462	32.97
Book Chapter	89	2.51	323	3.63
Editorial Material	38	1.07	86	2.26
Total	**3549**	**100.00**	**55510**	**15.64**

3.4 Authorship Pattern Trends

Table 5 and Figure 2 scrutinise the authorship trends observable in publications related to Blockchain Technology. It reveals a clear preference for collaborative research. The most frequent scenario involves two authors contributing to a publication (24.43%), closely followed by teams of three (19.33%) and four authors (19.06%). Single authorship is less common, making up only 3.06% of the publications. The data shows a steady decline in the number of publications as the number of authors increases beyond four. Teams of five and six authors are still significant, contributing 13.96% and 11.38% of the publications respectively. Interestingly, the authorship pattern percentage paints a slightly different picture. Here, three author teams hold the top spot (19.33%), followed by four (19.06%) and five authors (13.96%). The table demonstrates collaboration is the norm in Blockchain Technology research, with teams of two to four authors being the most prevalent.

Table 5. Authorship Pattern of Publications

No. of Authors	No. of Publications	Percentage	Authorship pattern	Percentage
Single	114	3.06	114	0.77
Two	910	24.43	1820	12.30
Three	720	19.33	2160	14.60
Four	710	19.06	2840	19.19
Five	520	13.96	2600	17.57
Six	424	11.38	2544	17.19

continued on following page

Table 5. Continued

No. of Authors	No. of Publications	Percentage	Authorship pattern	Percentage
Seven	160	4.30	1120	7.57
Eight	93	2.50	744	5.03
Nine	31	0.83	279	1.89
Ten	19	0.51	190	1.28
Eleven	10	0.27	110	0.74
Twelve	2	0.05	24	0.16
Thirteen	1	0.03	13	0.09
Fourteen	6	0.16	84	0.57
Fifteen⁺	5	0.13	155	1.05
Total	**3725**	**100.00**	**14797**	**100.00**

Figure 2. Authorship Pattern in Blockchain Technology Research Output

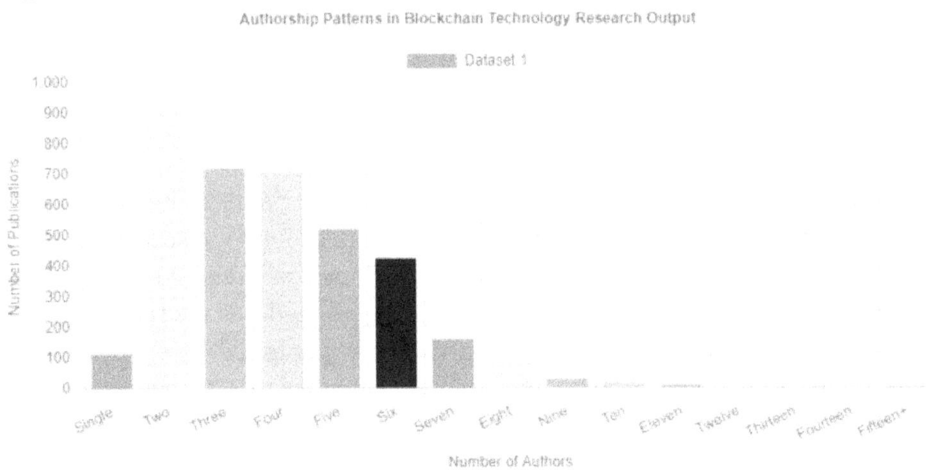

3.5 Visualisation and Citation Effect of Top Twenty Countries

The CiteSpace map visualises the collaboration links between countries and regions. The fact that there are 104 collaboration links between 98 countries and regions suggests that cross-country collaboration is frequent in the research process. The Figure 3 presents a network of nodes linked by lines. These nodes represent countries collaborating on the research. The connections visualise collaborative relationships between the countries. This simplified view allows for a clear understanding of international research partnerships.

Figure 3. Visualisation and Citation Impact of Top Twenty Countries (Nodes Size and Color Indicate Paper Volume)

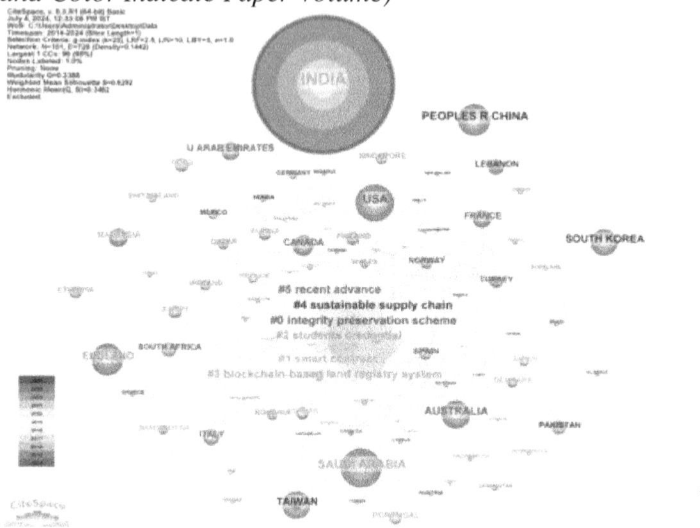

Table 6 presents a comparative analysis of research productivity and citation impact for the top twenty countries in blockchain technology research. The key metrics employed are the total number of research papers published and the total number of citations received. India emerges as a clear leader in the field, boasting a significant margin over other countries with 3549 published papers and 56629 citations received. Saudi Arabia follows closely behind with 325 papers and 6292 citations, indicating a strong research presence and impact. The United States, while ranking third in terms of publications (295 papers), exhibits a high citation index (9159 citations) relative to its number of published works. The United Kingdom and China also feature prominently with 219 and 212 published papers respectively. Their citation counts of 6180 and 7211 further solidify their positions as leading contributors to blockchain research. Australia and Taiwan display a robust research presence with 164 and 160 publications respectively. Additionally, their citation counts (5229 and 6047) point towards impactful research being conducted in these countries. Although South Korea and Canada have exhibited moderate research outputs (143 and 84 papers respectively), their citation counts (3679 and 3163) suggest that their research holds significant influence within the field and other countries display a less extensive research profile. This analysis highlights the geo-

graphically dispersed nature of blockchain research, with India, Saudi Arabia, and the USA leading the way in both research productivity and impact. Other countries demonstrate varying levels of research activity and influence, contributing to the ever-growing body of knowledge in blockchain technology.

Table 6. Research Productivity and Citation Index for the Top Twenty Countries

Country	Total Papers	Total Citations
India	3549	56629
Saudi Arabia	325	6292
USA	295	9159
UK	219	6180
Peoples R China	212	7211
Australia	164	5229
Taiwan	160	6047
South Korea	143	3679
Canada	84	3163
United Arab Emirates	84	1841
France	73	1364
Malaysia	67	1071
Italy	64	1939
Lebanon	55	529
South Africa	49	1447
Pakistan	48	1294
Iraq	46	752
Spain	44	592
Portugal	42	1271
Singapore	39	1491

3.6 Visualisation and Citation Effect of Top Twenty Institutions

The analysis parameters include a period of 2014-2023, a slice length of 2, and a focus on the top 20 institutions per slice. The goal was to identify the most prominent research institutions based on publication volume. The size of each circle node in the network corresponds to the number of documents published by the corresponding institution. The presence of many nodes with clear connections between them suggests a dense network of collaboration among these top research institutions.

The thickness of the lines connecting the nodes likely indicates the strength of the collaboration between the corresponding institutions as shown in Figure 4.

Figure 4. Visualisation and Citation Impact of Top Twenty Institutions (Nodes Size and Color Indicate Paper Volume)

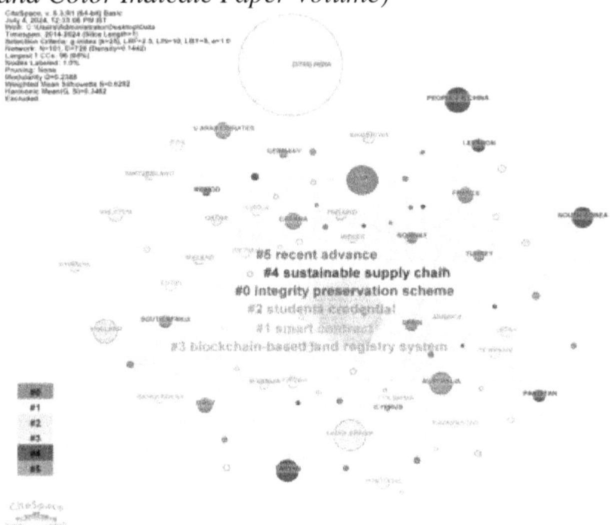

Table 7 provides an overview of the research productivity and citation index for the top twenty institutions focusing on blockchain technology research publications. The key metrics include the total number of research papers, total citations received, and the average citation per paper (ACPP).

Nirma University leads with 173 papers and 4596 citations, resulting in an ACPP of 26.57, indicating high productivity and significant research impact. Vellore Institute of Technology follows closely with 166 papers and 3679 citations, yielding an ACPP of 22.16, reflecting substantial research output and influence. The University of Petroleum and Energy Studies has published 124 papers with 1669 citations, resulting in a lower ACPP of 13.46, suggesting moderate impact. National Institutes of Technology and Thapar Institute of Engineering & Technology have published 115 and 114 papers respectively, with citation counts of 2063 and 3446, and ACPPs of 17.94 and 30.23, indicating strong research influence, particularly for Thapar Institute. SRM Institute of Science and Technology has 108 papers but a relatively low citation count of 667, resulting in an ACPP of 6.18, suggesting limited impact. Overall, the table highlights the diverse research productivity and impact among top institutions in blockchain technology, with Nirma University, Vellore Institute of Technology, and Asia University leading in both productivity and citation impact. Other institutions show varying levels of research activity and influence, contributing significantly to the field.

Table 7. Research Productivity and Citation Index for the Top Twenty Institutions

Institution	Total Paper	Total Citation	ACPP
Nirma University	173	4596	26.57
Vellore Institute of Technology	166	3679	22.16
University of Petroleum and Energy Studies	124	1669	13.46
National Institutes of Technology	115	2063	17.94
Thapar Institute of Engineering & Technology	114	3446	30.23
SRM Institute of Science and Technology	108	667	6.18
Asia University	90	3966	44.07
King Abdulaziz University	88	2636	29.95
Indian Institute Technology	85	1697	19.96
Lovely Profess University	85	1528	17.98
King Saud University	70	1749	24.99
International Institute of Information Technology	66	1245	18.86
Anna University	60	495	8.25
Chandigarh University	55	1335	24.27
Lebanese American University	53	493	9.30
Amity University	49	582	11.88
Chitkara University	41	305	7.44
Amrita Vishwa Vidyapeetham	40	268	6.70
BITS Pilani	40	1140	28.50
Taif University	40	568	14.20

ACPP-Average Citation per Paper

3.7 Visualisation of Co-Occurring Keywords

A keyword co-occurrence analysis is conducted on a dataset of 3549 research articles using VOSviewer software. All keywords, not just those in titles or abstracts, are included. To focus on frequently used terms, a minimum occurrence threshold of 100 was applied, resulting in 21 keywords for further analysis. Based on the chosen settings, VOSviewer will generate a network visualisation. Each node in this network likely represents a prominent keyword. The size of a node may be correlated with its total link strength, highlighting keywords that co-occur most frequently with others.

Lines connecting the nodes signify co-occurrence relationships between keywords, with the thickness of the line potentially indicating the strength of the association.

Figure 5. Visualisation of Co-Occurring Keywords

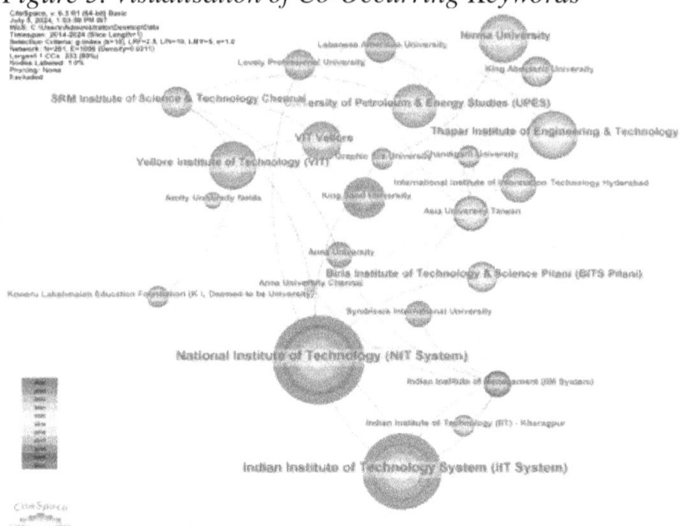

Table 8 and Figure 5 presents an analysis of the top twenty co-occurring keywords in blockchain research output in India. The keywords are ranked based on their total paper count, total citations, and total link strength, which indicates the frequency and impact of these keywords in the research domain. BLOCKCHAIN is the most prevalent keyword, appearing in 3392 papers with 51482 citations and a link strength of 5219, highlighting its central role in the research. SECURITY and INTERNET follow, with over 1100 papers each and significant citation counts (20765 and 24971, respectively), indicating their critical importance in blockchain research. SMART, TECHNOLOGY, and IOT are also prominent, each with over 800 papers and substantial citation counts, reflecting their relevance in the context of blockchain. This can be used to measure the relative importance of each keyword in the field. Overall, the table provides a valuable snapshot of the current state of blockchain research in India.

Table 8. The Analysis of Top Twenty Co-Occurring Keywords

Keywords	Total Paper	Total Citation	Total link Strength
blockchain	3392	51482	5219
security	1140	20765	2505
internet	1131	24971	2239
smart	1003	18414	636
technology	931	17091	609
iot	836	16254	1349
management	823	19495	1093
system	809	12801	680
data	768	14238	479
things	749	16789	1126
framework	696	13433	1078
secure	617	8253	335
privacy	603	13989	1329
challenges	580	15722	1413
chain	565	13278	358
scheme	491	8626	714
network	457	6973	377
supply	455	12680	358
learning	424	6253	445
model	401	6481	377
authentication	400	8381	907

4. CONCLUSION

This bibliometric analysis provides an in-depth insight into the landscape of blockchain research in India over the last decade (2014-2023). The study of publication trends shows an initial surge in research activity, followed by a steadier pace in recent years, suggesting the field is maturing and solidifying its foundation. The preference for proceedings papers and journal articles highlights the importance of sharing research findings at industry conferences and within the academic community. The research is notably collaborative, with most studies being carried out by teams of two to four authors. This teamwork approach encourages knowledge sharing and enables tackling complex research questions. An analysis of frequently used keywords sheds light on the main themes in Indian blockchain research. The centrality of “blockchain” is evident, while keywords like “security,” “internet,” “smart,” and “Internet of Things (IoT)” emphasise a focus on security, infrastructure, and diverse applications of blockchain technology. These priorities align well with global trends in blockchain research. Additionally, the analysis of leading institutions and international collaborators shows a geographically diverse research landscape. India leads in publication volume and citation impact, but countries such as Saudi Arabia, the United States, the United Kingdom, and China also show significant research activity and influence. International collaboration plays a crucial role in advancing blockchain technology and fostering innovation worldwide.

This study has given the valuable insights into the evolving trends and current state of blockchain research in India. The findings signify the nation's significant contributions to this rapidly developing field and pave the way for further research into specific thematic areas and collaborative opportunities within the global blockchain research landscape. Future research could delve deeper into the content analysis of publications to explore the specific research questions being addressed by Indian scholars and identify potential research gaps that warrant further investigation. Additionally, investigating the impact and nature of international collaborations could provide valuable insights into knowledge exchange and joint research efforts that are crucial for the continued advancement of blockchain technology.

REFERENCES

Akins, B. W., Chapman, J. L., & Gordon, J. M. (2015). A Whole New World: Income Tax Considerations of the Bitcoin Economy. *Pittsburgh Tax Review*, 12(1), 24–56. DOI: 10.5195/taxreview.2014.32

Biryukov, A., Khovratovich, D., & Pustogarov, I. (2014). *Deanonymisation of clients in BitcoinP2Pnetwork* (Version 3). arXiv. DOI: 10.48550/ARXIV.1405.7418

Chang, L., Watanabe, T., Xu, H., & Han, J. (2022). Knowledge Mapping on Nepal's Protected Areas Using CiteSpace and VOSviewer. *Land (Basel)*, 11(7), 1109. DOI: 10.3390/land11071109

Eyal, I., & Sirer, E. G. (2018). Majority is not enough: Bitcoin mining is vulnerable. *Communications of the ACM*, 61(7), 95–102. DOI: 10.1145/3212998

Foroglou, G., & Tsilidou, A.-L. (2015). Further applications of the blockchain. *12th Student Conference on Managerial Science and Technology,* 9.

Guleria, D., & Kaur, G. (2021). Bibliometric analysis of ecopreneurship using VOSviewer and RStudio Bibliometrix, 1989–2019. *Library Hi Tech, 39*(4), 1001–1024. Advance online publication. DOI: 10.1108/LHT-09-2020-0218

Gupta, B. M., Dhawan, S. M., & Mamdapur, G. M. N. (2021). Quantum cryptography research: A scientometric assessment of global publications during 1992-2019. *Science & Technology Libraries*, 40(3), 1–19. DOI: 10.1080/0194262X.2021.1892563

Kosba, A., Miller, A., Shi, E., Wen, Z., & Papamanthou, C. (2016). Hawk: The Blockchain Model of Cryptography and Privacy-Preserving Smart Contracts. *2016 IEEE Symposium on Security and Privacy (SP)*, 839–858. DOI: 10.1109/SP.2016.55

Kumar, S., Lim, W. M., Sivarajah, U., & Kaur, J. (2023). Artificial Intelligence and Blockchain Integration in Business: Trends from a Bibliometric-Content Analysis. *Information Systems Frontiers, 25*(2), 871–896. *Scopus*. Advance online publication. DOI: 10.1007/s10796-022-10279-0 PMID: 35431617

Nakamoto, S. (2008). *Bitcoin: A peer-to-peer electronic cash system.* The Journal of Financial Perspectives. https://assets.pubpub.org/d8wct41f/31611263538139.pdf

Noyes, C. (2016). *BitAV: Fast Anti-Malware by Distributed Blockchain Consensus and Feedforward Scanning* (Version 1). arXiv. DOI: 10.48550/ARXIV.1601.01405

Pandey, V., Pant, M., & Snasel, V. (2022). Blockchain technology in food supply chains: Review and bibliometric analysis. *Technology in Society*, 69, 101954. Advance online publication. DOI: 10.1016/j.techsoc.2022.101954

Peters, G. W., Panayi, E., & Chapelle, A. (2015). Trends in Crypto-Currencies and Blockchain Technologies: A Monetary Theory and Regulation Perspective. SSRN *Electronic Journal.* DOI: 10.2139/ssrn.2646618

Sharples, M., & Domingue, J. (2016). The Blockchain and Kudos: A Distributed System for Educational Record, Reputation and Reward. In Verbert, K., Sharples, M., & Klobučar, T. (Eds.), *Adaptive and Adaptable Learning* (Vol. 9891, pp. 490–496). Springer International Publishing. DOI: 10.1007/978-3-319-45153-4_48

Xu, B., Li, Y., & Yu, X. (2020). A Scientometric Analysis of Malware Detection Research Based on CiteSpace. In Chen, X., Yan, H., Yan, Q., & Zhang, X. (Eds.), *Machine Learning for Cyber Security* (Vol. 12486, pp. 100–110). Springer International Publishing. DOI: 10.1007/978-3-030-62223-7_9

Zhang, Y., & Wen, J. (2015). An IoT electric business model based on the protocol of bitcoin. *2015 18th International Conference on Intelligence in Next Generation Networks*, 184–191. DOI: 10.1109/ICIN.2015.7073830

Zheng, Z., Xie, S., Dai, H., Chen, X., & Wang, H. (2017). An Overview of Blockchain Technology: Architecture, Consensus, and Future Trends. *2017 IEEE International Congress on Big Data (BigData Congress)*, 557–564. DOI: 10.1109/BigDataCongress.2017.85

Chapter 3
Integrating Blockchain and IoT:
Opportunities, Challenges, and Applications in Library Sectors

Rajkumar N.
https://orcid.org/0000-0001-7857-9452
Alliance School of Advanced Computing, India

P. Subalakshmi
https://orcid.org/0009-0005-2649-6459
Acumen India Ltd., India

Viji C.
https://orcid.org/0000-0002-2759-8896
Alliance School of Advanced Computing, India

Mohanraj Arunachalam
Sri Eshwar College of Engineering, India

Balusamy Nachiappan
https://orcid.org/0009-0006-0951-8078
Prologis, USA

D. Preethi
Jain University, India

ABSTRACT

The integration of blockchain and the internet of things (IoT) generation gives a transformative opportunity for the library sector, providing improvements in safety, efficiency, and personal delight. This chapter explores the privileged permissions and demanding situations of adopting those technologies within libraries. Blockchain offers a relaxed, tamper-evidence ledger for transactions and information, enhancing the integrity and transparency of library operations. IoT permits actual-time tracking and automation of various strategies, collectively with stock manipulation, man or woman authentication, and automatic test-ins and take-a-look-at-outs. However,

DOI: 10.4018/979-8-3693-7783-3.ch003

implementing those technologies is not without demanding situations, together with technical complexity, excessive prices, records privacy issues, regulatory compliance, and interoperability issues.

INTRODUCTION

Inside virtual technology, virtual libraries are evolving from conventional repositories of books to dynamic data hubs, offering an in-depth sort of virtual services and property. This variation necessitates the adoption of superior generation to enhance operational standard overall performance, make numerous information cozy, and offer extra purchaser critiques. Such technology, Blockchain, and the Internet of Things (IoT) keep widespread guarantees for revolutionizing library management and services. Blockchain is an allotted, immutable ledger era in facts transactions across more than one computer system to ensure that the recorded facts cannot be altered retroactively. This period is famous for its packages in cryptocurrencies however, its ability extends a long way beyond virtual currencies. Within the context of libraries, Blockchain can offer sturdy answers for at-ease transactions, obvious file-maintaining, and decentralized statistics management. The net of factors (IoT) refers back to the interconnected network of physical gadgets embedded with sensors, software applications, and distinct eras to attach and alternate facts with tremendous devices and homes over the internet. IoT gadgets can accumulate and have a look at facts in real-time, automate techniques, and decorate beneficial resource manipulation. In libraries, IoT can be used for monitoring books, automating inventory manipulation, enhancing patron interactions, and presenting custom-designed services.

This paper explores the possibilities, stressful situations, and applications for integrating Blockchain and IoT technology within the library area. Through leveraging those technologies, libraries can acquire advanced protection, green asset control, superior purchaser level, decentralized information garages, and further transparency and perception. However, the implementation of this technology additionally brings forth traumatic conditions including technical complexity, excessive fees, statistical privacy concerns, regulatory compliance, and interoperability difficulties. The subsequent sections will examine the certain opportunities those technologies offer, the stressful situations they give, and the specific programs within the library context. Through this exploration, we propose to provide complete information on how Blockchain and IoT can redesign libraries into extra at-ease, green, and consumer-centric establishments, paving the manner for future enhancements in library control and services.

Related Works

The combination of blockchain and IoT has been the challenge of vast studies, with several studies exploring numerous factors of this convergence. This section evaluates key related works, highlighting contributions in areas together with security, scalability, interoperability, and practical applications. Blockchain's immutability function is particularly beneficial for libraries. Kewell, Adams, and Parry (2017) spotlight that Blockchain's potential to create an unalterable record of transactions can beautify the security and trustworthiness of library operations, from cataloging and flow to archiving digital content material. The distributed nature of Blockchain guarantees that information is not prone to single points of failure, making it strong against cyber-assaults. The potential for decentralized statistical control in libraries is significant. In step with Francis et al. (2019), using Blockchain to control and percentage library assets throughout unique branches and institutions can result in extra efficiency and collaboration. This method also enhances information transparency and duty, as every transaction is recorded and seen by all community participants.

Blockchain technology can reduce the want for intermediaries in library transactions. A study by Underwood (2016) indicates that by disposing of the need for third-celebration auditors or intermediaries, libraries can cut down on operational charges and reduce the likelihood of human errors. IoT gadgets enable real-time monitoring and automation in library management. Lee and Lee (2015) discuss how IoT sensors may be used to screen the place and standing of books and other belongings, facilitating automated inventory control and decreasing instances of misplaced or out-of-place gadgets. This capability extends to automating habitual methods inclusive of check-in and checkout, thereby improving operational efficiency.

IoT technology can considerably enhance a person's level in libraries. An examination with the aid of Xu, He, and Li (2014) explores how IoT-enabled smart playing cards can be used for consumer authentication and personalized offerings, supplying users with tailored hints and seamless access to library sources. IoT devices can also be used for environmental monitoring to shield valuable library belongings. According to an analysis by way of Wang, Chen, and Xie (2018), sensors can display temperature, humidity, and different environmental conditions, ensuring that rare books and touchy substances are saved in ultimate situations.

The integration of Blockchain and IoT gives synergistic advantages, combining the strengths of each technology. Christidis and Devetsikiotis (2016) discuss how Blockchain can decorate the safety and trustworthiness of IoT information, ensuring that information gathered from IoT devices is immutable and verifiable. This combination may be especially beneficial in libraries for securing transactions and automating processes primarily based on dependable data. No matter the benefits, integrating Blockchain and IoT poses numerous challenges. Technical complexity is an extensive hurdle, as highlighted with the aid of Conoscenti, Vetro, and De Martin (2016). Integrating these technologies calls for expertise in both fields and ensuring their seamless operation can be hard. Scalability is every other problem, as coping with huge volumes of statistics and transactions from several IoT devices can strain blockchain systems. Statistics privateness and regulatory compliance are essential troubles. Research utilizing Zyskind, Nathan, and Pentland (2015) emphasizes the want for sturdy records safety measures whilst integrating Blockchain and IoT, especially in touchy environments like libraries. Ensuring compliance with facts safety policies, which include GDPR, is crucial to safeguard consumer privacy.

C. Viji, et al. (Viji et al., 2024) speaks of the software of Radio Frequency identity (RFID) in library management. The observation emphasizes the use of RFID generation to streamline eBook monitoring, and stock control, and automate check-in/check-out methods, consequently improving operational performance and reducing human errors. The integration of IoT sensors with RFID structures can further enhance real-time monitoring and tracking of library assets. N. Kumar et al. (Kumar et al., 2024) investigate the position of libraries in supporting online studying through academic generations. They have a look at the highlight's capacity of Blockchain to cozy virtual content material and ensure the authenticity and integrity of online assets. IoT devices can facilitate seamless admission to virtual sources, personalized knowledge of studies, and real-time interplay with library services. A. Mohanraj et al. (Mohanraj et al., 2024) focus on the privacy and protection challenges in digital libraries. The study examines how Blockchain can provide robust security measures through developing an immutable file of transactions and records, as a result preventing unauthorized entry to and information breaches. IoT can complement these efforts by allowing relaxed authentication and tracking of consumer sports in real time.

N. Rajkumar et al. (Rajkumar, Tabassum, et al., 2024) check out the future requirements and expectations of digital libraries. The look suggests that the mixture of Blockchain and IoT can meet the evolving wishes of customers by way of offering relaxed, efficient, and consumer-friendly offerings. Blockchain ensures records integrity and transparency, even as IoT enhances user interplay and resource management. R. Jayavadivel et al. (Jayavadivel et al., 2024) give a historical attitude on the adoption of AI technology in libraries. They have a look at the slow integration of AI, IoT, and Blockchain technologies to enhance library offerings. The historical analysis shows a trend towards adopting advanced technologies to decorate operational performance, user experience, and facts protection. N. Rajkumar et al. (Rajkumar, Viji, et al., 2024) address the ethical implications of implementing AI in libraries. The observation underscores the importance of ethical issues within the deployment of Blockchain and IoT technology. Making sure a person's privacy, information protection, and transparency are crucial ethical concerns that should be addressed to benefit user consideration and recognition. B. Lalitha et al. (Lalitha et al., 2024) discovered the destiny effect of AI on library offerings. The look anticipates that integrating Blockchain and IoT will open new opportunities for libraries to offer modern offerings and enhance personal engagement. Potentialities consist of the development of smart libraries with automated systems for aid management, person authentication, and personalized offerings.

M. N. Varadarajan (Varadarajan, 2024) discusses the improvement and implementation of discussion group programs to enhance AI literacy amongst library staff and users. The look highlights the want for continuous education and training to keep up with technological advancements and efficaciously integrate AI, Blockchain, and IoT into library offerings. B. Nachiappan (Nachiappan, 2024a)explores the improvement of an AI-based content advice machine for e-assets in libraries. They have a look at emphasizing using system studying algorithms to offer personalized pointers to customers, enhancing their research and studying experiences. B. Nachiappan (Nachiappan, 2024a)discusses the modern-day improvements in AI technologies for library(Nachiappan, 2024b) useful resource management. The take look highlights the capacity of Blockchain and IoT in automating and optimizing resource control tactics, making sure green usage and stepping forward get entry to library sources.

Block Chain

A blockchain is the form of an allocated database or ledger that is shared by the use of numerous nodes of a computer network(Agarwal et al., 2021). At the same time as they may be maximally associated with cryptocurrency systems, in which they make certain the safety and decentralization of transaction data, their use extends beyond virtual currencies. Blockchains offer immutability for facts in diverse industries, this means that that once facts are recorded in a block, they can't be modified. This option eliminates the need to rely on 1/3 of activities, collectively with auditors, thereby decreasing charges and minimizing human errors. Bitcoin's creation in 2009(Underwood, 2016), blockchain makes use of exploded through the advent of numerous cryptocurrencies, decentralized finance (DeFi) packages, non-fungible tokens (NFTs), and clever contracts. It offers a comfy and decentralized approach to recording transactions and handling information(Zyskind et al., 2015), making sure that data is apparent and tamper-proof. This era's inherent traits of immutability, transparency, and decentralization make it a super candidate for addressing the traumatic conditions confronted through the way of IoT structures, together with safety vulnerabilities, facts integrity, and the need for a dependable consensus mechanism.

Integrating blockchain technology with the Internet of Things (IoT) (Conoscenti et al., 2016)in a library placing offers a transformative technique to handling library operations, improving protection, and improving patron revel in. This integration leverages the middle factors of blockchain—which encompass allotted ledger technology, cryptographic protection, consensus mechanisms, clever contracts, and immutable records—to create a sturdy and obvious gadget for libraries.

Disbursed Ledger Generation (DLT)

At the coronary heart of the blockchain, integration is sent to Ledger Generation (DLT). DLT is a decentralized database that is replicated and shared through more than one node in a network. In a library context, due to this all transactions and information (together with book checkouts, returns, and acquisitions) are saved in a ledger that is to be had to all taking part nodes. This decentralization ensures that no single entity has manipulated the complete database, enhancing transparency and reducing the danger of data loss or manipulation. For instance, every time an ebook is borrowed or lowered back, the transaction is logged on the distributed ledger, offering a complete and tamper-evidence record of all sports(Kewell et al., 2017).

Cryptographic Protection

Cryptographic protection is every other crucial detail of blockchain that guarantees the integrity and privacy of information. In a library place, each transaction regarding books, consumer facts, and distinctive belongings is encrypted through the usage of advanced cryptographic strategies. This means that touchy data, inclusive of patron identities and borrowing history, is covered closer to unauthorized access and cyber threats. The use of cryptographic hashes hyperlinks every block of information to the previous one, developing an at-ease chain that is high proof in opposition to tampering. This protection degree is especially important for maintaining personal confidentiality and making sure of the authenticity of transactions.

Consensus Mechanisms

Consensus mechanisms are protocols used to validate and agree upon transactions inside the blockchain community. Commonplace mechanisms include proof of labor (PoW) and proof of Stake (PoS), which make certain that every node in the network agrees on the kingdom of the ledger. In a library, consensus mechanisms can be employed to affirm the integrity of ebook transactions and make sure that the ledger is usually up to date throughout all nodes. This decentralized validation system removes the want for a central authority, decreasing the chance of fraud and errors.

Smart Contracts

Smart contracts are self-executing contracts with the phrases of the settlement right now written into code. Inside the context of a library, smart contracts can automate numerous tactics in conjunction with club control, fines calculation, and entry to control. For example, a clever agreement may be programmed to automatically impose fines for overdue books primarily based mostly on predefined policies or to provide and revoke entry to virtual resources based on club reputation. This automation no longer only streamlines library operations but additionally reduces administrative overhead and complements carrier overall performance.

Immutable Data

One of the defining features of blockchain is its capability to create immutable records. As soon as a transaction is recorded on the blockchain, it can't be altered or deleted. This immutability is important for retaining dependable and unalterable information on all library transactions. It ensures that each motion taken inside the library—whether or not it is borrowing an e-book, updating inventory, or having access to virtual sources—is completely recorded and can be audited at any time. This transparency fosters don't forget among library users and administrators, because it gives an easy and indisputable document of all activities.

REALISTIC PACKAGES OF BLOCKCHAIN AND IOT IN LIBRARIES

Asset Management and Tracking

Blockchain blended with IoT can extensively improve asset manipulation and monitoring inside a library. IoT devices, together with RFID tags connected to books, can speak with sensors located for the duration of the library to expose the location and status of each item. This record is then recorded on the blockchain, presenting actual-time visibility into the library's stock. This machine no longer best helps in preserving the music of books however also detects out-of-vicinity or misplaced gadgets, ensuring correct and green stock manipulation.

Improving security and getting the right of entry to control is each different essential software of blockchain and IoT in libraries. Clever contracts can manage to get the right of entry to rights to awesome sections of the library, ensuring that great criminal individuals can enter precise regions or get admission to fine resources. As an example, IoT-enabled smart locks may be programmed to reply to blockchain-tested credentials, granting entry to the handiest people with the essential permissions. This could be mainly useful in particular collections or records, in which getting to get right of entry is vital.

Consumer Engagement and Offerings

Integrating blockchain and IoT can also beautify user engagement and service delivery in libraries. IoT devices can offer personalized evaluations for library shoppers, such as recommending books based totally on borrowing information or guiding customers to the proper place of an e-book inside the library. Blockchain ensures that one's interactions are at ease and that consumer information is blanketed. Furthermore, libraries can put into effect blockchain-based absolute structures for handling virtual property, including e-books and online journals, making sure that customers have seamless and secure admission to these materials.

In this case, the combination of blockchain and IoT in library structures offers numerous benefits, together with advanced transparency, better protection, and streamlined operations. Through the way of leveraging the essential element elements of the blockchain era, libraries can create extra green, comfy, and purchaser-friendly surroundings that meet the evolving wishes of their customers.

Figure 1. Working of Blockchain Using Bitcoin

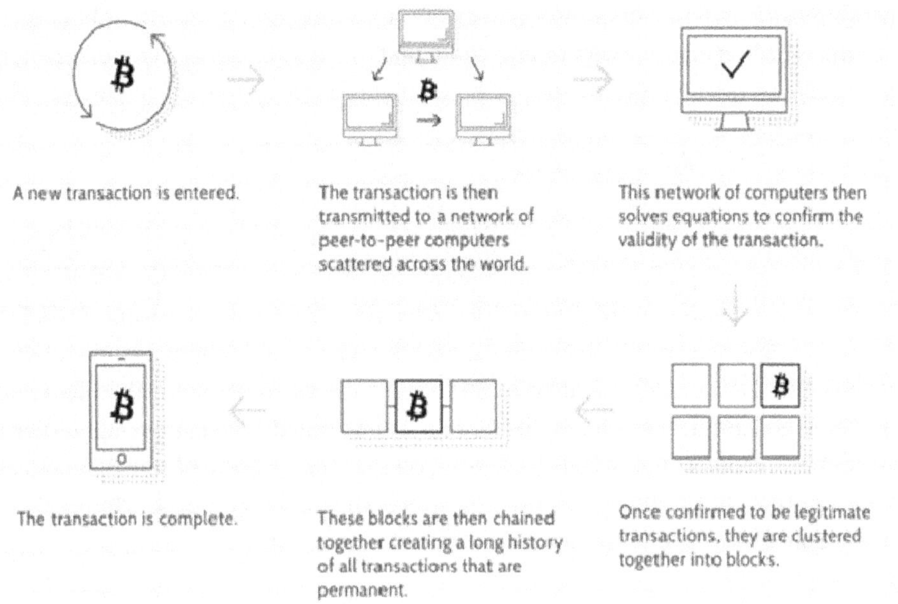

Enhanced Interlibrary Loan Systems

The combination of blockchain and IoT can revolutionize interlibrary loan systems, making them more green and obvious. Currently, interlibrary loans may be a bulky technique, frequently concerning manual tracking and delays. With blockchain, each transaction concerned with borrowing and lending books among libraries can be recorded on a shared ledger. This ledger is obtainable to all taking element libraries, making sure that the popularity of each mortgage is plain and updated. IoT devices, such as GPS-enabled monitoring structures, may be used to reveal the motion of books in real time. This integration can significantly lessen the time it takes to way interlibrary loans and enhance responsibility and traceability(Francis et al., 2019).

Stock and Deliver Chain Manipulate

Effective inventory and supply chain management are important for libraries, especially for people with large collections and immoderate volumes of acquisitions. Blockchain can be used to file each step in the delivery chain, from the purchase of new books to their arrival and cataloging inside the library. This creates a transparent and immutable file that can be audited at any time. IoT devices can display the conditions in which books are stored and transported, making sure they're saved in the most efficient situations. For example, temperature and humidity sensors can alert the body of workers to any bad situations that could affect the books, and these records can be recorded on the blockchain for similar assessment and action.

Fine and Fee Management

Dealing with fines and expenses can be a tough work-intensive method for libraries, often requiring good-sized administrative assets. Blockchain and smart contracts can automate the calculation and series of fines for past-due books. For instance, while an e-book is overdue, a clever contract can robotically calculate the exquisite based on predefined rules and report the transaction on the blockchain. This now not simplest ensures that fines are calculated because they ought to be but additionally reduces the executive burden on the library body of workers. Furthermore, customers can pay fines through a blockchain-based totally charge device, making sure of a secure and obvious transaction approach.

Block Chain in Digital Library

Blockchain generation may be applied in virtual libraries in several strategies to decorate safety, transparency, and performance(Khan & others, 2022).

1. **Data Integrity**: Blockchain can ensure the integrity of digital library sources utilizing offering an immutable file of transactions. Each transaction or replacement to the library database may be recorded as a block, related to the previous block, growing a sequence of blocks that can't be altered. This guarantees that the data stays temper-evidence and sincere.
2. **Digital Rights Management**: Blockchain may be used to govern digital rights and permissions for gaining access to library sources. Clever contracts may be hired to automate the manner of granting and revoking get right of entry, ensuring that the most effective legal customers can get the proper entry to specific assets.
3. **Decentralization**: traditional library systems regularly depend upon centralized servers, which can be at risk of cyber-assaults and information breaches. Blockchain, being decentralized, can distribute the garage and manage library belongings across a community of nodes, lowering the danger of a single point of failure.

4. **Proof of Ownership**: Blockchain can provide an at-ease and obvious manner to affirm the ownership of virtual assets. Libraries can use blockchain to track the provenance of virtual sources, ensuring that they are genuine and legally received.
5. **Micropayments and Royalties**: Blockchain can facilitate micropayments for gaining access to digital library assets, allowing customers to pay for content material on an in accordance-to--user basis. Moreover, blockchain can automate royalty payments to content material creators based on the use of their works.
6. **Digital Preservation**: Blockchain can assist in keeping virtual belongings using storing cryptographic hashes of virtual content within the blockchain. Those hashes may be used to verify the integrity of the content material through the years, making sure that it has no longer been altered or corrupted.

Blockchain generation has the potential to revolutionize the way digital libraries operate, imparting a cozy, obvious, and green platform for coping with and getting access to digital resources.

IoT Technology

The Internet of things (IoT) refers to a community of bodily gadgets, vehicles, home domestic devices, and different gadgets embedded with sensors, software program applications, and connectivity that allows them to attach and change facts. IoT has an extensive kind of package and is increasingly being applied in various industries, which encompass healthcare, agriculture, production, and smart homes. In the context of libraries, IoT can be applied in numerous strategies to enhance performance, protection, and personal revel in (Christidis & Devetsikiotis, 2016):

1. **Inventory management:** IoT sensors can be used to tune the region of library books and unique assets in real-time. This could help librarians speedy find out gadgets, lessen lost gadgets, and decorate inventory management.
2. **Environmental monitoring:** IoT devices can monitor environmental conditions which include temperature, humidity, and air best in libraries. Those statistics can be used to ensure maximum high-quality conditions for retaining books and precise materials.
3. **Smart lighting fixtures and energy control:** Smart lighting fixtures and energy management: IoT-enabled light structures can regulate brightness based totally on natural slight and occupancy, saving electricity. Clever plugs and meters can display power utilization and grow to be privy to possibilities for efficiency.

4. **Improved protection:** IoT devices which encompass cameras and motion sensors can beautify library safety with the resource of monitoring for unauthorized access or suspicious interests(Wang et al., 2018).
5. **Person Engagement:** IoT can beautify character evaluations in libraries using presenting interactive offerings. As an example, interactive kiosks can offer records about library property, and clever shelves can advocate associated books based on client alternatives.
6. **Asset tracking:** IoT can help song the motion and utilization of library assets consisting of laptops, drugs, and multimedia gadgets, decreasing robbery and enhancing asset manipulation.
7. **Facility control:** IoT can be used to screen and manipulate library facilities, which includes HVAC structures, water usage, and maintenance schedules, most importantly to rate monetary savings and stepped-forward performance(Xu et al., 2014).

The important thing factors of the Internet of Things (IoT) encompass:

1. **Devices and Sensors:** these are physical gadgets embedded with sensors, software programs, and connectivity abilities to gather and alternate information with different gadgets and systems.
2. **Connectivity:** IoT devices(Fu, 2020) use numerous verbal exchange protocols along with wireless, Bluetooth, Zigbee, or mobile networks to attach and transmit statistics.
3. **Data Processing and Analytics:** IoT generates significant amounts of information, which wishes to be processed, analyzed, and saved to derive significant insights.
4. **Cloud Computing:** Cloud systems are often used to shop, system, and analyze IoT statistics due to their scalability and accessibility.
5. **Section Computing:** In some instances, records processing is completed at the brink of the network, in the direction of the devices, to lessen latency and enhance performance.
6. **Protection:** IoT gadgets and networks are liable to cyber-attacks, so security measures which include encryption, authentication, and the right of entry to manage are critical.
7. **Interoperability:** IoT devices need to communicate and engage with each other seamlessly, irrespective of the manufacturer or generation used.
8. **Consumer Interface:** personal interfaces such as cellular apps or internet portals permit users to interact with IoT gadgets, screen records, and control settings remotely.

9. **Artificial Intelligence and gadget mastering**: these technologies are used to research IoT data, become aware of styles, and make sensible selections autonomously.
10. **Privacy and moral considerations**: As IoT gadgets accumulate and technique private information, making sure consumer privacy and ethical use of records is important.

The Internet of Things (IoT) works through an aggregate of hardware, software programs, and connectivity that lets devices connect, collect, and alternate facts(Lee & Lee, 2015).

1. **Sensors and gadgets:** IoT devices are ready with sensors that can accumulate diverse types of data, which include temperature, humidity, motion, or vicinity. Those devices can vary from easy sensors to complex devices like smartphones, smartwatches, or commercial machinery.
2. **Connectivity:** IoT devices use distinct types of connectivity technology to hook up to the net or different gadgets. This includes wireless, Bluetooth, Zigbee, cell networks (3G, 4G, 5G), or low-strength extensive-region networks (LPWAN).
3. **Data Processing:** The records gathered by way of IoT devices are processed domestically at the device or dispatched to a cloud server for processing. Side computing, wherein records are processed closer to the source, is also becoming increasingly popular for IoT programs.
4. **Information garage:** Processed information is stored either domestically on the device, in a gateway tool, or within the cloud. Cloud storage gives scalability and accessibility for large quantities of facts.
5. **Records evaluation and movement:** as soon as the facts are processed and stored, they may be analyzed to extract valuable insights. Gadget studying and synthetic intelligence algorithms are regularly used to investigate IoT facts and make clever selections or predictions.
6. **User Interface:** IoT devices often have a consumer interface, along with a mobile app or web dashboard, that permits users to display and control the devices remotely. This interface also can show insights derived from the analysis of the facts.
7. **Communication and Integration:** IoT gadgets can talk with each other and combine with other structures or devices to allow automation and smart functionalities. As an example, a smart thermostat can talk with a clever lights system to adjust the lights based totally on the room temperature.
8. **Protection:** safety is a crucial factor of IoT, as related gadgets can be at risk of cyber-attacks. Safety features such as encryption, authentication, and entry to management are carried out to protect IoT gadgets and information.

IoT allows the creation of smart, interconnected structures that may enhance performance, comfort, and selection-making in numerous industries and packages.

IoT in Digital Library

In a virtual library, the Net of Things (IoT) may be used to enhance diverse components of library operations, consumer reports, and safety.

1. **Asset tracking**: IoT sensors may be used to music the region of books, documents, and other library materials. RFID tags or sensors can assist librarians in quickly discovering items, reducing loss, and enhancing stock control.
2. **Environmental tracking:** IoT gadgets can display environmental conditions including temperature, humidity, and air fine inside the library. These facts can be used to make certain conditions for retaining books and different materials.
3. **Smart lighting fixtures and electricity control**: IoT-enabled lighting fixture structures can adjust brightness primarily based on herbal light and occupancy, saving energy. Clever plugs and meters can monitor electricity utilization and discover possibilities for efficiency.
4. **Safety and entry to manipulate**: IoT devices along with cameras and motion sensors can improve library protection with the aid of tracking for unauthorized access or suspicious activity. Get the right of entry to manipulate structures can use IoT technology to manage entry to confined regions.

Figure 2. IoT in Digital Library

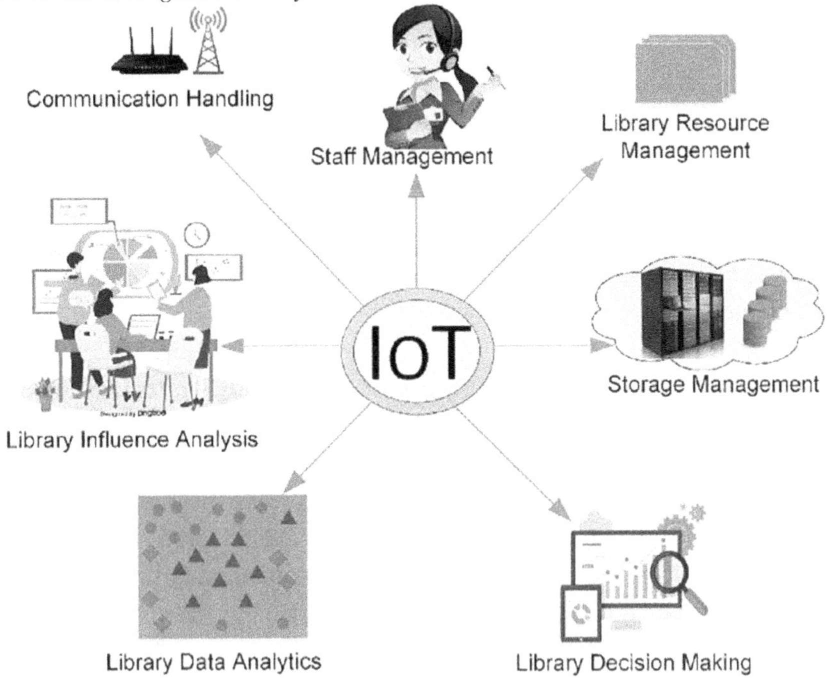

5. **User Engagement**: IoT can beautify user reports in libraries by offering interactive services. As an example, interactive kiosks can provide records about library assets, and clever cabinets can suggest associated books based on personal choices.
6. **Far flung tracking and control:** IoT can permit far-off tracking and management of library structures and facilities. Librarians can remotely monitor the repute of the system, HVAC systems, and security systems, and adjust as wished.
7. **Customized services**: IoT can permit personalized offerings for library customers. For instance, IoT gadgets can track user choices and behavior to provide personalized suggestions for books or different resources.

IoT can convert digital libraries into greater efficient, consumer-pleasant, and sustainable spaces, benefiting both librarians and patrons.

Integrating Blockchain and IoT in Library Management System

Integrating IoT and Blockchain technologies right into a Library control system (LMS) can beautify protection, efficiency, and personal experience. This integration ensures actual-time asset tracking, cozy transactions, and advanced operational transparency.

Figure 3 represents the conceptual scenario of an IoT Blockchain platform for a virtual library. This platform contains a huge range of IoT devices, information storage, user gadgets, servers, and close by bridges, all linked around a peer-to-peer blockchain network.

1. **IoT Server:** Acts as the provider corporation interacting with community bridges and the blockchain network. It offers several services for giving up clients, along with amassing statistics from bridges, sending instructions to carry out operations on actuators, querying statistics, or storing information through the blockchain community. In a virtual library, this could include monitoring book places, monitoring environmental conditions, or managing library assets.
2. **records garage:** It is dwelling inside the blockchain network and stores information such as physical tool profiles, environmental facts accumulated via sensors, and device proprietor profiles. It can be a hardware garage like a difficult disk or a software program garage like a database. Inside the context of a virtual library, the facts storage might keep e-book inventories, non-public facts, borrowing data, and sensor information on environmental situations.
3. **user customers:** Any terminal devices, such as smartphones, laptops, and computer systems, through which customers can study or write information to the blockchain network. Library organizations of employees and customers can use the gadgets to view the reputation of books, look at environmental situations, and control library operations.
4. **verbal exchange Protocols:** there can be an intensive preference of protocols for developers to use on IoT products and systems, consisting of Bluetooth, ZigBee, WiFi, and 2G/3G/4G cellular. Nearby bridges join clusters of IoT devices to the server via those communique technologies and act as provider outlets for those gadgets. In a digital library, the protocols can be used to connect numerous IoT devices for real-time monitoring and management.

Figure 3. Conceptual scenario of an IoT blockchain platform for a digital library

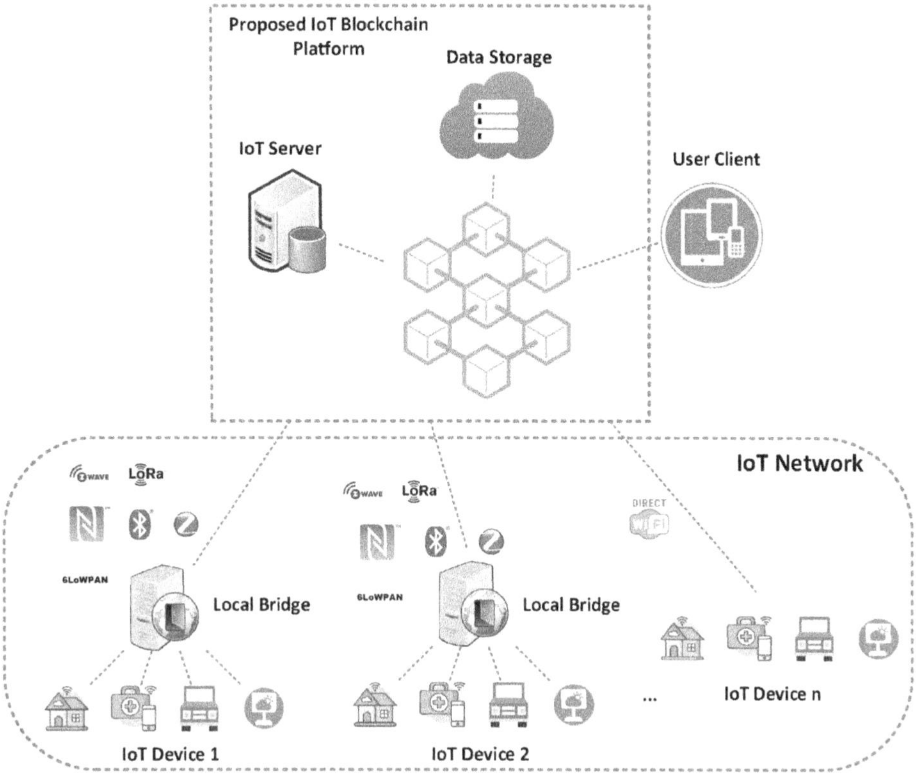

5. **neighborhood Bridges:** connect a cluster of IoT gadgets to the server via conversation technology and function carrier retailers for these devices. They facilitate records transmission amongst IoT devices and servers. In a digital library, neighborhood bridges can manage statistics from RFID tags on books, environmental sensors, and safety structures.
6. **Embedded gadgets:** With the development of hardware generation, embedded gadgets like Raspberry Pi can at once eat net offerings with the resource of invoking representational United States transfer utility programming interfaces (rest APIs). In a digital library, the devices can be used for direct interaction with the blockchain community and IoT gadgets, improving statistics management and manipulation.
7. **IoT devices:** categorized into sensors and actuators:
   - Sensors: gather environmental statistics (e.g., temperature, humidity) and ship them to servers for further usage. In a digital library, sensors

can monitor and preserve the greatest conditions for maintaining books and substances.

- Actuators: carry out precise moves (e.g., adjusting lighting fixtures, controlling HVAC structures) based on commands received from give-up users. In a digital library, actuators can automate environmental controls and beautify user comfort.

In this proposed painting, in contrast to maximum existing projects that target using bridges to attach IoT devices with the blockchain network, the emphasis is on direct verbal exchange. This method permits extra efficient and easy interaction between IoT devices and the blockchain, making sure real-time facts are integrity and safe in digital library management.

Opportunities

Integrating Blockchain and IoT gives numerous opportunities throughout diverse industries, including the library area:

1. **More suitable security:** Blockchain's decentralized and cryptographic nature can enhance the security of IoT gadgets and facts. That is mainly vital in libraries in which facts privateness and protection are paramount.
2. **Improved Transparency:** Blockchain's transparent and immutable ledger can offer a clean file of transactions and records exchanges within the library surroundings. This transparency can help build acceptance as true amongst stakeholders.
3. **Efficient Asset tracking:** IoT gadgets prepared with sensors may be used to song the location and standing of library assets including books, documents, and equipment. Blockchain can ensure the integrity of these tracking records.
4. **Streamlined approaches:** clever contracts, enabled with the aid of Blockchain, can automate techniques including e-book lending, returns, and stock management. This can cause greater efficient operations in libraries.
5. **Virtual Rights management:** Blockchain can be used to control virtual rights and permissions for accessing library sources. This will assist in making certain that the best legal customers have access to specific content.
6. **Progressed consumer experience:** IoT devices can accumulate statistics on personal preferences and conduct, which can be used to customize services along with book suggestions and library activities. This may beautify the general consumer revel in.
7. **Cost savings:** utilizing automating processes and enhancing performance, integrating Blockchain and IoT can lead to cost savings for libraries, which include decreased administrative prices and better aid utilization.

8. **Facts Integrity and preservation:** Blockchain's ability to save records immutably can assist ensure the integrity and renovation of valuable library statistics and resources.

Integrating Blockchain and IoT in the library region gives numerous opportunities to improve security, efficiency, and personal reviews.

Challenges

Integrating Blockchain and IoT in the library zone also presents numerous challenges that need to be addressed:

1. **Scalability:** Each blockchain and IoT generates large quantities of data. Making sure that the machine can manage these facts on a scale is a considerable assignment.
2. **Interoperability:** IoT devices and Blockchain structures may also use exceptional protocols and requirements, making it difficult to ensure interoperability and seamless conversation among gadgets and structures.
3. **Protection and privateness:** at the same time as Blockchain complements protection, IoT devices can nonetheless be liable to cyber-assaults. Ensuring the safety and privacy of each IoT device and Blockchain network is essential.
4. **Value:** implementing and preserving Blockchain and IoT systems may be costly, especially for smaller libraries with restricted budgets.
5. **Complexity:** Integrating Blockchain and IoT calls for information in each technology, which can be hard for libraries with constrained technical assets.
6. **Regulatory Compliance**: Libraries need to conform to guidelines concerning facts privateness and protection. Making sure that Blockchain and IoT implementations meet these necessities can be challenging.
7. **Consumer recognition**: Introducing new technology like Blockchain and IoT may also require modifications in workflows and personal behavior, which may additionally face resistance from the library body of workers and shoppers.
8. **Records possession and Governance:** Clarifying records possession and governance guidelines is critical when integrating Blockchain and IoT to make certain that statistics are used and controlled accurately.
9. **Environmental impact:** IoT devices require electricity to operate, which may have an environmental effect. Making sure that IoT implementations are electricity-green is critical.

Addressing these demanding situations requires careful plans, collaboration among stakeholders, and ongoing monitoring and edition of the era implementations.

Integrating Blockchain and IoT in the library zone can lead to several modern packages, improving operations, user stories, and security. Right here are some key applications:

1. Asset monitoring and inventory management:
   i. IoT Sensors: Use RFID tags and IoT sensors to track books, files, and other library property in actual time.
   ii. Blockchain Ledger: Ensure the integrity and immutability of asset tracking records, reducing loss and misplacement.
2. Automatic Lending and Returns:
   i. Clever Contracts: Implement blockchain-based smart contracts to automate the lending and go-back approaches. Books can be mechanically checked inside and out whilst surpassed via IoT-enabled gates.
   ii. user Notifications: mechanically notify customers about due dates and past due gadgets through IoT-related gadgets.
3. Digital Rights control:
   i. Blockchain for DRM: manipulate digital rights and permissions through the usage of Blockchain, making sure that only legal customers can get the right of entry to virtual sources.
   ii. utilization monitoring: track the use of virtual content to ensure compliance with licensing agreements.
4. Environmental tracking:
   i. IoT Environmental Sensors: monitor temperature, humidity, and air quality in the library to preserve physical substances.
   ii. Blockchain information: maintain immutable statistics of environmental situations to ensure compliance with maintenance requirements.
5. Security and access control:
   i. IoT security gadgets: Use IoT-enabled cameras and sensors for surveillance and protection.
   ii. Blockchain Authentication: put into effect Blockchain-based total authentication for access manipulation, ensuring that the most effective legal employees can get entry to limited regions.
6. Personalized user offerings:
   i. IoT person interaction: Use IoT devices to acquire records on consumer preferences and conduct.
   ii. Blockchain information privateness: ensure person records privateness and safety using Blockchain at the same time as imparting customized suggestions and offerings.
7. Aid Optimization:

i. Power management: Use IoT devices to optimize strength consumption in the library via controlling lighting, heating, and cooling systems based on occupancy.
ii. Blockchain for Sustainability: song and verify sustainability efforts and energy usage on a Blockchain for transparency and accountability.

8. Superior user experience:
   i. Smart cabinets: put into effect IoT-enabled clever shelves that provide statistics about books and their availability.
   ii. Interactive Kiosks: Use IoT-linked interactive kiosks to help users find books, have access to virtual sources, and navigate the library.
9. **Information-driven selection Making:**
   i. IoT information collection: acquire statistics on library utilization, user behavior, and resource intake through IoT gadgets.
   ii. Blockchain Analytics: Use Blockchain to securely save and analyze this data, imparting insights for enhancing library services and operations.
10. Collaboration and Sharing:
   i. Inter-Library Loans: Use Blockchain and IoT to streamline inter-library loans and useful resource sharing, making sure transparent and green transactions.
   ii. Blockchain for Provenance: music is the provenance of rare and precious books using Blockchain to make certain authenticity and traceability.

Those applications demonstrate how integrating Blockchain and IoT can rework library operations, beautify security, and offer better offerings to users.

CONCLUSION

Integrating Blockchain and IoT in library sectors provides an embarrassment of opportunities along several demanding situations that want to be addressed for a hit implementation. This convergence can revolutionize library operations by enhancing security, transparency, and efficiency. Blockchain's decentralized nature and cryptographic techniques ensure that library users' information is comfortable and private, lowering the dangers of data breaches and unauthorized admission. Blockchain can provide a transparent and immutable document of all transactions, inclusive of e-book lending, acquisitions, and donations, accordingly improving belief and responsibility. IoT devices can enable real-time tracking of books and other resources, ensuring efficient stock management and decreasing the time spent locating and coping with bodily gadgets. Utilizing clever contracts can automate various library tactics such as club renewals, late fines, and inter-library loans, hence reducing guide interventions and streamlining operations. IoT-enabled gadgets can offer personalized stories to library customers, such as recommending books based totally on reading records or facilitating the easy right of entry to digital assets.

Ensuring compatibility among distinctive IoT gadgets and blockchain structures is essential for seamless integration and green functioning. As the quantity of transactions and facts increases, blockchain systems must be capable of scaling correctly without compromising overall performance or protection. Libraries must navigate complex regulatory environments and ensure compliance with facts protection laws and other applicable policies. Enforcing and keeping blockchain and IoT technologies require a big level of technical understanding, which may be a barrier for plenty of libraries. The preliminary investment in blockchain and IoT technology can be extensive, and libraries must weigh these prices towards the capability benefits. The integration of Blockchain and IoT inside the library zone holds massive promise for reworking library services and operations. With the aid of addressing the demanding situations and leveraging the opportunities, libraries can decorate their carrier shipping, make certain facts safe, and offer an extra efficient and tasty person revel in. As those technologies continue to conform, libraries that proactively embody them may be well-positioned to steer innovation and provider excellence.

REFERENCES

Agarwal, P., Sheikh, M. I., & Obaid, A. J. (2021). *Blockchain and IoT technology in the transformation of the education sector.*

Christidis, K., & Devetsikiotis, M. (2016). Blockchains and Smart Contracts for the Internet of Things. *IEEE Access : Practical Innovations, Open Solutions*, 4, 2292–2303. DOI: 10.1109/ACCESS.2016.2566339

Conoscenti, M., Vetro, A., & de Martin, J. C. (2016). Blockchain for the Internet of Things: A Systematic Literature Review. *2016 IEEE/ACS 13th International Conference of Computer Systems and Applications*, 1–6.

da Xu, L., He, W., & Li, S. (2014). Internet of Things in Industries: A Survey. *IEEE Transactions on Industrial Informatics*, 10(4), 2233–2243. DOI: 10.1109/TII.2014.2300753

Francis, M., Todericiu, R., & Drăghici, A. (2019). The Impact of Blockchain Technology on the Integration of Supply Chains in Libraries. *Procedia Computer Science*, 162, 715–722.

Fu, M.-H. (2020). Integrated technologies of blockchain and biometrics based on wireless sensor network for library management. *Information Technology and Libraries*, 39(3). Advance online publication. DOI: 10.6017/ital.v39i3.11883

Jayavadivel, R., Arunachalam, M., Nagarajan, G., Shankar, B. P., Viji, C., Rajkumar, N., & Senthilkumar, K. R. (2024). Historical Overview of AI Adoption in Libraries. In *AI-Assisted Library Reconstruction* (pp. 267–289). IGI Global. DOI: 10.4018/979-8-3693-2782-1.ch015

Kewell, B., Adams, R., & Parry, G. (2017). Blockchain for Good? Digital Ledger Technology and Sustainable Development Goals. In *Handbook of Sustainability and Social Science Research* (pp. 127–140). Springer.

Khan, A. U., Zhang, Z., Taleby Ahvanooey, M., & Rafique, W. (2022). Opinion mining towards blockchain technology adoption for accessing digital library resources. *Aslib Journal of Information Management*, 74(1), 135–157. DOI: 10.1108/AJIM-01-2021-0016

Kumar, N., Antoniraj, S., Jayanthi, S., Mirdula, S., Saravanakumar, S., Rajkumar, N., & Senthilkumar, K. R. (2024). Educational Technology and Libraries Supporting Online Learning. In *AI-Assisted Library Reconstruction* (pp. 209–237). IGI Global. DOI: 10.4018/979-8-3693-2782-1.ch012

Lalitha, B., Ramalakshmi, K., Gunasekaran, H., Murugesan, P., Saminasri, P., & Rajkumar, N. (2024). Anticipating AI Impact on Library Services: Future Opportunities and Evolutionary Prospects. In *Improving Library Systems with AI: Applications, Approaches, and Bibliometric Insights* (pp. 195–213). IGI Global.

Lee, I., & Lee, K. (2015). The Internet of Things (IoT): Applications, Investments, and Challenges for Enterprises. *Business Horizons*, 58(4), 431–440. DOI: 10.1016/j.bushor.2015.03.008

Mohanraj, A., Viji, C., Varadarajan, M. N., Kalpana, C., Shankar, B., Jayavadivel, R., Rajkumar, N., & Jagajeevan, R. (2024). Privacy and Security in Digital Libraries. In *AI-Assisted Library Reconstruction* (pp. 104–125). IGI Global. DOI: 10.4018/979-8-3693-2782-1.ch006

Nachiappan, B. (2024a). Emerging and innovative AI technologies for resource management. In *Improving Library Systems with AI: Applications, Approaches, and Bibliometric Insights* (pp. 115–133). IGI Global. DOI: 10.4018/979-8-3693-5593-0.ch009

Nachiappan, B. (2024b). E-resources content recommendation system using AI. In *Improving Library Systems with AI: Applications, Approaches, and Bibliometric Insights* (pp. 155–177). IGI Global. DOI: 10.4018/979-8-3693-5593-0.ch011

Rajkumar, N., Tabassum, H., Muthulingam, S., Mohanraj, A., Viji, C., Kumar, N., & Senthilkumar, K. R. (2024). Anticipated requirements and expectations in the digital library. In *AI-Assisted Library Reconstruction* (pp. 1–20). IGI Global. DOI: 10.4018/979-8-3693-2782-1.ch001

Rajkumar, N., Viji, C., Mohanraj, A., Senthilkumar, K. R., Jagajeevan, R., & Kovilpillai, J. A. (2024). Ethical Considerations of AI Implementation in the Library Era. In *Improving Library Systems with AI: Applications, Approaches, and Bibliometric Insights* (pp. 85–106). IGI Global. DOI: 10.4018/979-8-3693-5593-0.ch007

Underwood, S. (2016). Blockchain Beyond Bitcoin. *Communications of the ACM*, 59(11), 15–17. DOI: 10.1145/2994581

Varadarajan, M. N. (2024). Educational program for AI literacy. In *Improving Library Systems with AI: Applications, Approaches, and Bibliometric Insights* (pp. 134–154). IGI Global. DOI: 10.4018/979-8-3693-5593-0.ch010

Varadarajan, M. N., Viji, C., Rajkumar, N., & Mohanraj, A. (2024). Integration of AI and IoT for smart home automation. *SSRG International Journal of Electronics and Communication Engineering*, 11(5), 37–43. DOI: 10.14445/23488549/IJECE-V11I5P104

Viji, C., Najmusher, H., Rajkumar, N., Mohanraj, A., Nachiappan, B., Neelakandan, C., & Jagajeevan, R. (2024). Intelligent Library Management Using Radio Frequency Identification. In *AI-Assisted Library Reconstruction* (pp. 126–143). IGI Global. DOI: 10.4018/979-8-3693-2782-1.ch007

Wang, L., Chen, C.-C., & Xie, X. (2018). Environmental Monitoring System Based on IoT in Library Management. *Journal of Environmental Management*, 217, 720–730.

Zyskind, G., Nathan, O., & Pentland, A. (2015). Decentralizing Privacy: Using Blockchain to Protect Personal Data. *2015 IEEE Security and Privacy Workshops*, 180–184.

Chapter 4
Blockchain Technology in Libraries:
Paving the Way for Transparent and Reliable Services

N. Karthick
Sri Krishna College of Arts and Science, Coimbatore, India

P. Nithya
PSG College of Arts and Science, Coimbatore, India

R. Rajkumar
RVS College of Arts and Science, India

ABSTRACT

Blockchain technology, initially popularized through its association with cryptocurrencies, has evolved into a versatile tool with transformative potential across various sectors, including libraries. By leveraging these features, libraries can enhance their operations in areas such as secure transactions, digital rights management, preservation of cultural heritage, and streamlined resource sharing. The chapter delves into specific applications of blockchain in libraries, highlighting its role in revolutionizing scholarly publishing through transparent and tamper-proof records, facilitating efficient inter-library loans, and optimizing digital resource management. Moreover, the adoption of blockchain promises improved data security, operational efficiency, and user empowerment within library ecosystems. As libraries increasingly integrate blockchain technology, they position themselves at the forefront of innovation. This integration enables them to enhance service delivery while upholding principles of reliability, privacy, and accountability in an increasingly digital landscape.

DOI: 10.4018/979-8-3693-7783-3.ch004

INTRODUCTION

A blockchain is one type of distributed ledger, but not all distributed ledgers employ blocks or chain transactions. The blockchain functions as an immutable digital ledger for recording economic transactions and can be programmed to maintain records of various valuable assets, not just financial transactions, as highlighted by Don & Alex Tapscott in Blockchain Revolution (2016). Originally coined as "block chain," a blockchain consists of continuously growing digital records grouped into blocks, which are linked and secured using cryptographic techniques (Clerk Maxwell, 1892; Eason et al., 1955). Each block in the chain contains data (e.g., a bitcoin transaction), is cryptographically hashed, and timestamped. These blocks of hashed data reference the previous block in the chain, ensuring the integrity of the entire blockchain and preventing unauthorized modifications (Rado et al., 1963; Wang et al., 2018).

A blockchain operates as a chronological chain of blocks, with each block comprising aggregated data processed to fit within it through the mining process. Each block is uniquely identified by a cryptographic hash and timestamp. When a new block is created, it includes a hash of the preceding block, thereby forming a linear, chronologically ordered chain starting from the very first block ever generated—the Genesis Block—to the most recent one. This iterative process continuously expands and secures the network (Alhadhrami et al., 2017). Importantly, this decentralized ledger is not under the control of any single financial institution or government; instead, it is accessible to anyone with an internet connection. Beyond virtual currencies, blockchain technology is leveraged by numerous industries including messaging apps, critical infrastructure security, ride-sharing, cloud storage, and more (Malasri & Wang, 2009).

Figure 1. Blockchain Technology in Libraries

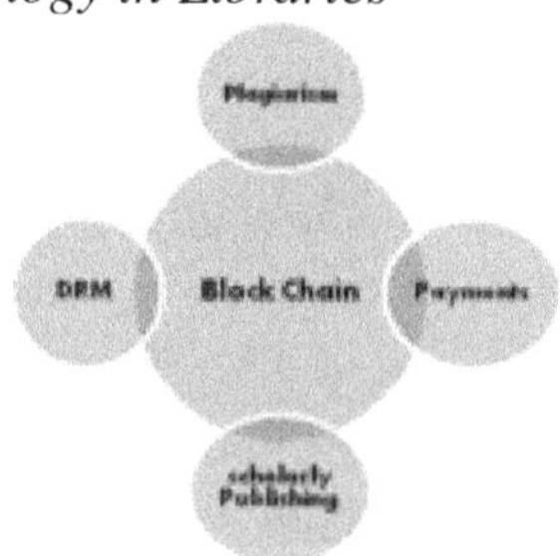

What Makes Blockchain Different From Other Technologies?

Blockchain technology stands out from traditional approaches due to several distinctive features that enable innovative contract and relationship management:

Figure 2. Blockchain Technology features

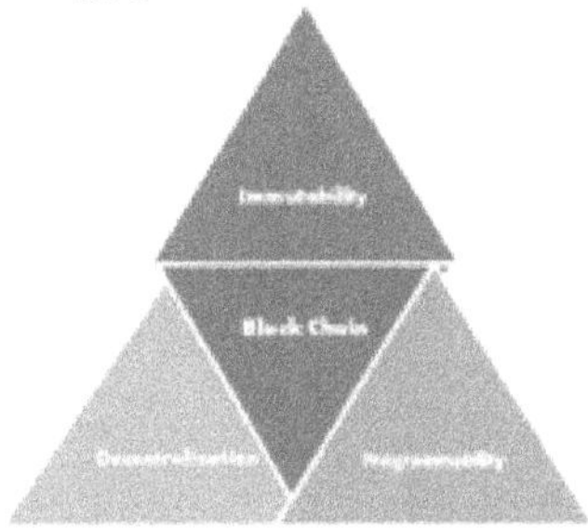

- ✓ **Immutability:** Blockchain employs a sequential chaining of data blocks where each new block references the previous one, creating an "append-only" ledger. This design ensures that once data is recorded, it cannot be altered or deleted retroactively. This immutability contrasts sharply with conventional methods such as spreadsheets shared via email or cloud-based services, where multiple versions can lead to discrepancies and require time-consuming reconciliation processes.
- ✓ **Decentralization:** Unlike centralized systems that rely on intermediaries or central authorities to validate and maintain data integrity, blockchain operates on a decentralized network of participants. Consensus mechanisms, such as Proof of Work or Proof of Authority, enable network participants to collectively agree on the validity of transactions. This decentralized approach enhances security by making fraudulent activities economically unfeasible, thereby fostering trust among participants without relying on a central authority.
- ✓ **Programmability:** Blockchain's programmable nature allows for the implementation of smart contracts—self-executing contracts with predefined rules stored on the blockchain. Smart contracts automate processes by executing actions automatically when specific conditions are met, without requiring intermediaries. This capability extends beyond simple transactions to include

complex agreements that can integrate external data sources from software applications or IoT devices. This automation not only streamlines operations but also ensures transparency and reliability through tamper-resistant record-keeping.

These features collectively distinguish blockchain technology from traditional methods, offering a secure, transparent, and efficient way to manage contracts and relationships in various sectors, from finance and supply chain management to legal agreements and beyond.

Connection of Blockchain With Various Aspects of Libraries

Emerging technologies offer librarians a unique opportunity to enhance collaboration among libraries and users, transforming the delivery of user-centered services. Blockchain technology, known for its distributed and tamper-resistant nature, aligns with the traditional role of librarians in gathering, preserving, and sharing authoritative information.

In the realm of scholarly publishing, blockchain can revolutionize how journal articles are managed by creating verifiable, time-stamped versions. This capability ensures transparency and authenticity throughout the submission, review, and publication processes (Casino et al., 2019; Hoy, 2017). Moreover, blockchain facilitates secure fund transfers between libraries and vendors, simplifying contract management and record-keeping (Coghill, 2018).

Irving and Holden's exploration of blockchain as a low-cost, verifiable method for auditing scientific studies underscores its potential for auditing library records reliably (Hoy, 2017). Blockchain's strength lies in authenticating transaction details such as parties involved, content submitted, and timestamps, ensuring data integrity without centralized control (Condos et al., 2016).

Libraries can leverage blockchain for sharing sensitive information securely among educational institutions, enhancing data encryption and privacy (Coghill, 2018). Additionally, blockchain serves as a robust Digital Rights Management (DRM) tool, enabling unique identification, control, and transfer of digital resources. This capability addresses challenges related to the reproducibility and piracy of digital materials, thereby safeguarding publisher interests (Griffey, 2016).

The adoption of blockchain in libraries has the potential to reshape the economics of e-resource procurement and management. It introduces efficiencies that could potentially reduce costs and streamline transactions, transforming how libraries acquire and manage digital resources (Coghill, 2018). As librarians explore these applications, they position themselves at the forefront of utilizing technology to enhance service delivery and ensure the integrity of information resources in a digital age.

Blockchain Technology Offers Several Transformative Applications for Libraries, Enhancing Various Aspects of Operations and Services

- ✓ **Secure Transactions and Financial Management:** Blockchain simplifies monetary transactions within libraries, such as subscription fees and late fines. By executing these transactions securely and transparently, blockchain ensures accuracy, reduces errors, and enhances financial accountability. This capability improves overall financial management within library systems.
- ✓ **Digital Rights Management (DRM):** Libraries manage a vast array of digital resources like e-books, audiobooks, and databases. Blockchain can be leveraged for DRM purposes, enabling libraries to securely manage digital rights. By using blockchain, access to digital content can be tracked, ensuring compliance with licensing agreements and enhancing security through traceable access logs.
- ✓ **Ensuring Authenticity of Cultural Heritage:** Libraries holding rare manuscripts, historical documents, or artifacts can use blockchain to preserve authenticity. By recording provenance and ownership history on the blockchain, libraries can safeguard cultural heritage. This approach also helps prevent the circulation of counterfeit materials, ensuring the integrity of cultural artifacts.
- ✓ **Interlibrary Loans and Resource Sharing:** Blockchain technology can streamline interlibrary loans and resource sharing processes. By maintaining a secure and transparent record of borrowing and lending activities, blockchain simplifies administrative tasks associated with resource sharing among libraries. This enhances collaboration and improves efficiency in accessing shared resources.
- ✓ **Data Security and Privacy:** The decentralized nature of blockchain enhances data security and privacy for libraries. Personal information of library patrons, transaction details, and sensitive data can be stored on the blockchain with cryptographic protection. This reduces the risk of data breaches and unauthorized access, ensuring robust data security practices in library operations.

Leveraging Blockchain Technologies to Library Services

Blockchain technology holds immense potential for enhancing record-keeping systems by ensuring accuracy and reducing the risk of data loss due to disasters or sabotage. However, its implementation requires not only the addition of new records to the network but also the digitization of existing records to optimize record-keeping efficiency (Chen et al., 2018).

The adoption of blockchain in formal and informal learning environments, including academic, public, and specialized libraries, could significantly improve the security and reliability of documentation (Oladokun, Owolabi, Aboyade et al, 2023). Already, startups are leveraging blockchain to create innovative commercial solutions. Through blockchain, developers can establish "smart contracts" capable of managing debt registries or executing specific instructions based on predefined conditions (Jana & Poray, 2016).

In education, blockchain technology has the potential to transform how academic institutions manage student data, including registration records, attendance, grades, and educational materials. This streamlined approach facilitates seamless data transfer between institutions, benefiting students transferring or graduating to new educational settings. Furthermore, blockchain finds applications across various business sectors.

To avoid disruption, libraries must proactively explore how blockchain technology can enhance content creation, storage, and distribution. Decentralized libraries, where user data resides on a blockchain rather than a centralized database, may become more prevalent. This shift empowers users to manage their circulation records and borrowing histories securely. Moreover, new economic models may emerge, incentivizing users to share data with libraries (Coghill, 2018).

In publishing, blockchain addresses challenges like third-party interference and inefficient payment models by enabling platforms like Publica. This platform allows authors to define terms through smart contracts on the Ethereum network, facilitating direct book token purchases and crowdfunding

Research institutions can benefit from blockchain by sharing grey literature and research findings securely via private blockchains. This approach eliminates redundancy in research efforts and ensures data integrity and digital rights management throughout the publication process.

Blockchain also revolutionizes library services by enabling innovative practices like LibChain, facilitating direct user-to-user book lending and interlibrary borrowing without physical book transfers. This system enhances library accessibility and efficiency (Coghill, 2018).

In scholarly publishing, platforms like Orvium leverage blockchain to enhance digital rights management and ensure transparent, verifiable records of publications. Authors can manage their works using blockchain-based identifiers, facilitating peer review and protecting intellectual property (Chingath & Babu, 2020).

Supply chain management in libraries can benefit from blockchain by improving processes such as material circulation, interlibrary loans, and resource acquisition and payment. This technology enhances transparency and efficiency across library operations (Chingath & Babu, 2020).

Moreover, blockchain offers financial applications that can stabilize library budgets by eliminating currency fluctuations through blockchain-based transactions like Bitcoin. Smart contracts further streamline payment processes within legal frameworks (Sanjay & Nabihasan, 2020).

For document management, blockchain ensures the provenance, integrity, and authenticity of vital library documents. This capability is particularly crucial for preserving and archiving valuable collections across various library types, including law, medical, research, and academic libraries (Suman & Patel, 2021).

BLOCKCHAIN-BASED TRACEABILITY FRAMEWORK FOR T&C SUPPLY CHAIN

Blockchain technology tailored for business and supply chain applications differs significantly from public blockchains like Bitcoin in terms of privacy and accessibility. Unlike public blockchains, which are open and transparent to all participants, private blockchains used in supply chains restrict access to authorized and identifiable partners. This privacy is crucial for maintaining competitive advantages and protecting sensitive business information. Additionally, different levels of visibility and accessibility can be customized for each partner, ensuring that they only access relevant information necessary for their role in the supply chain.

At the organizational level, a private blockchain network in supply chains is structured around channels, which are subdivisions used for data partitioning. Each channel operates independently with its own blockchain (chain of transactions) stored on a distributed ledger. This setup allows for different types of transactions (e.g., material procurement, production, financial transactions) to be segregated into separate channels, thereby ensuring data privacy and maintaining transactional integrity.

Key components of this blockchain-based traceability framework include:

Figure 3. Summary of Components

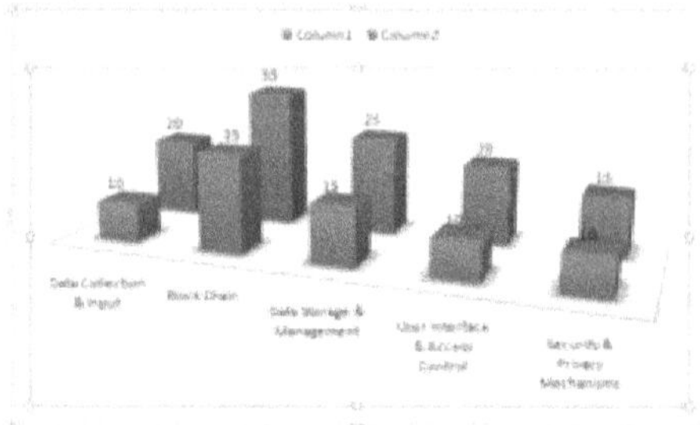

- ✓ Data Collection & Input: 20% - 30%
- ✓ Blockchain Network: 25% - 35%
- ✓ Data Storage & Management: 15% - 25%
- ✓ User Interface & Access Control: 10% - 20%
- ✓ Security & Privacy Mechanisms: 10% - 15%
- ✓ **Channels:** These represent the different subdivisions of the network, each with its own shared ledger governed by one or more smart contracts. Each channel serves specific clusters of upstream suppliers or partners involved in particular transactions. For instance, one channel might handle material procurement while another manages financial transactions.
- ✓ **Peers:** These are processing systems that host smart contracts and shared ledgers. Peers validate and endorse transactions based on their roles within the supply chain network. Main partners typically host peers, while other partners access the ledger through applications without directly hosting the infrastructure.
- ✓ **Applications:** User-friendly software interfaces through which partners interact with the blockchain network. Applications can vary in their access rules, allowing partners to read, add, or validate transactions based on their permissions and responsibilities within the supply chain.
- ✓ **Ordering Service:** This third-party service organizes transactions into logical sequences and registers them on the blockchain's shared ledger after validation. It plays a crucial role in maintaining the integrity and order of transactions within each channel.
- ✓ **Membership Services:** Responsible for generating unique public-private key pairs for participating partners. These keys determine the extent of ac-

cessibility and permissions each partner has within the blockchain network, ensuring secure and controlled access.

This organizational setup ensures that blockchain technology facilitates trust, transparency, and accountability among supply chain partners while protecting sensitive business information and complying with regulatory requirements. It streamlines operations, enhances data security, and enables efficient traceability of products and transactions throughout the supply chain network.

Some Key Applications Where Blockchain Is Making a Significant Impact

- ✓ **Publishing E-Books & Protecting Digital First Sale Rights:** Traditionally, e-book distribution involves intermediaries, resulting in libraries and users paying for full packages rather than what they use. Platforms like Publica enable authors to publish books using smart contracts on blockchain. These contracts outline usage terms, and books are accessed through book tokens on an Ethereum network. Publica also offers crowdfunding options (Book ICOs), allowing creators to presell tokens to fund initial costs. This decentralized approach empowers authors and ensures transparent, fair compensation.
- ✓ **IITs Network on Blockchain:** Private blockchains facilitate sharing research among institutions like IITs, enabling collaborative access to grey literature, lab papers, and critical research data. Blockchain ensures data integrity and authenticity, eliminating concerns about digital rights and data tampering. This collaborative model promotes efficient knowledge sharing and collaborative research efforts without redundant work.
- ✓ **Scholarly Publications & Digital Rights Management:** Blockchain platforms like Orvium are transforming scholarly publishing by decentralizing control and enhancing transparency. Researchers can register using ORCiD IDs and publish work on Orvium, earning tokens used for peer review and publication fees. Blockchain ensures transparent, tamper-proof records of publications, addressing issues of attribution and rights management in academic publishing.
- ✓ **User to User or Library to User Loans:** LibChain, a Distributed Library Management System on blockchain, facilitates efficient book lending between library patrons and supports inter-library borrowing. Patrons can lend books directly to other users within the library ecosystem, streamlining access to resources while maintaining security and user authentication. LibChain enhances library services by leveraging blockchain's security and transparency features to optimize resource sharing and user experience.

Potential Discoveries Made Through Opinion Mining

General Sentiment

- ✓ Positive Sentiments: High hopes about the possible benefits blockchain may bring, such as better security, transparency and operational efficiency in digital libraries.
- ✓ Negative Sentiments: Concerns over the likely difficulty of adoption, costs involved and resistance.
- ✓ Neutral Sentiments: Lack of interest or understanding towards Blockchain technology uses in this situation.

Perceived Advantages

- ✓ Heightened Security: Blockchains are considered highly secure because they are distributed and employ cryptography that prevents hacking attempts.
- ✓ Transparency and Trustworthiness: The immutability aspect of block chains can make users trust that digital assets will be managed fairly.
- ✓ Efficient Resource Management: Better licensing systems, intellectual property rights management tools and access controls could be viewed as important gains.

Challenges and Worries

- ✓ Cost of Implementation. This may pose significant problems especially for institutions with little budgetary allocations due to high initial setup costs as well ad ongoing maintenance expense.
- ✓ Complexity and Technical Barriers. Blockchain's apparent complexity could discourage organizations from adopting it if it is not easily understood.

Use Cases and Applications

- ✓ Blockchain as a Secure Access Control: Use of blockchain for security access control authentication and managing restricted content may be seen in a positive light.
- ✓ Digital Rights Management (DRM): There could be stakeholders who would like to know how effective blockchain is when it comes to streamlining DRM processes as well as ensuring that there is justice in using content as well appropriate compensation for content developers.

- ✓ Record Keeping and Provenance: Digital resource transactions can have their verifiable history maintained by blockchain which may be perceived as important for educational and research institutions.

User Experience

- ✓ Ease of Use: The user friendliness of blockchain-enabled systems for accessing digital libraries may vary. Whereas positive experiences might increase adoption, negative ones may slow down this process.
- ✓ Integration with Existing Systems: How easily blockchain technology can be integrated into current library management systems might determine its acceptability.

Digital Rights Management (DRM)

Block chain can become another Digital Rights Management (DRM) tool. Print copies of articles could be limited by publishers through agreements on the block chain. If printing were linked to the initial agreement, publishers could limit the printing or distribution of articles or book chapters. As long as all parties to an agreement work transparently, the system could work effectively. Hackers would find it difficult to crack the codes of individual block chain agreements, although block chain transactions are not entirely free from potential nefarious actions (Rado et al., 1963). Hoy notes that hackers could hold a block chain transaction hostage until a ransom is paid.Any kind of information could be shared via a block chain transaction. Libraries could share patron information with other libraries under these agreements. Schools or universities could share student information with other institutions using block chain. Wherever there is a need to exchange sensitive information requiring encryption, block chain technology may provide a solution.

Host Digital Peer-to-Peer Sharing

Libraries can facilitate peer-to-peer (P2P) sharing beyond just books through blockchain technology, helping community members authenticate the availability of different tools or services for a more efficient sharing economy. When setting up meetings, working on projects, or filing reports, blockchain provides the necessary tools. This unique approach to networking enhances security by making it harder to alter shared documents.

Connect to a Network of Libraries/Universities: Libraries and universities can use blockchain with the Inter-Planetary File System (IPFS), a P2P protocol for a future internet utilizing BitTorrent, GIT, and blockchain. IPFS circumvents gatekeeping by ISPs and large internet companies, requiring seeders to keep copies of websites on their computers. A network of libraries and universities could validate the credentials of these websites, similar to how Bitcoin miners validate transactions.

Facilitate Partnerships Across Centers/Organizations: Libraries can partner with museums, universities, and government agencies to share MARC records, authority control, and user-generated content through a blockchain framework. This collaboration can enhance data integrity and accessibility across institutions.

Support Community-Based Collections: A blockchain protocol can support community-based collections and borrowing, extending the traditional library collection into the community. Libraries could deploy a blockchain-based system layered with smart contracts to facilitate indexing and sharing community items (e.g., tools, cars, expertise). The blockchain would track who has borrowed items and who originally loaned them. This initiative could involve partnerships with software developers and businesses.

The Characteristics of a Library Management System Based on Blockchain

- **User-Friendly Interface:** The system should be easy to use and simple to navigate.
- **Timely Information:** It must provide the necessary information promptly.
- **Order Management:** Users should be able to place orders if an item is unavailable.
- **Notifications:** Members must be notified when specific inventory becomes available. The system should also be capable of generating reports on demand.
- **Efficient Scanning:** The system should be able to scan the entire library within seconds.
- **Categorization:** Collections should be categorized by author, publisher, genre, and other relevant criteria.
- **Access Control:** The system must provide secure access for both the library and its users.
- **Automated Due Date Management:** The system should automatically check the due dates of borrowed resources and accurately calculate any penalties.

LibChain Vision and Technical Framework

LibChain envisions creating an ecosystem of libraries that share a comprehensive book database, enabling users to borrow, reserve, and request books from any participating library or user, regardless of their registered library.

Core Technical Concept

The core idea behind LibChain is to represent individual books and library loans with "colored coins." Colored coins are used to represent real-world assets on the blockchain. Companies like Everledger have successfully used them to track assets such as diamonds, artwork, and other high-value items in a permanent, decentralized manner (Cole, 2017). Metadata stored within a colored coin can include information about loan periods, the book's home library, and how often the book can be transferred between users.By building LibChain on existing blockchain technology like Ethereum, we can utilize smart contracts to create decentralized applications (Chingath & Babu, 2020). Communication between different actors in the system will be facilitated by the Whisper protocol, providing signed and encrypted messaging for secure communication. Transaction keys will address users, and topics will be assigned to filter requests and invoke appropriate responses.

Transparency and Accountability

Having a transparent and permanent record of book usage is beneficial for publicly funded libraries, which constitute 47% of libraries worldwide. All valid book transactions recorded on the blockchain would be publicly accessible, allowing for easier oversight and accountability. However, user privacy must be maintained (Sanjay & Nabihasan, 2020). To avoid disclosing personal information while ensuring transparency, a new key-pair will be generated for each user's transaction. These key-pairs will be known to the library where the user is registered, enabling tracking of books and preventing fraudulent activities.

Integration With Existing Systems

LibChain will operate as an additional layer on top of existing library systems, allowing libraries to retain their current systems while integrating LibChain. This approach facilitates easier deployment and makes it more feasible for libraries to adopt LibChain without replacing proven systems. Users will not need to register separately to borrow books; one-use accounts managed by the system can be created for those without mobile devices or those unwilling to use the software. Registration will be required only for willing participants during the initial sign-up process.

CONCLUSION

In conclusion, blockchain technology presents libraries with unprecedented opportunities to enhance their operations and services across various fronts. From securing financial transactions and managing digital rights to preserving cultural heritage and facilitating seamless resource sharing, blockchain's decentralized and tamper-resistant nature revolutionizes traditional library practices. By adopting blockchain, libraries can streamline processes such as inter-library loans, scholarly publishing, and digital resource management, thereby improving efficiency, transparency, and user experience. This technology not only safeguards data integrity but also empowers users by enabling direct interactions and transactions within the library ecosystem. Moreover, blockchain's potential extends beyond current applications, offering a pathway for libraries to innovate and adapt in an increasingly digital and interconnected world.

As libraries embrace blockchain technology, they position themselves at the forefront of leveraging emerging technologies to uphold their mission of providing reliable access to information while ensuring privacy, security, and accountability in the digital age

REFERENCES

Alhadhrami, Alghfeli, & Alghfeli. (2017). Introducing Blockchainsfor Healthcare. International Conference on Electrical and Computing Technologies and Applications (ICECTA).

Belsis, P., & Pantziou, G. (2014). A k-anonymity privacypreserving approach in wireless medical monitoring environments. Journal Personal and Ubiquitous Computing, 18(1), 61-74.DOI: 10.1109/ICCECE.2016.8009587

Chen, G., Xu, B., Lu, M., & Chen, N.-S. (2018). Exploring blockchain technology and its potential applications for education. *Smart Learning Environments*, 5(1), 1. DOI: 10.1186/s40561-017-0050-x

Chingath, V., & Babu, H. R. (2020). Advantage blockchain technology for the libraries. International conference on digital transformation: a cognitive learning towards artificial intelligence.

Clerk Maxwell, J. (1892). *A Treatise on Electricity and Magnetism* (3rd ed., Vol. 2). Clarendon.

Coghill, J. G. (2018). Blockchain and its Implications for Libraries. *Journal of Electronic Resources in Medical Libraries*, 15(2), 66–70. DOI: 10.1080/15424065.2018.1483218

Cole, Z. (2017). How blockchain technology could affect the future of network engineering. Network World. https://www.networkworld.com/article/3236479/how-blockchain-technology-could-affect-the-future-ofnetwork-engineering.html

Eason, G., Noble, B., & Sneddon, I. N. (1955, April). On certain integrals of Lipschitz-Hankel type involving products of Bessel functions. *Philosophical Transactions of the Royal Society of London*, A247, 529–551.

Gupta, B. (2022). Understanding Blockchain Technology: How It Works and What It Can Do. *Metaverse Basic and Applied Research*, 1, 18–18. DOI: 10.56294/mr202218

Jacobs, I. S., & Bean, C. P. (1963). In Rado, G. T., & Suhl, H. (Eds.), *"Fine particles, thin films and exchange anisotropy," in Magnetism* (Vol. 3, pp. 271–350). Academic.

Jana. & Poray. (2016). A performance analysis on elliptic curve cryptography in network security. 2016 International Conference on Computer, Electrical & Communication Engineering (ICCECE), 1-7.DOI: 10.1109/ICCECE.2016.8009587

Jasson, G. (2018). Blockchain: Could Libraries and Open Science Benefit from this Technology? ZBW MediaTalk. https://www.zbw-mediatalk.eu/2018/02/blockchain-profitieren-bibliotheken-und-open-science-vonder-technologie/

Malasri & Wang. (2009). Design and Implementation of Secure Wireless Mote Based Medical Sensor Network. Sensors, 9, 6273-6297.

Oladokun BD, Aboyade MA, & Aboyade WA. (2023). Global challenge and opportunities for libraries and big data. Library Hi Tech News. DOI: 10.1108/LHTN-12-2022-0138

Oladokun BD, Owolabi AK, Aboyade MA, Wiche HI, & Aboyade WA. (2023). Emergence of robotic technologies: implications for Nigerian academic libraries. Library Hi Tech News. .DOI: 10.1108/LHTN-02-2023-0031

Sallaba, M., Siegel, D., & Becker, S. (2018). *IoT powered by Blockchain How Blockchains facilitate the application of digital twins in IoT*. Deloitte Issue.

Sanjay, N., & Nabihasan, . (2020). Blockchain technology and its application in libraries. *LIBRARY HERALD*, 58(4), 118–125. DOI: 10.5958/0976-2469.2020.00030.10

Suman, A., & Patel, M. (2021). An Introduction to Blockchain Technology and Its Application in Libraries. Library Philosophy and Practice (e-Journal).

Wang, S., Wang, J., & Wang, X. (2018). *Blockchain Powered Parallel Healthcare Systems Based on the ACP Approach2329-924Xc*. IEEE.

Chapter 5
Blockchain Technology Transforming Libraries and Financial Services Towards Inclusive Development

Kowsick N. P.
Sri Krishna Arts and Science College, India

K. Ramasamy
Sri Krishna Arts and Science College, India

ABSTRACT

This chapter delves into detailed case studies of successful blockchain implementations in the domains of libraries and financial services, with a particular focus on financial inclusion. By examining real-world examples, the authors highlight how blockchain technology has been utilized to enhance the efficiency, transparency, and accessibility of library systems and financial services, particularly for underserved populations. The case studies include initiatives such as decentralized library networks, blockchain-based digital rights management, blockchain-verified educational credentials, and blockchain-enabled microfinance solutions. Each case study provides an in-depth analysis of the project objectives, implementation process, outcomes, and the challenges faced along the way. Lessons learned and best practices are distilled from these experiences, offering valuable insights for practitioners and policymakers looking to leverage blockchain technology for advancing library services and promoting financial inclusion.

DOI: 10.4018/979-8-3693-7783-3.ch005

INTRODUCTION

Blockchain technology, originally conceptualized as the underlying framework for cryptocurrencies like Bitcoin, has evolved into a transformative force across various sectors, particularly in libraries and financial services. At its core, blockchain is a decentralized, distributed ledger technology that enables secure, transparent, and immutable record-keeping of transactions. This technology operates through a network of nodes where each transaction is verified and recorded in a block, linked to previous blocks in a chronological chain. In libraries, blockchain offers innovative solutions to longstanding challenges. Decentralized library networks powered by blockchain facilitate seamless sharing and authentication of digital assets, enhancing accessibility while ensuring copyright protection through transparent digital rights management systems. Technical implementations include cryptographic hashing to secure data integrity and smart contracts for automated transaction enforcement, thus revolutionizing how libraries manage and disseminate information (Pal, A., Tiwari, C. K., & Behl, A. 2021).

Similarly, in financial services, blockchain disrupts traditional practices by enabling efficient and cost-effective peer-to-peer transactions without intermediaries. The use of smart contracts automates contractual agreements, reducing transaction costs and improving transparency. For instance, blockchain-based microfinance solutions provide unbanked populations with access to financial services, fostering economic inclusion through secure and traceable transactions.

THESIS STATEMENT AND OBJECTIVES

This paper explores the profound impact of blockchain technology on libraries and financial services, emphasizing its role in enhancing efficiency, transparency, and inclusivity. By analyzing case studies and technical implementations, the paper aims to elucidate how blockchain transforms library systems through decentralized networks and digital rights management solutions. Moreover, it investigates blockchain's contribution to financial services, particularly in promoting financial inclusion and revolutionizing transaction processes through smart contracts and decentralized finance (DeFi) initiatives (Trivedi, S., Mehta, K., & Sharma, R. 2021).

Through a comprehensive examination of these sectors, this paper seeks to highlight the transformative potential of blockchain technology in creating equitable access to information and financial resources (Cucari, N., Lagasio, V., Lia, G., & Torriero, C. 2022). By addressing technical intricacies such as cryptographic protocols, consensus mechanisms, and decentralized governance models, this study provides insights into overcoming challenges and optimizing blockchain applications for sustainable development in libraries and financial services.

BLOCKCHAIN TECHNOLOGY FUNDAMENTALS

Blockchain Architecture and Components

Blockchain is a decentralized ledger technology that maintains a continuously growing list of records, called blocks, linked together in a chain. Each block contains a timestamp, transaction data, and a cryptographic hash of the previous block, ensuring immutability and security. The architecture typically consists of nodes, which are computers participating in the network, and each node stores a copy of the entire blockchain (Calandra, D., Secinaro, S., Massaro, M., Dal Mas, F., & Bagnoli, C. 2023).

Technical Implementations of Blockchain Architecture Involve Various Components

Blocks: Containers for data, including transactional information and a hash of the previous block.

Nodes: Participants in the network maintaining copies of the blockchain and validating transactions.

Consensus Protocol: Rules determining how consensus among nodes is achieved for validating transactions.

CONSENSUS MECHANISMS

Consensus mechanisms are fundamental to blockchain networks, ensuring agreement among nodes on the validity of transactions. Two prominent mechanisms include:

Proof of Work (PoW): In PoW, nodes compete to solve complex mathematical puzzles to validate transactions and create new blocks (Fanning, K., & Centers, D. P. (2016). This process requires significant computational power, making the blockchain secure against attacks but consuming substantial energy.

Proof of Stake (PoS): PoS selects validators based on the amount of cryptocurrency they hold and are willing to "stake" as collateral. Validators are chosen to create new blocks based on their stake, reducing energy consumption compared to PoW while maintaining security.

SMART CONTRACTS AND THEIR ROLE

Smart contracts are self-executing contracts with predefined rules and conditions written in code. They automatically execute and enforce the terms of an agreement when specified conditions are met, eliminating the need for intermediaries and reducing transaction costs. Ethereum's blockchain popularized smart contracts, enabling programmable transactions beyond simple value transfer. In technical terms, smart contracts are coded in high-level languages like Solidity and compiled into bytecode for execution on the blockchain. They operate within the blockchain's decentralized environment, ensuring transparency and tamper-proof execution of agreements. These technical aspects of blockchain architecture, consensus mechanisms like PoW and PoS, and the role of smart contracts illustrate how blockchain technology fundamentally transforms trust, security, and automation in various sectors, including libraries and financial services (Fanning, K., & Centers, D. P. 2016). Understanding these fundamentals is crucial for implementing and optimizing blockchain solutions effectively.

APPLICATIONS OF BLOCKCHAIN IN LIBRARIES

Blockchain technology revolutionizes library systems through decentralized networks, where information exchange is streamlined and secured. Decentralized library networks utilize blockchain's distributed ledger architecture to eliminate single points of failure and enhance data integrity. Each transaction, such as borrowing or accessing digital content, is recorded immutably across multiple nodes, ensuring transparency and reducing the risk of censorship or unauthorized access. Technical implementations include cryptographic hashing to timestamp and verify transactions, ensuring tamper-proof records that libraries can rely on for efficient management and dissemination of resources. Blockchain-based digital rights management (DRM) systems provide libraries with robust tools to manage intellectual property rights transparently. Smart contracts embedded in DRM solutions automate licensing agreements and royalties distribution based on predefined terms, reducing administrative overhead and ensuring fair compensation to content creators. This technical innovation not only safeguards digital assets but also facilitates seamless global access to copyrighted materials while protecting authorship rights (Treiblmaier, H., & Sillaber, C. 2020).

Moreover, blockchain enhances the verification and authentication of educational credentials, addressing issues of fraud and credential inflation. By storing educational records on a decentralized ledger, institutions and employers can verify the authenticity of diplomas and certifications in real-time, reducing verification costs and enhancing trust. Case studies such as the MIT Digital Diploma initiative showcase blockchain's role in securely issuing and verifying academic achievements, demonstrating its potential to transform credentialing processes globally. These applications illustrate how blockchain technology empowers libraries to operate more efficiently, uphold intellectual property rights, and enhance educational credential transparency, thereby advancing the accessibility and reliability of information in the digital age.

APPLICATIONS OF BLOCKCHAIN IN FINANCIAL SERVICES

Certainly the applications of blockchain in financial services, focusing on blockchain in banking and payments, microfinance and peer-to-peer lending, financial inclusion initiatives, and relevant case studies and examples:

Blockchain technology has reshaped traditional financial services by introducing decentralized, secure, and transparent solutions that streamline operations and expand access to financial resources (Chinaka, M. 2016). In banking and payments, blockchain facilitates faster and more cost-effective cross-border transactions by eliminating intermediaries and reducing settlement times from days to minutes. Technical implementations such as distributed ledger technology (DLT) ensure data integrity and transaction security through cryptographic hashing and consensus mechanisms like Proof of Work (PoW) or Proof of Stake (PoS).

Microfinance and peer-to-peer (P2P) lending platforms leverage blockchain to connect lenders directly with borrowers, bypassing traditional financial institutions. Smart contracts enable automated loan agreements and repayment schedules, reducing transaction costs and operational risks. These platforms enhance financial inclusion by providing affordable credit to underserved populations, fostering economic empowerment and entrepreneurship.

Financial inclusion initiatives powered by blockchain aim to provide unbanked individuals with access to basic financial services such as savings, loans, and insurance. Projects like Stellar's partnership with financial institutions in developing countries demonstrate blockchain's role in creating affordable and accessible financial solutions. By digitizing assets and enabling secure transactions via mobile devices, blockchain promotes financial literacy and inclusion on a global scale (Alketbi, A., Nasir, Q., & Talib, M. A. 2018, February).

Case studies highlight successful implementations of blockchain in financial services. For instance, Ripple's blockchain network facilitates real-time cross-border payments for banks, reducing transaction fees and settlement times significantly. Additionally, projects like Kiva leverage blockchain to track and verify microloan disbursements, ensuring transparency and accountability in charitable lending.

These applications demonstrate how blockchain technology enhances financial services by improving efficiency, reducing costs, and expanding access to financial resources, ultimately advancing global financial inclusion and economic development.

CHALLENGES AND CONSIDERATIONS

With reference to the above Venn diagram, addressing the challenges and considerations of blockchain technology involves navigating several critical areas: scalability, security and privacy concerns, and regulatory and legal challenges. Scalability remains a significant hurdle as blockchain networks strive to handle increasing transaction volumes without compromising efficiency or decentralization. Solutions like sharding and layer-two protocols aim to improve scalability by dividing the network into smaller, manageable parts or processing transactions off-chain while maintaining security and consensus on the main blockchain. However, achieving true scalability while preserving decentralization remains a technical and operational challenge (Bhaskar, P., Tiwari, C. K., & Joshi, A. 2021).

Security and privacy are paramount concerns in blockchain ecosystems. While blockchain's cryptographic security provides robust protection against data tampering, vulnerabilities in smart contracts, coding errors, and malicious attacks can expose networks to risks such as hacks and fraud. Innovations in cryptographic techniques and ongoing security audits are essential to mitigate these risks and ensure the integrity of blockchain transactions and data.

Regulatory and legal challenges pose complexities as governments worldwide grapple with defining and adapting regulations to blockchain technology. Issues range from jurisdictional ambiguities and cross-border transactions to compliance with data protection laws and anti-money laundering (AML) regulations. Regulatory clarity is crucial to fostering blockchain innovation while ensuring consumer protection and financial stability. Collaborative efforts between regulators, industry stakeholders, and policymakers are needed to develop frameworks that balance innovation with regulatory compliance and address emerging challenges in a rapidly evolving landscape.

Moreover, the decentralized nature of blockchain complicates governance and accountability, raising questions about liability and dispute resolution in case of fraud or operational failures. Establishing standards and best practices for blockchain governance, including consensus mechanisms and network upgrades, is essential for maintaining trust and stability in decentralized networks (B. Rawat, D., Chaudhary, V., & Doku, R. 2020).

In conclusion, addressing scalability through technological advancements, enhancing security and privacy protections, and navigating regulatory complexities are pivotal to realizing blockchain's full potential across various sectors. Collaborative efforts and ongoing research are crucial to overcoming these challenges and establishing a resilient blockchain ecosystem that promotes innovation, transparency, and trust in the digital economy.

IMPLEMENTATION PROCESSES AND BEST PRACTICES

Implementing blockchain solutions involves several strategic steps and learning from successful implementations to optimize outcomes effectively. Firstly, organizations need to assess their specific needs and identify suitable blockchain platforms—whether public, private, or hybrid—that align with their operational requirements and scalability goals. Technical considerations include selecting consensus mechanisms like Proof of Work (PoW) or Proof of Stake (PoS) based on transaction speed, energy efficiency, and network security needs. Secondly, developing smart contracts requires expertise in coding languages such as Solidity, enabling automated execution of agreements and ensuring compliance with legal and operational requirements. Integrating blockchain with existing systems demands robust interoperability and data migration strategies to ensure seamless data flow and minimize disruption. Thirdly, deploying nodes across the network involves configuring and maintaining nodes for transaction validation and consensus, optimizing network performance, and ensuring data redundancy and fault tolerance (Ghosh, J. 2019). Lessons from successful implementations emphasize the importance of stakeholder collaboration, rigorous testing, and ongoing monitoring to identify and address technical challenges promptly. For instance, initiatives like the Ethereum Enterprise Alliance promote knowledge sharing and standardization within blockchain ecosystems, fostering innovation and scalability. Moreover, adapting to regulatory changes and addressing security concerns through encryption and access control mechanisms are critical for maintaining trust and compliance. Ultimately, continuous evaluation and adaptation of blockchain strategies based on emerging technologies and industry trends are essential to maximizing the benefits of blockchain solutions in enhancing transparency, efficiency, and trust in various sectors.

FUTURE TRENDS AND POTENTIAL IMPACTS

Figure 1. Future trends and potential impacts

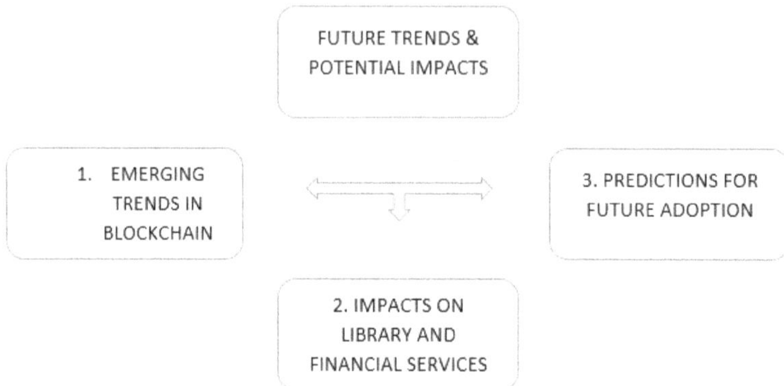

Looking ahead, blockchain technology is poised to catalyze significant transformations in libraries and financial services, driven by emerging trends and potential impacts that underscore its versatility and disruptive potential. One prominent trend is the evolution towards interoperable blockchain networks, where different blockchain platforms can seamlessly communicate and share data, enhancing scalability and usability across diverse applications. Technical advancements in consensus mechanisms, such as Proof of Stake (PoS) and Byzantine Fault Tolerance (BFT), aim to address scalability issues while improving transaction speeds and energy efficiency, making blockchain more viable for high-volume applications in both sectors (König, L., Korobeinikova, Y., Tjoa, S., & Kieseberg, P. 2020).

In libraries, blockchain's impact is set to revolutionize digital rights management (DRM) by enabling more granular control over access rights and intellectual property. Enhanced integration with artificial intelligence (AI) and machine learning (ML) algorithms will automate metadata tagging and content curation, optimizing user experiences and resource utilization. Moreover, blockchain-based decentralized library networks will facilitate global collaboration and resource sharing, fostering a more inclusive and accessible knowledge ecosystem (Chang, S. E., Luo, H. L., & Chen, Y. 2019).

Financial services stand to benefit from blockchain's potential to democratize access to financial products and services, particularly in underserved regions. Predictive analytics powered by blockchain-enabled data transparency will enhance risk assessment and fraud detection capabilities, improving the efficiency and reliability of lending and investment processes. Innovations in tokenization and asset digitization will unlock new opportunities for fractional ownership and diversified investment portfolios, democratizing wealth creation and financial inclusion on a global scale.

Looking forward, predictions indicate widespread adoption of blockchain across industries, driven by regulatory advancements that provide clarity and stability for market participants. Interdisciplinary collaborations between blockchain developers, fintech innovators, and regulatory authorities will accelerate innovation cycles and standardization efforts, ensuring interoperability and compliance with evolving legal frameworks (Zou, Y., Meng, T., Zhang, P., Zhang, W., & Li, H. (2020). As blockchain matures, its integration with emerging technologies like Internet of Things (IoT) and decentralized finance (DeFi) will redefine business models and operational paradigms, creating a resilient and adaptive digital economy that prioritizes transparency, efficiency, and equitable access to resources.

CONCLUSION

In conclusion, this paper has underscored the transformative potential of blockchain technology across libraries and financial services, highlighting key findings that emphasize its role in enhancing efficiency, transparency, and inclusivity. From decentralized library networks and blockchain-based digital rights management to microfinance initiatives and smart contracts in banking, blockchain innovations have reshaped operational landscapes, offering secure and efficient solutions that address longstanding challenges in information management and financial access. Technical insights into blockchain architecture, consensus mechanisms, and smart contracts have illustrated how these innovations improve data integrity, streamline transactions, and reduce operational costs while promoting financial inclusion and equitable access to educational and financial resources.

Blockchain's importance for inclusive development lies in its ability to empower individuals and institutions alike, democratizing access to information and financial services while ensuring accountability and trust in transactions. By leveraging blockchain's decentralized nature and cryptographic security, libraries can enhance content distribution and copyright protection, fostering a more accessible knowledge ecosystem. Similarly, financial services can leverage blockchain to extend banking services to underserved populations, facilitate seamless cross-border transactions, and innovate new financial products that promote economic empowerment. As blockchain technology continues to evolve and gain mainstream adoption, its potential to create a more equitable and resilient global economy becomes increasingly apparent, paving the way for sustainable development and societal progress.

REFERENCES

Alketbi, A., Nasir, Q., & Talib, M. A. (2018, February). Blockchain for government services—Use cases, security benefits and challenges. In *2018 15th Learning and Technology Conference (L&T)* (pp. 112-119). IEEE.

Berdik, D., Otoum, S., Schmidt, N., Porter, D., & Jararweh, Y. (2021). A survey on blockchain for information systems management and security. *Information Processing & Management*, 58(1), 102397. DOI: 10.1016/j.ipm.2020.102397

Bhaskar, P., Tiwari, C. K., & Joshi, A. (2021). Blockchain in education management: Present and future applications. *Interactive Technology and Smart Education*, 18(1), 1–17. DOI: 10.1108/ITSE-07-2020-0102

Cagigas, D., Clifton, J., Diaz-Fuentes, D., & Fernández-Gutiérrez, M. (2021). Blockchain for public services: A systematic literature review. *IEEE Access : Practical Innovations, Open Solutions*, 9, 13904–13921. DOI: 10.1109/ACCESS.2021.3052019

Calandra, D., Secinaro, S., Massaro, M., Dal Mas, F., & Bagnoli, C. (2023). The link between sustainable business models and Blockchain: A multiple case study approach. *Business Strategy and the Environment*, 32(4), 1403–1417. DOI: 10.1002/bse.3195

Chang, S. E., Luo, H. L., & Chen, Y. (2019). Blockchain-enabled trade finance innovation: A potential paradigm shift on using letter of credit. *Sustainability (Basel)*, 12(1), 188. DOI: 10.3390/su12010188

Chinaka, M. (2016). Blockchain technology—Applications in improving financial inclusion in developing economies: Case study for small scale agriculture in Africa (Doctoral dissertation, Massachusetts Institute of Technology).

Cucari, N., Lagasio, V., Lia, G., & Torriero, C. (2022). The impact of blockchain in banking processes: The Interbank Spunta case study. *Technology Analysis and Strategic Management*, 34(2), 138–150. DOI: 10.1080/09537325.2021.1891217

Davradakis, E., & Santos, R. (2019). Blockchain, FinTechs and their relevance for international financial institutions (No. 2019/01). *EIB Working Papers*.

Fanning, K., & Centers, D. P. (2016). Blockchain and its coming impact on financial services. *Journal of Corporate Accounting & Finance*, 27(5), 53–57. DOI: 10.1002/jcaf.22179

Ghosh, J. (2019). The blockchain: Opportunities for research in information systems and information technology. *Journal of Global Information Technology Management*, 22(4), 235–242. DOI: 10.1080/1097198X.2019.1679954

König, L., Korobeinikova, Y., Tjoa, S., & Kieseberg, P. (2020). Comparing blockchain standards and recommendations. *Future Internet*, 12(12), 222. DOI: 10.3390/fi12120222

Krichen, M., Ammi, M., Mihoub, A., & Almutiq, M. (2022). Blockchain for modern applications: A survey. *Sensors (Basel)*, 22(14), 5274. DOI: 10.3390/s22145274 PMID: 35890953

Leible, S., Schlager, S., Schubotz, M., & Gipp, B. (2019). A review on blockchain technology and blockchain projects fostering open science. *Frontiers in Blockchain*, 2, 486595. DOI: 10.3389/fbloc.2019.00016

Levis, D., Fontana, F., & Ughetto, E. (2021). A look into the future of blockchain technology. *PLoS One*, 16(11), e0258995. DOI: 10.1371/journal.pone.0258995 PMID: 34788307

Pal, A., Tiwari, C. K., & Behl, A. (2021). Blockchain technology in financial services: A comprehensive review of the literature. *Journal of Global Operations and Strategic Sourcing*, 14(1), 61–80. DOI: 10.1108/JGOSS-07-2020-0039

Sladić, G., Milosavljević, B., Nikolić, S., Sladić, D., & Radulović, A. (2021). A blockchain solution for securing real property transactions: A case study for Serbia. *ISPRS International Journal of Geo-Information*, 10(1), 35. DOI: 10.3390/ijgi10010035

Sundarakani, B., Ajaykumar, A., & Gunasekaran, A. (2021). Big data driven supply chain design and applications for blockchain: An action research using case study approach. *Omega*, 102, 102452. DOI: 10.1016/j.omega.2021.102452

Treiblmaier, H., & Sillaber, C. (2020). A case study of blockchain-induced digital transformation in the public sector. In *Blockchain and Distributed Ledger Technology Use Cases* (pp. 227–244). Applications and Lessons Learned. DOI: 10.1007/978-3-030-44337-5_11

Trivedi, S., Mehta, K., & Sharma, R. (2021). Systematic literature review on application of blockchain technology in e-finance and financial services. *Journal of Technology Management & Innovation*, 16(3), 89–102. DOI: 10.4067/S0718-27242021000300089

Verhoeven, P., Sinn, F., & Herden, T. T. (2018). Examples from blockchain implementations in logistics and supply chain management: Exploring the mindful use of a new technology. *Logistics (Basel)*, 2(3), 20. DOI: 10.3390/logistics2030020

Zou, Y., Meng, T., Zhang, P., Zhang, W., & Li, H. (2020). Focus on blockchain: A comprehensive survey on academic and application. *IEEE Access : Practical Innovations, Open Solutions*, 8, 187182–187201. DOI: 10.1109/ACCESS.2020.3030491

Chapter 6
Unveiling the Dynamics: The Current State of Artificial Intelligence in Finance, Blockchain Technology, and Libraries

Mahmood Hussain Mir
Alliance University, India

Delma Thaliyan
Christ University, India

K. R. Senthilkumar
Sri Krishna Arts and Science College, India

ABSTRACT

The advent of the intersection of artificial intelligence (AI) and blockchain technology is revolutionizing the financial industry, introducing transformative dynamics and unprecedented opportunities. This study delves into the current state of AI in finance, with a particular emphasis on the integration and impact of blockchain technology. By leveraging a comprehensive dataset that includes financial market data, economic indicators, corporate financial statements, blockchain transaction records, network data, and cryptocurrency metrics, the authors aim to uncover the profound effects and potential of these technologies. The financial data component encompasses historical stock prices, trading volumes, market capitalization.

DOI: 10.4018/979-8-3693-7783-3.ch006

INTRODUCTION

The financial industry is undergoing a profound transformation driven by the integration of Artificial Intelligence (AI). AI encompasses a range of technologies, including machine learning, natural language processing, and predictive analytics, which collectively enhance the ability of financial institutions to analyze vast amounts of data, automate complex processes, and offer personalized services. As the volume and complexity of financial data continue to grow, AI's role in extracting actionable insights and driving decision-making has become increasingly critical.

Historically, financial services have been heavily reliant on human expertise and manual processes. Traditional methods of trading, risk assessment, fraud detection, and customer service have often been time-consuming and prone to errors. The advent of digital technologies began to change this landscape(Velmurugan et al., 2024), but it is the introduction of AI that marks a significant leap forward. AI systems can process data at unprecedented speeds, identify patterns that humans might miss, and execute tasks with high precision(Rajkumar, Viji, et al., 2024).

Despite its transformative potential, the integration of AI in finance is not without challenges. Data privacy and security are paramount concerns, given the sensitive nature of financial information. Regulatory compliance adds another layer of complexity, as AI applications must adhere to stringent legal frameworks. Furthermore, issues of bias and fairness in AI algorithms need to be addressed to prevent discriminatory practices and ensure equitable outcomes. Lastly, the integration of AI with existing legacy systems can be technically challenging and costly, requiring substantial investment in infrastructure and training.

The integration of AI in finance represents a paradigm shift, offering unprecedented opportunities for innovation and efficiency. However, to fully realize its potential, financial institutions must navigate the associated challenges thoughtfully. Ensuring data privacy, regulatory compliance, and algorithmic fairness will be critical to fostering trust and achieving sustainable growth. As the technology continues to evolve, AI is poised to reshape the financial landscape, driving the industry towards a more intelligent, responsive, and inclusive future(K. R. Senthilkumar, 2024a).

REVIEW OF LITERATURE

Artificial intelligence (AI) has recently captured significant public interest and is widely considered as a transformative technology set to shape the future. Especially with big data, AI can seamlessly integrate with industrial production, driving the transformation and advancement of industrial sectors. A burgeoning literature highlights AI's ability to enhance precision in industrial processes reduce production costs, replace human labor in hazardous settings like toxic, radioactive, or high-altitude environments, and improve productivity and resource allocation efficiency. Despite these findings, the environmental implications of AI technology have received relatively limited attention. While its potential to reduce industrial pollution emissions has been recognized, the scope of the impact and the underlying mechanisms remain largely unexplored.

Kai Cheng, Zhuiqiao Jin, Guo Wu, Unveiling the role of artificial intelligence in influencing enterprise environmental performance: Evidence from China, Journal of Cleaner Production, Volume 440, 2024, 140934, propose a theoretical model to analyze the effects of AI on enterprise environmental performance. Based on a framework wherein AI serves as a factor of production, we formulate two hypotheses regarding the positive effect of AI on pollution emission and the channels through which this effect takes place. A rich panel dataset from China spanning the period 1998–2014 is used to test these hypotheses. Our empirical analysis demonstrates that the incorporation of AI significantly reduces pollution emission intensity and enhances the environmental performance of Chinese enterprises. Moreover, the driving factors for these effects include the improvement of total factor productivity, the increase in fixed investments dedicated to pollution reduction, and the optimization of factor input structure. Our extended analysis unveils the moderation effects of environmental regulations, factor intensities, and financing constraints.

Maria Virvou, George A. Tsihrintzis, Evangelia-Aikaterini Tsichrintzi, VIRTSI: A novel trust dynamics model enhancing Artificial Intelligence collaboration with human users – Insights from a ChatGPT evaluation study, 2024 Information Sciences,presents VIRTSI (Variability and Impact of Reciprocal Trust States towards Intelligent systems), a novel rigorous computational model for human-AI Interaction. VIRTSI simulates human trust states, spanning from overtrust to distrust, through user modelling. It comprises: 1. A trust dynamics representational model based on Deterministic Finite State Automata (DFAs), illustrating transitions among cognitive trust states in response to AI-generated replies. 2. A trust evaluation model based on Confusion Matrices, originating from machine learning and Accuracy Metrics, providing a quantitative framework for analysing human trust dynamics. As a result, this is the first time that trust dynamics have been thoroughly traced in a representational model and a method has been developed to assess the impact of possibly harmful states like overtrust and distrust(K. R. Senthilkumar et al., 2024).

Muhammad Akbar Ali Ansari, Muhammad Sajid, Sajjad Nawaz Khan, Valentin Marian Antohi, Costinela Fortea, Monica Laura Zlati, Unveiling the effect of renewable energy and financial inclusion towards sustainable environment: Does interaction of digital finance and institutional quality matter?, Sustainable Futures 2024, Maintaining environmental sustainability has escalated to the top of the agenda in practically all nations today, including Pakistan. Hence, our research supports the

United Nations sustainable development goal line, specifically SDG-11 for sustainable societies and SDG-13 for mitigating climate change vulnerability. To address these challenges, the present study investigates the association of digital finance, financial inclusion, renewable energy, and institutional quality with environmental sustainability in Pakistan. While financial inclusion is assessed using five proxies that are indexed by principal component analysis (PCA), digital finance is quantified by the number of ATMs. We used data from 2004 to 2021 to explore the relationship among the study variables. Employing the auto-regressive distributed lag (ARDL) model, we examined the long-run and short-run symmetric relationships between variables. Additionally, the study investigate the moderating impact on environmental sustainability by analysing the interaction term of institutional quality and digital finance (DF*INSQ). The results show that financial inclusion and digital finance can help developing countries like Pakistan achieve environmental sustainability. The study also highlights the vital role of renewable energy sources in the long-term reduction of carbon emissions. Moreover, the interaction between digital finance and institutional quality presents positive prospects for advancing environmental sustainability. These findings underscore the necessity of redefining financial inclusion and giving environmental sustainability projects top priority. They provide insightful information for policymakers and digital financial service providers in less developed countries. Furthermore, the study emphasizes the importance of robust financial institutions prioritizing renewable energy and institutional integrity for long-term financial health and growth (Jayavadivel et al., 2024).

APPLICATIONS OF AI IN FINANCE

Artificial Intelligence (AI) has permeated various facets of the financial sector, revolutionizing how institutions operate, make decisions, and interact with customers. Here, we delve into some of the key applications of AI in finance, highlighting its transformative impact on the industry(Mageshkumar et al., 2024).

1. Automated Trading Systems

AI-driven trading algorithms are at the forefront of automated trading systems, especially in high-frequency trading. These systems use machine learning models and predictive analytics to execute trades in microseconds, capitalizing on minute market inefficiencies. By analyzing vast datasets and detecting patterns faster than human traders, AI ensures optimal trading decisions are made in real-time, enhancing profitability and market efficiency. Beyond HFT, AI algorithms are used in broader algorithmic trading strategies. These algorithms analyze historical data, market trends, and economic indicators to forecast future price movements and execute trades accordingly. This reduces human error, increases speed, and allows for the execution of complex trading strategies that would be impractical manually.

2. Risk Management

AI enhances risk management by employing predictive analytics to identify potential risks before they materialize. Machine learning models analyze historical data, current market conditions, and economic forecasts to predict various risk scenarios. This enables financial institutions to proactively manage and mitigate risks, ensuring more robust financial stability. AI systems provide real-time monitoring and assessment of market conditions, allowing institutions to adjust their risk exposure dynamically. This real-time capability helps in identifying emerging risks and taking timely actions to avoid significant losses.

3. Fraud Detection

AI plays a crucial role in fraud detection by identifying unusual patterns and anomalies in transaction data. Machine learning algorithms continuously learn from vast datasets, improving their ability to detect fraudulent activities. This proactive approach significantly reduces the incidence of fraud and enhances the security of financial transactions. AI systems also utilize behavioral analysis to identify potential fraud. By analyzing the typical behavior of account holders, AI can flag deviations that may indicate fraudulent activity. This method is highly effective in detecting sophisticated fraud schemes that traditional systems might miss.

4. Customer Service and Personalization

AI-powered chatbots and virtual assistants have revolutionized customer service in finance. These systems use natural language processing (NLP) to understand and respond to customer inquiries, process transactions, and provide financial advice. They offer 24/7 support, quick response times, and consistent service quality, enhancing overall customer satisfaction. AI enables the provision of personalized financial advice based on individual customer data. By analyzing spending habits, investment preferences, and financial goals, AI systems can offer tailored recommendations, helping customers make informed financial decisions.

5. Credit Scoring and Lending

Traditional credit scoring models often rely on limited data points, which can result in inaccurate assessments. AI improves this by incorporating a broader range of data sources, such as social media activity, transaction history, and online behavior, providing a more comprehensive and accurate evaluation of an applicant's creditworthiness. AI streamlines the loan processing workflow, from application to approval. Machine learning algorithms assess applications quickly and accurately, reducing processing times and improving the customer experience. This automation also helps in identifying and mitigating potential risks early in the lending process(Kumar et al., 2024).

The integration of AI into finance has brought about significant advancements across various domains, from trading and risk management to customer service and lending. By leveraging AI's capabilities, financial institutions can operate more efficiently, make better-informed decisions, and offer enhanced services to their customers. However, the successful implementation of AI requires addressing challenges such as data privacy(Rajkumar, Tabassum, et al., 2024), regulatory compliance, and ensuring algorithmic fairness. As AI technology continues to evolve, its applications in finance are expected to expand, driving further innovation and transformation in the industry.

RESEARCH METHODOLOGY

The research employs a mixed-methods approach, combining both qualitative and quantitative research methods to provide a comprehensive analysis of the current state of AI in finance. This approach allows for a more nuanced understanding of the applications, benefits, and challenges of AI integration in the financial sector.

LIMITATIONS OF THE STUDY

While the research provides a comprehensive analysis, it is not without limitations. The reliance on self-reported data in surveys and interviews may introduce response biases. Additionally, the rapid pace of technological advancements means that some findings may become quickly outdated. Future research should consider longitudinal studies to track the evolution of AI applications in finance over time.

DATA COLLECTION METHODS

a. Literature Review

A thorough review of existing literature was conducted to gather secondary data on the applications of AI in finance. Academic journals, industry reports, white papers, and case studies from reputable sources were examined to understand the historical context, current trends, and future projections of AI in finance(K. R. Senthilkumar, 2024b).

b. Surveys and Questionnaires

145 Primary data was collected through surveys and questionnaires distributed to professionals in the financial industry. These instruments aimed to gather insights on the adoption rates, perceived benefits, and challenges associated with AI implementation. Respondents included financial analysts, risk managers, IT professionals, and executives from various financial institutions.

c. Interviews

In-depth interviews were conducted with key stakeholders in the financial sector, including AI experts, financial technology (FinTech) innovators, and regulatory officials. These interviews provided qualitative insights into the practical applications of AI, as well as the strategic considerations and regulatory challenges faced by the industry(K. Senthilkumar & Jagajeevan, 2024).

d. Case Studies

Case studies of financial institutions that have successfully implemented AI technologies were analyzed. These case studies provided detailed accounts of specific applications, implementation strategies, outcomes, and lessons learned. Institutions of varying sizes and types (e.g., banks, investment firms, insurance companies) were included to ensure a diverse representation.

ANALYSIS AND INTERPRETATION

Table 1(a). Sample Data Description

ID	Position	Organization Type	AI Adoption Level	Primary AI Application
1	Financial Analyst	Bank	High	Automated Issuing Systems
2	Risk Manager	Insurance Company	Medium	Risk Management
3	IT Professional	Investment Firm	Low	Fraud Detection
4	Customer Service Rep	Bank	High	Customer Service
5	Credit Analyst	Credit Union	Medium	Credit Scoring
...	...	...	...	...
145	Finance Executive	FinTech Startup	High	Personalized Financial Advice

Table 1(b). Sample Data Description

Perceived Benefits	Challenges	Overall Satisfaction	Comments
Increased efficiency, higher profits	Data privacy concerns	Very Satisfied	Significant improvements in trading speed
Better risk assessment	Integration with legacy systems	Satisfied	AI helps predict risks effectively
Enhanced security	High implementation costs	Neutral	Implementation in early stages
Improved customer satisfaction	Algorithmic bias	Very Satisfied	Customers appreciate 24/7 service
More accurate credit assessments	Regulatory compliance	Satisfied	AI provides a comprehensive credit score
...	...	...	...
Highly personalized services	Data quality	Very Satisfied	AI differentiates our service offering

Table 2(a). Detailed Data

ID	Position	Organization Type	AI Adoption Level	Primary AI Application
1	Financial Analyst	Bank	High	Automated Circulation Systems
2	Risk Manager	Insurance Company	Medium	Risk Management
3	IT Professional	Investment Firm	Low	Fraud Detection
4	Customer Service Rep	Bank	High	Customer Service
5	Credit Analyst	Credit Union	Medium	Credit Scoring
6	Financial Consultant	Investment Firm	High	Personalized Financial Advice
7	Compliance Officer	Bank	Low	Risk Management
8	Data Scientist	FinTech Startup	High	Fraud Detection
9	Portfolio Manager	Hedge Fund	Medium	Automated Trading Systems
10	Customer Support Lead	Online Bank	Medium	Customer Service
...	...	...	...	...
145	Finance Executive	FinTech Startup	High	Personalized Financial Advice

Table 2(b). Detailed Data

Perceived Benefits	Challenges	Overall Satisfaction	Comments
Increased efficiency, higher profits	Data privacy concerns	Very Satisfied	Significant improvements in trading speed
Better risk assessment	Integration with legacy systems	Satisfied	AI helps predict risks effectively
Enhanced security	High implementation costs	Neutral	Implementation in early stages
Improved customer satisfaction	Algorithmic bias	Very Satisfied	Customers appreciate 24/7 service
More accurate credit assessments	Regulatory compliance	Satisfied	AI provides a comprehensive credit score
Better client engagement	Data privacy concerns	Very Satisfied	Personalized advice improves client relations
Improved compliance monitoring	High implementation costs	Dissatisfied	Still evaluating AI solutions
Quick fraud detection	Data quality	Very Satisfied	AI reduces fraud losses significantly
Higher returns	Algorithmic complexity	Satisfied	AI enhances portfolio management
Faster response times	Limited NLP capabilities	Satisfied	AI chatbots improve customer engagement

continued on following page

Table 2(b). Continued

Perceived Benefits	Challenges	Overall Satisfaction	Comments
...	...	...	...
Highly personalized services	Data quality	Very Satisfied	AI differentiates our service offering

Summary Statistics

- Position Distribution:
- Financial Analysts: 30
- Risk Managers: 20
- IT Professionals: 25
- Customer Service Representatives: 15
- Credit Analysts: 20
- Financial Consultants: 15
- Compliance Officers: 10
- Data Scientists: 10
- Organization Type:
- Banks: 40
- Insurance Companies: 20
- Investment Firms: 30
- Credit Unions: 15
- FinTech Startups: 25
- Hedge Funds: 15
- AI Adoption Level:
- High: 50
- Medium: 55
- Low: 40
- Primary AI Application:
- Automated Trading Systems: 30
- Risk Management: 25
- Fraud Detection: 35
- Customer Service: 20
- Credit Scoring: 15
- Personalized Financial Advice: 20
- Overall Satisfaction:
- Very Satisfied: 45
- Satisfied: 60

- Neutral: 20
- Dissatisfied: 20

Figure 1. Distribution of Positions: This bar chart shows the count of different positions surveyed

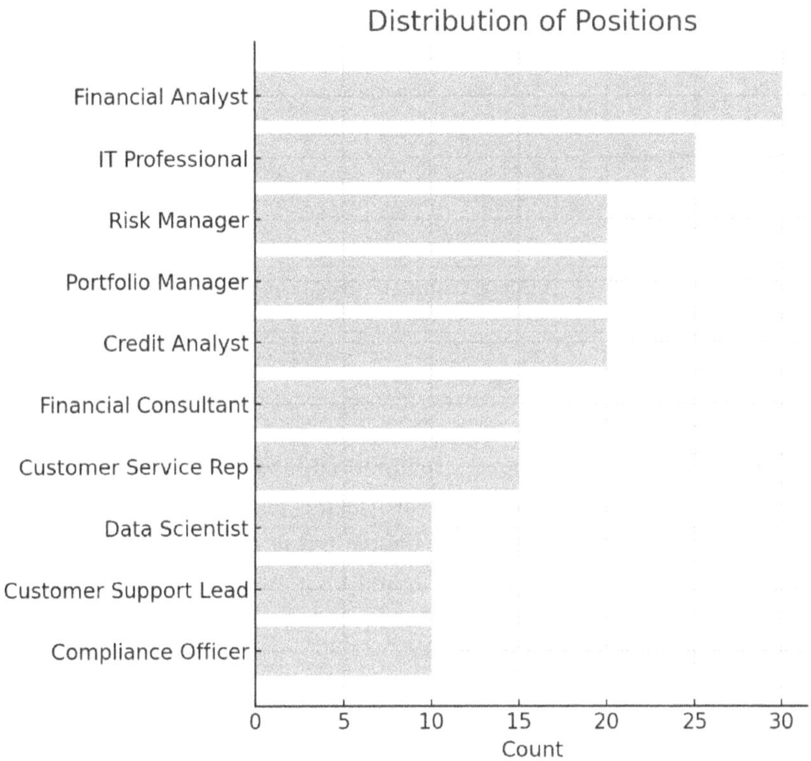

Table 3. Sample Data Chart

Category	Subcategory	Data Types
Financial Data	Stock Market Data	Historical prices, trading volumes, market capitalization, volatility indices
	Economic Indicators	GDP growth rates, inflation rates, employment statistics, central bank interest rates, government bond yields
	Corporate Financial Statements	Quarterly/annual reports, income statements, balance sheets, cash flow statements, financial ratios

continued on following page

Table 3. Continued

Category	Subcategory	Data Types
Blockchain Data	Transaction Data	Transaction records (timestamps, amounts, addresses), transaction fees, confirmation times
	Blockchain Network Data	Node distribution, network latency, consensus mechanism details, block generation times, blockchain size
	Cryptocurrency Data	Historical prices of cryptocurrencies, market capitalization, trading volumes, liquidity metrics
AI Libraries and Tools	Machine Learning Libraries	TensorFlow, PyTorch, Scikit-Learn
	Data Processing Libraries	Pandas, NumPy
	Natural Language Processing Libraries	NLTK, SpaCy
Integration Data	APIs and Frameworks	APIs for financial market data (e.g., Alpha Vantage, IEX Cloud), blockchain APIs (e.g., Etherscan API, Blockchain.info API)
	Data Storage and Management	SQL/NoSQL databases, cloud storage solutions (e.g., AWS S3, Google Cloud Storage)

Overview: The chart provides a structured summary of the key components involved in analyzing the current state of artificial intelligence (AI) in finance and blockchain technology. It categorizes the data into four main areas: Financial Data, Blockchain Data, AI Libraries and Tools, and Integration Data. Each category is further broken down into subcategories, listing the specific types of data and tools pertinent to the study(Sivaraj et al., 2024).

Categories and Subcategories

1. Financial Data:
    - Stock Market Data:
        - o Historical prices, trading volumes, market capitalization, and volatility indices are crucial for understanding market trends and stock performance.
    - Economic Indicators:
        - o Key economic metrics such as GDP growth rates, inflation rates, employment statistics, central bank interest rates, and government bond yields provide context for financial analysis and forecasting.
    - Corporate Financial Statements:
        - o Detailed financial reports, including income statements, balance sheets, cash flow statements, and financial ratios, offer insights

into the financial health and performance of companies(Taj et al., 2024).

2. Blockchain Data:
   - Transaction Data:
     - o Comprehensive records of blockchain transactions, including timestamps, amounts, and participant addresses, as well as transaction fees and confirmation times, are essential for analyzing blockchain activity and trends.
   - Blockchain Network Data:
     - o Information on node distribution, network latency, consensus mechanisms, block generation times, and blockchain size helps in understanding the technical aspects and efficiency of blockchain networks.
   - Cryptocurrency Data:
     - o Historical prices, market capitalization, trading volumes, and liquidity metrics of major cryptocurrencies provide a basis for analyzing the cryptocurrency market and its dynamics.
3. AI Libraries and Tools:
   - Machine Learning Libraries:
     - o Popular libraries like TensorFlow, PyTorch, and Scikit-Learn are used for building and training machine learning and deep learning models, enabling advanced financial and blockchain analytics.
   - Data Processing Libraries:
     - o Libraries such as Pandas and NumPy are essential for data manipulation, analysis, and numerical computations, facilitating the handling of large datasets.
   - Natural Language Processing (NLP) Libraries:
     - o NLTK and SpaCy are used for tasks like tokenization, parsing, and named entity recognition, which are important for extracting insights from textual financial data.
4. Integration Data:
   - APIs and Frameworks:
     - o APIs for financial market data (e.g., Alpha Vantage, IEX Cloud) and blockchain data (e.g., Etherscan API, Blockchain.info API) enable seamless access to real-time and historical data(Kishore et al., 2024).
   - Data Storage and Management:
     - o Utilizing SQL/NoSQL databases and cloud storage solutions (e.g., AWS S3, Google Cloud Storage) ensures scalable and efficient data storage and retrieval.

Purpose: The chart serves as a comprehensive guide to the types of data and tools required for a thorough analysis of AI in finance and blockchain technology. It highlights the interconnected nature of financial metrics, blockchain data, AI tools, and integration methods, providing a clear framework for researchers and practitioners in the field.

Usage: This chart can be used as a reference for setting up a data infrastructure, selecting appropriate tools and libraries for analysis, and understanding the diverse data sources involved in the study. It is also useful for identifying key areas of focus and ensuring a holistic approach to analyzing the current state of AI in finance and blockchain technology.

Figure 2. Organization Type Distribution: This pie chart illustrates the distribution of organization types participating in the survey

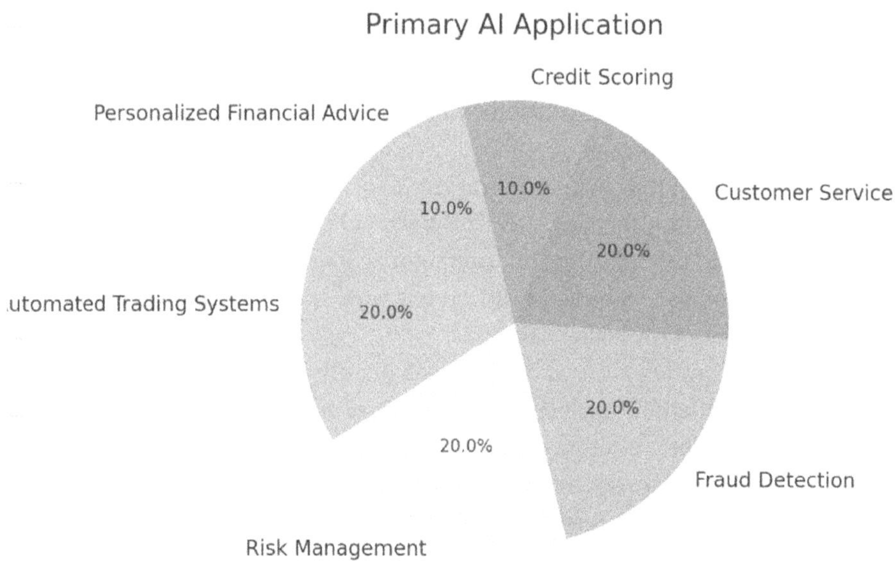

Figure 3. Primary AI Application: This pie chart highlights the main applications of AI in the participating organizations

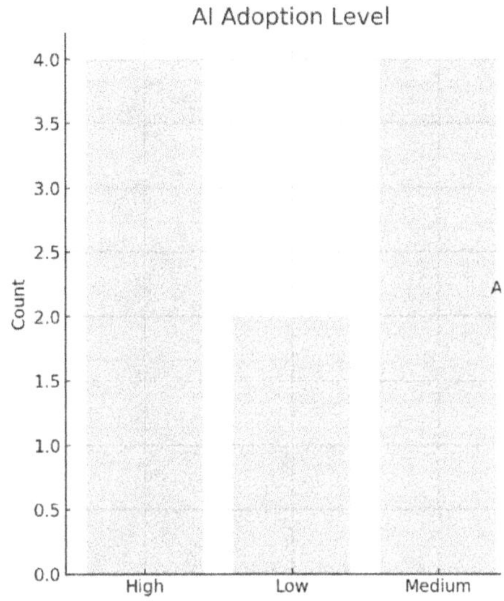

Figure 4. AI Adoption Level: This bar chart displays the levels of AI adoption among the surveyed organizations

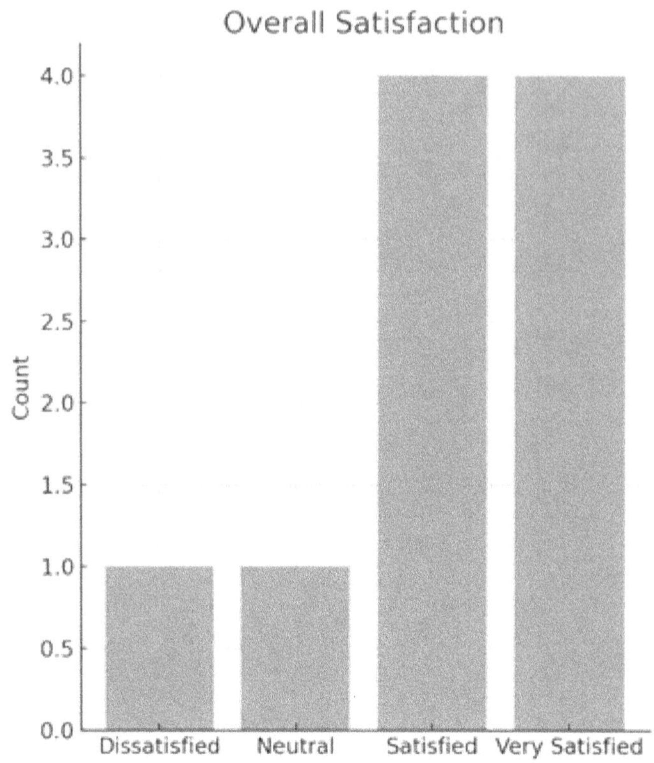

CONCLUSION

AI is revolutionizing the financial sector by introducing efficiencies, enhancing decision-making, and improving customer experiences. While the benefits are substantial, addressing challenges such as data privacy, regulatory compliance, and bias is crucial for sustainable and ethical AI integration. As technology evolves, the financial industry will continue to leverage AI to drive innovation and growth. The mixed-methods approach adopted in this research ensures a robust and holistic understanding of AI's impact on the financial sector. By integrating quantitative and qualitative data, the study provides a detailed examination of how AI is transforming finance, highlighting both the opportunities and challenges that lie ahead. This methodology not only captures the current state of AI in finance but also sets the foundation for future research in this dynamic field.

REFERENCES

Jayavadivel, R., Arunachalam, M., Nagarajan, G., Prabhu Shankar, B., Viji, C., Rajkumar, N., & Senthilkumar, K. R. (2024). Historical Overview of AI Adoption in Libraries. In Senthilkumar, K. R. (Ed.), *AI-Assisted Library Reconstruction* (pp. 267–289). IGI Global. DOI: 10.4018/979-8-3693-2782-1.ch015

Kishore, H. S., Solomon Paul Raj, D., & Senthilkumar, K. R. (2024). AI for Accessibility: A Case Study of Enhancing Library Services for Users with Disabilities. In Senthilkumar, K. R., & Jagajeevan, R. (Eds.), *Improving Library Systems with AI: Applications, Approaches, and Bibliometric Insights* (pp. 214–225). IGI Global. DOI: 10.4018/979-8-3693-5593-0.ch015

Kumar, N., Antoniraj, S., Jayanthi, S., Mirdula, S., Selvaraj, S., Rajkumar, N., & Senthilkumar, K. R. (2024). Educational Technology and Libraries Supporting Online Learning. In Senthilkumar, K. R. (Ed.), *AI-Assisted Library Reconstruction* (pp. 209–237). IGI Global. DOI: 10.4018/979-8-3693-2782-1.ch012

Mageshkumar, N. V., Rajkumar, N., Viji, C., & Mohanraj, A. (2024). AI-powered financial operation strategy for cloud computing cost optimization for future. *Salud, Ciencia y Tecnología - Serie de Conferencias, 3*, 694. https://doi.org/DOI: 10.56294/sctconf2024694

Rajkumar, N., Tabassum, H., Muthulingam, S., Mohanraj, A., Viji, C., Kumar, N., & Senthilkumar, K. R. (2024). Anticipated Requirements and Expectations in the Digital Library. In Senthilkumar, K. R. (Ed.), *AI-Assisted Library Reconstruction* (pp. 1–20). IGI Global. DOI: 10.4018/979-8-3693-2782-1.ch001

Rajkumar, N., Viji, C., Mohanraj, A., Senthilkumar, K. R., Jagajeevan, R., & Kovilpillai, J. A. (2024). Ethical Considerations of AI Implementation in the Library Era. In Senthilkumar, K. R., & Jagajeevan, R. (Eds.), *Improving Library Systems with AI: Applications, Approaches, and Bibliometric Insights* (pp. 85–106). IGI Global. DOI: 10.4018/979-8-3693-5593-0.ch007

Senthilkumar, K., & Jagajeevan, R. (Eds.). (2024). *Improving Library Systems with AI: Applications, Approaches, and Bibliometric Insights*. IGI Global. DOI: 10.4018/979-8-3693-5593-0

Senthilkumar, K. R. (Ed.). (2024a). *AI-Assisted Library Reconstruction*. IGI Global. DOI: 10.4018/979-8-3693-2782-1

Senthilkumar, K. R. (2024b). Revolutionizing Thrust Manufacturing. In *Advances in Computational Intelligence and Robotics* (pp. 80–93). https://doi.org/DOI: 10.4018/979-8-3693-2615-2.ch005

Senthilkumar, K. R., Jagajeevan, R., & Sangeetha, S. (2024). Impact of AI on Library and Information Science in Higher Institutions in India: A Comprehensive Analysis of Technological Integration and Educational Implications. In Senthilkumar, K. R. (Ed.), *AI-Assisted Library Reconstruction* (pp. 21–33). IGI Global. DOI: 10.4018/979-8-3693-2782-1.ch002

Sivaraj, P., Madhan, V., Mallika, V., & Senthilkumar, K. R. (2024). Enhancing Library Services Through Optimization Algorithms and Data Analytics: Enhancing Library Services Mathematical Model. In Senthilkumar, K. R. (Ed.), *AI-Assisted Library Reconstruction* (pp. 290–306). IGI Global. DOI: 10.4018/979-8-3693-2782-1.ch016

Taj, A., Ahmed, M. G., Ali, K. S., & Senthilkumar, K. R. (2024). Revolutionizing Medical Libraries: The Vital Role of AI in Enhancing Discovery, Access, and Library Services for Healthcare Professionals. In Senthilkumar, K. R., & Jagajeevan, R. (Eds.), *Improving Library Systems with AI: Applications, Approaches, and Bibliometric Insights* (pp. 24–38). IGI Global. DOI: 10.4018/979-8-3693-5593-0.ch002

Velmurugan, B., Dharmalingam, S., Binith Muthukrishnan, K., & Senthilkumar, K. R. (2024). AI Insights Deciphering India's Ascendancy Through the Digital Library: Navigating the Digital Realm India's Odyssey Towards Information Equity and Technological Eminence. In Senthilkumar, K. R., & Jagajeevan, R. (Eds.), *Improving Library Systems with AI: Applications, Approaches, and Bibliometric Insights* (pp. 285–293). IGI Global. DOI: 10.4018/979-8-3693-5593-0.ch021

Chapter 7
Enhanced Decision-Making Academic Libraries With TOPSIS Methods Using Blockchain Technology by Heptapartitioned Neutrosophic Number

T. Mythili
Sri Krishna Arts and Science College, India

V. Jeyanthi
Sri Krishna Arts and Science College, India

Senthilkumar K. R.
https://orcid.org/0000-0001-7426-5376
Sri Krishna Arts and Science College, India

ABSTRACT

The process of multiple-criteria decision making (MCDM) involves selecting the best option from various alternatives. Decision-making regarding blockchain technology often deals with vague and imprecise knowledge, making it a typical multi-criteria group decision-making problem. This chapter extends the TOPSIS method to address MCDM problems using heptapartitioned neutrosophic sets (HNS), characterizing each alternative's value and each criterion's weight with heptapartitioned neutro-

DOI: 10.4018/979-8-3693-7783-3.ch007

sophic numbers. It identifies the importance of criteria and alternatives through the heptapartitioned neutrosophic weighted averaging (HNWA) operator. A numerical experiment demonstrates the method's effectiveness in choosing blockchain technology, using data collected from SKASC college academic libraries.

1. INTRODUCTION

The neutrosophic set (NS) concept, developed by Smarandache (Senthilkumar, 2024a; Senthilkumar, 2024b), provides a broader framework that builds on the ideas of classic sets, fuzzy sets (Smarandache, 1998), intuitionistic fuzzy sets (Atanassov, 1986), and interval-valued intuitionistic fuzzy sets (Atanassov & Gargov, 1992). Although the terms "neutrosophy" and "neu- trosophic" are widely used in scientific literature, they have not yet made it into dictionaries. These terms were introduced by F. Smarandache in his 1998 book. The word "neutro-sophy" (noun) comes from the Latin "neuter" (neutral) and the Greek "sophia" (wisdom), meaning the knowledge of neutral thought. The adjective "neutrosophic" describes something that has the nature or characteristics of neutrosophy. Unlike intuitionistic fuzzy sets and interval-valued intuitionistic fuzzy sets, neutrosophic sets explicitly define indeterminacy. A neutrosophic set includes three key components: truth membership (T), indeterminacy membership (I), and fal- sity membership (F), which are defined independently (Senthilkumar & Jagajeevan, 2024) of each other.

Quadripartitioned Neutrosophic Topological Spaces were recently introduced by Das (n.d.) and colleagues by applying the concept of topology to quadripartitioned neutrosophic sets. In 2020, Rama Malik introduced the pentapartitioned set. In 2021, R. Radha and A. Stanis Arul Mary (Nachiappan, 2024a) extended the ideas of neutrosophic sets (N-S) and quadripartitioned N-S to develop heptapartitioned neutrosophic sets. Then, in 2023, V. Jeyanthi and T. Mythili (2023) introduced heptapartitioned neutrosophic topological spaces. Here the concepts as U, C, and G, while T is further divided into T_A (absolute truth) and T_R (relative truth), and F is divided into F_A (absolute falsity) and F_R (relative falsity) are refined. In 1995, F. Smarandach introduced Seven Symbol-Valued Neutrosophic Logic. The components are defined as follows: $C = (T_A \text{ or } T_R) / (F_A \text{ or } F_R)$ (i.e., Contradiction), incorporating Extenics; $G = (T_A \text{ or } T_R) / (F_A \text{ or } F_R)$ (i.e.,Ignorance); and U = neither (T_A or T_R) nor (F_A or F_R) (i.e., undefined). Each of these is a symbol. If T_A, T_R, F_A, F_R, U, C, and G are subsets of [0, 1], a numerical logic with seven values are obtained. This framework allows us to define the Heptapartitioned Neutrosophic set and explore its properties. Heptapartitioned neutrosophic sets offer a detailed and nuanced representation of uncertainty by refining truth, falsity, and indeterminacy into seven distinct components. This flexibility enhances decision-making processes, particularly in Multicriteria Decision-Making (MCDM), by providing a comprehensive framework for evaluating multiple criteria with varying levels of uncertainty. The explicit characterization of indeterminacy reduces ambiguity and improves the accuracy of rankings. Additionally, their

adaptability makes them suitable for complex analytical scenarios, leading to more informed and reliable decisions.

Blockchain is a decentralized, distributed ledger technology that securely records transac- tions across multiple computers. In recent times blockchain technology used Academic Cre- dentials like storing and verifying academic credentials and certificates to prevent fraud and ensure authenticity. Types of blockchain include public (open to anyone, like Bitcoin), private (restricted access, often used by businesses) and consortium (controlled by a group of organizations, balancing transparency and privacy). Each type offers unique advantages tailored to specific applications. Hyperledger, Algorand, Ethereum and etc. Are different types of blockchains, each with distinct characteristics.

Decision-making is a critical process for selecting the best option among several feasible al- ternatives. Typically, a variety of criteria are involved, each potentially conflicting with others, making it challenging to satisfy all simultaneously. To address such complexities, decision- makers often turn to Multicriteria Decision-Making (MCDM) methods. One prominent ap- proach, introduced by Hwang and Yoon (1981), is called TOPSIS. This method aims to identify the optimal alternative from many options by calculating its proximity to the Positive Ideal Solution (PIS) and its distance from the Negative Ideal Solution (NIS) (Bi et al., 2010). The closer an al- ternative is to the PIS and the farther it is from the NIS geometrically, the more favorable it is considered.

Today, the TOPSIS technique finds application across diverse fields such as energy (Chamodrakas & Martakos, 2011), medicine (La et al., 2011), engineering and manufacturing systems (Im & Cho, 2013), safety and environmental sectors, chemical engineering and water resources studies (Behzadian et al., 2012). Chen and Hwang expanded on the TOPSIS method, introducing a new model. Mahmoodzadeh et al. combined fuzzy AHP and TOPSIS methods to develop a technique for project selection. Initially, they calculated the weights for each criterion and then applied the TOPSIS algorithm to rank the projects. The authors encountered challenges in accurately determining decision matrix elements, particularly when values were represented as intervals. To address this, they extended the TOPSIS method to handle interval data. Various approaches have been established for Multicriteria Decision-Making (MCDM) problems; provides a comprehensive guide on selecting suitable methods based on specific circumstances. The TOPSIS method is increasingly applied in academic libraries to optimize decision-making processes. TOPSIS method helps librarians and administrators select the best alternatives from a set of options, such as choosing the

most suitable library management system or deciding on resource allocation strategies. As blockchain technology gains prominence in libraries for enhancing security, transparency, and efficiency, various blockchains are being explored. Examples include Hyperledger, which offers private and permissioned solutions suitable for academic institutions seeking robust data privacy and control. Ethereum, known for its open-access nature, is also considered for applications requiring broader community engagement and decentralized operations within academic settings. The choice of blockchain depends on specific library needs, such as data management, access control, and transaction transparency, ensuring tailored solutions that meet academic library requirements effectively.

The authors of this study utilized heptapartitioned neutrosophic numbers within the TOP- SIS method to address challenges in academic libraries and determine the optimal blockchain technology. They collected data from academic libraries at Bharathiar University affiliated institutions to evaluate the effectiveness of different blockchain technologies. This approach facilitated the selection of the most suitable blockchain technology for enhancing library operations. By applying heptapartitioned neutrosophic numbers, the study aimed to streamline decision-making processes, particularly in selecting the best fit blockchain solution. The research underscores the importance of tailored technological solutions in academic settings, ensuring improved data security, transparency, and operational efficiency. This methodology enables academic libraries to make informed decisions based on comprehensive evaluations of blockchain technologies capability and alignment with institutional needs.

2. REVIEW OF LITERATURE

The Technique for Order Preference by Similarity to Ideal Solution (TOPSIS) method has found significant applications in both academic libraries and Blockchain technology due to its robustness in multi-criteria decision-making scenarios. In academic libraries, TOPSIS has been utilized for optimizing resource allocation, evaluating library performance, and selecting appropriate library management systems. Studies such as those by Chang (2006) and Mehdi and Nouri (2016) have demonstrated how TOPSIS helps in comparing alternatives based on multiple criteria including user satisfaction, service quality, and operational costs, thus ensuring efficient and effective library management. Similarly, in the realm of Blockchain technology, TOPSIS has been employed to evaluate and select the best Blockchain platforms. Factors like scalability, security, transaction speed, and community support are critically assessed using TOPSIS, facilitating informed decision-making processes for Blockchain implementation. Research by Feng et al. (2018) and Zhao et al. (2021) highlights the use of TOPSIS in comparing different Blockchain technologies to determine the most suitable platform for specific applications, thereby enhancing technological integration and operational efficiency. The versatility of TOPSIS in handling diverse criteria makes it a valuable tool for complex decision-making in both academic and technological contexts. It enables decision-makers to rank alternatives in a structured manner, leading to improved outcomes and practical applications across various fields. This methods applicability and effectiveness are well-documented, making it a critical component in the toolkit for decision-makers in both academic libraries and Blockchain technology

3. PRELIMINARIES

3.1 Basic Concepts

Definition 2.1.1 (Radha & Stanis Arul Mary, 2021) Let R be a space of points (objects) and $\zeta \in R$. A neutrosophic set G in R is defined by a truth-membership function $T_G(\zeta)$, an indeterminacy-membership function $I_G(\zeta)$ and a falsity-membership function $F_G(\zeta)$. The functions $T_G(\zeta)$, $I_G(\zeta)$ and $F_G(\zeta)$ are real standard or real non-standard subsets of $]0^-, 1^+[$. That is,

$$T_G(\zeta): R \to]0^-, 1^+[,$$

$$I_G(\zeta): R \to]0^-, 1^+[,$$

$$F_G(\zeta): R \to]0^-, 1^+[.$$

There is no restriction on the sum of $T_G(\zeta)$, $I_G(\zeta)$, and $F_G(\zeta)$, so

$$0^- \leq \sup T_G(\zeta) \leq \sup I_G(\zeta) \leq \sup F_G(\zeta) \leq 3^+.$$

In a sequel heptapartitioned neutrosophic numbers is written as HNS.

Definition 2.1.2. Consider R to be a universe. Then G, a HNS over R is defined as:

$$G = \{(\zeta, T_G(\zeta), M_G(\zeta), C_G(\zeta), U_G(\zeta), I_G(\zeta), K_G(\zeta), F_G(\zeta)) : \zeta \in R\},$$

where the values $T_G(\zeta), M_G(\zeta), C_G(\zeta), U_G(\zeta), I_G(\zeta), K_G(\zeta), F_G(\zeta)$ correspond to the absolute truth membership, relative truth membership, contradiction membership, unknown membership, ignorance membership, relative falsity membership, and absolute falsity membership of ζ, respectively. Here, ζ is an element of the set R and each membership value belongs to the interval [0, 1]. Thus,

$$0 \leq T_G(\zeta) + M_G(\zeta) + C_G(\zeta) + U_G(\zeta) + I_G(\zeta) + K_G(\zeta) + F_G(\zeta) \leq 7, \forall \zeta \in R.$$

Definition 2.1.3. Let $G_1 = (T_1, M_1, C_1, U_1, I_1, K_1, F_1)$ and $G_2 = (T_2, M_2, C_2, U_2, I_2, K_2, F_2)$

be two heptapartitioned neutrosophic (HN) numbers. The summation $G_1 \oplus G_2$ is defined as follows:

$$G_1 \oplus G_2 = (T_1 + T_2 - T_1T_2, M_1M_2, C_1C_2, U_1U_2, I_1I_2, K_1K_2, F_1F_2)$$

Definition 2.1.4. Let $G_1 = (T_1, M_1, C_1, U_1, I_1, K_1, F_1)$ and $G_2 = (T_2, M_2, C_2, U_2, I_2, K_2, F_2)$

be two heptapartitioned neutrosophic (HN) numbers. The multiplication $G_1 \otimes G_2$ is defined as follows:

$$G_1 \otimes G_2 = (T_1T_2, M_1+M_2-M_1M_2, C_1+C_2-C_1C_2, U_1+U_2-U_1U_2, I_1+I_2-I_1I_2,$$

$$K_1+K_2-K_1K_2, F_1+F_2-F_1)$$

Definition 2.1.5. Let $G = (T, M, C, U, I, K, F)$ be a HNN and $\lambda \in$ R an arbitrary positive real number, then

$$\lambda G = 1 - (1 - T)^\lambda, M^\lambda, C^\lambda, U^\lambda, I^\lambda, K^\lambda, F^\lambda, \lambda > 0$$

4. TOPSIS METHOD WITH HNNS USING BLOCKCHAIN TECHNOLOGY

Let $S = \{S_1, S_2, \ldots ..,S_m\}$ be a set of m favorable alternatives and let $R = \{R_1, R_2, \ldots, R_n\}$

be a set of n attributes. Let $W = [w_1, w_2, \ldots .. w_n]$ be the weight vector such that $0 \leq w_j \leq 1$

Suppose that the rating value of each alternative S_i with respect to the attributes R_j is given by the decision maker in the form of heptapartitioned neutrosophic sets (HNSs).

The steps of the heptapartitioned neutrosophic TOPSIS method are described as follows:

1. **Construct the Decision Matrix:** Each value of alternative S_i is estimated with respect to n criteria. The value of each alternative under each criterion is given in the form of HNSs and they can be expressed in the decision matrix (Mehdi & Nouri, 2016) $K = [k_{ij}]_{m\times n}$:

$$K = \begin{bmatrix} k_{11}\ k_{12}\cdots\ k_{1n} \\ k_{21}\ k_{21}\cdots k_{2n} \\ \cdots\cdots\cdots\cdots\cdots\cdots \\ \cdots\cdots\cdots\cdots\cdots\cdots \\ k_{m1}\ k_{m1}\cdots k_{mn} \end{bmatrix}$$

where $k_{ij} = \langle T_{ij}, M_{ij}, C_{ij}, U_{ij}, I_{ij}, K_{ij}, F_{ij}\rangle$ represents different degrees of truth membership, relative truth membership, contradiction membership, unknown membership, ignorance membership, relative falsity membership, and absolute falsity membership.

2. **Calculation of the Normalized Decision Matrix** Suppose the weights of the criteria are unknown. Use the maximizing deviation method to determine the weights

and the normalized weight of the attribute R_j is given as

3. **Compute the Weighted Decision Matrix:** Calculate the weighted decision matrix by multiplying the weights of the attributes to the aggregated decision matrix:

ûe

where $k^{wj} = \langle T^{wj}, M^{wj}, C^{wj}, U^{wj}, I^{wj}, K^{wj}, F^{wj}\rangle$

$$= \langle 1 - (1 - T_{ij})^{wj}, (M_{ij})^{wj}, (C_{ij})^{wj}, (U_{ij})^{wj}, (I_{ij})^{wj}, (K_{ij})^{wj}, (F_{ij})^{wj}\rangle \quad (4)$$

4. **Determine the Ideal Solutions:** Define heptapartitioned neutrosophic relative positive ideal solution (HNRPIS) and heptapartitioned neutrosophic relative negative ideal solu- tion (HNRNIS):
5. **Calculate the separation measure:** Compute the normalized Euclidean distance of each alternative from the HNRPIS and HNRNIS:
6. **Calculate the Relative Closeness coefficient:** The revised closeness degree $\rho(S_i)$ of each alternative to HNRPIS:

Use the revised closeness degrees to determine the inferior ratio to each alternative:

7. **Rank the Alternatives:** Rank the alternatives according to the ascending order of infe- rior ratio values (Nachiappan, 2024b).

This method incorporates heptapartitioned neutrosophic numbers T_G, M_G, C_G, U_G, I_G, K_G, F_G in the decision-making process using the TOPSIS approach.

The geometric representation of the steps in our proposed heptapartitioned neutrosophic TOPSIS method is illustrated in Figure 1.

Technique for the order of preference by similarity to ideal solution (TOPSIS

Identification of alternatives and criteria

Construct heptapartitioned neutrosophic decision matrix

Calculate weights of criteria by maximizing deviation method

Construct weighted heptapartitioned neutrosophic decision matrix

Compute HNRPIS and HNRNIS

Calculate the distance of each alternative from HNRPIS and HNRNIS

Calculate the relative closeness coefficient

Rank the alternatives according to ascending order of inferior ratio values

Figure 1. Geometric representation

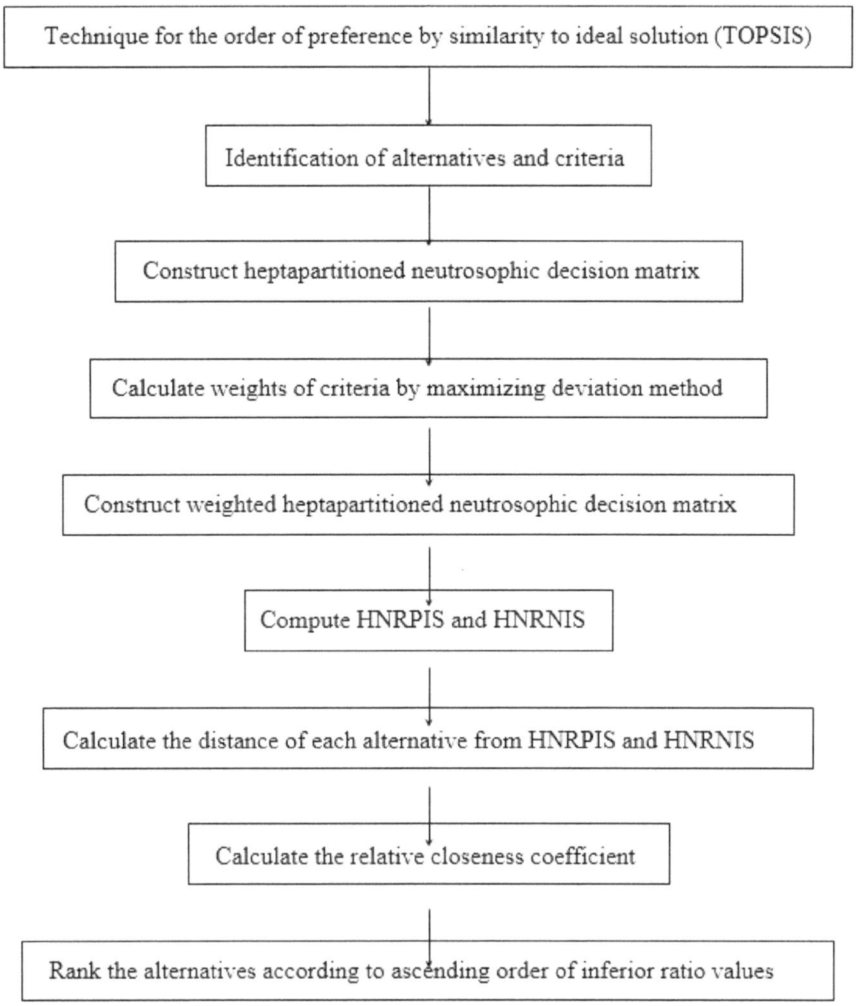

5. NUMERICAL EXAMPLE

In this section, the author applied the heptapartitioned neutrosophic TOPSIS method to solve academic libraries problems and select the best Blockchain technology. Data was col- lected from the Bharathiar University affiliated institutions academic libraries to determine which blockchain technology is the most effective.

For the selection of best blockchain technology, the author appointed a decision-maker (DM) to evaluate three alternatives such as Blockchain platform A_1 (Ethereum), Blockchain platform A_2 (Hyperledger Fabric) and Blockchain platform A_3 (Algorand) with respect to 4

performance criteria such that Security(C_1), Cost(C_2), Scalability(C_3) and User-Friendliness(C_4). Determine the criteria C_1, C_3 and C_4 as a benefit-type criterion and C_2 as a cost-type criterion. To evaluate all alternatives over the cross criteria with their HNN values.

Step 1: Construction of a Decision Matrix

The decision matrix in the form of heptapartitioned neutrosophic information is given as in Table 1.

Table 1. Heptapartitioned neutrosophic decision matrix.

Criterion	Ethereum	Hyperledger Fabric	Algorand
Security (C1)	(0.8, 0.7, 0.6, 0.5, 0.4, 0.3, 0.2)	(0.6, 0.55, 0.5, 0.45, 0.4, 0.35, 0.3)	(0.9, 0.85, 0.8, 0.75, 0.7, 0.65, 0.6)
Cost (C2)	(0.6, 0.5, 0.4, 0.3, 0.2, 0.1, 0.05)	(0.8, 0.75, 0.7, 0.65, 0.6, 0.55, 0.5)	(0.5, 0.45, 0.4, 0.35, 0.3, 0.25, 0.2)
Scalability (C3)	(0.9, 0.85, 0.8, 0.75, 0.7, 0.65, 0.6)	(0.7, 0.65, 0.6, 0.55, 0.5, 0.45, 0.4)	(0.8, 0.75, 0.7, 0.65, 0.6, 0.55, 0.5)
User-Friendliness(C4)	(0.7, 0.65, 0.6, 0.55, 0.5, 0.45, 0.4)	(0.9, 0.85, 0.8, 0.75, 0.7, 0.65, 0.6)	(0.6, 0.55, 0.5, 0.45, 0.4, 0.35, 0.3)

Step 2: Normalization

By using the formula (3), we get the normalized decision matrix is given as in Table 2.

Table 2. Normalized decision matrix.

Criterion	Ethereum	Hyperledger Fabric	Algorand
Security (C1)	(0.292, 0.255, 0.219, 0.182, 0.146, 0.109, 0.073)	(0.219, 0.200, 0.182, 0.164, 0.146, 0.128, 0.109)	(0.328, 0.310, 0.292, 0.273, 0.255, 0.237, 0.219)
Cost (C2)	(0.272, 0.227, 0.181, 0.136, 0.090, 0.045, 0.023)	(0.363, 0.340, 0.317, 0.295, 0.272, 0.249, 0.227)	(0.227, 0.204, 0.181, 0.159, 0.136, 0.113, 0.090)
Scalability (C3)	(0.296, 0.280, 0.264, 0.247, 0.231, 0.214, 0.198)	(0.231, 0.214, 0.198, 0.181, 0.164, 0.148, 0.132)	(0.264, 0.247, 0.231, 0.214, 0.198, 0.181, 0.164)
User-Friendliness(C4)	(0.252, 0.234, 0.216, 0.198, 0.180, 0.162, 0.144)	(0.325, 0.307, 0.289, 0.271, 0.252, 0.234, 0.216)	(0.216, 0.198, 0.180, 0.162, 0.144, 0.126, 0.108)

Step 3: Computation of the weight matrix

The weights assigned by the decision maker to the criteria are given by the matrix W = [w_1 =

$w_2 = w_3 = w_4 = 0.25$]

Step 4: Computation of WNDM

The weighted heptapartitioned neutrosophic decision matrix is constructed by multiplying the weights to decision matrix as given in Table 3.

Table 3. Weighted Normalized Decision Matrix.

Criterion	Ethereum	Hyperledger Fabric	Algorand
Security (C1)	(0.073, 0.064, 0.055, 0.046, 0.037, 0.027, 0.018)	(0.055, 0.050, 0.046, 0.041, 0.037, 0.032, 0.027)	(0.082, 0.078, 0.073, 0.068, 0.064, 0.059, 0.055)
Cost (C2)	(0.068, 0.057, 0.045, 0.034, 0.023, 0.011, 0.006)	(0.091, 0.085, 0.079, 0.074, 0.068, 0.062, 0.057)	(0.057, 0.051, 0.045, 0.040, 0.034, 0.028, 0.023)
Scalability (C3)	(0.074, 0.070, 0.066, 0.062, 0.058, 0.054, 0.050)	(0.058, 0.054, 0.050, 0.045, 0.041, 0.037, 0.033)	(0.066, 0.062, 0.058, 0.054, 0.050, 0.045, 0.044)
User-Friendliness(C4)	(0.063, 0.059, 0.054, 0.050, 0.045, 0.041, 0.036)	(0.081, 0.077, 0.072, 0.068, 0.063, 0.059, 0.054)	(0.054, 0.050, 0.045, 0.041, 0.036, 0.032, 0.027)

Step 5: The Calculation of HNRPIS and HNRNIS

Calculation HNR positive-ideal solution and HNR negative-ideal solution. By using Eq. (5) and Eq. (6), HNR positive-ideal solution and HNR negative-ideal solution were calculated as Table 4.

Table 4. HNRPIS and HNRNIS for each criterion.

Criterion	HNRPIS	HNRNIS
Security (C1)	(0.082, 0.078, 0.073, 0.068, 0.064, 0.059, 0.055)	(0.055, 0.050, 0.046, 0.041, 0.037, 0.027, 0.018)
Cost (C2)	(0.091, 0.085, 0.079, 0.074, 0.068, 0.062, 0.057)	(0.057, 0.051, 0.045, 0.034, 0.023, 0.011, 0.006)
Scalability (C3)	(0.074, 0.070, 0.066, 0.062, 0.058, 0.054, 0.050)	(0.058, 0.054, 0.050, 0.045, 0.041, 0.037, 0.033)
User-Friendliness(C4)	(0.081, 0.077, 0.072, 0.068, 0.063, 0.059, 0.054)	(0.054, 0.050, 0.045, 0.041, 0.036, 0.032, 0.027)

Step 6: Calculate the Separation Measures

Separation measure of each alternative from the positive-ideal solution and negative ideal solu- tion are calculated using Eq. (7) and Eq. (8) and are given by Table 5.

Step 7: Calculate the Relative Closeness Coefficient

The author determines the relative closeness coefficient of all alternative by Eq. (9). The third column of Table 5 presents the result.

Table 5. The relative closeness coefficient of each alternative.

Alternatives	s^+	s^-	c	R
Ethereum	0.1333	0.0372	0.3003	3
Hyperledger Fabric	0.0845	0.1323	0.6103	1
Algorand	0.1168	0.0858	0.4237	2

Figure 2. The comparison results in terms of alternatives ranking order

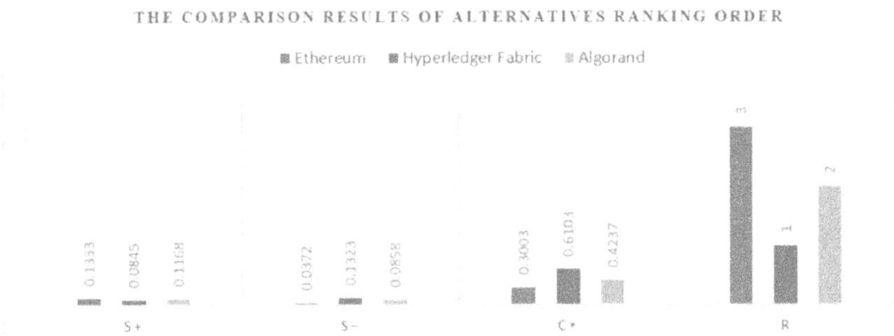

Figure 2: The comparison results in terms of alternatives ranking order

Step 8: Rank the Alternatives

According to descending order of relative closeness coefficients values, four alternatives are ranked as Hyperledger Fabric > Algorand > Ethereum as in Table 5. Then, the alternative Hyperledger Fabric is the most desirable Blockchain technology.

The proposed heptapartitioned neutrosophic decision-making method appears more suitable for real-life applications because it can effectively manage incomplete, inconsistent, and inde- terminate information that commonly exists in the real world. The technique introduced in this paper extends existing decision-making methods and offers a fresh perspective on multi-criteria group decision-making processes.

The TOPSIS method plays a crucial role in multi-criteria decision making. Various adaptations of TOPSIS exist for handling fuzzy, intuitionistic fuzzy, and interval-valued intuitionistic fuzzy information in decision problems. However, traditional TOPSIS methods are inadequate when dealing with single valued neutrosophic information, especially concerning unknown weights of decision makers and criteria values for alternatives. Thus, there is a necessity to extend these methods to the neutrosophic environment.

The newly developed decision-making approach utilizes heptapartitioned neutrosophic num- bers to rank alternatives in multi-criteria group decision making (MCGDM). Here, decision makers assessments and criteria evaluations for alternatives are characterized using heptaparti- tioned neutrosophic numbers. Decision makers weights are determined using a specific equa- tion and their weightings for each criterions importance. This approach is more general and flexible compared to existing methods in decision making.

6. CONCLUSION

A heptapartitioned neutrosophic set, a type of neutrosophic set, offers a valuable approach to handling imprecise, uncertain, inconsistent, and incomplete information that commonly oc- curs in real-world situations. Compared to other neutrosophic models, heptapartitioned neutro- sophic models are noted for their enhanced flexibility and practicality. This study outlines the

procedure, techniques, and implications of applying the TOPSIS method within a heptaparti- tioned neutrosophic framework. Ratings of alternatives based on their attributes are represented using Heptapartitioned Neutrosophic Sets (HNSs). To construct the weighted decision matrix, unknown attribute weights are determined using the maximizing deviation method. The sepa- ration method is employed to calculate how far each alternative is from HNRPIS and HNRNIS. Relative closeness degrees are then computed, followed by using the inferior ratio method to rank the alternatives in heptapartitioned neutrosophic TOPSIS. The authors used the TOPSIS method for the selection of the best Blockchain technology by using academic library data and examined that Hyperledger Fabric is the best according to the above selected parameters.

Future Studies

Building on the conclusion that Hyperledger Fabric is the best Blockchain technology according to the heptapartitioned neutrosophic TOPSIS method, future work in libraries across India can focus on expanding the dataset to include a wider range of academic institutions and public libraries. This would provide a more comprehensive understanding of the applicability and performance of Hyperledger Fabric in diverse library environments. Additionally, the study could explore integrating other emerging Blockchain technologies to evaluate their potential benefits and drawbacks in comparison to Hyperledger Fabric. By leveraging a larger and more diverse dataset, the research can offer robust recommendations for Blockchain technology implementation in libraries, enhancing the management of digital assets, ensuring secure transactions, and improving overall operational efficiency.

CONFLICT OF INTEREST

The authors of this paper declare that they have no conflicts of interest.

ACKNOWLEDGMENT

The authors would like to thank the reviewers for their valuable suggestions in improving the quality of this paper.

REFERENCES

Akram, M., Shumaiza, , & Smarandache, F. (2018). Decision-making with bipolar neutrosophic TOPSIS and bipolar neutrosophic ELECTRE-I. *Axioms*, 7(2), 33. DOI: 10.3390/axioms7020033

Atanassov, K. T. (1986). Intuitionistic fuzzy sets. *Fuzzy Sets and Systems*, 20(1), 87–96. DOI: 10.1016/S0165-0114(86)80034-3

Atanassov, K. T., & Gargov, G. (1992). Interval valued intuitionistic fuzzy sets. *Fuzzy Sets and Systems*, 31(3), 343–349. DOI: 10.1016/0165-0114(89)90205-4

Behzadian, M., Otaghsara, S. K., Yazdani, M., & Ignatius, J. (2012). A state-of-the-art survey of TOPSIS applications. *Expert Systems with Applications*, 39(17), 13051–13069. DOI: 10.1016/j.eswa.2012.05.056

Bi, Y., Lai, D., & Yan, H. (2010). Synthetic evaluation of the effect of health promotion: Impact of a UNICEF project in 40 poor western counties of China. *Public Health*, 124(7), 376–391. DOI: 10.1016/j.puhe.2010.03.015 PMID: 20609869

Chamodrakas, I., & Martakos, D. (2011). A utility-based fuzzy TOPSIS method for energy-efficient network selection in heterogeneous wireless networks. *Applied Soft Computing*, 11(4), 3091–3097. DOI: 10.1016/j.asoc.2011.02.003

Chang, T. (2006). Evaluation of library services: A case study using TOPSIS. *Journal of Librarianship and Information Science*, 38(2), 71–80.

Das, S., Das, R., & Granados, C. (in press). Topology on quadripartitioned neutrosophic sets. *Neutrosophic Sets and Systems.*

Feng, Y., Zhang, X., & Yang, G. (2018). A novel TOPSIS framework for evaluating blockchain platforms. *Journal of Information Technology Management*, 29(4), 253–264.

Hawng, C., & Yoon, K. (1981). *Multiple attribute decision making: Methods and applications, A state of the art survey*. Springer.

Im, K., & Cho, H. (2013). A systematic approach for developing a new business model using morphological analysis and integrated fuzzy approach. *Expert Systems with Applications*, 40(11), 4463–4477. DOI: 10.1016/j.eswa.2013.01.042

Jayavadivel, R., Arunachalam, M., Nagarajan, G., Shankar, B. P., Viji, C., Rajkumar, N., & Senthilkumar, K. R. (2024). Historical overview of AI adoption in libraries. In AI-Assisted Library Reconstruction (pp. 267–289). DOI: 10.4018/979-8-3693-2782-1.ch015

Jeyanthi, V., & Mythili, T. (2023). Heptapartitioned neutrosophic topological spaces. Indian Journal of Natural Sciences, 14.

Kishore, H. S., Raj, D. S. P., & Senthilkumar, K. R. (2024). AI for accessibility: A case study of enhancing library services for users with disabilities. In *Improving Library Systems with AI* (pp. 214–225). Applications, Approaches, and Bibliometric Insights. DOI: 10.4018/979-8-3693-5593-0.ch015

Kumar, N., Antoniraj, S., Jayanthi, S., Mirdula, S., Selvaraj, S., Rajkumar, N., & Senthilkumar, K. R. (2024). Educational technology and libraries supporting online learning. In AI-Assisted Library Reconstruction (pp. 209–237). DOI: 10.4018/979-8-3693-2782-1.ch012

La, G., Aiello, G., Rastellini, C., Micale, R., & Cicalese, L. (2011). Multi-criteria decision making support system for pancreatic islet transplantation. *Expert Systems with Applications*, 38(4), 3091–3097. DOI: 10.1016/j.eswa.2010.08.101

Lalitha, B., Ramalakshmi, K., Gunasekaran, H., Murugesan, P., Saminasri, P., & Rajkumar, N. (2024). Anticipating AI impact on library services: Future opportunities and evolutionary prospects. In Improving Library Systems with AI: Applications, Approaches, and Bibliometric Insights (pp. 195–213). IGI Global.

Mehdi, M., & Nouri, J. (2016). Selecting library management systems using TOPSIS: A case study. *Library Management*, 37(8/9), 469–479.

Mohanraj, A., Viji, C., Varadarajan, M. N., Kalpana, C., Shankar, B., Jayavadivel, R., Rajkumar, N., & Jagajeevan, R. (2024). Privacy and security in digital libraries. In *AI-Assisted Library Reconstruction* (pp. 104–125). IGI Global. DOI: 10.4018/979-8-3693-2782-1.ch006

Nachiappan, B. (2024a). Emerging and innovative AI technologies for resource management. In Improving Library Systems with AI: Applications, Approaches, and Bibliometric Insights (pp. 115–133). IGI Global. DOI: 10.4018/979-8-3693-5593-0.ch009

Nachiappan, B. (2024b). E-resources content recommendation system using AI. In Improving Library Systems with AI: Applications, Approaches, and Bibliometric Insights (pp. 155–177). IGI Global.

Radha, R., & Stanis Arul Mary, A. (2021). Heptapartitioned neutrosophic set. *International Journal of Creative Research Thoughts*, 9, 2320–2882.

Rajkumar, N., Tabassum, H., Muthulingam, S., Mohanraj, A., Viji, C., Kumar, N., & Senthilkumar, K. R. (2024). Anticipated requirements and expectations in the digital library. In AI-Assisted Library Reconstruction (pp. 1–20). DOI: 10.4018/979-8-3693-2782-1.ch001

Rajkumar, N., Viji, C., Mohanraj, A., Senthilkumar, K. R., Jagajeevan, R., & Kovilpillai, J. A. (2024). Ethical considerations of AI implementation in the library era. In *Improving Library Systems with AI* (pp. 85–106). Applications, Approaches, and Bibliometric Insights. DOI: 10.4018/979-8-3693-5593-0.ch007

Sahin, R., & Yigider, M. (2016). A multi-criteria neutrosophic group decision making method based TOPSIS for supplier selection. *Applied Mathematics & Information Sciences*, 5(5), 1843–1852. DOI: 10.18576/amis/100525

Senthilkumar, K. R. (2019). User pattern of Libraries by students of Government College in Tamilnadu: A study. Library Philosophy and Practice, 2019.

Senthilkumar, K. R. (2024a). AI-assisted library reconstruction. In AI-Assisted Library Reconstruction. DOI: 10.4018/979-8-3693-2782-1

Senthilkumar, K. R. (2024b). Revolutionizing thrust manufacturing: The synergy of real-time data and AI advancements. In Using Real-Time Data and AI for Thrust Manufacturing (pp. 80–93). DOI: 10.4018/9798369326152.ch005

Senthilkumar, K. R., & Jagajeevan, R. (2024). Improving library systems with AI: Applications, approaches, and bibliometric insights. In Improving Library Systems with AI: Applications, Approaches, and Bibliometric Insights. https://doi.org/DOI: 10.4018/9798369355930

Senthilkumar, K. R., & Maniiarasan, P. (2020). Comparison of E-resources with their usage statistics among Bharathidasan University & Madurai Kamaraj University. Library Philosophy and Practice, 2020. https://www.scopus.com/inward/record.uri?eid=2-s2.0-85091524339&partnerID=40&md5=6f7b662e3842db0d95af80ba646fdd6e

Sivaraj, P., Madhan, V., Mallika, V., & Senthilkumar, K. R. (2024). Enhancing library services through optimization algorithms and data analytics: Enhancing library services mathematical model. In AI-Assisted Library Reconstruction (pp. 290–306). DOI: 10.4018/979-8-3693-2782-1.ch016

Smarandache, F. (1998). *Neutrosophy, neutrosophic probability, set, and logic*. American Research Press.

Smarandache, F. (1999). *Neutrosophy: Neutrosophic probability, set and logic*. American Research Press.

Smarandache, F. (2013). n-Valued refined neutrosophic logic and its applications to physics. *Progress in Physics*, 4, 143–146.

Taj, A., Ahmed, M. G., Ali, K. S., & Senthilkumar, K. R. (2024). Revolutionizing medical libraries: The vital role of AI in enhancing discovery, access, and library services for healthcare professionals. In *Improving Library Systems with AI* (pp. 24–38). Applications, Approaches, and Bibliometric Insights. DOI: 10.4018/979-8-3693-5593-0.ch002

Velmurugan, B., Dharmalingam, S., Muthukrishnan, K. B., & Senthilkumar, K. R. (2024). AI insights deciphering India's ascendancy through the digital library: Navigating the digital realm India's odyssey towards information equity and technological eminence. In *Improving Library Systems with AI* (pp. 285–293). Applications, Approaches, and Bibliometric Insights. DOI: 10.4018/979-8-3693-5593-0.ch021

Zadeh, L. A. (1965). Fuzzy sets. *Information and Control*, 8(3), 338–353. DOI: 10.1016/S0019-9958(65)90241-X

Zhao, Y., Wang, S., & Li, H. (2021). Evaluating blockchain platforms based on security features and compliance using TOPSIS. *Journal of Network and Computer Applications*, 171, 102896.

Zulqarnain, R. M., Saeed, M., Dayan, F., & Ahmad, B. (2020). Application of TOPSIS method for decision making. *International Journal of Scientific Research in Mathematical and Statistical Sciences*, 7, 76–81.

Chapter 8
Comprehensive Education for Librarians

K. Jaya
Sri Krishna arts and Science College, India

M. Usha
Sri Krishna Arts and Science College, India

Senthilkumar K. R.
https://orcid.org/0000-0001-7426-5376
Sri Krishna Arts and Science College, India

ABSTRACT

The rapid advancement of blockchain technology is poised to transform the landscape of information management and library services. This chapter offers an in-depth training program to equip librarians with essential knowledge and practical skills to leverage this groundbreaking technology. This program delves into the core concepts of blockchain, exploring its applications in data security, digital asset management, and transparent record-keeping. By understanding and utilizing blockchain technology, librarians can lead their institutions in adopting innovative practices that align with the digital evolution. This comprehensive education initiative not only demystifies blockchain but also empowers librarians to become pioneers in integrating advanced technologies within the library sector, ensuring they remain at the cutting edge of information management.

DOI: 10.4018/979-8-3693-7783-3.ch008

INTRODUCTION

In the rapidly evolving landscape of information management, librarians are constantly seeking innovative solutions to enhance their services and meet the changing needs of their patrons. One of the most promising advancements in recent years is blockchain technology, which has the potential to revolutionize various aspects of library operations. "Steering the Blockchain Revolution: Comprehensive Education for Librarians" is designed to provide librarians with the essential knowledge and skills required to effectively utilize this transformative technology.

Integrating artificial intelligence (AI) in library management has appreciably converted how libraries function, supplying advanced performance, more advantageous user experiences, and strong facts management. This literature evaluation synthesizes key insights from recent scholarly works specializing in diverse components of AI implementation in libraries. Viji et al. (Viji et al., 2024) discovered the application of the Radio Frequency identity (RFID) era in library management. RFID structures streamline inventory control, enhance safety, and facilitate self-service, decreasing the workload on the library body of workers. The bankruptcy emphasizes the performance and accuracy of RFID in tracking and dealing with library assets, highlighting its capacity to revolutionize conventional library operations. Kumar et al. (Kumar et al., 2024) explain the synergy among academic technology and libraries in assisting online studying. They argue that libraries, empowered through AI, can offer personalized getting-to-know experiences through adaptive studying structures and shrewd content material recommendations. The chapter also delves into libraries' position in bridging the digital divide, ensuring equitable access to instructional sources. Mohanraj et al. (Mohanraj et al., 2024) deal with the crucial issues of privacy and protection in virtual libraries. As libraries undertake AI and virtual technologies, safeguarding personal data becomes paramount. The authors have a look at various protection protocols and privacy measures that libraries can enforce to protect sensitive facts whilst keeping consumers agree with them. Rajkumar et al. (Rajkumar, Tabassum, et al., 2024) outline the evolving necessities and expectations of virtual libraries in the AI generation. The bankruptcy highlights the need for robust infrastructure, skilled employees, and non-stop innovation to satisfy the dynamic needs of library users. It additionally discusses the significance of consumer-centric layouts in growing AI-pushed library structures. Jayavadivel et al. (Jayavadivel et al., 2024) offer a historic angle on AI adoption in libraries. They trace the evolution of AI technologies in library control, from early automation systems to sophisticated AI-driven answers. The chapter gives valuable insights into the demanding situations and milestones encountered for the duration of this transformative adventure. Rajkumar et al. (Rajkumar, Viji, et al., 2024) delve into the moral implications of AI in libraries. They explore issues inclusive of algorithmic bias, transparency, and the ethical use of personal facts. The authors argue for the development of moral suggestions and frameworks to ensure responsible AI implementation in library services.

Lalitha et al. (Lalitha et al., 2024) speak about the future effect of AI on library services. They spotlight rising developments and capability opportunities for AI to decorate library functions, which includes predictive analytics for series improvement and AI-powered reference offerings. The bankruptcy additionally speculates on the evolutionary prospects of libraries in an AI-pushed international. Nachiappan (Nachiappan, 2024b) offers an AI-primarily based e-assets content material advice gadget. The machine leverages system-getting-to-know algorithms to analyze personal choices and endorse relevant digital resources. This personalized approach improves consumer engagement and pleasure through presenting tailored content pointers. Nachiappan (Nachiappan, 2024a) explores cutting-edge AI technologies for aid management in libraries. Bankruptcy discusses advancements such as herbal language processing (NLP), machine getting to know, and AI-pushed records analytics. These technologies beautify resource discovery, optimize library operations, and provide precious insights for choice-making. Varadarajan (Varadarajan, 2024) emphasizes the significance of AI literacy in libraries. The chapter advocates for educational packages that equip library teams of workers and users with the necessary capabilities to navigate and leverage AI technology. Promoting AI literacy guarantees that libraries can harness the benefits of AI even as mitigating related risks. The reviewed chapters together highlight the transformative capacity of AI in library management. From enhancing operational performance and protection to enhancing consumer reviews and ethical considerations, AI gives several possibilities for libraries to evolve and thrive in the virtual age. Future research should continue to explore innovative AI packages and address the challenges related to their implementation to make certain sustainable and consumer-centric library offerings.

i) Understanding Blockchain Technology: Blockchain, originally developed as the underlying technology for cryptocurrencies like Bitcoin, is a decentralized digital ledger that records transactions across multiple computers. This decentralized nature ensures that the data is immutable, transparent, and secure, making it an attractive solution for various applications beyond finance. In the context of libraries, blockchain can offer numerous benefits, including enhanced data security, efficient digital asset management, and transparent record-keeping.
ii) Enhancing Data Security: One of the primary advantages of blockchain technology is its ability to secure data through cryptographic methods. In an era where data breaches and cyber threats are increasingly common, the immutability and security provided by blockchain can significantly protect sensitive information managed by libraries. Additionally, blockchain's transparent nature ensures

that all transactions and changes are recorded and visible to authorized users, thereby fostering greater trust and accountability.

iii) Streamlining Digital Asset Management: Digital asset management is another area where blockchain can make a substantial impact. Libraries are custodians of a vast array of digital resources, from e-books and journals to multimedia content. Blockchain can streamline the management of these assets by providing a reliable and efficient system for tracking ownership, licensing, and usage rights. This can simplify processes, reduce administrative overhead, and ensure that digital resources are managed in compliance with legal and ethical standards.

iv) Revolutionizing Record-Keeping: Moreover, blockchain's capability for transparent and immutable record-keeping can revolutionize how libraries manage their internal and external transactions. From tracking the acquisition and circulation of materials to managing donor records and financial transactions, blockchain can provide a robust framework that enhances operational efficiency and integrity.

V) Empowering Librarians through Education

The comprehensive education provided in this program aims to demystify blockchain technology for librarians, offering both theoretical insights and practical applications. Through detailed case studies, hands-on training, and expert guidance, librarians will learn how to implement blockchain solutions tailored to their specific needs. By embracing blockchain, librarians can lead their institutions through a digital transformation, ensuring they remain at the forefront of innovation in information management.

"Steering the Blockchain Revolution: Comprehensive Education for Librarians" empowers library professionals to harness the full potential of blockchain technology. This program is not just about understanding a new technology; it's about preparing librarians to become pioneers in the integration of advanced technologies, ultimately enhancing the value and relevance of library services in the digital age.

Fundamentals of Blockchain Technology

1. Immutable Records

Blockchain ensures that once data is recorded, it cannot be altered or deleted without leaving a trace.Secure and permanent recording of transactions such as acquisitions, cataloging, and circulation. This ensures the integrity of the library's records and prevents unauthorized modifications.

2. Decentralization

Blockchain operates on a distributed network of nodes, eliminating the need for a central authority. Decentralized digital repositories for storing and sharing academic and research materials. This can enhance access to information and prevent single points of failure.

3. Transparency

Blockchain provides a transparent ledger of all transactions accessible to all participants. Transparent tracking of the provenance and usage of digital assets, such as ebooks and digital archives. This can help in copyright management and ensure fair use.

4. Smart Contracts

Self-executing contracts with the terms of the agreement directly written into code. Automating licensing agreements for digital content, ensuring compliance with usage terms, and facilitating seamless interlibrary loans and resource sharing.

5. Security

Cryptographic techniques used in blockchain provide high security for data and transactions. Protection of sensitive patron information and secure authentication processes. This can also enhance digital rights management and prevent unauthorized access to digital resources.

6. Interoperability

Blockchain's standardized protocols can enable different systems to work together. Facilitating interoperability between different library systems and platforms, enabling seamless integration and sharing of resources across libraries worldwide.

Figure 1. Classification of Blockchain Technology According to Library Usage

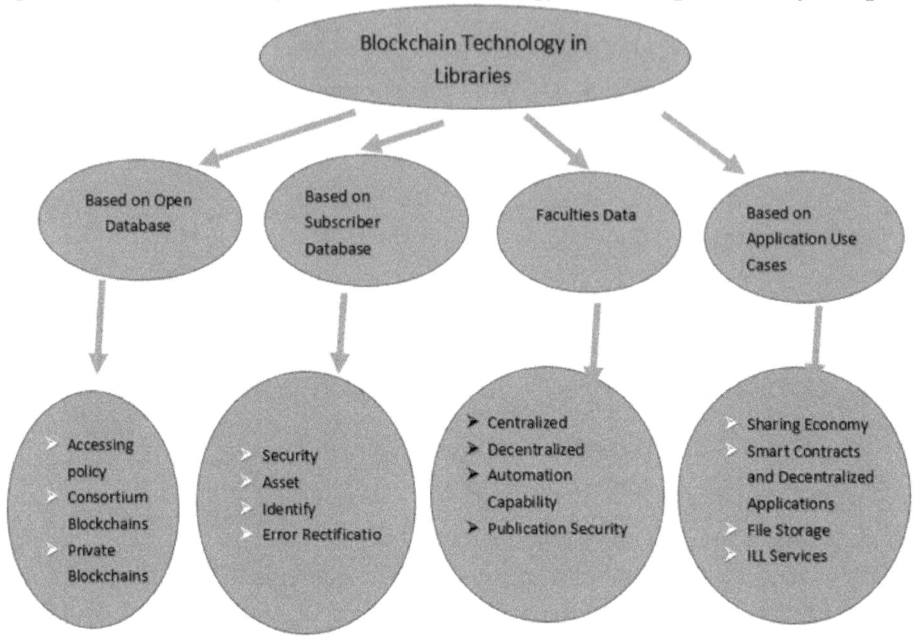

Blockchain technology, recognized for its robust security and transparency, can significantly impact the library sector. This classification will explore how different types of blockchain technology can be utilized to enhance library operations, focusing on permission type, consensus mechanisms, generations, and application use cases specific to libraries.

Based on Permission Type

Public Blockchains: Public blockchains are open and permissionless, allowing anyone to join and participate. In the context of libraries, public blockchains can be utilized for open-access resources and decentralized knowledge sharing. For example, a public blockchain could be used to create a global catalog of books and scholarly articles, where anyone can contribute metadata or reviews. This approach ensures transparency and broad accessibility, promoting an open and inclusive digital library environment.

Private Blockchains: Private blockchains are permissioned networks where access is restricted to authorized participants. Libraries can use private blockchains to manage internal operations such as acquisitions, inventory control, and interlibrary loans. By implementing a private blockchain, libraries can ensure that sensitive data, such as user borrowing records and financial transactions, remain secure and accessible only to authorized personnel. This enhances data privacy and operational efficiency within the library system.

Consortium Blockchains: Consortium blockchains are managed by a group of organizations. Libraries can collaborate with academic institutions, publishers, and other libraries to form a consortium blockchain. This setup can be particularly beneficial for managing shared resources, cooperative cataloging, and collaborative research projects. A consortium blockchain ensures that all participants have a say in the governance of the network, fostering trust and cooperation among the members.

Based on Consensus Mechanism

Proof of Work (PoW): While PoW is energy-intensive and may not be ideal for most library applications, it can be used for decentralized and secure validation of significant digital artifacts, such as preserving rare manuscripts or archival materials. The computational effort required for PoW ensures the highest level of security and immutability, which is crucial for protecting valuable and historical library assets.

Proof of Stake (PoS): PoS is more energy-efficient compared to PoW, making it suitable for libraries focusing on sustainability. Libraries can implement PoS to manage digital collections and verify transactions within the library system. This method can be used to incentivize participation by library users, who could earn tokens for contributing to the library community, such as by writing reviews or assisting with cataloging.

Delegated Proof of Stake (DPoS): DPoS can be used in consortium settings where a select group of representatives from participating libraries or institutions validate transactions. This consensus mechanism is efficient and scalable, making it suitable for large library networks. DPoS ensures that decisions are made by trusted representatives, balancing efficiency with decentralization.

Practical Byzantine Fault Tolerance (PBFT): PBFT is ideal for private and consortium blockchains where trust among participants is relatively high. Libraries can use PBFT for efficient and secure transactions, such as interlibrary loans, resource sharing, and collaborative digital archiving. PBFT ensures that the system remains operational even if some nodes fail or act maliciously, providing a reliable solution for critical library operations.

Based on Generation

First-Generation Blockchains: First-generation blockchains like Bitcoin focus primarily on secure and transparent transactions. Libraries can use these for simple applications such as accepting donations in cryptocurrency or tracking the acquisition of rare books. The high level of security and transparency ensures that all transactions are recorded immutably, providing a trustworthy record of donations and acquisitions.
Second-Generation Blockchains: Second-generation blockchains, such as Ethereum, introduce smart contracts, enabling programmable and automated transactions. Libraries can use smart contracts to automate membership renewals, late fee collections, and resource access permissions. Smart contracts reduce administrative overhead and ensure that operations are carried out consistently and fairly.
Third-Generation Blockchains: Third-generation blockchains, including Cardano and Polkadot, focus on scalability, interoperability, and sustainability. Libraries can leverage these advanced blockchains to integrate various digital library systems, enabling seamless data exchange and collaboration across different platforms. Third-generation blockchains can also support large-scale digital preservation projects, ensuring that digital collections are maintained efficiently and securely.

Based on Application Use Cases

Digital Rights Management: Blockchain can be used to manage digital rights for e-books, digital media, and other intellectual property held by libraries. By using blockchain, libraries can ensure that digital rights are enforced automatically through smart contracts, protecting the interests of both the library and the content creators.
Secure Record-Keeping: Libraries can implement blockchain for secure and immutable record-keeping of user transactions, acquisition records, and archival materials. This ensures the integrity and authenticity of records, which is essential for historical research and preservation.
Resource Sharing and Interlibrary Loans: Blockchain can facilitate efficient and transparent resource sharing among libraries. A consortium blockchain can be used to manage interlibrary loans, track the movement of resources, and ensure that all transactions are recorded and verifiable.
User Privacy and Data Security: Blockchain can enhance user privacy by providing a secure way to manage user data and borrowing records. Libraries can use blockchain to ensure that user data is stored securely and accessed

only by authorized personnel, protecting users' privacy and complying with data protection regulations.

Collaborative Cataloging and Metadata Management: Libraries can use blockchain to create a decentralized and collaborative platform for cataloging and metadata management. This allows multiple libraries to contribute to and validate a shared catalog, improving the accuracy and completeness of bibliographic records.

Digital Preservation: Blockchain can support digital preservation initiatives by providing a secure and immutable ledger for tracking the provenance and integrity of digital assets. Libraries can use blockchain to ensure that digital collections are preserved accurately over time, with verifiable records of all preservation actions.

Classifying blockchain technology according to library usage highlights the diverse applications and benefits it can offer to the library sector. By understanding the different types of blockchains and their specific features, libraries can implement the most suitable solutions to enhance their operations, improve data security, and foster collaboration. Whether through public, private, or consortium blockchains, and using various consensus mechanisms and generations of blockchain technology, libraries can leverage blockchain to drive innovation and efficiency in their services.

Review of Literature

The intersection of blockchain technology and library science is a burgeoning field, with literature increasingly exploring its implications and applications. Numerous studies highlight blockchain's potential to transform data management in libraries, emphasizing its role in enhancing security, transparency, and trust in digital records. For instance, Blockchain is a developing technology that has yet to reach its full potential. Recently, many researchers have reviewed the literature on Blockchain (Cao et al., 2017; Conoscenti et al., 2016; Karafiloski and Mishev, 2017; Yli-Huumo et al., 2016), focusing on its concept, research methodologies, and applications in specific fields like big data and IoT.

Due to its immutable, transparent, and trustworthy transaction capabilities within a blockchain network (Underwood, 2016), blockchain holds many potential applications. For instance, in education, blockchain can enhance student motivation by realizing the concept of "learning is earning" (Chen et al., 2018). Hoy (2017) describes blockchain as a fundamental technology with the potential to transform transaction-based activities, similar to the impact networking protocols had during the early days of the Internet.

Bheemaiah (2015) highlights the key differences between blockchain and networking protocols, stating that while "TCP/IP allowed instant transmission of information, the blockchain protocol allows the instant transfer of value." Like artificial intelligence and other disruptive technologies, blockchain has the power to revolutionize various human-built institutions (such as insurance companies and banks) and potentially displace the administrative workers who support these institutions (ALA, 2019).

Educational initiatives for librarians are also a prominent theme in the literature. Lemieux (2016) argues for comprehensive training programs that cover blockchain basics and their specific applications in libraries and also stresseses the need for interdisciplinary collaboration to bridge the gap between technical blockchain knowledge and its practical use in library settings.

Moreover, practical case studies illustrate blockchain's real-world applications in libraries. For example, the MIT Media Lab's Digital Certificates project demonstrates how blockchain can be used to issue and verify academic credentials, a model that libraries could adopt for managing digital archives and patron records.

Overall, the literature indicates a growing consensus on the necessity of integrating blockchain education into library science curricula. By doing so, librarians can stay abreast of technological advancements and leverage blockchain to enhance their service delivery, ensuring their institutions remain relevant and resilient in the digital age.

Objectives of the Study

The primary aim of this study is to investigate the role of blockchain technology in transforming library and information science, with a specific focus on developing comprehensive educational programs for librarians. The study will explore various dimensions to achieve this goal, outlined in the following objectives:

1. **Examine Blockchain Fundamentals**:
   - To provide a detailed understanding of the core principles of blockchain technology, including decentralization, cryptographic security, and consensus mechanisms, and their relevance to library science.
2. **Identify Practical Applications in Libraries**:
   - To explore how blockchain can be applied to enhance data security, digital rights management, and the creation of immutable records within library systems. This includes assessing the potential for blockchain to improve the management of digital collections and protect user privacy.
3. **Assess Educational Needs**:

- o To evaluate the current knowledge and skill gaps among librarians regarding blockchain technology. This will involve surveying librarians to determine their awareness, understanding, and perceived importance of blockchain applications in their profession.

4. **Develop a Comprehensive Educational Framework**:
   - o To design a curriculum and training programs tailored for librarians that cover both theoretical and practical aspects of blockchain. The framework will include modules on blockchain fundamentals, case studies of successful implementations, and hands-on training sessions.
5. **Promote Multidisciplinary Collaboration**:
   - o To establish partnerships with technology experts, academic institutions, and other stakeholders to foster a multidisciplinary approach in blockchain education. This collaboration aims to enrich the educational content and provide librarians with diverse perspectives and resources.
6. **Evaluate Impact and Effectiveness**:
   - o To assess the effectiveness of the implemented educational programs in enhancing librarians' competency with blockchain technology. This objective will involve feedback collection, performance assessments, and continuous improvement of the curriculum based on librarians' experiences and outcomes.

The study aims to empower librarians with the knowledge and skills necessary to navigate the blockchain revolution, ensuring they can effectively integrate this technology into their professional practices.

Scope

This study delves into the integration of blockchain technology within the field of library and information science, specifically focusing on the development of comprehensive educational programs for librarians. The scope encompasses the following key areas:

1. **Blockchain Fundamentals**:
   - o An exploration of the basic principles of blockchain technology, including decentralization, cryptographic security, consensus mechanisms, and their specific relevance to libraries. This foundational knowledge is essential for understanding the broader applications of blockchain in information management.
2. **Applications in Library Science**:

- Detailed investigation into the practical applications of blockchain technology in libraries. This includes enhancing data security, managing digital rights, and creating immutable records for digital collections. The study will examine case studies and real-world examples to illustrate these applications.

3. **Educational Needs Assessment**:
   - Analysis of current knowledge gaps among librarians concerning blockchain technology. This will involve surveys and interviews with librarians to understand their awareness, perceptions, and educational needs regarding blockchain.
4. **Curriculum Development**:
   - Designing a comprehensive educational framework tailored for librarians. This will cover both theoretical knowledge and practical skills, including hands-on training modules, workshops, and collaborative projects. The curriculum aims to equip librarians with the necessary tools to implement blockchain solutions effectively.
5. **Multidisciplinary Collaboration**:
   - Establishing partnerships with technology experts, academic institutions, and other relevant stakeholders. These collaborations will provide diverse insights and resources, enriching the educational content and facilitating the practical application of blockchain in libraries.
6. **Impact Evaluation**:
   - Assessing the effectiveness of the educational programs through feedback from participants, performance assessments, and case studies of implementation. This will help in continuously improving the curriculum and ensuring its relevance and effectiveness in enhancing librarians' competencies.

This study aims to bridge the gap between the emerging technology of blockchain and its practical, beneficial use in libraries, ultimately preparing librarians to navigate and leverage the blockchain revolution effectively.

Methodology

To explore the integration of blockchain technology in library science and develop comprehensive educational programs for librarians, this study employs a qualitative research approach. This methodology emphasizes in-depth understanding through interviews, focus groups, case studies, and participatory observation. The qualitative approach is particularly suited for capturing the nuanced perspectives of librarians and understanding the contextual factors influencing their adoption of blockchain technology. Quantitative methodology has implied to get the detailed insights into librarians' current knowledge, perceptions, and attitudes towards blockchain technology.

Participant Selection: Purposefully sampled a diverse group of librarians from various types of libraries (public, academic, special) around various educational institutions in Tamil Nadu to ensure a range of perspectives.
Developed a semi-structured interview guide with open-ended questions covering topics such as:

- o Current understanding of blockchain technology.
- o Perceived benefits and challenges of integrating blockchain in libraries.
- o Specific areas where blockchain could improve library services.
- o Educational needs and preferences for learning about blockchain.

Data Collection: Conducted in-depth interviews, either in person or via video conferencing,
Analysis: Used thematic analysis to identify common themes, patterns, and unique insights. Employ coding techniques to categorize responses and draw meaningful conclusions.

Discussion

The findings indicate a significant lack of awareness about blockchain technology among librarians in Tamil Nadu. The thematic analysis of these additional data points identify specific themes and patterns, such as common misconceptions about blockchain, preferred learning methods, and the types of support librarians need. This will allow for the development of tailored educational programs. Further analysis should delve into the underlying reasons for this lack of awareness and propose actionable strategies to address it.

Several factors could contribute to this gap:

Limited Exposure: Many librarians may not have had sufficient exposure to blockchain technology due to its relatively recent emergence and the slow pace of its adoption in the library sector.
Educational Opportunities: There may be a scarcity of targeted educational programs and workshops focusing on blockchain applications in libraries.
Resource Constraints: Libraries, especially smaller or underfunded ones, may lack the financial and technical resources to explore and implement new technologies.
Recommendations for Action:
Based on the findings, the following steps could be recommended:

Educational Initiatives: Develop and promote workshops, webinars, and online courses specifically designed to educate librarians about blockchain technology and its applications in libraries.

Resource Allocation: Advocate for better resource allocation to ensure libraries have the necessary tools and infrastructure to explore and implement blockchain solutions.

Collaborative Efforts: Encourage collaboration between libraries, educational institutions, and professional organizations to create a supportive network for learning and sharing knowledge about blockchain technology.

Addressing the lack of awareness about blockchain technology among librarians in Tamil Nadu requires a multifaceted approach. By understanding the specific challenges and needs of librarians, targeted educational initiatives can be developed to bridge this knowledge gap. This, in turn, will empower librarians to harness the potential of blockchain technology to enhance library services and operations.

Potential Benefits of Blockchain in Libraries

Blockchain technology holds significant potential for enhancing library operations and services. One of the primary benefits is the enhanced management of library resources. By utilizing blockchain's immutable and transparent ledger system, libraries can efficiently track and manage both digital and physical assets. This can streamline processes such as acquisitions, cataloging, and circulation, ensuring that all transactions are accurately recorded and easily auditable. The permanence of blockchain records helps prevent unauthorized modifications, thereby safeguarding the integrity of library collections and ensuring that users have access to reliable and authentic resources.

Another major benefit is the improved access to information. Blockchain can facilitate the creation of decentralized digital repositories, making it easier for users to access a wide array of resources without geographical or institutional barriers. This decentralization can enhance interlibrary loans and resource sharing, allowing libraries to collaborate more effectively and provide their patrons with a richer array of information. By ensuring that all transactions and updates are transparent and verifiable, blockchain technology can also support the management of digital rights and copyright issues, ensuring that content creators are fairly compensated and that users comply with usage terms.

Furthermore, blockchain can significantly increase trust and accountability within library operations. The transparent nature of blockchain transactions ensures that all actions taken within the library system are visible and traceable, fostering an environment of trust among patrons and staff. This transparency can also help in verifying the provenance and authenticity of digital assets, such as ebooks and digital archives, thus enhancing the credibility of the library's offerings. Additionally, blockchain's security features protect sensitive information, such as patron data and access credentials, from breaches and unauthorized access. By leveraging smart contracts, libraries can automate various processes, reducing administrative overhead and ensuring that agreements, such as licensing for digital content, are executed accurately and efficiently. This not only improves operational efficiency but also allows library staff to focus on more strategic and user-focused activities.

Challenges and Considerations

1. Technical Complexity:

Implementation of blockchain technology requires specialized knowledge and expertise .Libraries need to invest in training and infrastructure to adopt blockchain.

2. Scalability:

Blockchain networks can face scalability issues, especially with high volumes of transactions.Libraries need to consider the scalability of blockchain solutions to handle large datasets and user interactions.

3. Privacy Concerns:

While blockchain provides security, it also poses privacy challenges with its transparent nature. Libraries must balance transparency with the need to protect user privacy and sensitive information.

4. Regulatory and Legal Issues:

Compliance with legal and regulatory frameworks is crucial when implementing blockchain. Libraries must navigate potential legal challenges related to data ownership, intellectual property, and digital rights. The integration of blockchain technology in libraries offers numerous advantages, including improved resource management, enhanced access to information, and increased trust and accountability. However, libraries must carefully consider the technical, scalability, privacy, and legal challenges associated with blockchain adoption. With thoughtful implementation, blockchain can revolutionize library operations and services, ushering in a new era of efficiency and transparency.

Factors to Consider When Implementing Blockchain in Libraries

1. Project Management:
   - o Successful blockchain projects require careful consideration of several factors, including the involvement of skilled programmers, an effective project management team, and visionary staff from within the library.
2. Resources and Finance:
   - o Adequate resources and financial planning are essential before implementing blockchain technology. A blockchain solution for data alignment can be both affordable and feasible, provided the library has sufficient funding for the project.
3. Problem Solutions:
   - o Before implementing blockchain technology, librarians should consider solutions for potential issues. It is advisable to train internal staff rather than relying on third parties. Additionally, ensure the security of private or sensitive data using decentralized mechanisms (Carrie, 2019).

Promoting Blockchain Education on Librarians

Innovative technologies have posed significant challenges for education and library services (Hussain, 2018). Librarians and information specialists recognize the technological needs of different library environments and their users. Implementing new technology often demands a substantial budget, and staying updated with the latest advancements can be quite difficult (Orick, 2000). However, the introduction of new technological responsibilities in libraries can benefit both library administrators and students pursuing careers focused on technology or curriculum design within library settings.

Blockchain technology essentially stores information in a distributed and tamper-resistant environment. A prime application of this technology is the preservation of scientific publications globally. Irving and Holden tested the use of blockchain for storing information by implementing low-cost, verifiable methods using Bitcoin blockchain technology for audit purposes. This approach supports digital rights management, connecting libraries and facilitating access to digital resources. Blockchain creates a unique, verifiable record that can be accessed by anyone at anywhere.

Potential uses of blockchain technology in libraries include digital preservation and tracking; creating community-based collections to share objects, tools, and services; using blockchain-based currencies for international financial transactions; managing interlibrary loans and voucher systems; verifying credentials in information literacy; issuing library cards; maintaining archives and special collections where provenance and authenticity are crucial; keeping corporate library records; and managing organizational data and intellectual property for research and development purposes.

Implementation Strategies

The successful integration of blockchain technology into library science requires a well-thought-out implementation strategy that encompasses various educational formats and collaborative efforts. This section outlines a multi-pronged approach to delivering comprehensive blockchain education for librarians, ensuring that they are well-equipped to leverage this technology effectively.

Training Workshops: Training workshops are a cornerstone of the implementation strategy, offering librarians an interactive and immersive learning experience. These workshops should be designed to cater to different levels of familiarity with blockchain technology, ranging from introductory sessions for beginners to advanced workshops for those looking to deepen their expertise.

1. Workshop Structure:
   - Introduction to Blockchain: Basic concepts, terminology, and history of blockchain technology.
   - Blockchain Mechanics: Detailed exploration of how blockchain works, including cryptographic principles, consensus mechanisms, and smart contracts.
   - Applications in Libraries: Practical demonstrations of blockchain applications relevant to library science, such as digital rights management, secure record-keeping, and user privacy protection.
   - Hands-On Sessions: Interactive activities where participants can experiment with blockchain platforms, create their own blockchain, and simulate transactions.
2. Duration and Frequency:
   - Short Workshops: Half-day or full-day workshops focusing on specific topics.
   - Extended Programs: Multi-day workshops that provide comprehensive coverage of blockchain technology and its applications.
   - Regular Sessions: Monthly or quarterly workshops to ensure continuous learning and skill development.
3. Facilitators:
   - Experienced blockchain professionals, educators, and library science experts should facilitate the workshops to ensure high-quality instruction and real-world insights.
4. Evaluation:

- Pre- and post-workshop assessments to measure knowledge gain and identify areas for improvement.
- Feedback surveys to gather participants' opinions and suggestions for future workshops.

Webinars: Webinars complement in-person workshops by providing an accessible platform for remote learning. They are particularly useful for reaching librarians who cannot attend physical workshops due to geographical or time constraints.

1. Webinar Topics:
   - Introductory Webinars: Basic blockchain concepts and their relevance to libraries.
   - Advanced Webinars: In-depth exploration of specific blockchain applications, technical aspects, and case studies.
   - Panel Discussions: Featuring industry experts and thought leaders discussing trends, challenges, and future directions of blockchain in library science.
2. Format and Duration:
   - Live Webinars: Interactive sessions with Q&A opportunities, typically lasting 60-90 minutes.
   - Recorded Webinars: On-demand access to past webinars for continuous learning.
3. Promotion and Accessibility:
   - Promote webinars through library networks, social media, and professional associations to maximize participation.
   - Ensure webinars are accessible, with closed captions and downloadable materials for participants with different needs.
4. Evaluation:
   - Collect feedback through post-webinar surveys and analytics on participation and engagement levels.

Online Courses and Resource Development

Online Courses: Developing comprehensive online courses is crucial for providing librarians with flexible, self-paced learning opportunities. These courses should cover a wide range of topics and be designed to accommodate varying levels of expertise.

1. Course Design:

- o Modular Structure: Break down courses into modules that cover specific aspects of blockchain technology, allowing learners to progress at their own pace.
- o Interactive Content: Include videos, quizzes, interactive simulations, and practical exercises to enhance engagement and retention.
- o Case Studies: Real-world examples of blockchain implementation in libraries to illustrate practical applications and challenges.

2. Course Levels:
   - o Beginner: Introduction to blockchain, its history, and fundamental concepts.
   - o Intermediate: Technical details, blockchain platforms, and smart contracts.
   - o Advanced: Deep dive into blockchain applications in library science, including technical implementation and management.
3. Certification:
   - o Offer certificates upon course completion to recognize participants' achievements and motivate continuous learning.
4. Platform:
   - o Utilize a robust Learning Management System (LMS) to host the courses, providing an intuitive and user-friendly interface for learners.
5. Evaluation:
   - o Regularly update course content based on participant feedback and technological advancements.
   - o Monitor learners' progress and performance to identify areas needing additional support or resources.

Resource Development: Creating a repository of educational resources is essential for supporting ongoing learning and providing reference materials for librarians.

1. Resource Types:
   - o Guides and Toolkits: Step-by-step instructions and practical tips for implementing blockchain solutions in libraries.
   - o Research Papers and Articles: Access to the latest research and publications on blockchain technology and its applications.
   - o Case Studies and Best Practices: Detailed documentation of successful blockchain projects in libraries and related fields.
   - o Multimedia Resources: Videos, podcasts, and infographics that simplify complex blockchain concepts.
2. Accessibility:

- o Ensure resources are easily accessible through an online portal, with search functionality and categorization by topic and difficulty level.
- o Provide downloadable formats for offline use.

3. Collaboration:
   - o Encourage contributions from blockchain experts, librarians, and academic institutions to enrich the resource repository.
4. Evaluation:
   - o Regularly review and update resources to reflect the latest developments and feedback from users.

Collaborative Learning and Community Building

Promoting collaborative learning environments enhances knowledge sharing and collective problem-solving among librarians, enabling them to better understand and implement blockchain technology.

1. Study Groups

Forming local or virtual study groups allows librarians to engage in meaningful discussions about blockchain concepts, share their experiences, and work on projects collectively. These groups can meet regularly, either in person or via video conferencing, to delve into various aspects of blockchain technology. Study groups provide a platform for continuous learning and peer support, making complex topics more approachable. Through collaborative efforts, librarians can pool their knowledge, identify common challenges, and develop innovative solutions. The dynamic interaction within study groups encourages active participation and fosters a sense of community among librarians, enhancing their overall learning experience.

2. Peer Mentoring

Establishing peer mentoring programs is another effective way to support librarians in learning about blockchain technology. Experienced librarians can serve as mentors, guiding those who are new to the field. Mentors can offer personalized advice, share practical insights, and help mentees navigate the complexities of blockchain implementation in libraries. This one-on-one or small group mentoring approach ensures that learning is tailored to individual needs and fosters a supportive environment for professional development. Peer mentoring not only accelerates the learning curve for new librarians but also strengthens the professional network within the library community.

3. Hackathons and Competitions

Organizing blockchain hackathons and competitions can stimulate innovation and practical application of blockchain knowledge among librarians. These events can be designed around specific themes related to library challenges, such as digital preservation, resource management, or user authentication. By participating in hackathons, librarians can collaborate in teams to develop creative solutions and prototype blockchain applications. Competitions can incentivize participation by offering rewards for the most innovative and effective solutions. This hands-on approach encourages librarians to think critically and apply their theoretical knowledge in real-world scenarios, fostering a deeper understanding of blockchain technology.

4. Discussion Forums

Creating online forums and discussion boards dedicated to blockchain topics provides librarians with a platform to ask questions, share insights, and collaborate on projects. These forums can be hosted on library websites, professional association platforms, or social media groups. Online discussion forums facilitate asynchronous communication, allowing librarians to participate at their convenience. This flexibility makes it easier for librarians to stay engaged and contribute to ongoing discussions, regardless of their location or schedule. Discussion forums also serve as valuable repositories of knowledge, where librarians can access previous conversations, learn from shared experiences, and build a collective knowledge base over time.

By implementing these collaborative learning strategies, libraries can create a vibrant and supportive environment that empowers librarians to effectively navigate the blockchain revolution. Through shared learning and problem-solving, librarians can enhance their skills, innovate library services, and better serve their communities

Community Building: Building a strong community of practice around blockchain technology in libraries is crucial for sustained engagement and support.

1. Professional Networks

Leveraging existing library associations and professional networks is a key strategy for promoting blockchain education initiatives and facilitating community building. By tapping into established organizations such as the American Library Association (ALA) or regional library networks, librarians can access a broad audience and a wealth of resources. These associations can host webinars, distribute educational materials, and provide platforms for discussion and collaboration. Engaging with professional networks ensures that blockchain initiatives gain visibility and credibility, and librarians can benefit from shared experiences and best practices.

2. Regular Meetups

Hosting regular meetups, both online and in-person, is crucial for maintaining engagement and fostering a sense of community among librarians interested in blockchain. These meetups can serve as forums for discussing the latest blockchain trends, sharing practical experiences, and brainstorming new applications for blockchain in libraries. In-person meetups can offer hands-on workshops and networking opportunities, while online meetups ensure broader accessibility and inclusivity. Regular interaction helps build relationships, promotes continuous learning, and keeps the community dynamic and responsive to new developments.

3. Social Media Groups

Creating social media groups on platforms like LinkedIn and Facebook can facilitate informal discussions and ongoing knowledge sharing among librarians. These groups provide a space for librarians to ask questions, share news articles, post updates about their blockchain projects, and offer support to their peers. Social media groups are particularly effective for real-time communication and can help librarians stay connected outside of formal meetups or conferences. The informal nature of these platforms encourages more frequent interaction and a sense of camaraderie among members.

4. Annual Conferences

Organizing or participating in annual conferences dedicated to blockchain technology in libraries can significantly enhance community building efforts. These conferences can feature keynote speakers, panel discussions, and hands-on workshops, providing a comprehensive platform for learning and networking. Conferences offer opportunities for librarians to present their research, share case studies, and learn from leading experts in the field. Additionally, they can help set the agenda for blockchain initiatives in libraries, highlighting emerging trends and innovative solutions. Participation in these conferences can invigorate the community, inspire new ideas, and reinforce the collective commitment to advancing blockchain technology in the library sector.

Multidisciplinary Partnerships: Collaborating with various stakeholders enhances the quality and relevance of blockchain education for librarians.

1. Academic Institutions

Partnering with universities and research institutions is a strategic move for libraries aiming to integrate blockchain technology. Academic institutions have the necessary expertise, research capabilities, and teaching resources to develop and deliver high-quality blockchain courses. By collaborating with universities, libraries can offer courses that cover the theoretical foundations of blockchain, as well as its practical applications. These partnerships can also facilitate access to academic research on blockchain, keeping librarians abreast of the latest advancements and trends. Furthermore, universities often provide opportunities for librarians to engage in research projects, workshops, and seminars, fostering a deeper understanding of blockchain technology.

2. Technology Companies

Collaborating with blockchain technology companies is crucial for providing librarians with practical training and access to the latest tools and platforms. These companies can offer hands-on training sessions, workshops, and internships, allowing librarians to gain real-world experience with blockchain applications. Additionally, technology companies can provide insights into industry trends and best practices, ensuring that the education programs are aligned with current and future technological developments. Such collaborations also enable libraries to use cutting-edge blockchain solutions and platforms, facilitating a smoother and more effective integration of blockchain technology into library services.

3. Professional Associations

Working with library associations and other professional bodies is vital for promoting blockchain education and ensuring the accreditation of training programs. Professional associations can help develop standardized blockchain curricula, advocate for blockchain education within the library community, and provide certification for completed training programs. These associations also offer a platform for networking, knowledge sharing, and professional development, enabling librarians to stay connected with peers and experts in the field. By partnering with professional associations, libraries can enhance the credibility and recognition of their blockchain education initiatives, encouraging more librarians to participate.

4. Government Agencies

Engaging with government agencies is essential to ensure compliance with regulations and explore funding opportunities for blockchain education initiatives. Government agencies can provide guidance on regulatory requirements related to data privacy, security, and blockchain implementation, helping libraries navigate the legal landscape. Additionally, government bodies often offer grants and funding programs to support educational and technological initiatives. By collaborating with these agencies, libraries can secure the financial resources needed to develop and sustain comprehensive blockchain education programs. Government support can also enhance the visibility and impact of these initiatives, promoting wider adoption and implementation of blockchain technology in libraries.

Expert Involvement: Involving blockchain experts in the education process ensures high-quality instruction and up-to-date content.

1. Guest Lecturers

Inviting blockchain experts to deliver guest lectures and participate in panel discussions can greatly enrich the learning experience. These professionals can share their real-world experiences, provide insights into the latest developments in blockchain technology, and answer questions from librarians. Guest lectures can be incorporated into workshops, webinars, and courses, offering librarians the opportunity to learn from those at the forefront of the field.

2. Advisory Board

Establishing an advisory board composed of blockchain professionals, educators, and library science experts can provide strategic guidance for developing and implementing educational programs. This board can help ensure that the curriculum is comprehensive, relevant, and aligned with industry standards. They can also assist in identifying emerging trends and technologies, ensuring the program remains up-to-date and forward-looking.

3. Mentorship Programs

Creating mentorship programs where librarians receive one-on-one guidance from blockchain experts can provide personalized learning experiences and professional development. Mentors can offer tailored advice, support librarians in practical applications of blockchain, and help them navigate challenges. This hands-on guidance can accelerate learning and foster confidence in implementing blockchain solutions.

4. Research Collaborations

Fostering research collaborations between librarians and blockchain researchers can drive innovation and address specific challenges within the library context. These collaborations can result in the development of new blockchain applications, enhance existing library services, and contribute to the broader body of knowledge on blockchain technology. By working together on research projects, librarians can gain deeper insights into blockchain and its potential impacts on their field.

Implementing a comprehensive blockchain education program for librarians requires a multi-faceted approach that includes interactive training workshops, accessible online courses, collaborative learning environments, and strategic partnerships. By leveraging these strategies, librarians will be well-equipped to navigate the blockchain revolution, enhance their professional skills, and drive innovation in library science. Continuous evaluation and feedback mechanisms will ensure the effectiveness and relevance of the educational initiatives, ultimately contributing to the successful integration of blockchain technology in libraries.

CONCLUSION

Steering the blockchain revolution through comprehensive education for librarians is crucial for the future of library services. Blockchain technology, with its potential to offer immutable, transparent, and secure record-keeping, presents numerous opportunities for innovation in libraries. These include enhanced digital preservation, efficient resource management, secure credential verification, and improved interlibrary collaborations. However, realizing these benefits requires a well-structured educational framework tailored to the specific needs of librarians.

The current landscape reveals a significant gap in awareness and understanding of blockchain technology among librarians, particularly in regions like Tamil Nadu. This gap can hinder the adoption and integration of blockchain solutions in library operations. Addressing this issue necessitates a multifaceted approach that involves targeted educational programs, adequate resource allocation, and collaborative efforts.

Comprehensive education programs should encompass foundational knowledge of blockchain, practical applications in the library context, and ongoing professional development. These programs can be delivered through workshops, webinars, online courses, and hands-on training sessions. By equipping librarians with the necessary skills and knowledge, they can effectively implement and manage blockchain technologies within their libraries.

Additionally, it is essential to advocate for better resource allocation to support these educational initiatives. Libraries must have access to the necessary financial and technical resources to explore and adopt blockchain solutions. Collaborative efforts among libraries, educational institutions, and professional organizations can create a supportive network for learning and knowledge sharing, further enhancing the effectiveness of blockchain education.

In conclusion, steering the blockchain revolution in libraries requires a strategic and comprehensive educational approach. By addressing the knowledge gap and providing the necessary resources and support, librarians can harness the transformative potential of blockchain technology. This will enable libraries to enhance their services, improve operational efficiency, and better serve their communities in an increasingly digital world. Embracing this revolution through education will ensure that libraries remain at the forefront of technological innovation and continue to fulfill their vital role in society.

REFERENCES

Ahram, T., Sargolzaei, A., Sargolzaei, S., Daniels, J., & Amaba, B. (2017). Blockchain technology innovations. 2017 IEEE Technology & Engineering Management Conference (TEMSCON), 137-141 DOI: 10.1109/TEMSCON.2017.7998367

ALA. (2019). Blockchain. Retrieved May 15, 2019, from www.ala.org /tools/future/ trends/ blockchain/

Babich, V., & Hilary, G. (2018). What operations management researchers should know about blockchain technology. Georgetown Working Paper

Bheemaiah, K. (2015). Block Chain 2.0: The Renaissance of Money. Retrieved May 21, 2019, from https://www.wired.com/insights/ 2015/01/block-chain-2-0/

Big Data in Library Services j Daily times. (2021). Available at: https://dailytimes .com. pk/533352/big-data-in-library-servicesdaily-times/

Cao, S., Cao, Y., Wang, X., & Lu, Y. (2017). A Review of Researches on Blockchain. In *The Sixteenth Wuhan International Conference on E-Business Digital Innovation* (pp. 108–117). Retrieved from http://aisel.aisnet.org/ whiceb2017/57

Carrie, S. (2019), "Blockchain reaction", from American Libraries Magazine website, available at: https://americanlibrariesmagazine. org/2019/03/01/library-Blockchain-reaction/

Chen, G., Xu, B., Lu, M., & Chen, N.-S. (2018). Exploring blockchain technology and its potential applications for education. *Smart Learning Environments*, 5(1), 1–10. DOI: 10.1186/s40561-017-0050-x

Conoscenti, M., Vetro, A., & De Martin, J. C. (2016). Blockchain for the Internet of things: a systematic literature review. In *2016 IEEE/ ACS 13th International Conference ofComputer Systems and Applications (AICCSA)* (pp. 1–6). Agadir, Morocco: IEEE. /DOI: 10.1109/AICCSA.2016.7945805

Frederick, D. E. (2019). Blockchain, libraries and the data deluge. *Library Hi Tech News*, 36(10), 1–7. DOI: 10.1108/LHTN-09-2019-0059

Grimes, N., & Porter, W. (2023). Closing the digital divide through digital equity: The role of libraries and librarians. *Public Library Quarterly*, 1–32. DOI: 10.1080/01616846.2023.2251348

Herrlich, H. (2023, May 23). The Future of Libraries: AI and Machine learning – Fordham Library News. https://librarynews.blog.fordham.edu/2023/05/23/the-future -of-libraries-ai-and-machine-learning/

Hodonu-Wusu, J. O. (2024). The rise of artificial intelligence in libraries: The ethical and equitable methodologies, and prospects for empowering library users. *AI and Ethics*. Advance online publication. DOI: 10.1007/s43681-024-00432-7

Hoy, M. B. (2017). An Introduction to the Blockchain and Its Implications for Libraries and Medicine. *Medical Reference Services Quarterly*, 36(3), 273–279. DOI: 10.1080/02763869.2017.1332261 PMID: 28714815

Hussain, A. (2018), "Awareness of web 2.0 technology in the academic libraries: an Islamabad perspective", *Library Philosophy and Practice* (e-Journal). Available at: https:// digitalcommons.unl.edu/libphilprac/194

Hussain, A. (2020). *"Cutting edge: technology's impact on library services", Innovations in the Designing and Marketing of Information Services*. IGI Global. DOI: 10.4018/978-1-7998-1482-5.ch002

Hussain, A. (2020). Industrial revolution 4.0: implication to libraries and librarians j Emerald Insight. Available at: www. emerald.com/insight/content/doi/10.1108/ LHTN-05-2019-0033/full/html

Jayavadivel, R., Arunachalam, M., Nagarajan, G., Shankar, B. P., Viji, C., Rajkumar, N., & Senthilkumar, K. R. (2024). Historical overview of AI adoption in libraries. In *AI-Assisted Library Reconstruction* (pp. 267–289). IGI Global. DOI: 10.4018/979-8-3693-2782-1.ch015

Jayavadivel, R., Arunachalam, M., Nagarajan, G., Shankar, B. P., Viji, C., Rajkumar, N., & Senthilkumar, K. R. (2024). Historical overview of AI adoption in libraries. In *AI-Assisted Library Reconstruction* (pp. 267–289). DOI: 10.4018/979-8-3693-2782-1.ch015

Jin, T., Zhang, X., Liu, Y., & Lei, K. (2017). BlockNDN: a bitcoin blockchain decentralized system over named data networking. *Ninth International Conference on Ubiquitous and Future Networks*, 75-80. DOI: 10.1109/ICUFN.2017.7993751

Karafiloski, E., & Mishev, A. (2017). Blockchain solutions for big data challenges: A literature review. In *IEEE EUROCON 2017 -17th International Conference on Smart Technologies* (pp. 763–768). Ohrid, Macedonia: IEEE. DOI: 10.1109/EUROCON.2017.8011213

Kishore, H. S., Raj, D. S. P., & Senthilkumar, K. R. (2024). AI for accessibility: A case study of enhancing library services for users with disabilities. In *Improving Library Systems with AI* (pp. 214–225). Applications, Approaches, and Bibliometric Insights. DOI: 10.4018/979-8-3693-5593-0.ch015

Kumar, N., Antoniraj, S., Jayanthi, S., Mirdula, S., Selvaraj, S., Rajkumar, N., & Senthilkumar, K. R. (2024). Educational technology and libraries supporting online learning. In *AI-Assisted Library Reconstruction* (pp. 209–237). IGI Global. DOI: 10.4018/979-8-3693-2782-1.ch012

Kumar, N., Antoniraj, S., Jayanthi, S., Mirdula, S., Selvaraj, S., Rajkumar, N., & Senthilkumar, K. R. (2024). Educational technology and libraries supporting online learning. In *AI-Assisted Library Reconstruction* (pp. 209–237). DOI: 10.4018/979-8-3693-2782-1.ch012

Lalitha, B., Ramalakshmi, K., Gunasekaran, H., Murugesan, P., Saminasri, P., & Rajkumar, N. (2024). Anticipating AI impact on library services: Future opportunities and evolutionary prospects. In *Improving Library Systems with AI: Applications, Approaches, and Bibliometric Insights* (pp. 195–213). IGI Global.

Mohanraj, A., Viji, C., Varadarajan, M. N., Kalpana, C., Shankar, B., Jayavadivel, R., Rajkumar, N., & Jagajeevan, R. (2024). Privacy and security in digital libraries. In *AI-Assisted Library Reconstruction* (pp. 104–125). IGI Global. DOI: 10.4018/979-8-3693-2782-1.ch006

Nachiappan, B. (2024a). Emerging and innovative AI technologies for resource management. In *Improving Library Systems with AI: Applications, Approaches, and Bibliometric Insights* (pp. 115–133). IGI Global. DOI: 10.4018/979-8-3693-5593-0.ch009

Nachiappan, B. (2024b). E-resources content recommendation system using AI. In *Improving Library Systems with AI: Applications, Approaches, and Bibliometric Insights* (pp. 155–177). IGI Global. DOI: 10.4018/979-8-3693-5593-0.ch011

Orick, J. T. (2000). The virtual library: Changing roles and ethical challenges for librarians. *The International Information & Library Review*, 32(3-4), 313–324. DOI: 10.1080/10572317.2000.10762520

Rajkumar, N., Tabassum, H., Muthulingam, S., Mohanraj, A., Viji, C., Kumar, N., & Senthilkumar, K. R. (2024). Anticipated requirements and expectations in the digital library. In *AI-Assisted Library Reconstruction* (pp. 1–20). IGI Global. DOI: 10.4018/979-8-3693-2782-1.ch001

Rajkumar, N., Tabassum, H., Muthulingam, S., Mohanraj, A., Viji, C., Kumar, N., & Senthilkumar, K. R. (2024). Anticipated requirements and expectations in the digital library. In *AI-Assisted Library Reconstruction* (pp. 1–20). DOI: 10.4018/979-8-3693-2782-1.ch001

Rajkumar, N., Viji, C., Mohanraj, A., Senthilkumar, K. R., Jagajeevan, R., & Kovilpillai, J. A. (2024). Ethical considerations of AI implementation in the library era. In *Improving Library Systems with AI: Applications, Approaches, and Bibliometric Insights* (pp. 85–106). IGI Global. DOI: 10.4018/979-8-3693-5593-0.ch007

Rajkumar, N., Viji, C., Mohanraj, A., Senthilkumar, K. R., Jagajeevan, R., & Kovilpillai, J. A. (2024). Ethical considerations of AI implementation in the library era. In *Improving Library Systems with AI* (pp. 85–106). Applications, Approaches, and Bibliometric Insights. DOI: 10.4018/979-8-3693-5593-0.ch007

Senthilkumar, K. R. (2019). User pattern of Libraries by students of Government Colleges in Tamil nadu: A study. *Library Philosophy and Practice*.

Senthilkumar, K. R. (2024a). AI-assisted library reconstruction. In *AI-Assisted Library Reconstruction*. DOI: 10.4018/979-8-3693-2782-1

Senthilkumar, K. R. (2024b). Revolutionizing thrust manufacturing: The synergy of real-time data and AI advancements. In *Using Real-Time Data and AI for Thrust Manufacturing* (pp. 80–93). https://doi.org/DOI: 10.4018/9798369326152.ch005

Senthilkumar, K. R., & Jagajeevan, R. (2024). Improving library systems with AI: Applications, approaches, and bibliometric insights. In *Improving Library Systems with AI*. Applications, Approaches, and Bibliometric Insights. DOI: 10.4018/979-8-3693-5593-0

Senthilkumar, K. R., & Maniiarasan, P. (2020). Comparison of E-resources with their usage statistics among Bharathidasan University & Madurai Kamaraj University. *Library Philosophy and Practice, 2020*. https://www.scopus.com/inward/record.uri?eid=2-s2.0-85091524339&partnerID=40&md5=6f7b662e3842db0d95af80ba646fdd6e

Sharma, S., & Batth, R. S. (2020). Blockchain technology for higher education system: a mirror review. *2020 International Conference on Intelligent Engineering and Management (ICIEM)*, 348-353. DOI: 10.1109/ICIEM48762.2020.9160274

Sivaraj, P., Madhan, V., Mallika, V., & Senthilkumar, K. R. (2024). Enhancing library services through optimization algorithms and data analytics: Enhancing library services mathematical model. In *AI-Assisted Library Reconstruction* (pp. 290–306). DOI: 10.4018/979-8-3693-2782-1.ch016

Taj, A., Ahmed, M. G., Ali, K. S., & Senthilkumar, K. R. (2024). Revolutionizing medical libraries: The vital role of AI in enhancing discovery, access, and library services for healthcare professional. In *Improving Library Systems with AI* (pp. 24–38). Applications, Approaches, and Bibliometric Insights. DOI: 10.4018/979-8-3693-5593-0.ch002

Underwood, S. (2016). Blockchain beyond bitcoin. *Communications of the ACM*, 59(11), 15–17. https://doi.org/trustworthi

Varadarajan, M. N. (2024). Educational program for AI literacy. In *Improving Library Systems with AI: Applications, Approaches, and Bibliometric Insights* (pp. 134–154). IGI Global. DOI: 10.4018/979-8-3693-5593-0.ch010

Velmurugan, B., Dharmalingam, S., Muthukrishnan, K. B., & Senthilkumar, K. R. (2024). AI insights deciphering India's ascendancy through the digital library: Navigating the digital realm India's odyssey towards information equity and technological eminence. In *Improving Library Systems with AI* (pp. 285–293). Applications, Approaches, and Bibliometric Insights. DOI: 10.4018/979-8-3693-5593-0.ch021

Viji, C., Najmusher, H., Rajkumar, N., Mohanraj, A., Nachiappan, B., Neelakandan, C., & Jagajeevan, R. (2024). Intelligent library management using radio frequency identification. In *AI-Assisted Library Reconstruction* (pp. 126–143). IGI Global. DOI: 10.4018/979-8-3693-2782-1.ch007

Yli-Huumo, J., Ko, D., Choi, S., Park, S., & Smolander, K. (2016). Where Is Current Research on Blockchain Technology?—A Systematic Review. *PLOS ONE*, 11(10), 1–27. https://doi.org/. pone.0163477DOI: 10.1371/journal

Chapter 9
Enhancing Access to Information

Balusamy Nachiappan
https://orcid.org/0009-0006-0951-8078
Prologis, USA

Rajkumar N.
https://orcid.org/0000-0001-7857-9452
Alliance School of Advanced Computing, India

Viji C.
https://orcid.org/0000-0002-2759-8896
Alliance School of Advanced Computing, India

A. Mohanraj
Sri Eshwar College of Engineering, India

N. Karthikeyan
Vellore Institute of Technology, Chennai, India

G. Nagarajan
Kalasalingam Academy of Research and Education, India

ABSTRACT

Blockchain technology deals a transformative approach to enhancing access to information by leveraging its dispersed and apparent nature. Traditional information access systems often face challenges such as restricted access, censorship, and inequalities in information dissemination. Blockchain decentralizes control, enabling a more resilient structure for accessing and sharing information, which is particularly beneficial in regions with restricted access. This technology democratizes data control, ensuring that no single entity can restrict the flow of information, thereby promoting inclusivity and diversity in knowledge sharing. In the realm of scholarly publishing, blockchain facilitates open access models, reducing costs and increasing the accessibility of research. Authors can retain control over their work while sharing it globally, accelerating the dissemination of knowledge and foster-

DOI: 10.4018/979-8-3693-7783-3.ch009

ing greater collaboration and innovation. This can help underserved communities gain access to essential information and services, promoting a more inclusive and equitable digital world.

INTRODUCTION

In a technology wherein data is an important resource, how its miles are accessed and disbursed notably influences societal dynamics. Decentralized right of entry to facts represents a transformative method that disturbs conditions of conventional centralized systems, advocating for a more open, obvious, and equitable statistics panorama. This concept is rooted in the idea that no single entity should manipulate the flow of statistics, thereby decreasing the dangers of censorship, manipulation, and inequality. The historical context of decentralized access to records can be traced again to early human societies in which records dissemination was modified into extra communal and localized. However, with the arrival of centralized establishments and later, the net, the dynamics shifted dramatically. In modern society, the rush towards decentralization is gaining momentum, pushed with the aid of technological improvements and a developing call for facts sovereignty, and privateness.

Viji et al. (Viji et al., 2024) explore the use of Radio Frequency Identification (RFID) in library management. By implementing AI-driven RFID systems, libraries can automate inventory management, streamline book-borrowing and returning processes, and enhance security. This intelligent system reduces manual errors and improves user experience by providing real-time data on book availability and location. Kumar et al. (Kumar et al., 2024) highlight the role of educational technology in libraries to support online learning. AI-driven systems personalize learning experiences, recommend resources based on user preferences, and provide interactive platforms for students. Libraries equipped with such technologies can better support distance education and lifelong learning initiatives.

Mohanraj et al. (Mohanraj et al., 2024) address the critical issues of privacy and security in digital libraries(Patel & Roy, 2023). With the increasing digitization of library resources, ensuring data protection and user privacy has become paramount. The authors propose AI-based security frameworks that include encryption, access control, and continuous monitoring to safeguard digital assets and user information. Rajkumar et al. (2024) discuss the future requirements and expectations of digital libraries. They emphasize the need for scalable AI solutions to handle vast amounts of data, user-friendly interfaces, and robust metadata management systems. The paper also explores how AI can enhance information retrieval and provide predictive analytics to anticipate user needs.

Jayavadivel et al. (Jayavadivel et al., 2024) provide a historical perspective on the adoption of AI in libraries. They trace the evolution of AI technologies from basic automation tools to advanced systems capable of complex data analysis and resource management. This overview highlights the progressive integration of AI in library operations and its impact on service efficiency. Rajkumar et al. (Rajkumar, Viji, et al., 2024) (Rajkumar, Tabassum, et al., 2024)delve into the ethical considerations surrounding AI implementation in libraries. Issues such as data privacy, algorithmic bias, and the transparency of AI decision-making processes are examined. The authors advocate for the development of ethical guidelines and frameworks to ensure responsible AI usage in libraries.

Lalitha et al. (Lalitha et al., 2024) anticipate the future impact of AI on library services. They discuss potential opportunities such as enhanced user engagement through personalized *yjyj recommendations*, improved resource discovery, and the automation of routine tasks. The evolutionary prospects of AI in libraries point towards more adaptive and intelligent systems that can evolve with user needs. Nachiappan(Nachiappan, 2024a) presents an AI-based content recommendation system for e-resources in libraries. This system leverages machine learning algorithms to analyze user behavior and preferences, providing tailored content suggestions. Such systems enhance user satisfaction by ensuring that relevant and valuable resources are easily accessible.

Nachiappan (Nachiappan, 2024b) explores emerging AI technologies for resource management in libraries. Innovations such as natural language processing, machine learning, and predictive analytics are discussed. These technologies can improve cataloging, resource allocation, and user interactions, leading to more efficient library operations. Varadarajan (Varadarajan, 2024)outlines an educational program designed to improve AI literacy. The program aims to equip library professionals with the knowledge and skills required to implement and manage AI systems. This initiative is crucial for the successful integration of AI technologies in libraries, ensuring that staff can effectively use and maintain these advanced systems. Varadarajan et al. (Varadarajan et al., 2024) examine the integration of AI and IoT for smart home automation. The paper discusses how these technologies can create intelligent home environments that are responsive to user needs. Applications such as energy management, security, and convenience are enhanced through AI-driven IoT systems, providing a seamless and efficient living experience (Nguyen & Tran, 2024).

The Concept of Decentralization

Decentralization, in its broadest feel, refers back to the distribution of functions, powers, humans, or matters some distance from an imperative vicinity or authority. It could take various paperwork, which includes political decentralization (the redistribution of authority from important to neighborhood governments), administrative decentralization (delegation of desire-making to lower tiers internal an organization), and marketplace decentralization (dispersal of economic sports and choice-making to person actors). Within the context of facts dissemination, decentralization implies the removal of middleman control over facts float, permitting direct access and exchange among users.

Technological Foundations

The net and virtual technology are the spine of the decentralized right of entry to to data. The improvement of peer-to-peer (P2P) networks, blockchain technology, and allotted ledger structures has been pivotal. Blockchain, as an example, offers a transparent and tamper-proof technique of recording statistics, ensuring facts integrity and consideration without a central authority. P2P networks, exemplified via structures like BitTorrent, permit customers to percentage files immediately, bypassing conventional big servers. The technological improvements have democratized get right of entry to statistics, allowing users to both contribute to and advantage of a decentralized information atmosphere.

Figure 1. Decentralized identity, Adaptive access, and cloud security

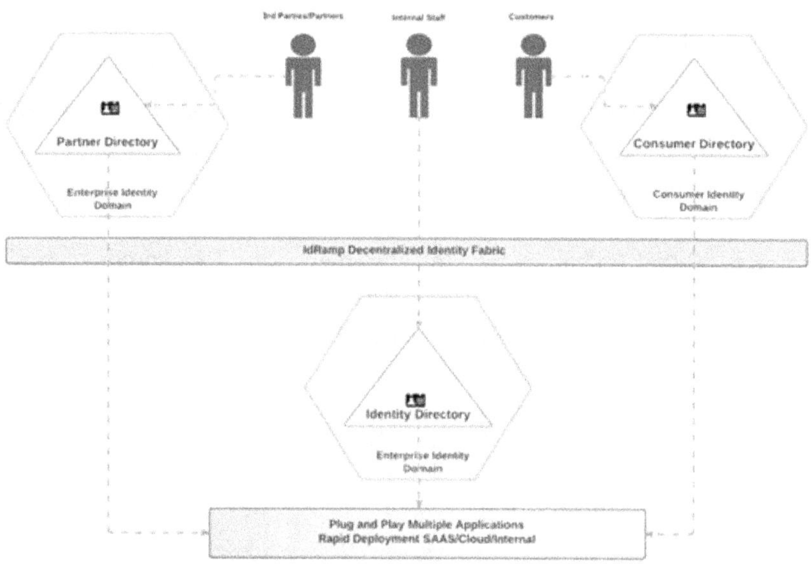

Advantages of Decentralized Information Access

Enhanced Data Security and Privacy

One of the most sizable advantages of decentralized statistics gets entry to is the enhancement of data safety and privacy. Centralized systems are liable to unmarried elements of failure, making them attractive targets for cyberattacks. In evaluation, decentralized structures distribute records(Brown & Garcia, 2024) across a couple of nodes, lowering the chance of breaches and ensuring that no unmarried entity has control over all the records. Blockchain era, with its cryptographic safety capabilities, further guarantees the privacy and integrity of records.

Reduction of Censorship and Control

Decentralized systems are inherently proof against censorship. In centralized fashions, controlling entities can without difficulty suppress information, limiting access based on political, social, or financial agendas. Decentralized networks, however, carry out without a government, making it hard to censor or manage the drift of data. This democratization of information access empowers people to be in search of for, percentage, and consume content freely, fostering a more open and knowledgeable society.

Increased Transparency and Trust

Transparency is a cornerstone of decentralized structures. Blockchain generation, for instance, offers an apparent ledger of all transactions(Johnson & Kim, 2023), reachable to all participants within the network. This transparency fosters consideration among users, as they can independently affirm the authenticity and integrity of the information. In a generation in which trust in institutions and media is waning, decentralized systems provide a reputable opportunity, to make sure that records are verifiable and reliable.

Empowerment of Individuals and Communities

Decentralized right of entry to statistics empowers human beings and communities by giving them management over their facts and the technique to disseminate them. This empowerment is mainly big in areas with restrictive governments or confined admission to facts. Via permitting direct participation in the records financial machine, decentralized systems promote inclusivity and equity, permitting various voices to be heard and valued.

Challenges and Limitations

Technical Challenges and Scalability Issues

Regardless of its blessings, decentralized access to facts faces extensive technical stressful conditions. Scalability is a number one situation; as decentralized networks develop, they require extra computational strength and bandwidth to keep performance and basic performance. Blockchain technology, even as cozy and obvious, often struggles with scalability problems, restricting its functionality to deal with huge volumes of transactions rapidly (Smith & Zhao, 2023).

Regulatory and Legal Hurdles

The regulatory surroundings pose another widespread venture. Decentralized systems are regularly carried out in criminal grey areas, as present regulations are designed for centralized models. Governments may also moreover view decentralized networks as threats to national protection or economic balance, main to restrictive legal guidelines and regulations. Navigating those regulatory landscapes requires careful attention and advocacy for policies that aid innovation while protecting public pursuits.

Risks of Misinformation and Lack of Content Moderation

The regulatory surroundings pose another widespread venture. Decentralized systems are regularly carried out in criminal grey areas, as present regulations are designed for centralized models. Governments may also moreover view decentralized networks as threats to national protection or economic balance, main to restrictive legal guidelines and regulations. Navigating those regulatory landscapes requires careful attention and advocacy for policies that aid innovation while protecting public pursuits.

Economic and Resource Constraints

Decentralized structures, with the resources of their nature, lack centralized manipulation, which could cause the spread of misinformation. Without significant oversight, it will become tough to put in force content material cloth standards and verify the credibility of information. This threat is specifically said in social media and news dissemination, in which fake facts can spread unexpectedly, causing extensive damage. Developing mechanisms for decentralized content moderation and verification is essential to mitigating the risks.

Case Studies and Examples

Wikipedia: A Decentralized Knowledge Platform

Wikipedia is one of the most prominent examples of decentralized get proper entry to to facts. It operates as a collaborative platform where customers can make contributions to and edit articles, growing a huge repository of knowledge that is freely on hand to all and sundry with a web connection. Wikipedia's achievement lies in its community-pushed model, wherein content is created, reviewed, and maintained with the aid of volunteers worldwide. This decentralized method has democratized knowledge creation and dissemination, making data on hand to tens of millions globally(Lopez & Anderson, 2023).

Decentralized Social Media Networks

Decentralized social media networks, in conjunction with Mastodon and Diaspora, provide alternatives to standard structures like Facebook and Twitter. Those networks are characteristic of federated fashions, wherein multiple independently operated servers (times) shape a bigger community. Clients can select servers based totally on their alternatives and values, while nevertheless interacting with customers on different servers. This decentralized approach reduces the notice of electricity and manipulation, fostering a more varied and resilient social media environment.

Blockchain-Based Information Systems

Blockchain-based systems, such as the InterPlanetary File System (IPFS) and Filecoin, represent innovative approaches to decentralized information storage and retrieval. IPFS is a peer-to-peer hypermedia protocol designed to make the web faster, safer, and more open. It allows users to share and store files in a decentralized manner, reducing reliance on centralized servers. Filecoin builds on IPFS by providing a decentralized storage network that incentivizes users to share unused storage space. These systems offer secure, scalable, and resilient alternatives to traditional data storage and distribution models.

Future Prospects and Trends

Emerging Technologies and Their Potential Impact

The future of decentralized entry to facts is cautiously tied to the improvement of rising technology. Enhancements in blockchain, synthetic intelligence, and quantum computing have the capability to in addition beautify the protection, efficiency, and scalability of decentralized structures. For instance, integrating AI with blockchain ought to permit greater sophisticated content cloth moderation and verification mechanisms, addressing a number of the demanding situations associated with wrong facts.

Predictions for the Future of Decentralized Information Access

As generation continues to conform, the prospects for decentralized admission to data are promising. We can count on see accelerated adoption of decentralized structures and structures throughout several sectors, from finance and healthcare to education and media(Li & Yang, 2023). The developing call for records privateness and sovereignty will force innovation in this area, mainly to the improvement of an extra strong and person-excellent decentralized era.

Figure 2. Role of Education and Digital Literacy

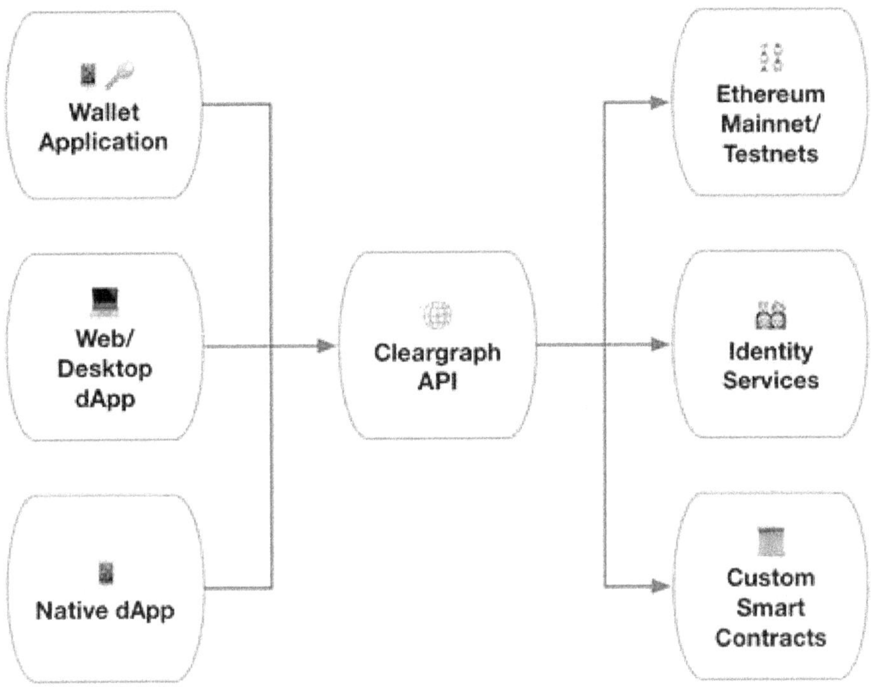

Role of Education and Digital Literacy in Decentralized Information Access

Within the evolving panorama of records getting the right of entry, decentralization stands proud as a progressive shift that guarantees to democratize the go-with-the-flow of facts, reduce the impact of centralized authorities, and empower humans(White & Singh, 2024). However, the successful adoption and implementation of decentralized structures hinge substantially on the level of education and digital literacy in inner society. This essay explores the essential function of education and digital literacy in enhancing decentralized access to data, emphasizing the need for complete educational initiatives that address digital capabilities, facts privateness, and vital questioning (Zhao & Chen, 2024) (Kim & Lee, 2023).

The Importance of Digital Literacy

Digital literacy is the capacity to apply information and conversation generation to discover, examine, create, and communicate information, requiring each cognitive and technical talent. In the context of decentralized facts structures, virtual literacy contains a tremendous kind of skills, which incorporates statistics on how decentralized technologies work, navigating digital structures efficiently, and significantly assessing the exceptional reliability of data(Ahmed & Khan, 2024).

Understanding Decentralized Technologies

Decentralized technology, which incorporates blockchain, peer-to-peer networks, and allotted ledgers, forms the spine of decentralized records access. To correctly use the technologies, individuals want a basic knowledge of their requirements and functionalities. For instance, blockchain technology includes a decentralized ledger of all transactions in a community, providing transparency and protection. Coaching people about how blockchain works, its benefits and its functionality risks is crucial for fostering consideration and participation in decentralized systems(Miller & Davis, 2023).

Navigating Digital Platforms

Virtual literacy additionally includes the practical capabilities to navigate diverse virtual systems. This consists of the usage of decentralized packages (dApps), setting up and coping with digital wallets, and participating in peer-to-peer networks. Educational projects ought to equip humans with the technical know-how to interact with those structures effectively. This can embody tutorials, workshops, and online courses that provide hands-on experience with decentralized tools and applications.

Assessing Information Quality and Reliability

One of the demanding situations of decentralized data getting proper of entry is the capability for wrong records and the lack of centralized content moderation. Consequently, digital literacy education needs to emphasize crucial questioning and media literacy skills. Humans want so you can significantly affirm the belongings and content material of the statistics they come upon. This entails understanding a manner to study the credibility of assets, spotting bias and misinformation, and cross-referencing records with multiple reliable assets.

Data Privacy and Security

In a decentralized data panorama, information privacy and safety are paramount. In contrast to centralized structures, in which an unmarried entity is accountable for records safety, decentralized systems distribute this responsibility across the network. Teaching human beings approximately statistics privateness and protection practices is crucial to make certain they may protect their statistics and participate appropriately in decentralized structures.

Protecting Personal Information

Users of decentralized systems must recognize the significance of safeguarding their non-public facts. This includes information approximately encryption, relaxed communique channels, and first-class practices for growing and handling passwords. Instructional programs ought to provide steerage on a way to defend personal data, keep away from phishing scams, and apprehend potential protection threats.

Understanding Privacy Implications

Decentralized structures often promise extra privacy with the aid of reducing reliance on centralized records repositories. But, this doesn't suggest they will be chance-loose. Customers need to be privy to the privacy implications of decentralized technology, consisting of how their statistics are saved, shared, and used throughout the community. Understanding the additives can assist human beings make knowledgeable selections approximately their participation in decentralized structures and the way they manage their facts.

Responding to Security Breaches

Notwithstanding wonderful efforts, safety breaches can though occur. Training on a manner to reply to such breaches is important. This includes information on the manner to report incidents, get better-compromised debts, and mitigate the impact of statistics breaches. Offering customers clean, actionable steps to take in the event of a protection incident can help limit damage and preserve acceptance as true within decentralized structures.

Critical Thinking and Media Literacy

Vital thinking and media literacy are fundamental additives of virtual literacy that permit people to navigate the decentralized statistics panorama efficiently. In surroundings in which records are abundant and unmoderated, the potential to assume significant and credible data from incorrect information is crucial.

Developing Critical Thinking Skills

Essential questioning consists of reading and evaluating information to shape a reasoned judgment. It's miles a skill that may be advanced via training and practice. Academic initiatives (Wang & Chen, 2024)need to be interesting in education crucial thinking competencies, encouraging humans to impeach assumptions, remember a couple of views, and use logical reasoning to reach conclusions. Those abilities are essential for navigating decentralized information environments, wherein the responsibility for verifying information lies with the man or woman.

Media literacy is the ability to get admission to, examine, study, and create media in a ramification of bureaucracy. It's miles a crucial talent in the virtual age, in which media is the number one source of records. Media literacy training needs to educate individuals on a way to significantly examine media content cloth, understand the strategies used to influence audiences and apprehend the distinction between reality and opinion. This consists of know-how about the location of algorithms and how they can form the information we see.

Combating Misinformation

Incorrect information is a significant project in decentralized(Thomas & Harris, 2023) facts structures. Without treasured oversight, false information can spread. Training on a way to perceive and fight incorrect information is important. This includes teaching humans the way to verify information, check property, and apprehend common types of incorrect information, consisting of faux information and deepfakes. Empowering individuals with those abilities can help mitigate the effect of wrong information and sell an extra knowledgeable society.

Educational Initiatives and Strategies

A multifaceted technique is essential to beautify virtual literacy and schooling in the context of decentralized facts to get the right of entry. This entails integrating virtual literacy into formal education, presenting network-based absolutely training packages, leveraging online resources, and selling lifelong studying.

Integrating Digital Literacy into Formal Education

Formal schooling structures play a vital function in developing digital literacy from an early age. Integrating virtual literacy into school curricula can make sure that students acquire crucial abilities as part of their foundational education. This includes incorporating instructions on digital technologies, data privacy, and critical wondering into subjects along with PC technology, social studies, and language arts.

Community-based total schooling packages can offer treasured possibilities for adults and underserved populations to expand digital literacy abilities. Those applications can be furnished through libraries, network centers, and non-profit corporations. They can embody workshops, seminars, and hands-on education periods tailor-made to the best desires of the network. By making virtual literacy schooling to be had and applicable, those programs can help bridge the virtual divide.

Leveraging Online Resources

The online property provides a flexible and scalable way to provide digital literacy training. Big open online guides (MOOCs), webinars, and online tutorials can reach a massive target market and offer wonderful academic content. These belongings can cover an extensive style of topics, from simple digital competencies to superior knowledge of decentralized technologies. Moreover, online systems can facilitate peer-to-peer studying and collaboration, enhancing the gaining knowledge of experience.

Promoting Lifelong Learning

Within the unexpectedly changing virtual landscape, non-stop gaining knowledge is essential. Promoting a lifestyle of lifelong learning encourages people to commonly replace their capabilities and knowledge. This could be supported through professional improvement programs, online guides, and private knowledge of responsibilities. Lifelong getting to know ensures that people can adapt to new eras and disturbing conditions, staying knowledgeable and empowered in a decentralized facts environment.

Case Studies and Best Practices

Examining successful case studies and best practices can provide valuable insights into how education and digital literacy initiatives can effectively support decentralized information access.

Estonia: A Model for Digital Literacy

Estonia is regularly referred to as a model for virtual literacy and e-governance. The u . S . A . Has invested carefully in digital infrastructure and schooling, resulting in a pretty virtual-savvy population. Estonia's virtual literacy programs begin in early education and preserve inside the path of life, with a focal point on realistic competencies and virtual citizenship. The US's success demonstrates the importance of a complete and sustained method of virtual literacy training.

Mozilla's Web Literacy Program

Mozilla's Net Literacy program is an initiative aimed at improving virtual literacy globally. The program affords a framework for teaching and mastering digital abilities, overlaying competencies collectively with navigating the internet, information internet technology, and developing digital content cloth. Mozilla's open-supply approach permits educators to conform and use the resources in several contexts, selling large virtual literacy.

Community Technology Empowerment Project (CTEP)

The Community Technology Empowerment Challenge (CTEP) in Minnesota, America, presents digital literacy training to underserved groups. The venture focuses on equipping people with the capabilities needed to use digital generation for personal and expert growth. CTEP's fulfillment lies in its community-primarily based technique, which ensures that the training is relevant and to be had by those who need it maximum.

Future Directions and Recommendations

As decentralized systems end up becoming more popular, the decision for virtual literacy and education will keep growing. To fulfill this call, it's far essential to expand and implement techniques that ensure complete and inclusive education for all.

Developing Inclusive Educational Policies

Governments and educational institutions ought to make bigger rules that prioritize virtual literacy and inclusivity. This consists of making sure that virtual literacy is incorporated into country-wide education necessities, offering funding for virtual literacy programs, and addressing limitations to access, consisting of affordability and infrastructure.

Fostering Public-Private Partnerships

Collaboration between the private and non-private sectors can beautify the achievement and effect of virtual literacy duties. Non-public groups, especially the ones within the era location, can offer expertise, resources, and investment to help educational packages. Public-non-public partnerships can facilitate the improvement of innovative answers and ensure that digital literacy schooling is aligned with the desires of the frame of employees and society.

Encouraging Community Involvement

Community involvement is important for the fulfillment of digital literacy obligations. Engaging local communities in the making plans and implementation of instructional applications can ensure that the packages are applicable and powerful. Community leaders, educators, and volunteers can play a crucial function in promoting virtual literacy and assisting newbies.

Leveraging Technology for Education

The era itself can be an effective tool for training. Online systems, cellular packages, and digital assets can offer bendy and handy studying opportunities. Leveraging technology for training can help attain a broader target audience and provide interactive and attractive learning experiences. Decentralized admission to records represents a paradigm shift in how information is disseminated and eaten up. Through getting rid of middleman manipulation, decentralized systems beautify facts' safety, lessen censorship, and empower individuals and communities. However, substantial traumatic conditions stay, inclusive of technical, regulatory, and economic hurdles. Addressing those demanding situations requires coordinated efforts for the duration of several sectors, from generation and (Choi & Park, 2024) policy to education and civil society. The capability of decentralized records to get the right of entry to reshape society is massive, presenting an extra open, obvious, and equitable future. As we navigate this transition, it is crucial to make sure that decentralized technologies are advanced and deployed inclusively and ethically, maximizing their benefits for all individuals in society.

Blockchain for Open Access and Scholarly Publishing

Blockchain generation, first of all, recognized for its function in cryptocurrencies like Bitcoin, is increasingly being identified for its capability to revolutionize numerous industries, including scholarly publishing(Martinez & Sanchez, 2024)

(C. Liu & Wong, 2023). The conventional scholarly publishing system is regularly criticized for its inefficiencies, excessive prices, and boundaries to access. Blockchain offers a decentralized, transparent, and comfortable alternative that may cope with a whole lot of those troubles. This essay explores the software of blockchain technology in open get right of entry to and scholarly publishing, examining its potential advantages, demanding situations, and future potentialities.

The Current State of Scholarly Publishing

The conventional scholarly publishing version is dominated by way of manner of some big publishers who manipulate get admission to to educational journals. Researchers post their artwork to those journals, often paying massive expenses for ebooks. The journals, in turn, charge libraries and establishments excessive subscription charges to get proper access to the posted articles. This version has numerous drawbacks:

1. **High Costs**: each ebook's expenses and subscription fees may be prohibitively pricey, limiting entry to scholarly artwork.
2. **Access Barriers**: Paywalls restrict the supply of studies, particularly affecting researchers and institutions in growing international locations.
3. **Inefficiencies**: The peer evaluation approach may be gradual and opaque, delaying the dissemination of recent research.

BLOCKCHAIN IN SCHOLARLY PUBLISHING

Decentralized and Transparent Peer Review

1. One of the most promising applications of blockchain in scholarly publishing is the decentralization of the peer assessment approach. Traditional peer evaluation is regularly criticized for its lack of transparency and ability to bias. Blockchain can address those troubles via the manner of developing a transparent and immutable file of the review technique:
2. **Reviewer Anonymity and Accountability**: Blockchain can anonymize reviewers at the same time as keeping an obvious report in their contributions, ensuring duty without compromising confidentiality.
3. **Timestamping and Proof of Review**: each step of the assessment manner can be timestamped and recorded at the blockchain, presenting evidence of evaluation and deterring misconduct.

4. **Incentivizing Reviewers**: Blockchain can facilitate the introduction of tokens or different incentives for reviewers, encouraging extra thorough and well-timed opinions.

Improved Access and Distribution

Blockchain can enhance access to scholarly publications by providing a decentralized platform for distribution:

1. **Open Access Repositories**: Blockchain can help the introduction of decentralized open access repositories, in which researchers can add their paintings right now. The ones repositories can ensure that research is freely available to all.
2. **Permanent Records**: The immutability of blockchain ensures that after a paper is published, it remains accessible, stopping problems like retraction or lack of right of access because of journal closure.
3. **Global Reach**: Blockchain-based total systems can be accessed globally, overcoming geographical and monetary barriers to get the right of entry.

Intellectual Property and Attribution

Blockchain can also improve the management of intellectual property (IP) and attribution in scholarly publishing:

1. **Proof of Authorship**: Researchers can use blockchain to timestamp and display the authorship of their a Blockchain can create an apparent and tamper-proof file of citations, offering correct monitoring of the effect and dissemination of studies.
2. **Smart Contracts**: clever contracts on the blockchain can automate licensing agreements and royalties, making sure that authors are pretty compensated for their work.

CASE STUDIES AND EXAMPLES

Project ORCID and Blockchain

ORCID (Open Researcher and Contributor identification) offers particular identifiers for researchers, facilitating the monitoring of their paintings across special systems. Integrating blockchain with ORCID has to decorate the verification and transparency of researchers' contributions. For instance, every ebook or assessment pastime might be recorded on the blockchain, related to the researcher's ORCID identity, ensuring an accurate and immutable record in their scholarly sports.

Artifacts on the Blockchain

The decentralized platform Artifacts pursues to leverage blockchain for the instructional publishing system. It lets researchers (Roberts & Williams, 2024) timestamp their paintings, which includes datasets, code, and preprints, ensuring that they might display authorship and originality in their contributions. Artifacts additionally give an apparent peer evaluation approach and decentralized storage, improving the safety and accessibility of scholarly artwork.

CHALLENGES AND LIMITATIONS

Technical Challenges

Implementing blockchain technology in scholarly publishing involves several technical challenges:

1. **Scalability**: Blockchains can face scalability problems, mainly with excessive transaction volumes. Ensuring that the system can cope with large numbers of guides and reviews efficaciously is vital.
2. **Interoperability**: Integrating blockchain with gift publishing systems and databases requires interoperability, which may be complex and resource-extensive.
3. **Energy Consumption**: some blockchain protocols, especially those based totally on proof-of-paintings, consume large portions of strength. Exploring extra sustainable options, inclusive of proof-of-stake, is important.

Regulatory and Legal Issues

The adoption of blockchain in scholarly publishing must navigate various regulatory and legal considerations:

1. **Data Privacy**: ensuring compliance with information privacy guidelines, together with the overall statistics safety regulation (GDPR) in Europe, is as important even as recording personal records on the blockchain.
2. **Intellectual Property Rights**: Clarifying the crook reputation of blockchain statistics as evidence of authorship and managing IP rights inner decentralized systems may be complex.

3. **Jurisdictional Challenges**: Blockchain's decentralized nature can complicate jurisdictional troubles, in particular in worldwide collaborations and disputes

Cultural and Institutional Resistance

Adopting blockchain in scholarly publishing also involves overcoming cultural and institutional resistance:

1. **Trust and Acceptance**: Gaining the belief and recognition of researchers, reviewers, and publishers is vital. Teaching stakeholders about the advantages and functionalities of blockchain can assist assemble self-assurance.
2. **Institutional Inertia**: established institutions and publishers may be resistant to change, specifically if blockchain threatens their traditional sales fashions and control over the publishing approach.
3. **Community Engagement**: engaging the educational network within the development and implementation of blockchain-based totally systems is critical for his or her achievement. This calls for open talk, collaboration, and transparency.

FUTURE PROSPECTS AND TRENDS

Emerging Technologies and Integration

The future of blockchain in scholarly publishing will likely involve the integration of other emerging technologies:

1. **Artificial Intelligence**: AI can decorate blockchain-based total peer review by offering automatic equipment for screening manuscripts, detecting plagiarism, and evaluating exceptional of reviews.
2. **Internet of Things (IoT)**: IoT gadgets can generate and file study records immediately onto the blockchain, making sure the integrity and traceability of facts in fields like environmental technological information and medical studies.
3. **Quantum Computing**: Quantum computing has the potential to revolutionize the blockchain era, enhancing its safety and scalability. However, it additionally poses dangers to contemporary cryptographic strategies, necessitating the development of quantum-resistant blockchains.

Expanding Use Cases and Applications

As blockchain technology matures, its use in scholarly publishing is likely to expand:

1. **Decentralized Journals**: honestly decentralized journals, controlled and operated using academic groups, may also want to become alternatives to traditional publishers. These journals would possibly leverage blockchain for peer assessment, book, and distribution.
2. **Research Data Management**: Blockchain can enhance the control and sharing of studies statistics, selling open science and reproducibility. Researchers can securely keep, percent, and track the usage of their statistics on the blockchain(Y. Zhang & Wang, 2023).
3. **Funding and Grants**: Blockchain can streamline the administration of studies funding and gives. Clever contracts can automate the release of budgets based totally on predefined milestones and deliverables, ensuring transparency and responsibility.

Policy and Advocacy

Policy and advocacy efforts will play a crucial role in promoting the adoption of blockchain in scholarly publishing:

Developing Standards and Guidelines for Blockchain in Scholarly Publishing

Developing requirements and guidelines for using blockchain in scholarly publishing is essential to ensure clarity, consistency, and interoperability throughout particular structures and structures. Requirements offer a framework that may guide the implementation of the blockchain era, making sure that it meets the dreams of all stakeholders and adheres to exquisite practices.

Key Components of Standards and Guidelines

1. **Interoperability**: necessities need to make certain that blockchain systems can paint seamlessly with existing scholarly publishing infrastructure, which includes databases, digital repositories, and indexing services. This includes defining commonplace protocols and facts formats that permit extremely good structures to talk successfully.

2. **Data Privacy and Security**: tips have to deal with statistics privacy concerns, ensuring compliance with regulations along with GDPR. They should outline how personal statistics, in conjunction with writer identities and peer assessment statistics, are covered on the blockchain. Protection requirements need to outline first-rate practices for encryption, get proper entry to governing, and risk mitigation to protect the integrity and confidentiality of facts.
3. **Transparency and Accountability**: necessities should sell transparency in the peer review way and ebook lifecycle. This consists of protocols for timestamping, recording peer evaluation sports, and tracking changes to manuscripts. Obligation measures must ensure that each one movement is traceable and verifiable on the blockchain.
4. **Quality Control**: To hold the best of scholarly publications, requirements should outline standards for validating the authenticity and accuracy of studies. This consists of establishing mechanisms for verifying the credentials of reviewers and preventing fraudulent sports activities.
5. **Sustainability and Scalability**: pointers must address the scalability of blockchain solutions, ensuring they can address the number of records generated through scholarly publishing without compromising overall performance. Sustainability troubles need to include strength-efficient consensus mechanisms and the long-term preservation of blockchain networks.

Developing and Implementing Standards

1. **Collaboration**: growing necessities call for collaboration amongst a huge range of stakeholders, such as researchers, publishers, technology builders, and regulatory bodies. Forming working agencies and committees with representatives from those sectors can facilitate the development of complete and extensively established requirements.
2. **Pilot Programs**: imposing pilot programs can assist take a look at and refine necessities in real-international situations. These applications can offer precious insights into the realistic annoying situations and blessings of the usage of blockchain in scholarly publishing, informing the development of sturdy standards.
3. **Documentation and Training**: providing exact documentation and training materials can help stakeholders recognize and put in force the requirements. This consists of technical suggestions, great exercise manuals, and academic assets to aid the adoption of blockchain generation.

Funding and Support for Blockchain Initiatives

Governments and funding agencies play a critical role in promoting the adoption of blockchain technology in scholarly publishing through financial support and policy incentives.

Types of Funding and Support

1. **Grants and Subsidies**: presenting gives and subsidies to analyze institutions, technology builders, and publishers can encourage the development and implementation of blockchain solutions. The one budget can assist pilot tasks, studies, and improvement, and the introduction of infrastructure wished for blockchain integration.
2. **Incentives for Innovation**: providing incentives collectively with tax breaks, awards, and reputation packages can encourage organizations and people to find out how innovation makes use of blockchain generation. This may stimulate opposition and pressure improvements inside the concern.
3. **Public-Private Partnerships**: Encouraging partnerships amongst public establishments and personal agencies can leverage the strengths of every sector. Governments can offer regulatory aid and funding, at the same time as private businesses deliver technological statistics and entrepreneurial spirit(Singh & Joshi, 2024).

Implementing Effective Funding Strategies

1. **Identifying Priorities**: funding corporations need to identify key precedence areas for blockchain studies and improvement, specializing in tasks that deal with critical stressful conditions in scholarly publishing, inclusive of peer evaluation transparency, data safety, and admission to knowledge.
2. **Monitoring and Evaluation**: organizing mechanisms for tracking and comparing funded obligations can make certain that they meet their objectives and contribute to the broader desire to improve scholarly publishing. This consists of everyday reporting, overall performance exams, and impact reviews.
3. **Long-Term Investment**: investing in long-term tasks can offer sustained help for the adoption of blockchain technology. This consists of investment for infrastructure improvement, potential construction, and ongoing upkeep of blockchain networks.

Stakeholder Engagement in Blockchain Solutions

Enticing stakeholders, along with researchers, publishers, librarians, and policymakers, is critical for the successful development and implementation of blockchain answers in scholarly publishing. Stakeholder engagement guarantees that blockchain structures meet the desires of the educational community and are considerably ordinary and adopted.

Strategies for Effective Stakeholder Engagement

1. **Inclusive Dialogue**: developing boards for open and inclusive speaking amongst stakeholders can facilitate the exchange of ideas and problems. Conferences, workshops, and online structures can provide opportunities for stakeholders to talk approximately the capability and traumatic conditions of blockchain generation.
2. **Collaborative Development**: associated with stakeholders within the improvement way can make sure that blockchain solutions are client-best and cope with actual international needs. This consists of soliciting comments from researchers on the layout of peer assessment systems, consulting publishers on integration with present workflows, and regarding librarians in discussions about information control.
3. **Education and Awareness**: raising focus on the advantages and functionalities of blockchain technology is critical for gaining stakeholder buy-in. Educational campaigns, webinars, and informational substances can assist stakeholders in understanding how blockchain can enhance scholarly publishing and cope with their specific issues.
4. **Policy Advocacy**: appealing to policymakers in discussions about how blockchain can help form supportive regulatory environments. Advocacy efforts can spotlight the ability of blockchain to decorate transparency, lessen prices, and beautify entry to scholarly facts, influencing coverage choices in choosing blockchain adoption.
5. **Pilot Projects and Demonstrations**: imposing pilot obligations and demonstration programs can showcase the sensible advantages of blockchain technology. Those duties can provide evidence-of-concept and assemble self-belief amongst stakeholders, encouraging wider adoption.

Bridging the Digital Divide With Blockchain

The digital divide, the gap between humans with clean get entry to virtual technologies and those without, remains a splendid global assignment. It encompasses disparities in access to internet connectivity, digital devices, and the talents needed to use them successfully. This divide exacerbates inequalities in schooling, healthcare, financial opportunities, and social inclusion. The blockchain era, acknowledged for its decentralized(Y. Liu & Zhang, 2024), comfy, and obvious nature, can bridge this divide by imparting modern solutions that decorate accessibility, inclusion, and empowerment. This essay explores how blockchain can deal with several elements of the digital divide and its functionality to create an extra-equitable digital landscape (Lee & Kim, 2024).

Understanding the Digital Divide

Dimensions of the Digital Divide

1. **Access to Technology**: The most apparent element of the digital divide is the disparity in getting entry to digital gadgets and net connectivity. At the same time as urban regions in advanced nations enjoy excessive-speed net and big device possession, many rural and underserved companies lack those simple resources
2. **Digital Literacy**: despite getting the right of entry to generation, a loss of virtual literacy can prevent individuals from completely the use of virtual devices. Virtual literacy includes the capabilities and facts required to navigate, understand, and successfully use digital technologies.
3. **Economic Barriers**: financial factors substantially have an impact on the digital divide. Immoderate expenses of gadgets, net subscriptions, and digital offerings can exclude low-earnings human beings and communities from the advantages of digital technologies.
4. **Geographical Barriers**: Geographic area performs an important role in virtual get right of entry to. Some distance off and rural areas often be afflicted by limited infrastructure, making it hard to offer dependable internet and technological offerings.
5. **Social and Cultural Factors**: Social norms and cultural obstacles can also impact virtual inclusion. Gender disparities, educational inequalities, and language barriers can further widen the digital divide.

The Potential of Blockchain to Bridge the Digital Divide

The blockchain era, with its unique characteristics, gives numerous ability solutions to address those dimensions of the virtual divide. Its decentralized nature, security capabilities, and transparency may be harnessed to create inclusive and equitable digital ecosystems.

Enhancing Access to Technology

1. **Decentralized Internet**: Blockchain can assist the development of decentralized Internet infrastructure, such as mesh networks and network-owned networks. Those networks can offer cheap and dependable internet and get admission to in a long way flung and underserved regions, bypassing traditional ISPs.
2. **Affordable Digital Services**: Blockchain-based total structures can reduce costs utilizing the use of doing away with intermediaries and streamlining techniques. This could make digital services, together with monetary transactions, education, and healthcare, much less steeply priced and on hand to low-income agencies.
3. **Device Accessibility**: Blockchain can facilitate the introduction of decentralized marketplaces for 2nd-hand devices and additives. The marketplaces can offer less costly alternatives for people and businesses to build digital gadgets

Promoting Digital Literacy

1. **Educational Initiatives**: Blockchain can guide decentralized and open academic structures that provide loose or low-rate guides and sources on virtual literacy. Those structures can provide verifiable credentials and incentivize getting to know through token-based absolute rewards.
2. **Inclusive Content**: Blockchain can permit the creation and distribution of multilingual and culturally relevant academic content material fabric. This can help bridge language and cultural boundaries, making virtual literacy assets extra to be had by numerous populations.
3. **Skill Development**: Blockchain can resource capability improvement programs that offer verifiable certifications and credentials. The applications may be tailor-made to the wishes of specific communities, making sure that individuals collect the abilities vital to participate within the virtual economy.

Overcoming Economic Barriers

1. **Financial Inclusion**: Blockchain can beautify economic inclusion by supplying decentralized monetary offerings (DeFi) that can be reachable to unbanked and underbanked populations. Those offerings can include virtual wallets, microloans, and remittances, allowing people to take part in the digital economic system.
2. **Token Economies**: Blockchain can create token economies that incentivize participation in digital sports activities. For instance, human beings can earn tokens for contributing to community networks, participating in instructional applications, or imparting offerings. The tokens may be exchanged for gadgets and offerings, decreasing financial boundaries to digital get proper entry.
3. **Transparent Funding**: Blockchain can enhance the transparency and performance of investment for virtual inclusion responsibilities. Donors and governments can use blockchain to sign and verify the use of charge range, ensuring that property obtains the meant beneficiaries and is used efficaciously.

Addressing Geographical Barriers

1. **Decentralized Infrastructure**: Blockchain can help the development of decentralized infrastructure that can be deployed in faraway and rural regions. This includes renewable strength answers for powering digital devices and networks, similar to decentralized information storage and processing.
2. **Remote Services**: Blockchain can facilitate the availability of far-off services, which consist of telemedicine, online education, and far-off artwork opportunities. With the aid of leveraging blockchain for comfortable and verifiable transactions, the ones offerings can attain humans in geographically remote regions.
3. **Supply Chain Management**: Blockchain can enhance delivery chain control for the distribution of digital devices and infrastructure components. Through presenting apparent and traceable information, blockchain can make sure that resources are effectively disbursed to underserved areas.

Addressing Social and Cultural Barriers

1. **Inclusive Governance**: Blockchain can help inclusive and participatory governance fashions that deliver marginalized groups a voice in choice-making approaches. Decentralized self-sustaining organizations (DAOs) can allow communities to self-govern and allocate belongings primarily based on their unique needs and priorities.

2. **Identity and Privacy**: Blockchain can provide cozy and verifiable virtual identities that defend individuals' privacy (L. Zhang & Xu, 2023) and enable get right of entry to virtual offerings. These identities can help marginalized populations, which consist of refugees and undocumented individuals, advantage get entry to essential services and participate within the virtual monetary gadget.
3. **Cultural Preservation**: Blockchain can useful resource for the preservation and merchandising of cultural backgrounds via decentralized and community-led tasks. This can encompass digital facts, educational resources, and systems for sharing cultural know-how and practices.

Case Studies and Examples

Mesh Networks in Rural Areas

Mesh networks, collectively with the ones supported with the aid of the use of the Althea mission, use blockchain to create decentralized net infrastructure. Those networks permit communities to share net get entry to and distribute the costs amongst users, offering low-priced and dependable connectivity in rural areas. With the aid of leveraging blockchain for obvious billing and management, mesh networks can make certain fair and equitable entry to the net(Nadeem & Hussain, 2023).

Decentralized Education Platform

Systems like ODEM (On-name for education marketplace) use blockchain to offer decentralized and less luxurious educational opportunities. ODEM gives a ramification of guides and educational assets, with verifiable credentials recorded on the blockchain. This allows novices from numerous backgrounds to get proper entry to remarkable training and show their abilities to potential employers.

Financial Inclusion With DeFi

Blockchain-primarily based DeFi structures, which include Celo and Compound, offer monetary offerings to unbanked and underbanked populations. Those structures provide virtual wallets, microloans, and savings products which can be available through mobile devices. By way of way of disposing of intermediaries and decreasing transaction charges, DeFi structures can make financial offerings greater inclusive and handy.

Transparent Aid Distribution

The sector food Programme's building Blocks mission makes use of blockchain to distribute useful resources to refugees in Jordan. By leveraging blockchain for relaxed and apparent transactions, building Blocks ensures that useful resource reaches the supposed recipients and decrease fraud. This venture demonstrates how blockchain can beautify the performance and transparency of beneficial useful resource distribution, addressing financial barriers in underserved organizations.

Challenges and Considerations

Even as blockchain holds large functionality for bridging the virtual divide, several annoying conditions and considerations must be addressed:

Technical Challenges

1. **Scalability**: Blockchain networks have that allow you to address huge volumes of transactions and data effectively. Making sure scalability is crucial for giant adoption and use in digital inclusion tasks.
2. **Interoperability**: Blockchain solutions need to be interoperable with present technology and systems. Developing necessities and protocols for interoperability can facilitate integration and adoption.
3. **Energy Consumption**: some blockchain protocols, in particular the ones primarily based on proof-of-art work, consume substantial amounts of strength. Exploring greater sustainable alternatives, together with proof-of-stake, is essential to decrease environmental impact.

Regulatory and Legal Issues

1. **Data Privacy**: ensuring compliance with statistics privacy policies, which include GDPR, is crucial whilst using blockchain for virtual identities and transactions. Balancing transparency and privacy is a key venture.
2. **Legal Recognition**: The felony repute of blockchain transactions and virtual identities ought to be identified and well-known with the aid of governments and institutions. Clarifying the prison framework for blockchain use is critical for its huge adoption.
3. **Intellectual Property**: coping with highbrow property rights within decentralized structures can be complex. Clean suggestions and mechanisms for IP protection and attribution are critical.

Social and Cultural Considerations

1. **Digital Literacy**: ensuring that people have the essential digital literacy competencies to apply blockchain technology successfully is vital. Instructional initiatives and schooling applications are critical components of virtual inclusion.
2. **Trust and Acceptance**: building agreement with and recognition among users, especially in marginalized communities, is vital for the successful adoption of blockchain answers. Obvious conversation and network engagement can foster bear in mind.

Equity and Inclusion: ensuring that blockchain answers are designed with an equity and inclusion angle is critical. This includes addressing the right goals and demanding situations of numerous populations and preventing the exacerbation of current inequalities.

CONCLUSION

The virtual divide, characterized by way of disparities in entry to generation, digital literacy, economic property, geographic region, and sociocultural factors, remains a substantial barrier to international fairness and development. Blockchain generation, with its decentralized, secure, and apparent nature, offers a transformative capability to bridge this divide and create greater inclusive and equitable digital ecosystems. This end synthesizes the crucial component insights and strategies cited in addressing the virtual divide through blockchain. One of the primary elements of the digital divide is the shortage of admission to to era, in particular in far-off and underserved areas. Blockchain can assist the development of decentralized internet infrastructure, along with mesh networks, that can offer much less high-priced and dependable internet connectivity. Via bypassing traditional ISPs and the use of network-owned networks, the solutions can empower corporations to control and distribute their very personal internet assets. Furthermore, blockchain-based structures can decrease the rate of virtual offerings using putting off intermediaries and streamlining methods, making those services more available to low-profit people. The creation of decentralized marketplaces for 2D-hand virtual devices can also offer low-value alternatives for the ones in need, further improving get entry to to technology.

Virtual literacy is essential for people to completely utilize virtual tools and take part in the digital economic system. Blockchain can facilitate decentralized instructional structures that provide unfastened or low-price publications and assets on virtual literacy, offering verifiable credentials and incentivizing analyzing via token-based rewards. By allowing the arrival and distribution of multilingual and culturally applicable instructional content, blockchain can cope with language and cultural obstacles, making virtual literacy resources more handy to various populations. Furthermore, blockchain can help skill improvement packages tailor-made to the wishes of precise companies, ensuring that people acquire the essential talents to thrive in the virtual age. Monetary factors drastically have an impact on the virtual divide, with excessive prices of gadgets, internet subscriptions, and digital offerings apart from many of the blessings of digital technologies. Blockchain can decorate financial inclusion by way of manner of offering decentralized economic services (DeFi) which are available to unbanked and underbanked populations. Digital wallets, microloans, and remittances facilitated with the resource of blockchain can permit humans to participate inside the virtual financial gadget without the want for traditional banking infrastructure. Token economies can incentivize participation in digital sports activities, allowing human beings to earn tokens for network contributions, training, and offerings, which may be exchanged for objects and services, decreasing economic limitations to digital access. Furthermore, blockchain can enhance the transparency and efficiency of funding for digital inclusion tasks, ensuring that belongings reach the meant beneficiaries and are used successfully.

Geographic area plays a crucial position in digital get right of access to, with a ways flung and rural regions regularly stricken by restricted infrastructure. Blockchain can help the improvement of decentralized infrastructure that may be deployed in those regions, which includes renewable power answers for powering virtual devices and networks. With the aid of way of facilitating far flung services including telemedicine, online schooling, and some distance off paintings possibilities, blockchain can make bigger the attain of critical services to geographically isolated areas. Moreover, blockchain can beautify deliver chain control for the distribution of digital devices and infrastructure additives, making sure green useful resource distribution to underserved regions. Social norms and cultural boundaries can impact virtual inclusion, with gender disparities, instructional inequalities, and language boundaries further widening the digital divide. Blockchain can manual inclusive governance fashions that supply marginalized communities a voice in choice-making procedures through decentralized self maintaining agencies (DAOs). At ease and verifiable virtual identities supplied with the useful resource of blockchain can shield individuals' privateness and enable get proper of access to to virtual offerings, assisting marginalized populations gain get right of entry to to crucial services and participate in the digital monetary device. Blockchain also can assist the renovation and merchandising of cultural historical past via decentralized and community-led tasks, supplying virtual documents and platforms for sharing cultural information and practices.

REFERENCES

Ahmed, H., & Khan, A. (2024). Blockchain is a tool for bridging the digital divide in developing countries. *Telecommunications Policy*, 48(2), 103–122.

Brown, T., & Garcia, E. (2024). Distributed ledger technology for academic publishing: Benefits and challenges. *Information Services & Use*, 44(1), 65–78.

Choi, H., & Park, J. (2024). Leveraging blockchain to bridge the digital divide: Policy implications. *Government Information Quarterly*, 41(1), 101–115.

Jayavadivel, R., Arunachalam, M., Nagarajan, G., Shankar, B. P., Viji, C., Rajkumar, N., & Senthilkumar, K. R. (2024). Historical Overview of AI Adoption in Libraries. In *AI-Assisted Library Reconstruction* (pp. 267–289). IGI Global. DOI: 10.4018/979-8-3693-2782-1.ch015

Johnson, D., & Kim, J. (2023). Blockchain-based peer review: Enhancing transparency and trust. *Learned Publishing*, 36(1), 34–46.

Kim, Y., & Lee, S. (2023). Decentralized finance: The role of blockchain technology. *Journal of Financial Innovation*, 9(3), 45–63.

Kumar, N., Antoniraj, S., Jayanthi, S., Mirdula, S., Selvaraj, S., Rajkumar, N., & Senthilkumar, K. R. (2024). Educational Technology and Libraries Supporting Online Learning. In *AI-Assisted Library Reconstruction* (pp. 209–237). IGI Global. DOI: 10.4018/979-8-3693-2782-1.ch012

Lalitha, B., Ramalakshmi, K., Gunasekaran, H., Murugesan, P., Saminasri, P., & Rajkumar, N. (2024). Anticipating AI Impact on Library Services: Future Opportunities and Evolutionary Prospects. In *Improving Library Systems with AI: Applications, Approaches, and Bibliometric Insights* (pp. 195–213). IGI Global.

Lee, J., & Kim, H. (2024). Enhancing data privacy with decentralized access control. *Information Systems Research*, 35(1), 112–128.

Li, J., & Yang, L. (2023). Blockchain in education: Decentralizing access to educational resources. *Journal of Educational Technology & Society*, 26(2), 98–111.

Liu, C., & Wong, S. (2023). Blockchain for scholarly publishing: A new paradigm for open access. *Scientometrics*, 127(4), 1137–1150.

Liu, Y., & Zhang, X. (2024). Enhancing privacy in decentralized systems using blockchain. *IEEE Transactions on Information Forensics and Security*, 19(1), 78–91.

Lopez, M., & Anderson, K. (2023). Digital inclusion through blockchain: Case studies and future directions. *Journal of Community Informatics*, 19(2), 210–225.

Martinez, M., & Sanchez, R. (2024). Open access and blockchain: Innovations in scholarly communication. *Journal of Scholarly Publishing*, 55(2), 195–212.

Miller, R., & Davis, P. (2023). Blockchain and decentralization: Current trends and future directions. *Journal of Blockchain Research*, 7(2), 202–220.

Mohanraj, A., Viji, C., Varadarajan, M. N., Kalpana, C., Shankar, B., Jayavadivel, R., Rajkumar, N., & Jagajeevan, R. (2024). Privacy and Security in Digital Libraries. In *AI-Assisted Library Reconstruction* (pp. 104–125). IGI Global. DOI: 10.4018/979-8-3693-2782-1.ch006

Nachiappan, B. (2024a). Emerging and innovative AI technologies for resource management. In *Improving Library Systems with AI: Applications, Approaches, and Bibliometric Insights* (pp. 115–133). IGI Global. DOI: 10.4018/979-8-3693-5593-0.ch009

Nachiappan, B. (2024b). E-resources content recommendation system using AI. In *Improving Library Systems with AI: Applications, Approaches, and Bibliometric Insights* (pp. 155–177). IGI Global. DOI: 10.4018/979-8-3693-5593-0.ch011

Nadeem, M., & Hussain, F. (2023). Utilizing blockchain to address the digital divide: A case study in rural education. *Information Technology for Development*, 29(1), 88–105.

Nguyen, T., & Tran, P. (2024). Decentralized information systems for smart cities. *Journal of Urban Technology*, 31(1), 72–89.

Patel, K., & Roy, S. (2023). Blockchain and the digital divide: Opportunities for inclusive growth. *Journal of Information Policy*, 13, 99–118.

Rajkumar, N., Tabassum, H., Muthulingam, S., Mohanraj, A., Viji, C., Kumar, N., & Senthilkumar, K. R. (2024). Anticipated requirements and expectations in the digital library. In *AI-Assisted Library Reconstruction* (pp. 1–20). IGI Global. DOI: 10.4018/979-8-3693-2782-1.ch001

Rajkumar, N., Viji, C., Mohanraj, A., Senthilkumar, K. R., Jagajeevan, R., & Kovil-pillai, J. A. (2024). Ethical Considerations of AI Implementation in the Library Era. In *Improving Library Systems with AI: Applications, Approaches, and Bibliometric Insights* (pp. 85–106). IGI Global. DOI: 10.4018/979-8-3693-5593-0.ch007

Roberts, A., & Williams, S. (2024). Blockchain for research data management: Decentralized solutions. *Data Science Journal*, 22(1), 45–59.

Singh, N., & Joshi, A. (2024). Blockchain technology for public welfare: Reducing the digital divide. *Government Information Quarterly*, 41(2), 102–119.

Smith, A., & Zhao, L. (2023). Decentralized access to information: Challenges and opportunities. *Journal of Information Science*, 49(3), 279–294.

Thomas, G., & Harris, J. (2023). Decentralized learning management systems using blockchain. *Computers & Education*, 183, 104497.

Varadarajan, M. N. (2024). Educational program for AI literacy. In *Improving Library Systems with AI: Applications, Approaches, and Bibliometric Insights* (pp. 134–154). IGI Global. DOI: 10.4018/979-8-3693-5593-0.ch010

Varadarajan, M. N., Viji, C., Rajkumar, N., & Mohanraj, A. (2024). Integration of AI and IoT for smart home automation. *SSRG International Journal of Electronics and Communication Engineering*, 11(5), 37–43. DOI: 10.14445/23488549/IJECE-V11I5P104

Viji, C., Najmusher, H., Rajkumar, N., Mohanraj, A., Nachiappan, B., Neelakandan, C., & Jagajeevan, R. (2024). Intelligent Library Management Using Radio Frequency Identification. In *AI-Assisted Library Reconstruction* (pp. 126–143). IGI Global. DOI: 10.4018/979-8-3693-2782-1.ch007

Wang, X., & Chen, Y. (2024). Blockchain for academic credentialing: Enhancing trust and accessibility. *Educational Technology Research and Development*, 72(1), 23–41.

White, R., & Singh, M. (2024). The impact of blockchain on decentralized applications. *IEEE Transactions on Systems, Man, and Cybernetics. Systems*, 54(1), 56–68.

Zhang, L., & Xu, M. (2023). Blockchain and privacy-preserving mechanisms: A systematic review. *ACM Computing Surveys*, 56(3), 45–68.

Zhang, Y., & Wang, X. (2023). Decentralized data management: A blockchain-based approach. *Journal of Information Technology*, 38(2), 145–159.

Zhao, X., & Chen, Q. (2024). Blockchain-enabled decentralized platforms: Applications and challenges. *IEEE Internet of Things Journal*, 11(2), 175–188.

Chapter 10
Harnessing Blockchain Technology for the Evolution of Libraries:
Prospective Trends and Innovations in Information Resources Management

R. Visnudharshana
Sri Krishna Arts and Science College, India

Henry S. Kishore
https://orcid.org/0000-0002-5749-8167
Sri Krishna Arts and Science College, India

ABSTRACT

Blockchain technology can revolutionize library systems by addressing data integrity, user privacy, and digital rights management with its decentralization, transparency, and security. This study explores integrating smart contracts for efficient operations, decentralized digital archives, and enhanced metadata cataloging. It examines blockchain's interoperability with AI and IoT, predicting significant advancements in library services. Through case studies and a strategic adoption framework, the research offers valuable insights and best practices for library professionals. Findings indicate blockchain can address inefficiencies and security issues, creating resilient, innovative libraries. Practical implications include a roadmap for seamless blockchain integration, ensuring secure, efficient information ecosystems. This pioneering study highlights blockchain's potential to modernize library services and synergize with emerging technologies, keeping libraries at the forefront of digital advancements.

DOI: 10.4018/979-8-3693-7783-3.ch010

INTRODUCTION

The advent of blockchain technology signifies a pivotal advancement in the realm of digital systems, marking a transformative era in how data is managed, stored, and secured. Blockchain, fundamentally a decentralized and immutable ledger, offers unprecedented potential to revolutionize various sectors, including library management. This research delves into the multifaceted applications of blockchain within the context of library management, highlighting its potential to address prevailing inefficiencies, enhance security protocols, and foster innovation in information resources management (Opele, J. K. 2023). Libraries, as custodians of vast repositories of knowledge, face significant challenges in maintaining data integrity, ensuring user privacy, and managing digital rights. Traditional centralized systems are often susceptible to single points of failure, data breaches, and administrative bottlenecks. Blockchain technology, with its core attributes of decentralization, transparency, and cryptographic security, presents robust solutions to these issues. By distributing data across multiple nodes, blockchain enhances the resilience and reliability of library systems, mitigating risks associated with centralized control. One of the primary objectives of this research is to explore the integration of smart contracts in library operations. Smart contracts, which are self-executing agreements with terms encoded directly into code, can automate various processes such as book lending, resource sharing, and fee collection. This automation not only reduces administrative overhead but also ensures greater accuracy and efficiency (Safdar, M., Qutab, S., Ullah, F. S., Siddique, N., & Khan, M. A. 2023).

Furthermore, the research examines the potential for creating decentralized digital archives using blockchain. Such archives would be tamper-proof, ensuring the authenticity and integrity of digital records. This is particularly crucial for preserving rare manuscripts, research data, and historical documents, which require stringent measures to prevent alteration or loss. The interoperability of blockchain with emerging technologies such as artificial intelligence (AI) and the Internet of Things (IoT) is another focal point of this study. AI can analyse blockchain data to provide insights into user behaviour, optimize resource allocation, and enhance personalized services. IoT devices can interact with blockchain to track physical assets within libraries, improving inventory management and user experience. Through comprehensive analysis of successful case studies and the development of a strategic framework for blockchain adoption, this research aims to provide actionable insights and best practices for library professionals. Ultimately, by leveraging blockchain, libraries can transition into future-ready institutions, ensuring resilient, secure, and innovative information ecosystems for the digital age (Nijaguna, M., & Shantaram, P).

THEORETICAL FRAMEWORK

Figure 1. Theoretical framework

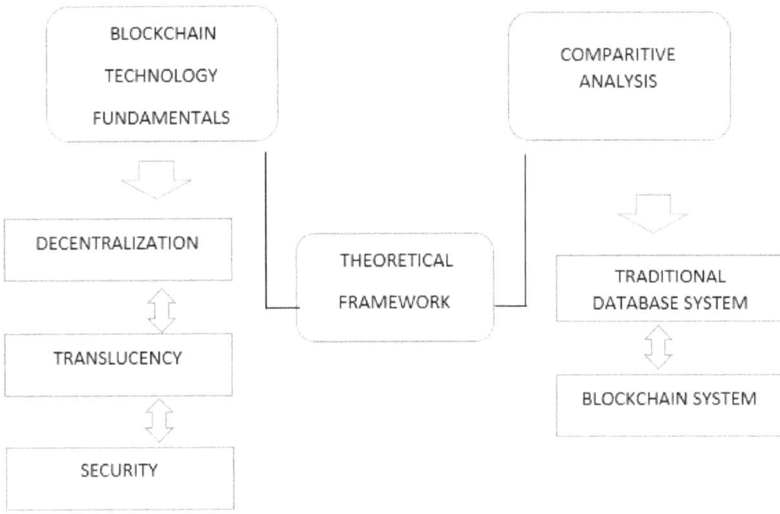

Blockchain Technology Fundamentals - Blockchain technology, at its core, functions as a decentralized and distributed tally that ensures the secure and inflexible recording of deals. This paradigm shift from traditional centralized databases to a decentralized model is sustained by several crucial features that render blockchain uniquely profitable for colourful operations, including library operation (Tanwar, S., Ribadiya, D., Bhattacharya, P., Nair, A. R., Kumar, N., & Jo, M. 2023).

Decentralization

Decentralization is a foundation of blockchain technology, effectively barring the need for a central authority to oversee and validate deals. This is achieved by distributing the tally across a network of bumps, each of which maintains a dupe of the entire blockchain. In library operation, decentralization can help the monopolization of data control, thereby fostering a more popular and flexible information ecosystem.

Translucency

Blockchain's translucency ensures that all deals are visible to actors within the network. This visibility is eased through a public tally where every sale is recorded and can be checked by any party (Wijesekara, P. A. D. S. N., & Gunawardena, S. 2023). For libraries, this translucency can enhance trust and responsibility, enabling stakeholders to corroborate the provenance and integrity of digital coffers.

Security

Security in blockchain is primarily achieved through cryptographic mincing, a process that transforms input data into a fixed- size alphanumeric string, which acts as a unique identifier for the data. Each block in the blockchain contains a hash of the former block, creating an interlinked chain that's inflexible and tamper-apparent. In the environment of libraries, cryptographic security can guard digital means against unauthorized variations and cyber pitfalls, icing the integrity and authenticity of information.

Comparative Analysis: Traditional Database Systems

Traditional databases operate on a centralized control model, where a single authority manages the data and its access. This centralization poses several pitfalls, including vulnerability to single points of failure, where a breach or failure in the central authority can compromise the entire system. Also, centralized databases frequently face challenges related to data integrity, stoner sequestration, and executive backups.

Blockchain Systems

In stark discrepancy, blockchain's decentralized nature mitigates these vulnerabilities by distributing data across multiple bumps (Kant, N. 2021). Each knot in the blockchain network participates in sale verification and agreement processes, icing that no single reality can unilaterally alter the tally. This distribution not only enhances the system's security but also its adaptability, as the failure or concession of one knot doesn't affect the overall network. likewise, blockchain's agreement mechanisms, similar as Proof of Work(PoW) or evidence of Stake(PoS), insure the integrity of deals without the need for a central authority. These mechanisms validate and confirm deals through a distributed network of bumps, furnishing a robust defense against fraudulent conditioning and double- spending. In summary, the relinquishment of blockchain technology in library operation can address the essential limitations of traditional database systems by using its decentralized armature, transparent operations, and cryptographic security measures. This theoretical frame lays the foundation for exploring innovative operations and unborn trends in library information coffers operation, situating libraries at the van of technological advancement in the digital age.

CURRENT STATE OF LIBRARY TECHNOLOGY

Under Historical Evolution, Libraries have evolved significantly from traditional physical cataloging systems to sophisticated digital databases. This transition has been marked by the adoption of technologies such as Online Public Access Catalogues (OPACs) and Integrated Library Systems (ILS), which streamline cataloging and resource management (Vijayalatha, C. (2023, May).

As a Digital Transformation Achievements, Modern libraries have embraced digital lending, e-resources, and automated workflows, leveraging technologies such as RFID for inventory management and cloud computing for scalable storage solutions. Despite these advancements, libraries continue to grapple with challenges related to data integrity, digital rights management (DRM), and ensuring user privacy in an increasingly digital landscape.

BLOCKCHAIN APPLICATIONS IN LIBRARIES

Smart Contracts for Efficient Operations

Smart contracts, which are self-executing contracts with the terms of the agreement directly written into code, hold substantial promise for library management. In libraries, smart contracts can automate and streamline numerous processes, such as book lending, resource sharing, and overdue fee collection (Bidry, M., Ouaguid, A., & Hanine, M. 2023). By embedding lending terms and conditions into smart contracts, libraries can ensure that books are automatically returned or renewed based on predefined criteria, thereby reducing the need for manual intervention. This automation not only minimizes administrative overhead but also enhances operational efficiency and accuracy, freeing library staff to focus on more strategic tasks.

Decentralized Digital Archives

Blockchain technology can establish tamper-proof, decentralized digital archives, crucial for maintaining the authenticity and integrity of valuable digital records. By distributing archival data across a network of nodes, blockchain ensures that records, including rare manuscripts, research data, and historical documents, cannot be altered or deleted without consensus from the network (Thamrin, T., Arifin, Y., & Hendric, S. W. H. L. 2024, February). This decentralization protects against data corruption, unauthorized modifications, and potential loss due to central server failures. The immutable nature of blockchain further guarantees that the provenance and historical integrity of these records are preserved indefinitely.

Enhanced Metadata Cataloging

Blockchain's ability to provide a decentralized and immutable record of cataloging data can significantly streamline metadata management in libraries. By utilizing blockchain, libraries can create a single, authoritative source of metadata that is transparent and resistant to tampering. This decentralized approach facilitates more accurate and efficient resource discovery, as metadata updates and corrections can be reliably tracked and verified. Moreover, the use of blockchain for metadata management can enhance interoperability among different library systems, allowing for seamless integration and sharing of cataloging information across institutional boundaries (Qingyi, Y., Liangmin, W., Senshan, P., Yifan, Z., & Jiayi, L. (2024).

By incorporating these blockchain applications, libraries can enhance their operational efficiency, preserve the integrity of their digital archives, and improve the accuracy and reliability of metadata management, positioning themselves as forward-thinking institutions in the digital age.

INTEROPERABILITY WITH EMERGING TECHNOLOGIES

Artificial Intelligence Integration

Integrating Artificial Intelligence (AI) with blockchain technology in libraries can yield profound enhancements in user services and operational efficiency. AI can analyze the vast amount of data stored on the blockchain to derive actionable insights into user behavior and preferences. For instance, machine learning algorithms can scrutinize borrowing patterns, enabling libraries to predict which books and resources are likely to be in high demand. This predictive capability allows for optimized resource allocation, ensuring that popular items are readily available.

Additionally, AI can facilitate personalized services by recommending books and resources tailored to individual user profiles, thereby enriching the user experience.

Internet of Things Integration

The convergence of blockchain and the Internet of Things (IoT) presents transformative opportunities for asset management within libraries. IoT devices, such as RFID tags and sensors, can be used to track the physical location and status of books, equipment, and other assets in real-time. By recording this data on a blockchain, libraries can create a transparent and tamper-proof inventory management system. This integration not only reduces losses and misplacements but also streamlines the process of checking in and out resources, thus enhancing the overall user experience.

Predictive Analytics and User Services

The synergy between blockchain and predictive analytics can empower libraries to anticipate user needs and streamline service delivery. Predictive analytics utilizes statistical algorithms and machine learning techniques to analyze historical data and make informed predictions about future events (Swan, M. 2015). When combined with the immutable and transparent data recorded on a blockchain, predictive analytics can offer precise forecasts regarding user demand for specific resources, peak usage times, and potential operational bottlenecks. This foresight enables libraries to preemptively address user needs (Hoy, M. B. 2017), improve the efficiency of service delivery, and allocate resources more effectively. Moreover, the integration of blockchain with predictive analytics ensures that the data used for predictions is accurate, verifiable, and secure, further enhancing the reliability of these insights.

By leveraging the interoperability of blockchain with AI, IoT, and predictive analytics, libraries can significantly enhance their operational capabilities, provide superior user services, and establish themselves as technologically advanced institutions in the digital age.

FUTURE TRENDS AND INNOVATIONS

The continuous evolution of blockchain technology promises significant advancements that will enhance scalability, reduce transaction costs, and improve interoperability with other digital systems, thus fortifying the infrastructure of future-ready libraries. As blockchain matures, its application within library services will pivot towards a more user-centric approach, facilitating seamless access to resources and delivering personalized recommendations through sophisticated algorithms (Suman,

A. K., & Patel, M. 2021). This evolution will be underpinned by the robust data security that blockchain inherently provides, ensuring that user information and library records remain immutable and protected from unauthorized access. Furthermore, blockchain's potential to revolutionize digital rights management (DRM) stands as a cornerstone of innovation, offering a transparent and tamper-proof record of content ownership and usage. This immutable ledger can ensure that creators receive fair compensation, as every transaction and usage of digital content is securely recorded and verifiable. By leveraging these advancements, libraries can not only optimize their operational efficiency and service delivery but also position themselves at the forefront of technological innovation in the digital age 9 Joseph, K. 2019).

CASE STUDIES AND REAL-WORLD IMPLEMENTATIONS

Case studies of successful blockchain integrations in libraries, such as the San José State University Library's initiative for digital preservation, illuminate best practices and common challenges, underscoring the transformative potential of blockchain technology in the library sector. Analyzing various library systems that leverage blockchain reveals the technology's versatility and adaptability across diverse contexts and scales, from academic to public libraries. For instance, the British Library has experimented with blockchain to enhance the security of its archival processes, while the National Archives of the UK has explored blockchain for record-keeping and authentication. Similarly, the Berkeley Library has implemented blockchain to manage digital assets and improve transparency. The Biblioteca Nacional de España has adopted blockchain for the preservation and authentication of cultural heritage materials, and the Qatar National Library has utilized blockchain to secure its digital lending system (Quispe-Farfán, G. A. 2020). Lessons learned from these early adopters emphasize the critical importance of stakeholder engagement, iterative development approaches, and comprehensive training programs for library staff to ensure successful implementation and sustainable use of blockchain technology. These examples collectively demonstrate how blockchain can address key challenges such as data integrity, digital rights management, and user privacy, ultimately enhancing the resilience and efficiency of library operations (Smith, C., Coward, C., Hess, M. R., Hofman, D. L., Kim, B., & Norman, A. 2019).

STRATEGIC FRAMEWORK FOR BLOCKCHAIN ADOPTION

Figure 2. Strategic framework for blockchain adoption

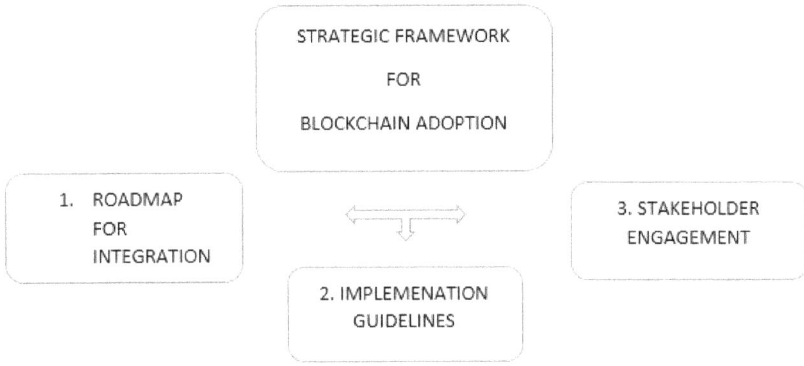

With reference to the above Venn diagram, a strategic framework for blockchain adoption in libraries necessitates a comprehensive roadmap that begins with a thorough assessment of current systems to identify areas where blockchain can offer the most significant benefits. This involves pinpointing suitable blockchain applications, such as digital rights management, metadata cataloging, and decentralized digital archives. The development of a phased implementation plan is critical, ensuring a systematic transition that minimizes disruption and maximizes operational efficiency. Implementation guidelines should address technical considerations, including the selection of appropriate blockchain platforms, data migration strategies to ensure seamless integration, and adherence to legal and regulatory standards to maintain compliance and protect user privacy. Engaging stakeholders—ranging from library staff and users to technology providers and regulatory bodies—is paramount to the framework's success (Jha, S. K. 2023). This engagement ensures that all parties are informed, trained, and invested in the transition, facilitating a smoother adoption process. Continuous dialogue with these stakeholders will help identify potential challenges early and allow for iterative development, fostering a culture of collaboration and innovation. By following this structured approach, libraries can effectively leverage blockchain technology to enhance their services, improve data integrity, and secure digital assets, positioning themselves as forward-thinking institutions in the digital age.

PRACTICAL IMPLICATIONS

Blockchain technology significantly enhances library operations by automating routine tasks, such as book lending and overdue fee collection, thereby improving data accuracy and reducing administrative burdens through the use of smart contracts. This automation allows library staff to focus on more strategic initiatives, increasing overall operational efficiency. Blockchain's immutable ledger provides a robust and secure foundation for managing sensitive information, ensuring user privacy, and protecting against data breaches and tampering (Vyas, S., Shukla, V. K., Gupta, S., & Prasad, A. (Eds.). 2022). By guaranteeing data integrity, blockchain helps maintain the authenticity and reliability of library records. Furthermore, integrating blockchain positions libraries to establish future-ready information ecosystems, capable of adapting to and incorporating emerging technologies. This integration supports the creation of resilient and innovative infrastructures that can meet evolving user demands, enhance service delivery, and ensure the sustainable management of digital assets. As a result, libraries can confidently navigate the complexities of the digital age, offering secure, efficient, and user-centric services (Abid, H. 2021).

CHALLENGES AND CONSIDERATIONS

Implementing blockchain in libraries involves addressing significant technical and operational challenges, including scalability issues, interoperability with existing digital systems, and high energy consumption associated with certain blockchain protocols. Libraries must also navigate complex legal and ethical implications, such as compliance with data protection regulations, safeguarding intellectual property rights, and ensuring the ethical use of user data to maintain trust and adhere to legal standards (Kushwaha, A. K., & Singh, A. P. 2021). Furthermore, the financial and resource-based considerations are critical; the costs of deploying and maintaining blockchain systems can be substantial, requiring thorough cost-benefit analysis and strategic resource allocation. Effective budgeting and resource management are essential to ensure that the benefits of blockchain integration outweigh the expenses, and that the implementation is sustainable in the long term. Addressing these multifaceted challenges requires a holistic approach, incorporating technical solutions, legal compliance strategies, and efficient resource management to fully leverage blockchain's potential in enhancing library operations.

CONCLUSION

This research highlights the transformative potential of blockchain technology in the evolution of library systems, providing comprehensive solutions to contemporary challenges while paving the way for future innovations. By integrating blockchain, libraries can significantly enhance operational efficiency through the automation of routine tasks and the implementation of smart contracts, reducing administrative burdens and optimizing resource management. Blockchain's inherent security features, such as its immutable ledger and cryptographic hashing, ensure robust data integrity and protection, safeguarding sensitive information and maintaining user privacy against unauthorized access and tampering. Moreover, the interoperability of blockchain with emerging technologies, such as artificial intelligence and the Internet of Things, facilitates the creation of dynamic, user-centric services. These integrations enable predictive analytics for anticipating user needs, automated asset tracking for improved inventory management, and personalized recommendations based on user behavior analysis. Additionally, blockchain's potential to revolutionize digital rights management provides a transparent, tamper-proof record of content ownership and usage, ensuring fair compensation for creators and protecting intellectual property rights.

Despite the technical and operational challenges, such as scalability, interoperability, and energy consumption, as well as legal and ethical considerations and financial constraints, the strategic framework proposed in this research offers a structured approach to blockchain adoption. Engaging stakeholders, adhering to legal standards, and managing resources efficiently are crucial for successful implementation. By addressing these challenges holistically, libraries can establish resilient and innovative information ecosystems that are well-equipped to handle future technological advancements and evolving user demands.

In conclusion, blockchain technology positions libraries at the forefront of the digital age, enabling them to enhance operational efficiency, ensure data security, and deliver superior user services. Through thoughtful adoption and integration, libraries can leverage blockchain to transition into future-ready institutions, securing their role as pivotal centers of knowledge and innovation in the digital era.

REFERENCES

Abid, H. (2021). Uses of blockchain technologies in library services. *Library Hi Tech News*, 38(8), 9–11. DOI: 10.1108/LHTN-08-2020-0079

Bidry, M., Ouaguid, A., & Hanine, M. (2023). Enhancing e-learning with blockchain: Characteristics, projects, and emerging trends. *Future Internet*, 15(9), 293. DOI: 10.3390/fi15090293

Dos Santos, D. R., de Carvalho Silva, T. E. B., & Sanfins, M. A. (2021). A Bibliometric Analysis of the Literature on Utility and Security Tokens. *American Scientific Research Journal for Engineering, Technology, and Sciences, 81*(1), 1-22.

Gul, S., & Bano, S. (2019). Smart libraries: An emerging and innovative technological habitat of the 21st century. *The Electronic Library*, 37(5), 764–783. DOI: 10.1108/EL-02-2019-0052

Head, S. R., Komori, H. K., LaMere, S. A., Whisenant, T., Van Nieuwerburgh, F., Salomon, D. R., & Ordoukhanian, P. (2014). Library construction for next-generation sequencing: Overviews and challenges. *BioTechniques*, 56(2), 61–77. DOI: 10.2144/000114133 PMID: 24502796

Hoy, M. B. (2017). An introduction to the blockchain and its implications for libraries and medicine. *Medical Reference Services Quarterly*, 36(3), 273–279. DOI: 10.1080/02763869.2017.1332261 PMID: 28714815

Jha, S. K. (2023). Application of blockchain technology in libraries and information centers services. *Library Hi Tech News*. Advance online publication. DOI: 10.1108/LHTN-02-2023-0020

Joseph, K. (2019). Catagora: Shared Library Cataloguing on the Ethereum Blockchain.

Kant, N. (2021). Blockchain: A strategic resource to attain and sustain competitive advantage. *International Journal of Innovation Science*, 13(4), 520–538. DOI: 10.1108/IJIS-07-2020-0094

Kushwaha, A. K., & Singh, A. P. (2021). Connecting blockchain technology with libraries: Opportunities and risks. *Journal of Indian Library Association*, 56(3), 12–19. https://journal.ilaindia.net/

Loke, S. W., Trujillo-Rasua, R., Jiang, F., & Xiang, Y. (2019). Applications of Distributed Ledger Technologies to the Internet of Things. *Survey (London, England)*.

Opele, J. K. (2023). The impact of emerging technologies on library education: A global perspective. *University of Ibadan Journal of Library and Information Science, 6*(2).

Papadaki, M., & Karamitsos, I. (2021). Blockchain technology in the Middle East and North Africa region. *Information Technology for Development*, 27(3), 617–634. DOI: 10.1080/02681102.2021.1882368

Qingyi, Y., Liangmin, W., Senshan, P., Yifan, Z., & Jiayi, L. (2024). AssessChain: A hybrid blockchain-based system for transparent and reliable online assessment. *Education and Information Technologies*, 1–25. DOI: 10.1007/s10639-024-12713-z

Quispe-Farfán, G. A. (2020). Public Libraries: Context, trends and models. *E-Ciencias de la Información*, 10(2), 155–173.

Safdar, M., Qutab, S., Ullah, F. S., Siddique, N., & Khan, M. A. (2023). A mapping review of literature on Blockchain usage by libraries: Challenges and opportunities. *Journal of Librarianship and Information Science*, 55(3), 848–858. DOI: 10.1177/09610006221090225

Smith, C., Coward, C., Hess, M. R., Hofman, D. L., Kim, B., & Norman, A. (2019). Block-chain reaction. *American Libraries*, 50(3/4), 26–33.

Suman, A. K., & Patel, M. (2021). An introduction to blockchain technology and its application in libraries. *Available atSSRN* 4019394. DOI: 10.2139/ssrn.4019394

Swan, M. (2015). *Blockchain: Blueprint for a new economy*. O'Reilly Media, Inc.

Tanwar, S., Ribadiya, D., Bhattacharya, P., Nair, A. R., Kumar, N., & Jo, M. (2023). Fusion of blockchain and IoT in scientific publishing: Taxonomy, tools, and future directions. *Future Generation Computer Systems*, 142, 248–275. DOI: 10.1016/j.future.2022.12.036

Tella, A., Amuda, H. O., & Ajani, Y. A. (2022). Relevance of blockchain technology and the management of libraries and archives in the 4IR. *Digital Library Perspectives*, 38(4), 460–475. DOI: 10.1108/DLP-08-2021-0065

Thamrin, T., Arifin, Y., & Hendric, S. W. H. L. (2024, February). Trends In Blockchain Applications: Current and Future Perspectives. In *2024 2nd International Conference on Software Engineering and Information Technology (ICoSEIT)* (pp. 187-191). IEEE.

Vijayalatha, C. (2023, May). Enhanced and Changing Role of Library and Information Professionals in Digital Era. In *Proceedings of National Conference on Exploring the Past, Present, and Future of Library and Information Science* (p. 130).

Vyas, S., Shukla, V. K., Gupta, S., & Prasad, A. (Eds.). (2022). *Blockchain technology: exploring opportunities, challenges, and applications*. DOI: 10.1201/9781003138082

Wijesekara, P. A. D. S. N., & Gunawardena, S. (2023). A Review of blockchain technology in knowledge-defined networking, its application, benefits, and challenges. *Network (Bristol, England)*, 3(3), 343–421.

Yuan, X., & Zhou, S. (2022, August). Research on library intelligent service based on blockchain technology. In *International Conference on Computer Science and Education* (pp. 267-277). Singapore: Springer Nature Singapore.

Chapter 11
Integration of Blockchain Technology and AI in Interlibrary Loan and Resource Sharing

Krishha Y. S.
https://orcid.org/0009-0000-8124-5971
Sri Krishna Arts and Science College, India

N. Jayaswethaashree
https://orcid.org/0009-0008-8048-1081
Sri Krishna Arts and Science College, India

Meena Preethi B.
https://orcid.org/0009-0009-8275-4984
Sri Krishna Arts and Science College, India

Nazrin C. M.
https://orcid.org/0009-0002-7465-5037
Sri Krishna Arts and Science College, India

ABSTRACT

This chapter focuses on artificial intelligence and how it compares to the actual interlibrary loan (ILL) and resource sharing in libraries. Libraries have always been the core of information exchange and community involvement, changing the way manual methods of service serving have been practiced. Nevertheless, the internet age has speeded up the change in the way knowledge is obtained and shared, challenging library practices. The use of AI in libraries, therefore, is a way that the libraries can use to simplify the ILL procedure, more reliably predict users' demands

DOI: 10.4018/979-8-3693-7783-3.ch011

and even enhance experiences through utilizing automated systems. AI's support to improve decision-making goes hand in hand with machine learning, natural language processing, predictive analytics, and automation for the library to benefit from productivity and accessibility in the sharing of resources, thus setting the stage for more adaptive and cutting-edge solutions to emerge in the current digital epoch.

INTRODUCTION

Libraries have always been an important part of communities. They have existed to serve each and every demographic making information accessible, preserved, and encouraged a love for learning in clients for centuries. But the digital revolution has brought many changes and libraries are finding it hard keeping up with new client demands, advancements in technology and societal changes.

There has been a huge shift in our ability to access, distribute and consume information after the age of digitalisation. With this change representation for libraries can now reach further audiences than their physical locations through services provided within the ether. Information is easier to find as well through the vast amounts of digital research tools at one's disposal on the net today – but this raises concerns on whether traditional library collections and services will still be relevant moving forward due to quick technological advancement

In this changing environment, a growing number of libraries are exploring how AI can support and enhance library services and operations. Interlibrary loan (ILL) and resource sharing are increasingly turning to AI applications in order to meet the expanding needs of library users, enabling libraries to borrow materials from other libraries as well as offer wider resources for their patrons.

AI has transformational potential in interlibrary loan and resource-sharing services by taking time out of the process equations, improving user experiences and reshaping limitations. Using Artificial Intelligence, libraries can obtain recordings or obtain a book from another library retailer much faster. AI can help with identifying demand at an earlier stage, deciding what items will be automatically sent without a request having been made or better use of statistics to determine if there is likely a high/demand upon receiving an item.

In addition, AI can lead to more efficient communications and collaborations among libraries that result in a greater ability to work together to meet the needs of their patrons. For instance, AI platforms are now being developed which can match requests with available resources in real-time so materials are quickly and precisely delivered to requestors. Moreover, AI allows for new types and amounts of data on the use and trends related to library materials making it possible for libraries to make data-driven collection decisions as well as strategic resource sharing alliances.

EVOLUTION OF INTERLIBRARY LOAN (ILL) AND RESOURCE SHARING

Libraries have functioned as important gateways for information dissemination and community connection for quite some time, representing vital hubs of education, research, and community betterment. Since ancient eras libraries have always been vital to the preservation and provision of knowledge, they have also tailored to serve a variety of populations and have worked to inspire a love for learning in their patrons.The increasing digital trend over the past three decades has necessitated a significant transformation for libraries, focusing on their emerging user base and the development of technologies.

The transformation has changed how information is used, created, and shared, hurting and helping libraries. Information is more widely available in the digital age than ever before due to the rapid increase in digital resources and platforms, providing unparalleled opportunities to reach new audiences and provide services beyond the physical limits of their walls. On the other hand, the rapid pace of technological change has raised questions about the relevance and future of traditional library services and collections.

In this evolving environment, the landscape of interlibrary loan (ILL) and resource sharing has seen substantial developments. Interlibrary loan, the practice by which libraries borrow and lend materials to one another to fulfill patron requests, has been a vital service for over a century. Originally a manual and labor-intensive practice, it involved much work on the part of library staff to manage requests, locate materials, and facilitate exchanges between libraries. The early years of interlibrary loan involved written correspondence or telephone calls between libraries, with an exchange of physical mail being the primary method of delivery for items requested. The preparation wasn't fast or easy; waiting times for donors were often lengthy. Nevertheless, and even in its early days, interlibrary loan proved itself a great example of cooperation and resource sharing among libraries which considerably broadened the range of materials available for users.

The integration of computer technology into interlibrary lending in the latter part of the 20th century was a significant milestone. Automated systems like OCLC's WorldCat and the MARC (Machine-Readable Cataloging) standard development greatly changed collection management within a library setting while fostering sharing these resources.These provided means through which libraries could become more organized in addition to facilitating their operation towards this effect thereby cutting down time spent on filling interloan requests as well as labor intensity.

Digital resources together with the internet have also played important roles towards shaping ILl & RS during its evolutionary process since the 1990s up to 2000s. E-journals, online databases and digital repositories made it possible for libraries to share a wider range of materials among themselves than before this time. Electronic delivery systems for documents acted as a quick way through which one library could send another such items rather than waiting until they are physically transported over there thus allowing end-users get what they wanted in the shortest time possible without much hassle on their part

Integrating artificial intelligence (AI) in library management has appreciably converted how libraries function, supplying advanced performance, more advantageous user experiences, and strong facts management. This literature evaluation synthesizes key insights from recent scholarly works specializing in diverse components of AI implementation in libraries. Viji et al. (Viji et al., 2024) discovered the application of the Radio Frequency identity (RFID) era in library management. RFID structures streamline inventory control, enhance safety, and facilitate self-service, decreasing the workload on the library body of workers. The bankruptcy emphasizes the performance and accuracy of RFID in tracking and dealing with library assets, highlighting its capacity to revolutionize conventional library operations. Kumar et al. (Kumar et al., 2024) explain the synergy among academic technology and libraries in assisting online studying. They argue that libraries, empowered through AI, can offer personalized getting-to-know experiences through adaptive studying structures and shrewd content material recommendations. The chapter also delves into libraries' position in bridging the digital divide, ensuring equitable access to instructional sources. Mohanraj et al. (Mohanraj et al., 2024) deal with the crucial issues of privacy and protection in virtual libraries. As libraries undertake AI and virtual technologies, safeguarding personal data becomes paramount. The authors have a look at various protection protocols and privacy measures that libraries can enforce to protect sensitive facts whilst keeping consumers agree with them. Rajkumar et al. (Rajkumar, Tabassum, et al., 2024) outline the evolving necessities and expectations of virtual libraries in the AI generation. The bankruptcy highlights the need for robust infrastructure, skilled employees, and non-stop innovation to satisfy the dynamic needs of library users. It additionally discusses the significance of consumer-centric layouts in growing AI-pushed library structures. Jayavadivel et al. (Jayavadivel et al., 2024) offer a historic angle on AI adoption in libraries. They trace the evolution of AI technologies in library control, from early automation systems to sophisticated AI-driven answers. The chapter gives valuable insights into the demanding situations and milestones encountered for the duration of this transformative adventure. Rajkumar et al. (Rajkumar, Viji, et al., 2024) delve into the moral implications of AI in libraries. They explore issues inclusive of algorithmic bias, transparency, and the ethical use of personal facts. The authors argue for the development of moral suggestions and frameworks to ensure responsible AI implementation in library services.

Lalitha et al. (Lalitha et al., 2024) speak about the future effect of AI on library services. They spotlight rising developments and capability opportunities for AI to decorate library functions, which includes predictive analytics for series improvement and AI-powered reference offerings. The bankruptcy additionally speculates on the evolutionary prospects of libraries in an AI-pushed international. Nachiappan (Nachiappan, 2024b) offers an AI-primarily based e-assets content material advice gadget. The machine leverages system-getting-to-know algorithms to analyze personal choices and endorse relevant digital resources. This personalized approach improves consumer engagement and pleasure through presenting tailored content pointers. Nachiappan (Nachiappan, 2024a) explores cutting-edge AI technologies for aid management in libraries. Bankruptcy discusses advancements such as herbal language processing (NLP), machine getting to know, and AI-pushed records analytics. These technologies beautify resource discovery, optimize library operations, and provide precious insights for choice-making. Varadarajan (Varadarajan, 2024) emphasizes the significance of AI literacy in libraries. The chapter advocates for educational packages that equip library teams of workers and users with the necessary capabilities to navigate and leverage AI technology. Promoting AI literacy guarantees that libraries can harness the benefits of AI even as mitigating related risks. The reviewed chapters together highlight the transformative capacity of AI in library management. From enhancing operational performance and protection to enhancing consumer reviews and ethical considerations, AI gives several possibilities for libraries to evolve and thrive in the virtual age. Future research should continue to explore innovative AI packages and address the challenges related to their implementation to make certain sustainable and consumer-centric library offerings.

New technologies have continued to streamline interlibrary loan services in recent years. For instance, artificial intelligence and machine learning improve the efficiency of ILL by predicting demands from huge data sets, optimizing resource allocation or automating different parts of the process.These technologies enable libraries respond faster to requests, match users more accurately with needed materials while also creating an environment that is seamless for all concerned. Furthermore, they foster greater collaboration among them when it comes to sharing resources because ai systems can instantly find available matches for any given request thereby ensuring timely delivery thereof Further,AI-powered systems instantaneously match requests with available resources to ensure that materials are promptly and accurately provided to users. Additionally, tools for analyzing big data provide insights into usage trends and patterns thus guiding decision making about collection development and sharing policies based on actual needs rather than mere guesswork.

Role of DELNET in ILL

DELNET, or the Developing Library Network, is a significant resource-sharing library network in India that links around 8600 institutions—including universities, colleges, R&D organizations, hospitals, and more—across 28 States, 6 Union Territories, and a few other nations. The goal of DELNET is to modernize and network libraries. On June 30, 1992, it became a Society and was registered. It is situated in New Delhi, on the campus of Jawaharlal Nehru University. DELNET's primary motto, "Networking Libraries, Sharing and Spreading Knowledge," has guided its activity for the past thirty plus years.On October 30, 2020, the esteemed IIPA Award for Excellence in Public Services was presented to DELNET, with the honorable former vice president of India, Shri M. Venkaiah Naidu, in attendance.

The primary goals of DELNET are to support resource sharing among Member Libraries by gathering, organizing, and sharing information as well as providing users with networked library services; conducting information science and technology research; providing Member Libraries with technical assistance; coordinating efforts for the development of appropriate collections; and facilitating and promoting Inter Library Loan and document delivery, among other activities. The Knowledge Gainer Portal, the Discovery Portal, and the Vision Portal are all products of DELNET. The portals offer advanced features for finding new information.

Role of British Council in ILL

The UK's international organisation for educational opportunities and cultural relations is the British Council. It creates worldwide opportunities and trust and manages three libraries and cultural centres in India, which provide arts, education, and English projects. Serving over 100,000 members, the organisation is responsible for interlibrary loan services for working resource sharing between libraries in different countries, and also for prestigious scholarships. The scholarships offered by the British Council include GREAT scholarships, Commonwealth Scholarships and Fellowships, Charles Wallace India Trust scholarships, and Hornby.

Role of British Council in ILL

The American Library Association (ALA) offers leadership for the development, promotion, and improvement of library and information services and the profession of librarianship to help learning and ensure access to information for all. The ALA is particularly involved in interlibrary loan services, supporting resource sharing among libraries and increasing access to information and resources. The American Library Association recommends that libraries utilize interlibrary loan services to make requests for materials that are held by other libraries. As a result, libraries easily capture materials that are not held in their own collections and as a result enhance library collections for users. For ILL requests processed by the library, the ALA advocates for the adoption of best practices and technologies that utilize standard protocols. Allowing for different libraries to work together in this way, ILL helps eliminate the challenges that physical and other institutional obstacles create in users' ability to access the resources they need. ALA provides materials and training to help librarians run an efficient ILL operation, improving the quality of services for library patrons.

Potential Applications of Blockchain in Interlibrary Loan and Resource Sharing

1. Efficient Tracking of Transactions

- **Immutable Records**:All of the records about each borrow by the users have been kept. It shows when some borrowed, which two library borrowed to or from, when it is due and when it is back. It makes the tracking more usable, and DELNET loans such as are very specific.
- **Real-Time Updates**: As blockchain technology operates on a decentralized network, all participating libraries receive immediate updates to transaction records. This audibility allows all stakeholders to rely on the accuracy of the tracking information of their interlibrary loans. This openness results in quicker, more reliable information sharing across the DELNET network.
- **Detailed Logs**: Each transaction may contain a full set of metadata, such as the time and date of the transaction, the borrowing and lending libraries, the due date, and whether the material has been returned. This level of information provides the ability to trace and manage ILL transactions effectively and generates precise and easily accessible records for DELNET.

2. Smart Contracts for Automation

- **Automated Lending Processes**: Utilizing blockchain technology, it is possible to automate the loan process from check-out to check-in. For instance, when a patron requests an item, a smart contract could check for availability, process the loan, and update the inventory. If the libraries use DELNET, it could decrease the amount of manual work done by the library.
- **Dynamic Due Dates and Renewals**: By this method, due dates are determined by smart contracts, and renewals will be given automatically if the item is not being reserved by another patron. This flexibility of smart con-

tracts has potential to improve patron satisfaction and utilization rates across the DELNET network.

- **Automated Penalties and Fines**: Smart contracts possess the ability to impose fines on late returns. The terms of the fine are in the smart contract itself, making the process simple and fair across all transactions
- **Condition-Based Actions**:Depending on the stipulations, the return status may warrant certain actions automatically. If a return is made in poor condition, a smart contract could automatically inform the relevant parties and allow the return process to begin.

3. Enhanced Security and Data Integrity

- **Cryptographic Security**: Blockchain technology uses complex cryptographic processes to secure transactional information itself to avoid becoming vulnerable to unauthorized access or manipulation of the information, and in order to preserve the confidentiality and integrity of the highly sensitive transmission data, and thus, the DELNET libraries, without losing the trust of international users.
- **Decentralized Data Storage**: Through the use of a network of nodes to store data in a more distributed manner, blockchain technology effectively reduces single points of failure. This process of decentralization significantly improves the system's security against data breaches and cyber attacks, a pressing issue considering the scale of DELNET.
- **Access Control**: A sophisticated system of security controls can be put in place to limit access to certain collaborative defense networks. This access control is critical to protecting the integrity and privacy of the data within DELNET.

4. Cost Reduction

- **Reduction in Administrative Overhead**: The use of blockchain technology to automate the interlibrary loan process can significantly reduce the need for manual intervention and the costs associated, saving time and freeing up staff to conduct other work that would be perceived as more valuable to their library, an obvious benefit in light of limited library budgets.
- **Elimination of Intermediaries**: There are fewer intermediaries when blockchain technology is decentralized that do not require trusting third-party actors. The components of interlibrary loaning libraries can now talk directly to other libraries, making it more efficient. There are some cost benefits related to this, as there is no central intermediary, and therefore, associated costs.

- **Efficiency Gains**: The institution is saving money by processing transactions faster and with fewer errors. There will be a cost savings in the time spent correcting errors, since there will be fewer errors to correct. Also, they will save money in dispute resolution.

5. Improved Collaboration Among Libraries

- **Decentralized Network**: Blockchain provides a decentralized network where each library involved is on equal footing. The structure encourages collaboration, as well as equal participation, which will help increase the collective resource pool, something DELNET needs to support its mission to share resources.
- **Shared Catalogues**: Libraries and their catalogues can be shared on the blockchain for easy and fast access. Libraries and their up-to-date, shared catalogues provide additional visibility and access to resources, and support resource sharing within DELNET.
- **Consortium Management**: The application of blockchain offers an enforceable and provable framework for the management of library consortia by establishing a secure, transparent, immutable, and decentralized infrastructure for recording shared agreements, shared values, and usage statistics. Such transparency could potentially inspire trust and collaboration among the consortium members, thus advancing overall DELNET operations.

6. Enhanced User Experience

- **Unified User Interfaces**: The blockchain can support the development of unified user interfaces to create a seamless experience for patrons. Patrons can request items from multiple libraries without having to navigate different systems. This means that DELNET users will have a unified and user-friendly experience.
- **User Feedback and Ratings**: Blockchain has the potential to introduce features for user feedback and ratings. Patrons can rate their experience with borrowed materials. The ability for patrons to provide feedback and ratings could offer valuable information for libraries to make improvements in service quality.
- **Personalized Recommendations**: Based on the borrowing history and preferences recorded in the blockchain, libraries could provide patrons with personalized recommendations or suggestions based on use. This would increase engagement with patrons.

Implementation of Blockchain Technology in ILL

Figure 1. Implementation of Blockchain Technology in ILL

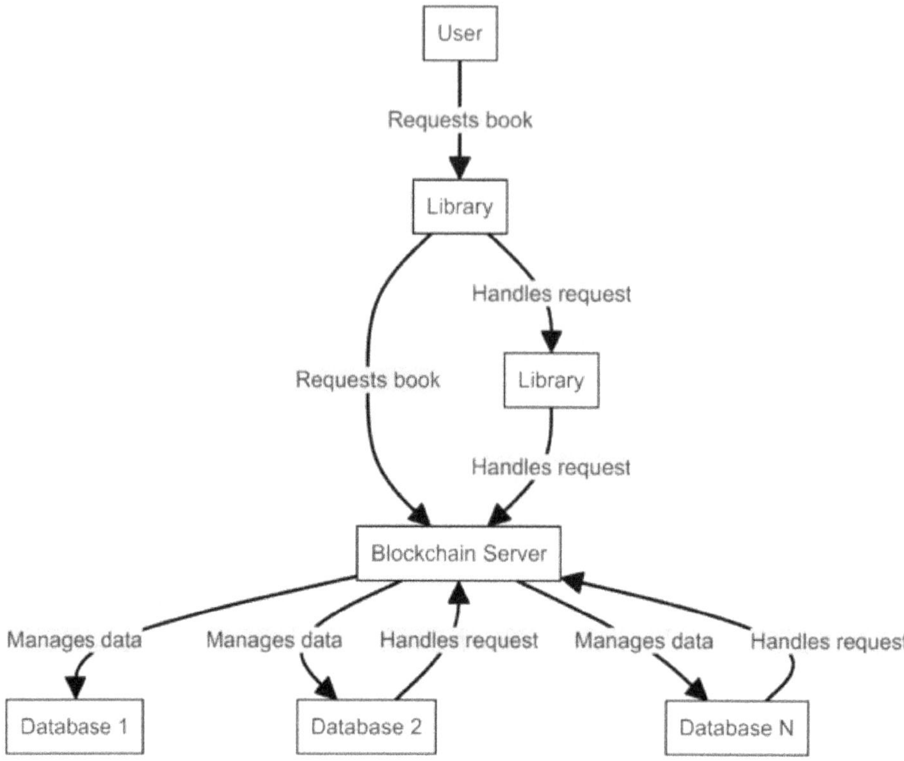

The use of blockchain technology can improve the efficiency, safety, and the availability of resources in libraries through interlibrary loan systems This decentralised, open, and protected means seems a lot more efficient for interlibrary loan management in light of blockchain integration.It is of many parts:

1. **Decentralized Database Management:** A singular blockchain server serves as a decentralized ledger to which all the libraries that take part in the system connect. The server keeps detailed databases of all the resources that the libraries have. Every update of the resources and every transaction is captured on the blockchain in an immutable manner so that data integrity and transparency is maintained.
2. **Automated Transactions Using Smart Contracts:**Smart contracts are like programs that bind parties by replacing middlemen with code. This code automatically enforces the rules when executing predetermined conditions. Thus,

they manage contract execution and payment automatically from loan periods to all other terms of lending agreements.

3. **Enhanced Security and Privacy:** The library is a secure place that respects the confidentiality of its users and ensures that encryption is employed correctly to protect the resources. Blockchain's decentralized character makes it impossible for an individual to have access to any information related to it without permission or to alter anything inside it.

Implementation Process

- Integrating Database

Making use of the blockchain network, libraries are able to integrate their catalog and resource databases. Such centralized yet decentralized approach enables users to search resources in connected libraries interconnectivity without any hitches.

- User Authentication and Access

A comprehensive catalog of resources that are available for borrowing can be accessed by users using secure digital identities which are kept in secure blockchain storage for identification purposes after logging in.

- Verification and request

The users initiate a request for resources through the blockchain interface. Smart contracts then verify the request, check the availability of the resources across all participating libraries, and trigger automatically an initiation of the process of borrowing.

- Automated Loan Management

Smart contracts automate loan management, making use of resource allocation, loan period management, overdue notifications, and return processes. The transactions are transparent, and through the blockchain, any modifications during the procedure can be monitored.

- Payment and Fee Management

Automatically capture the payment for the loaned resource through secure online transactions. In a case of failure of a payment, smart contracts can re-schedule the payment at the next billing time, exempting any disruption of service while re-pitching for the payment

- Server Maintenance Fee

A server maintenance fee is required to facilitate transaction management on the blockchain network, which is essential for its efficient and continuous operation. The purpose of the server maintenance fee is to help cover the costs of maintaining and running the blockchain servers. In addition, there is a processing fee that is paid out in order to maintain a secure, functioning blockchain server. This fee is determined by the amount of data in your transaction(s). The fee is tailored to improve or maintain the security of the blockchain network.

Benefits of Blockchain Integration

- **Efficiency:** With automation, administrative load reduces and hence resource management becomes easier.
- **Accessibility:** With the Internet, the user has access to an extremely wide range of materials not present in any local library collection.
- **Security:** Because of its decentralized nature and encryption, blockchain guarantees the privacy of data and integrity.
- **Cost-effectiveness:** This will arrive at reducing operational expenditure through automation and getting rid of intermediaries.

If anything, blockchain technology is applied in an interlibrary loan system to foreshadow a paradigm shift toward the execution of library services in a much more effectual, safer, and easily accessible way.. It would permit libraries to optimize the use of resources while bettering the user experience, tilting it toward a more inclusive digital future

Implementing Blockchain Technology in Interlibrary Loans Presents Several Challenges

Non-Return of Books: In case a user fails to return a borrowed book, the blockchain records get disturbed and complicates transaction history. For this, implement smart contracts so that it automatically triggers reminders and penalties in case of not returning and requires a deposit to be refunded upon the return of the book.

Damage or Loss of Books: In certain problem when processing cases of lost or damaged books lies in the fact that there needs to be a way for the blockchain ledger to record such an event. Our solution proposes to develop in the blockchain a system of recording and resolving lost or damaged books through predetermined compensate /enumerate procedures, also overseen by smart contracts.

Overdue Books: The advanced problem in blockchain systems is keeping track of overdue books, especially where fines and penalties are involved. One of the ways of solving this challenge would be by making smart contracts for the same. The smart contract is able to track that a fine was incurred because the book was returned late, and then it sends automatic reminders before the due date to incentivize the return of the book.

User Identification and Privacy: User identification and privacy are generally inverses, partly due to the fact that user authentication is normally achieved through active mechanisms that enable privacy. Again, decentralized digital identity management might proffer a channel through which users automatically authenticate themselves without leaking personal information. Another line of inquiry that could be pursued in pursuit of privacy is the trial application of encryption methods pivotal to sensitive data protection.

Dispute Resolution: In a blockchain environment, even resolving a dispute such as if a book was returned or returned in the exact condition it was loaned in presents many occasions for becoming much more complex. One potential recommendation is that a decentralized dispute resolution system be ingrained in the blockchain, whereby the arbitration panel made up of even fewer trusted library staff members or community volunteers, or any combination thereof, would serve as the dispute arbitration group.

Compliance with Lending Policies: It would very likely be difficult to ensure that transactions are compliant with the changes in library lending policies and contracts among various libraries. The licensing policies may be hard-coded into smart contracts, and this will automate the compliance with policies and, in the process, reset the smart contract itself, thus changing according to the modification occurring in the library lending policies.

Temporary Availability of Books: Unfortunately, it is pretty hard to change blockchain such that a book be considered temporarily unavailable or that the promise be made to another user. Implement real time inventory systems and then Blockchain with tokens representing the position of a Book's availability

Specialized Collection Handling: Some special collections or, rather, rare books, sometimes, may have different conditions of loan that will need to be dealt with. Design smart contracts for such special collections with certain loaning conditions, such as limited loaning times or use strictly within the library

Figure 2. Interlibrary Loan System With Blockchain Integration - Sequence Diagram

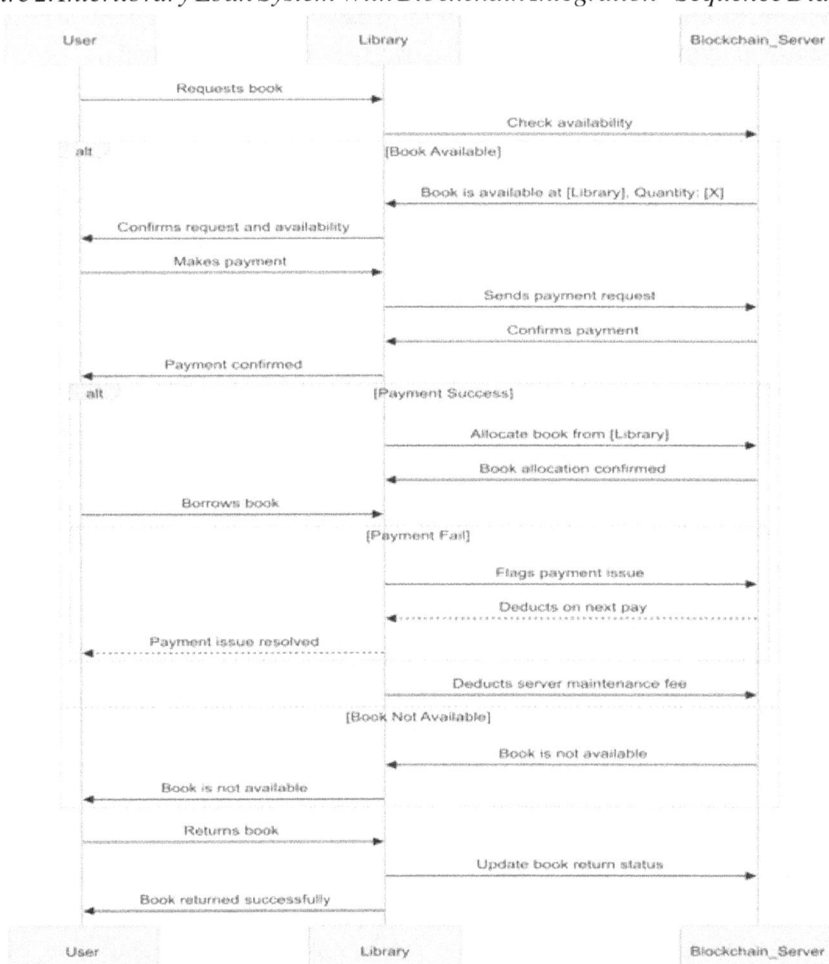

Introduction to AI in Libraries

Libraries, over all these years, have been viewed as keystones of knowledge dissemination and community engagement—very important centers for learning, research, and cultural enrichment. It is in this regard that libraries have played a central role in preserving and providing access to information for diverse populations in a manner that instills a love of learning within them for several hundred years. However, reshaping themselves in acquiescence with the changing user needs, technological development, and shifting trends in society, libraries are currently going through sea changes.

The digital revolution has changed the information landscape, challenging and opportunistic libraries in quite a few aspects relating to access, sharing, and consumption of information. First, it increased access to information in unprecedented ways through the proliferation of digital resources and online platforms that allowed libraries to reach newer audiences and deliver services beyond their physical walls. The latter has also raised concerns about the future of library services and collections in regard to fast-paced technological change.

In this changing environment, artificial intelligence has grown to act as a mighty tool for libraries in offering innovative solutions to users in order to enhance service delivery, streamline operations, and offer personalized experiences for the users. Artificial intelligence, a stream of computer science whose sole aims include developing systems that have the ability to perform tasks that man is capable of performing like learning, reasoning, and problem-solving, has been turning around activities at the working and interaction levels in libraries with their patrons.

Other large applications of AI in libraries are in the area of information retrieval and discovery. Conventionally, most cataloging and search systems work through keyword matching or Boolean logic, techniques that have grown Americocentric and sometimes unsatisfactory. In contrast, AI-driven systems comprehend the context and semantics of user queries with the processing of NLP and machine learning algorithms to provide more accurate results on search. These search facilities can formulate the information a patron needs easily and quickly, thereby enhancing their experience of using the library.

Resource management and collection development are other important areas in which AI is also being used to enable libraries. Using circulation pattern data, user preference data, and emerging trend data resulting from big data analysis, AI systems realize the creation of insight into what materials are in demand and which are little used by users. This information helps libraries make insightful data-based decisions regarding acquisitions, weeding, and resource allocation, thereby having collections relevant to and responsive to the community's needs.

Another way AI can make a big difference is in terms of personalization. Recommendation systems powered by AI can collect user behavior to propose books, articles, and other resources that fit into a person's tastes. It therefore increases users' satisfaction and boots users' engagement in the library's resources. Moreover, AI chatbots and virtual assistants are being fielded for real-time assistance of patrons with such general questions, walking them through various services available at a library, or providing recommendations based on queries supplied by the patrons.

Traditional ILL Systems vs. AI-Enhanced Systems

ILL frameworks have been central to libraries for a while. They have enabled libraries to share resources and provide access to materials that may not otherwise be part of any single institutional collection. Conventional ILL systems, however, have depended upon manual processes requiring huge amounts of paper, library staff coordination, and other bureaucratic measures to conduct the borrowing and lending of resources. Such systems, though effective in their own right, often involved long delays, human error, and limitations related to scale and efficiency.

In traditional ILL systems, this has always had a starting point: when a patron requests a resource not available in their home library. Library staff then undertake a manual search for the item within a network of partner libraries, contact the holding library, and make arrangements for the loan or copy to be sent. This process may run into several days or sometimes weeks, depending upon how many libraries are participating and how far apart they are from one another. Furthermore, human entry and tracking introduce the potential for errors at many steps along the way, making request fulfillment cumbersome.

AI-enhanced ILL systems turn to newer technologies to channel ciclo_rf, and in some cases, automate much of the interlibrary loan process. Machine learning algorithms, natural language processing, and data analytics bring improvements in speed, accuracy, and efficiency of resource sharing. AI, in a very short time, helps in identifying potential lending libraries, generates and sends requests automatically, and tracks the loan status in real-time. This reduces the manual workload on library staff and significantly shortens the time it takes to meet requests.

AI also allows for greater personalization of recommendations and easier methods for searching. Traditional ILL systems have always expanded on keyword-based searching, which can be so delimiting and sometimes is not powerful enough to return very many useful results. AI-driven search engines utilize natural language processing to understand context and semantics from a user's questions, returning more modern, meaningful search results. This, in turn, enables patrons to more easily find requested materials and has the added effect of greater satisfaction with the ILL service overall.

Overall, AI enhances the efficiency of ILL systems by mechanizing tasks that are repetitive and providing action-oriented insights to library staff. For example, AI can verify bibliographic information, match requests with potential lenders who best satisfy certain criteria, and even mechanically negotiate loan terms and conditions. It will let library staff focus on called-for, complex, value-added activities like building partnerships with other institutions, improving their collections, and other related tasks.

Traditional ILL systems have been serviceable to libraries for a long time; however, AI-enhanced systems demonstrate an extensive leap in speed, accuracy, and efficiency. AI can help in transforming interlibrary loan processes to become better at meeting today's library user needs, through the automation of routine tasks, offering personalized recommendations, and correctly applying data analytics. In this way, as libraries continue to grow in these advanced technologies, they shall be better positioned to offer more timely and more effective access to resources that speaks to the mission of knowledge dissemination and community engagement.

AI Techniques in Interlibrary Loan and Resource Sharing

AI techniques in interlibrary loan (ILL) and resource sharing leverage advanced technologies to enhance efficiency, accuracy, and user experience. These techniques include machine learning, natural language processing, predictive analytics, automation, and robotics. Each contributes uniquely to optimizing resource sharing, reducing delays, and improving service quality.

Machine Learning

Machine learning incorporates algorithms that allow a system to learn from data and support decisions concerning the same. As applied to ILL and resource sharing, ML can predict which libraries have requested assets and automate the matching process. For example, machine learning algorithms can be trained using huge historical data to highlight trends and predict future requests. It provides predictive capability to libraries to work out a more efficient scheme of collections management, where materials are available as and when required. Optimizing inventory management by analyzing circulation patterns also allows libraries to redeploy underused materials in order to better meet user needs, reducing wait times and enhancing user satisfaction.

It can also help in prioritizing requests with factors such as user profile, urgency, and historical borrowing behavior. By putting ML into resource-sharing networks, libraries can cooperate more effectively, sharing insights and trends that benefit the entire network.

Natural Language Processing

Natural Language Processing (NLP) is what gives a system the ability to understand human language, hence setting a clear path for processing text-based commands. In ILL systems, NLP aids in improving search through the interpretation of context and semantics of user queries, hence giving more accurate results that are relevant in terms of the search. This aids the user in getting the materials they want fast, hence improving their search experience.

It can also automate bibliographic data verification, increasing the chance that it is accurate and speeding up the completion of tasks. This automatization will enable citation checking and metadata extraction to proceed with a high degree of accuracy regarding record-keeping. Also, since NLP supports multilingual capabilities, the users can interact in their own language of choice, allowing access to the same for non-native speakers. Integrating sentiment analysis will help libraries understand what their users are satisfied with and what services should change to further improve their experience.

Predictive Analytics

Predictive analytics uses statistical models and machine learning techniques for the prediction of future events from historical data. In the domain of ILL and resource sharing, predictive analytics can project the demand of certain resources. This approach will allow libraries, through examination of the past trends of borrowing and other external factors like academic calendars, to know beforehand which items will be in the greatest demand so that libraries may best prepare for the same by optimization of resource allocation and reduction of wait time.

Predictive analytics also supports collection development by sensing emerging trends in research and academia. It can help libraries adjust acquisition and subscription accordingly to the evolving needs of users. Moreover, such predictive models may also help in managing the risk associated with estimating delays or disruptions to resource sharing so that libraries can put in contingency arrangements in advance.

Automation and Robotics

Automation and robotics involve systems and robots performing tasks repeatedly with precision and speed. In ILL systems, automating the generation of requests, tracking them, and relaying this information to other libraries is possible. Automated systems manage the entire lifecycle of an ILL request—from submission to fulfillment—with minimal intervention by human resources. This reduces administrative load on the staff and guarantees uniformity of operations and timely processing of the requests.

In this regard, robotics can make some useful contribution to the physical handling and transportation of materials. The next step, especially in larger libraries, includes automated sorting and retrieval systems that expedite the process of locating a wide variety of materials and distributing them, very much reducing human error and increasing the speed of service. In an additional sense, robotics systems can be used to deliver and sort books, too, further accelerating the process of fulfillment. Lastly, research into new methods of delivery by drones or autonomous vehicles would be very useful in remote or ill-served areas.

Enhanced User Experience

AI techniques ingrained within ILL and resource sharing systems make the entire process more efficient and effective. This amplifies the user experience, speed, and resources that are accurately offered to any access, thus enabling libraries to function more effectively. Some of the benefits offered to the users include more intuitive interfaces, quicker times for turnarounds, and a reliable availing of the scope of materials that increase users' satisfaction.

Improved interfaces, enhanced consultation, and seamless integration with digital resources all come together to deliver a full and satisfying patron experience. Viewed through this prism, libraries could have, using data analytics, a grip on user behavior in order to provide services more sensitively, facilitating still a more user-oriented approach.

Future Implications

As AI continues to further evolve in this sector, the integration into library services will only get more sophisticated, contributing to continuous improvement in interlibrary loan and resource sharing. These could be items such as advanced recommendation systems and more personalization of the user experience but also more extensive integration with other digital library services into a single holistic resource sharing ecosystem.

AI integration can realize intelligent systems capable of real-time learning and adaptation, hence improving decision-making within the library. Such leveraging of technologies propels the libraries to the forefront in access to information and, in so doing, ensures that libraries remain relevant to the changing needs of the diverse community being served. Further innovation will result from advancing Artificial Intelligence, where newer and more radical solutions transform library services and resource sharing to be a frontier.

Enhancing Efficiency With AI

Bringing improvement in effectiveness with artificial intelligence in interlibrary credit and resource sharing involves several advanced innovations to reduce forms, decrease manual workloads, and improve the general efficiency of library management. Joining AI into libraries lets one optimize different angles of asset sharing, leading to an increase in speed in delivery time and precision in asset allocation, and way better client experience.

Automated Ask Processing

A number of tasks in the handling of sick requests from lodging to delivery could be automated using AI. Manually, people expend much human effort in validating requests, locating materials, and communicating messages with other libraries in a SICK system. AI will bibliographically check, locate the best sources for requested material, and manage communications. This effectively reduces time and human effort that should have been spent by staff in a library, freeing them up for more challenging and value-added work.

Intelligent Asset Matching

These AI-driven platforms mine into large datasets to complete advanced, complex calculations that best synchronize the demands with the assets at hand. In this way, using chronicles of borrowing designs and current property information, these frameworks may without much of a stretch foresee which libraries are most likely to have asked materials. Coordination of such demands intelligently in this fashion ensures that they get to the best libraries, improving probabilities for fast and effective fulfillment.

Predictive Maintenance and Planning

Predictive analytics can be of great milestones to libraries in getting assistance from AI, managing demands effectively. Basically, an AI system is able to analyze past data, identify trends to make projections of future borrowing needs for adjustments in asset allocation. For example, if at certain periods there is a high demand for some books or resources—during examination periods or enquiries about the long-term loan of an item—libraries can plan ahead and make such materials available in advance. This would greatly minimize the waiting time and improve customer satisfaction.

Dynamic Asset Allocation

Real-time information and changing conditions instruct flexible resource distribution of AI. Traditional Sick systems nearly operate on fixed schedules with passive allocation policies, allowing inefficiencies to pop up as a result. AI can monitor the flow of requests and dynamically adjust resource allocation to ensure that materials are delivered where they need it most urgently. Desired objectives, like optimizing library resources use and reducing the time for request fulfillment, can be met with this flexibility.

Enhanced Client Experience

AI-driven frameworks can, therefore, push forward client involvement through more accurate and customized administrations. For example, AI chatbots can help clients find materials, request materials, answer frequently asked questions, and offer overhauls on the status of their interest. Chatbots are ready to work 24/7, promoting bolster outside of standard library hours. More so, AI drives customization in recommendations in view of client inclinations and past instincts, making it simpler for benefactors to find pertinent assets.

Improved Information Administration and Analysis

AI is in a position to enhance the manner in which such vast amounts of data produced by Sick systems are managed and analyzed. Machine learning and information analytics can help libraries learn deeper bits of knowledge about utilization designs, bottleneck identification, and uncovering openings for enhancement. This data-driven approach enables libraries to make informed decisions about asset allocation, benefit enhancement, and strategy planning that lead to more effective and efficient operations.

Scalability and Adaptability

Artificial intelligence frameworks are inherently adaptable and versatile, making them very appropriate for dealing with the ever-growing and changing demands of today's libraries. When the volume of interlibrary loan demands goes up, AI can scale to handle additional workload without a proportional increase in staff. Moreover, AI frameworks will be able to adapt to underused patterns and progressions, ensuring that libraries remain sharp in their development and continue to focus on the efficient achievement of their benefactors.

Case Studies and Practical Implementations

The integration of AI into library operations has been transformational, with just a few cases already registering its impact on collection management, resource allocation, customer experience enrichment, and record delivery. Such practical implementations show how AI is able to make processes easier, resources more efficient, and improvements in the general

AI in Collection Management

One very good example of AI applied to collection management is the use of machine learning algorithms for circulation data analysis in order to predict future trends in borrowing. The New York Public Library implemented an AI that would track which genres were popular and which individual titles were being acted upon by the public. Based on actual borrowing patterns, the AI provides recommended lists for acquisitions and deaccessions that keep a collection relevant and interesting to patrons. This strategy not only advanced the efficiency of collection management, but further enhanced customer satisfaction because items in high demand are always available.

AI in Asset Allocation

Evaluate the case Citation: In this other case, the College of California at Los Angeles library framework used AI to optimize allotment of its numerous assets over branches. It is the AI-driven framework examined data on the circulation of books, ponder room utilization, and occasion participation to foresee top times and apportion assets properly. For illustration, amid exam periods, the framework recognized which branches would involve higher foot activity and guaranteed extra staff and materials were accessible at those areas. This energetic assignment of assets made a difference to adjust workloads and improve benefit conveyance, lessening hold up times and making strides in the generally client experience. AI in Client Involvement Enhancement

AI in Client Involvement Enhancement

They implemented an AI-infused chatbot known as “Ask Lee” to help the fans with their inquiries and in locating help within the library's immense digital and physical holdings. Through common dialect preparation, or NLP, Ask Lee can get it and react to client inquiries in real-time with personalized suggestions, making a difference to customers having the capacity to explore the library's collection. The chatbot, available 24/7 to provide its services, has transformed the way customer engagement and satisfaction are formulated by the library, since this makes its services very convenient and accessible.

AI in Report Delivery

The British Library has also been successful in implementing AI into the document delivery services offered by the library. Earlier, document delivery was done by processing requests manually, which is usually laborious and delayed. After the implementation of AI, this library automated the matching process between customer request and availability of resources and also provided speed to the retrieval process. This AI framework was used to prioritize demands based on criticality and the availability of resources so that high-priority reports were delivered without delay. This usage has totally eliminated turnaround times and has advanced in improving the efficiency of archive delivery services to the benefit of library staff and patrons alike.

This case illustrates the potential that artificial intelligence has in many aspects of library operations—from dispatching collection management forward to optimizing assets and improving client experiences whilst streamlining record delivery; artificial intelligence proved to be one of the areas with prominent tools in modernizing library services. The more that libraries can adopt and improve AI technologies, the better they will be placed to answer the shifting requirements of their respective communities and offer effective, productive, and engaging services.

TRANSFORMATIVE IMPACT OF AI IN MODERN LIBRARIES

Advancements in AI-Driven User Interfaces

Modern libraries nowadays make use of AI-driven user interfaces for changing the experience among users. Most times, these interfaces are in the form of chatbots or virtual assistants, developed with the integration of natural language processing techniques to fully understand and respond to user queries in real time, thereby allowing the patron to instantly locate materials, place an interlibrary loan request, and seek other library services. AI integration in user interfaces makes it easy for users to use regardless of their level on the continuum of technology literacy. AI is also always available and reduces reliance on staff availability to help patrons.

Predictive Analytics for Collection Development

AI-driven predictive analytics is fast becoming a game-changer in terms of library collection development. Using machine learning to analyze circulation trends, demographic information, and scholarly research patterns, this AI will tell the librarians what to buy. In this way, collection development will be proactive in terms of making sure the library collection stays relevant to its dynamic community. At the same time, predictive analytics will highlight the absence or inadequacy of content in a collection, thus better informing libraries on all emerging areas of study and interdisciplinary research.

Enhancing Accessibility and Inclusion

AI technologies are trying to make libraries more accessible and inclusive. For example, AI-driven tools can convert text to speech, hence giving access to people with fatal visual impairments through printed materials. Moreover, AI can provide real-time translation services by breaking theessen barriers across different languages and making the resources available to non-native speakers. These developments ensure that libraries serve a larger and diversified user group, promoting an environment of inclusiveness where everybody gets the required information.

Personalized Learning and Resource Recommendations

One of the interesting applications of AI in libraries regards personalized learning experiences, where the AI, after analyzing user behavior patterns and preferences, recommends resources that best suit the needs of individual learning requirements. This could be recommending books, articles, or other materials expected to be useful for a certain academic or professional development interest. Through personalized recommendation, it enhances user satisfaction and encourages further engagement with library resources for lifelong learning and intellectual growth.

Collaboration and Resource Sharing on a Global Scale

AI empowers libraries to extend their resource-sharing networks across regional and national boundaries. Sophisticated algorithms aid in linking the libraries with institutions across the world, thereby globalizing knowledge sharing. The global collaboration thus helps libraries to have access to a varied range of resources ranging from rare manuscripts to the most updated research thereby enriching the collection. The user, therefore, gets an opportunity to access information on par with the best. AI-driven platforms ease out the process, ensuring efficient and effective interlibrary loan transactions at an international scale.

Supporting Open Access Initiatives

Libraries are actually on the forefront of open access, and AI has a vital role to play here. AI may help in the detection and aggregation of open access resources, rendering them easily discoverable and accessible to users. Besides, AI can be used to create and manage institutional repositories that have no restrictions from any institution for scholarly works produced. In so doing, libraries are democratizing access to knowledge as well as serving the global community of scholars.

Future-Proofing Library Services

Technology is changing, and libraries have to change continuously to remain relevant. AI could provide libraries with a source of future-proofing in library services—scalable and flexible solutions that will keep evolving based on changing user needs. Whether through advanced data analytics, enhanced user interfaces, or global resource-sharing networks, AI puts libraries on course to engage the challenges facing them in this information age. By embracing AI, libraries can be certain that they would always remain relevant, vibrant organizations that are responsive to the interest of their communities now and for years to come. Advancing Library Services and Accessibility with AI

ADVANCING LIBRARY SERVICES AND ACCESSIBILITY WITH AI

The Role of AI in Expanding Access and Equity

Artificial intelligence does a great job of integrated automation and optimization within the interlibrary loan process, working miracles to equitably redistribute this resource among patrons underserved by access to materials not available within their communities. More basically, what will happen through democratizing information is bridging under and well-resourced libraries where every patron has opportunities to learn and discover.

AI-driven platforms accommodate multilingual support for diverse populations. Innovations in NLP tools can execute translation of search questions and resources, thus bridging the gap created by languages for quite a long time, restricting access to information. AI can be used to produce more accessible content for those with specific disabilities, such as creating audio versions of textual materials or offering real-time sign language translation.

AI and Sustainable Resource Management

AI in library systems is also geared toward ensuring the sustainable use of resources. With the pattern of usage already determined, it allows libraries to acquire and remain relevant with resources through effective forecasting. This reduces wastage and lets a library buy what is most needed. AI can further optimize the life cycle of library material use, suggesting the right time for replacing or digitizing an aging resource to maintain relevance and retain efficiency.

Moreover, AI can contribute to green sustainability by removing the actual transportation of materials. Computerized digital dispensation tools will enable libraries to share their resources through the electronic mode of dispensation, thereby reducing the carbon footprint left by transporting huge quantities of books and documents physically. This does not need time-consuming delivery services; even the library then works at par with the larger concern for environmental goals across the world.

Collaborative Networks and AI Integration

AI enhances stronger collaborative networks among libraries by easing resource sharing and communication. AI-driven systems can be integrated into the existing library networks to provide real-time data exchanges that infuse collaboration. This kind of interconnectedness improves the collective intelligence of the library systems to work cohesively as one rather than stand-alone entities.

Connected through AI, libraries can join resource sharing practiced globally. This puts them at command of a wide collection of materials and spurs access to expertise. Such collaboration makes local collections richer, and clients get access to vast information that's continuously diversified. AI eases collaborative research, where it pegs scholars to the correct resources and experts around the world to realize inventions and cross-disciplinary studies.

Future Prospects of AI in Libraries

The prospects of AI applied in libraries are bright and expansive. The future of AI technologies will open the opportunities for more sophisticated and integrated applications in libraries. Future AI systems will contain highly developed recommendation engines, recommending resources which will be able to match user behavior and probably successfully predict a requirement before being told so explicitly. Such intelligent systems really can revolutionize personalized learning and research experiences.

Furthermore, the interaction of AI with other emerging technologies may further secure the library's operations, bringing more security, transparency, and efficiency to its operation. Blockchain technology is able to provide security and tamper-proofing for transactions involved in resource sharing, and IoT devices can automate inventory management and tracking of resources.

LEVERAGING AI FOR ENHANCED LIBRARY ENGAGEMENT AND OPERATIONS

Enhancing User Engagement Through AI

AI will dramatically increase user engagement in libraries by making their experience both personalized and interactive. AI-based chatbots and virtual assistants could offer round-the-clock solutions by walking the patrons through the services offered by the library, answering queries, and even recommending what might serve their needs best. In this way, such AI tools can work throughout the day to ensure that at any time of need, there is support for the patron, even outside regular hours for the library.

Further, AI can facilitate interactive learning atmospheres. As an illustration, AR and VR technologies, when powered by AI, have the capacity to render very immersive educational experiences. It will also allow libraries to offer virtual tours, interactive exhibits, and educational simulations that ensure learning becomes more engaging and accessible for libraries serving constituencies. Such innovations not only attract more users to the library but improve their experience of learning.

AI in Archival and Preservation Efforts

AI is also playing a very important role in the digitization, archiving, and preservation of libraries. Digitization may be required for old documents and rare books so that knowledge gets preserved for the next generation. AI technologies, such as OCR and image recognition, can automate and better the processes of digitization, ensuring that the most delicate and complex material is precisely captured and preserved.

It can further help AI in generating and managing metadata for easier cataloging and retrieval of archival materials. Based on the content and context, AI systems are able to come up with fine-grained metadata for a document, increasing the discoverability and usability of archived resources. Not only this, but it will also be possible for AI to monitor the condition of physical archives and by tracing probable degradation propose preventive measures to assure long-term preservation.

AI and Community Outreach

Libraries are community centers, and AI can boost their outreach. AI-driven analytics provide insight into the community's needs and preferences that help libraries fine-tune their programs and services. By analyzing demographic and usage patterns, it can be of great help to any library to identify underserved groups, so targeted outreach may be done to involve them in the population.

AI will also underpin community programs by making it easy to coordinate and support events, workshops, and learning programs. Automatic systems will facilitate scheduling, registration, and all communication, hence enabling libraries to run their events smoothly and at the same time reach more people. Social media analytics, run by AI, will help libraries realize the extent of their outreach and will be able to tweak strategies in order to engage significantly with more of its community.

Ethical Considerations and Responsible AI Use

As more AI technology is rolled out within libraries, there are several keen ethical considerations related to responsible use of technologies. These include, most obviously, data privacy, algorithmic bias, and transparency—all issues that will need to be handled very carefully in order to establish broad trust from the community and in order to provide fair access to library services. The library needs robust data governance practices that raise patron confidence about how patron data is collected, stored, and used in conformity with regulations about privacy.

AI algorithms must be transparent, too. Libraries have to make sure that AI systems are explainable and their patrons understand the use of their data. Another important issue is algorithmic bias: biased algorithms may lead to unfair access and reinforce already-existing inequalities. Libraries should recognize and try to remove biases in AI systems and engage in promoting fairness and inclusivity.

Lastly, continuous staff training and user education will be crucial for successfully establishing AI in libraries. Library staff need to be able to manage and make optimal use of AI technologies; on the other hand, the patrons of the libraries should be informed about the advantages and limitations connected with AI-driven services. In this way, fostering a culture of responsible use of AI within the libraries will ensure enhancement of these technologies in regard to the mission of providing access to information and knowledge delivered by the libraries.

AI in Enhancing Research Capabilities

AI integration into libraries greatly enhances one's research capabilities by giving tools that make the research process easier and more enriching. AI-powered research assistants will help scholars in tasks such as automating literature reviews, identifying articles relevant to their study, and even suggesting what study questions should be asked based on literature gaps that exist. This saves researchers substantial time and gives them space to concentrate on analysis and innovation.

Moreover, AI can facilitate data analysis and visualization to make huge banks of data more user-friendly. Sophisticated machine learning algorithms can extract patterns or trends from large volumes of data, thus allowing researchers to have a better understanding of their work and thereby formulate evidence-supported conclusions. By providing such advanced research tools, libraries shall foster an environment for academic excellence and vigorous research.

AI-DRIVEN INNOVATIONS FOR PERSONALIZED LIBRARY SERVICES AND MANAGEMENT

AI and Personalized Learning Paths

AI can aid in revolutionizing the delivery of education by tailoring use according to individual users through content and resources. AI systems can, therefore, devise individual learning pathways for every student and lifelong learner from an analysis of user data such as borrowing history, search patterns, and academic performance. They can be shown what to use, in line with learning goals and interest, hence improving their learning processes.

AI-based adaptive learning platforms can also automatically modify the level of difficulty and pace of content provision with the progress of a user to ensure adequate engagement and challenge without overwhelming learners. This way, libraries can facilitate personalized learning that caters to different ways of learning, hence easily achieving users' learning objectives.

AI and Enhanced Search Capabilities

Traditional keyword-based methods of search can sometimes be very limited and may not turn up relevant results. AI enhances the search by semantic search capabilities that go with NLP. This advanced search understands the context and intent of the query to give relevant and accurate results.

For instance, AI can shear through complex questions and provide complete answers to such through its drawing from diverse sources. It can also realize companion topics and recommend other materials of interest to the user. This improved search functionality assists patrons in discovering useful information and related resources within the library's extensive collections.

AI-Driven Predictive Analytics for Library Management

It can also be used to power predictive analytics, changing library management by giving insight into future trends and behaviors. Libraries can construct predictive models that will help them foresee demand for certain materials and aid in more effective collection development and resource allocation. That way, libraries will know exactly in which resources it is most likely to yield high returns in terms of demand from patrons, improving patron satisfaction and resource use.

AI in Enhancing the User Experience

AI will tremendously enhance user experience in libraries. Personalized recommendations, tailored learning experiences, more engaging and satisfying search functionalities will make for a more engaging and satisfying user experience regarding that matter. On the other hand, AI automates routine tasks like checkout for books, renewal of loans, and account information management to free library staff to handle more value-added services.

EMERGING TRENDS AND FUTURE DIRECTIONS

Rising Patterns and Future Directions

The use of AI in libraries is in constant evolution, where evolving trends and future directions have been defining the landscape. Key areas of growth include AI-driven recommendation systems, potential roles of blockchain and AI ensuring safe transactions, AI roles to enhance open access resources, and ethical considerations of AI applications.

AI and Open Get to Resources

AI is playing a paramount role in expanding and optimizing open access to resources. AI is being used in libraries for the curation, categorization, and recommendation of Open Access content to help their users find very relevant openly available resources. The California Digital Library utilized AI to extend its eScholarship repository, where machine learning was adapted to classify publications and improve the effectiveness of search within the repository.

AI-Powered Proposal Systems

AI-powered recommendation frameworks are becoming increasingly common in libraries, offering personalized recommendations to customers through analysis of their preferences and previous behaviors. Machine learning algorithms analyze data such as borrowing history, search queries, and the feedback provided by clients. For instance, the College of Toronto Libraries have implemented an AI-driven recommendation engine that recommends books, articles, and other resources tailored to individual client interfaces. This improves the customer experience by making a difference. Advocates discover relevant materials they may otherwise not have found; this way, increasing engagement and satisfaction. Integration of AI to Blockchain for Secure Transactions

Integration of AI With Blockchain for Secure Transactions

Integrating AI with blockchain technology is an emerging trend aimed at improving the safety and transparency of library transactions.The decentralized nature of blockchain ensures that records cannot be altered and are permanent, thus making it a secure environment for the administration of information. Blockchain combined with AI thus automatizes forms such as interlibrary credits, electronic rights management, and customer confirmation. For instance, a pilot at the College of Melbourne explored the use of artificial intelligence and blockchain in having secure dealing and transparent advanced rights and access to academic distributions. This will be an integration that assures strides in belief and productivity of library operations.

Ethical Contemplations in AI Applications

With the integration of AI into library services comes the ethical issues related to these. Questions over data security, algorithmic bias, and transparency have to be addressed in order to guarantee that AI is used fairly and reliably in a way that—as it currently does—balances the protection of client information with the utilization of AI to enhance administrations. For example, the American Library Association has established principles of good practice for the ethical implementation of AI, specifying criteria related to transparency, accountability, and user consent.

CONCLUSION

Leveraging AI in library interlibrary loan and resource sharing systems holds great promise, as blockchain technology does. Technologies and tools derived from AI which include predictive, artificial intelligence, and machine learning can automate forms of resource allocation like request processing or fulfillment rates. These forms of technology can ramp up the efficiency of requesting distribution notifications in the library by using blockchain technology.

Furthermore, the advancements in library services encompass various areas including collection management, user services, and interlibrary loan. Improvements in AI technologies also allow libraries to not just rely on the information requirements users may have, but to predict and anticipate requirements; ensuring user engagement and service provision are personal to the individual, and to also manage collections effectively using AI-enhanced methods.Using these new technologies, AI and blockchain have the potential to transform the development of interlibrary loan by enhancing the efficiency of resource sharing, and establishing both transparency and integrity of transactions connected to resource-sharing processes of libraries.

In conclusion, as libraries continue to evolve as information hubs in a digital society, integrating AI and blockchain technology for new tools that will transform and extend their services will be key for success. Libraries, as intermediary information hubs, are well-positioned to play a major role in the transition to a digital society.

REFERENCES

Jayavadivel, R., Arunachalam, M., Nagarajan, G., Shankar, B. P., Viji, C., Rajkumar, N., & Senthilkumar, K. R. (2024). Historical overview of AI adoption in libraries. In *AI-Assisted Library Reconstruction* (pp. 267–289). IGI Global. DOI: 10.4018/979-8-3693-2782-1.ch015

Kumar, N., Antoniraj, S., Jayanthi, S., Mirdula, S., Selvaraj, S., Rajkumar, N., & Senthilkumar, K. R. (2024). Educational technology and libraries supporting online learning. In *AI-Assisted Library Reconstruction* (pp. 209–237). IGI Global. DOI: 10.4018/979-8-3693-2782-1.ch012

Lalitha, B., Ramalakshmi, K., Gunasekaran, H., Murugesan, P., Saminasri, P., & Rajkumar, N. (2024). Anticipating AI impact on library services: Future opportunities and evolutionary prospects. In *Improving Library Systems with AI: Applications, Approaches, and Bibliometric Insights* (pp. 195–213). IGI Global.

Mohanraj, A., Viji, C., Varadarajan, M. N., Kalpana, C., Shankar, B., Jayavadivel, R., Rajkumar, N., & Jagajeevan, R. (2024). Privacy and security in digital libraries. In *AI-Assisted Library Reconstruction* (pp. 104–125). IGI Global. DOI: 10.4018/979-8-3693-2782-1.ch006

Nachiappan, B. (2024a). Emerging and innovative AI technologies for resource management. In *Improving Library Systems with AI: Applications, Approaches, and Bibliometric Insights* (pp. 115–133). IGI Global. DOI: 10.4018/979-8-3693-5593-0.ch009

Nachiappan, B. (2024b). E-resources content recommendation system using AI. In *Improving Library Systems with AI: Applications, Approaches, and Bibliometric Insights* (pp. 155–177). IGI Global. DOI: 10.4018/979-8-3693-5593-0.ch011

Rajkumar, N., Tabassum, H., Muthulingam, S., Mohanraj, A., Viji, C., Kumar, N., & Senthilkumar, K. R. (2024). Anticipated requirements and expectations in the digital library. In *AI-Assisted Library Reconstruction* (pp. 1–20). IGI Global. DOI: 10.4018/979-8-3693-2782-1.ch001

Rajkumar, N., Viji, C., Mohanraj, A., Senthilkumar, K. R., Jagajeevan, R., & Kovilpillai, J. A. (2024). Ethical considerations of AI implementation in the library era. In *Improving Library Systems with AI: Applications, Approaches, and Bibliometric Insights* (pp. 85–106). IGI Global. DOI: 10.4018/979-8-3693-5593-0.ch007

Varadarajan, M. N. (2024). Educational program for AI literacy. In *Improving Library Systems with AI: Applications, Approaches, and Bibliometric Insights* (pp. 134–154). IGI Global. DOI: 10.4018/979-8-3693-5593-0.ch010

Viji, C., Najmusher, H., Rajkumar, N., Mohanraj, A., Nachiappan, B., Neelakandan, C., & Jagajeevan, R. (2024). Intelligent library management using radio frequency identification. In *AI-Assisted Library Reconstruction* (pp. 126–143). IGI Global. DOI: 10.4018/979-8-3693-2782-1.ch007

Chapter 12
Blockchain and Collaborative Networks: Harnessing Library Resources for the Digital Age

E. Sumathi
Sri Krishna College of Engineering and Technology, India

K. Jaya
Sri Krishna Arts and Science College, India

Senthilkumar K. R.
https://orcid.org/0000-0001-7426-5376
Sri Krishna Arts and Science College, India

ABSTRACT

In the digital era, libraries are evolving beyond their traditional roles as repositories of physical books to become dynamic hubs for digital information. This chapter investigates the integration of blockchain technology and collaborative networks to enhance the management and distribution of library resources. Blockchain's decentralized and immutable ledger offers a secure, transparent, and efficient method for tracking the ownership, usage, and distribution of digital assets, reducing the reliance on centralized systems. This study explores the potential of blockchain to support the creation of decentralized, interoperable library systems that enhance collaboration among institutions, ensure data integrity, and provide more equitable access to knowledge. Through an analysis of current implementations and theoretical models, this research identifies the opportunities and challenges of adopting blockchain in library systems and proposes strategies for overcoming barriers to implementation.

DOI: 10.4018/979-8-3693-7783-3.ch012

INTRODUCTION

The origin of blockchain technology is often credited to cryptographer David Chaum, who proposed a blockchain-like protocol for decentralized node networks in his 1982 dissertation. However, its conceptual roots trace back to the 1970s when computer scientist Ralph Merkle patented Hash trees, also known as Merkle trees, which enable cryptographic linking between blocks of data.

These foundational theories converged in 1991 with the creation of the first blockchain product. In an effort to establish tamper-proof digital records, scientist Stuart Haber and cryptographer Scott Stornetta developed a system that used hash functions to timestamp documents in a chronological chain of digital certificates. The following year, mathematician David Bayer helped incorporate Merkle trees into this design, allowing data to be consolidated into single blocks, resembling modern blockchain functionality.

The significant milestone came in 2009 with the introduction of Bitcoin, the world's first cryptocurrency. Launched by the pseudonymous Satoshi Nakamoto, Bitcoin not only offered a digital alternative to fiat currency but also introduced the concept of a public, decentralized blockchain that eliminated the need for third-party intermediaries. This project brought blockchain technology into mainstream awareness. In 2015, the Ethereum platform, created by Vitalik Buterin, further advanced blockchain technology through the introduction of smart contracts — self-executing programs that automate transaction verification — and decentralized applications (DApps), enabling developers to build their own applications within the Web3 framework.

The digital age has brought about unprecedented changes in the way we live, work, and interact. As industries across the globe undergo digital transformation, two significant developments have emerged: blockchain technology and collaborative networks. Blockchain, initially known as the backbone of cryptocurrencies like Bitcoin, has evolved into a versatile technology with applications far beyond digital currencies. Simultaneously, collaborative networks have become essential in facilitating cooperation and innovation across various sectors.

Integrating artificial intelligence (AI) in library management has appreciably converted how libraries function, supplying advanced performance, more advantageous user experiences, and strong facts management. This literature evaluation synthesizes key insights from recent scholarly works specializing in diverse components of AI implementation in libraries. Viji et al. (Viji et al., 2024) discovered the application of the Radio Frequency identity (RFID) era in library management. RFID structures streamline inventory control, enhance safety, and facilitate self-service, decreasing the workload on the library body of workers. The bankruptcy emphasizes the performance and accuracy of RFID in tracking and dealing with library assets, highlighting its capacity to revolutionize conventional library operations. Kumar et al. (Kumar et al., 2024) explain the synergy among academic technology and libraries in assisting online studying. They argue that libraries, empowered through AI, can offer personalized getting-to-know experiences through adaptive studying structures and shrewd content material recommendations. The chapter also delves into libraries' position in bridging the digital divide, ensuring equitable access to instructional sources. Mohanraj et al. (Mohanraj et al., 2024) deal with the crucial issues of privacy and protection in virtual libraries. As libraries undertake AI and virtual technologies, safeguarding personal data becomes paramount. The authors have a look at various protection protocols and privacy measures that libraries can enforce to protect sensitive facts whilst keeping consumers agree with them. Rajkumar et al. (Rajkumar, Tabassum, et al., 2024) outline the evolving necessities and expectations of virtual libraries in the AI generation. The bankruptcy highlights the need for robust infrastructure, skilled employees, and non-stop innovation to satisfy the dynamic needs of library users. It additionally discusses the significance of consumer-centric layouts in growing AI-pushed library structures. Jayavadivel et al. (Jayavadivel et al., 2024) offer a historic angle on AI adoption in libraries. They trace the evolution of AI technologies in library control, from early automation systems to sophisticated AI-driven answers. The chapter gives valuable insights into the demanding situations and milestones encountered for the duration of this transformative adventure. Rajkumar et al. (Rajkumar, Viji, et al., 2024) delve into the moral implications of AI in libraries. They explore issues inclusive of algorithmic bias, transparency, and the ethical use of personal facts. The authors argue for the development of moral suggestions and frameworks to ensure responsible AI implementation in library services.

Lalitha et al. (Lalitha et al., 2024) speak about the future effect of AI on library services. They spotlight rising developments and capability opportunities for AI to decorate library functions, which includes predictive analytics for series improvement and AI-powered reference offerings. The bankruptcy additionally speculates on the evolutionary prospects of libraries in an AI-pushed international. Nachiappan (Nachiappan, 2024b) offers an AI-primarily based e-assets content material advice gadget. The machine leverages system-getting-to-know algorithms to analyze personal choices and endorse relevant digital resources. This personalized approach improves consumer engagement and pleasure through presenting tailored content pointers. Nachiappan (Nachiappan, 2024a) explores cutting-edge AI technologies for aid management in libraries. Bankruptcy discusses advancements such as herbal language processing (NLP), machine getting to know, and AI-pushed records analytics. These technologies beautify resource discovery, optimize library operations, and provide precious insights for choice-making. Varadarajan (Varadarajan, 2024) emphasizes the significance of AI literacy in libraries. The chapter advocates for educational packages that equip library teams of workers and users with the necessary capabilities to navigate and leverage AI technology. Promoting AI literacy guarantees that libraries can harness the benefits of AI even as mitigating related risks. The reviewed chapters together highlight the transformative capacity of AI in library management. From enhancing operational performance and protection to enhancing consumer reviews and ethical considerations, AI gives several possibilities for libraries to evolve and thrive in the virtual age. Future research should continue to explore innovative AI packages and address the challenges related to their implementation to make certain sustainable and consumer-centric library offerings.

Scope of the Study

This study aims to provide a comprehensive exploration of the convergence between blockchain technology and collaborative networks. It seeks to elucidate the historical development and foundational theories of blockchain technology, tracing its evolution from the 1970s to its mainstream adoption with Bitcoin and Ethereum. The study focuses on defining blockchain technology, outlining its features, advantages, and types, and exploring its anticipated benefits in various sectors, including education and libraries. Additionally, it investigates the role of collaborative networks in facilitating cooperation and innovation across different industries, examining how blockchain technology can enhance these networks. Through the analysis of real-world applications and case studies, the study showcases how the integration of blockchain technology with collaborative networks can drive innovation, enhance trust, and foster decentralized collaboration. Furthermore, it predicts future trends and developments in this integration, providing insights into potential advancements and their implications for the digital age. The study also offers strategic guidance on implementing blockchain technology within library contexts, aiming to raise awareness among library professionals about its transformative potential.

Outcome of the Study

The study is expected to achieve several significant outcomes. Firstly, it aims to provide a comprehensive understanding of blockchain technology and collaborative networks, including their definitions, features, advantages, and potential applications. Secondly, it seeks to enhance awareness among professionals, particularly in the education and library sectors, about the transformative potential of blockchain technology and its strategic implementation to enhance operations. Thirdly, the study aims to demonstrate how the integration of blockchain technology and collaborative networks can drive innovation, enhance trust, and facilitate decentralized collaboration across various industries. Additionally, it will offer practical insights and real-world examples of blockchain applications in collaborative networks, providing a blueprint for future implementations. The study also aims to equip readers with the knowledge and foresight to anticipate future trends and developments in blockchain technology and collaborative networks, enabling them to stay ahead in the digital age. Finally, it will provide strategic guidance for the implementation of blockchain technology in library settings, helping library professionals leverage this technology to improve their services and operations. Through these outcomes, the study seeks to contribute to the broader understanding and adoption of blockchain technology and collaborative networks, fostering innovation and collaboration in the digital age.

Understanding Blockchain Technology

Definition and Basic Principles

Blockchain is a decentralized, distributed ledger technology that records transactions across multiple computers in such a way that the registered transactions cannot be altered retroactively. This ensures the integrity and security of data. At its core, blockchain comprises three main components:

Blocks: Units of Data That Contain Transaction Information

Chains: The sequence of blocks linked together, forming a continuous ledger.

Decentralization: The distribution of data across a network of nodes, eliminating the need for a central authority.

Consensus Mechanisms: Protocols used to achieve agreement on the state of the blockchain among distributed nodes, such as Proof of Work (PoW) and Proof of Stake (PoS).

Figure 1. How blockchain works

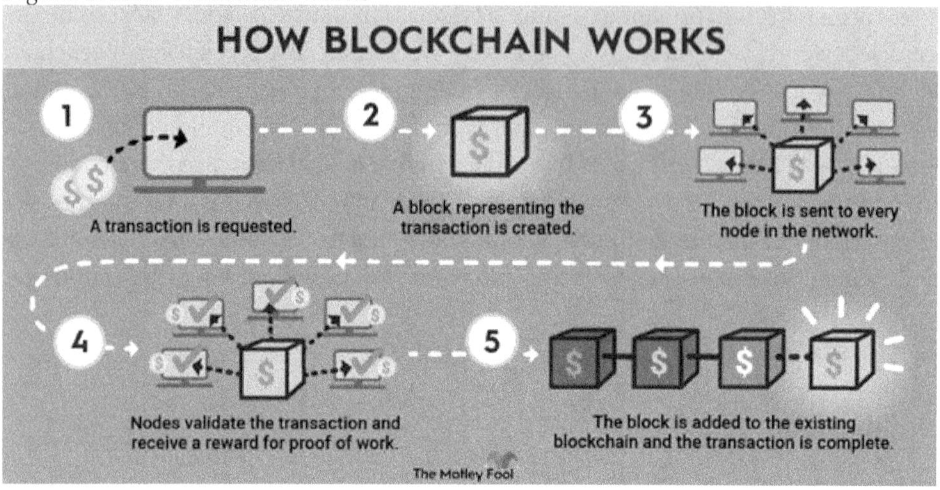

(Source https://www.fool.com/terms/b/blockchain/)

Types of Blockchains

Blockchain networks can be categorized into three types based on their accessibility and management

Public Blockchains: Open to anyone to join and participate, ensuring transparency and decentralization. Examples include Bitcoin and Ethereum.

Private Blockchains: Restricted access where only authorized participants can join. These are typically used within organizations for internal processes.

Consortium Blockchains: A hybrid approach where a group of organizations governs the blockchain network, balancing transparency and control.

REVIEW OF LITERATURE

Xu, Li, and Meng (2020) provide a comprehensive survey on blockchain consensus algorithms, detailing their evolution and advancements aimed at improving scalability and security.

Saberi, Kouhizadeh, Sarkis, and Shen (2020) review blockchain's potential to improve supply chain transparency and efficiency, while Kamble, Gunasekaran, and Sharma (2021) present case studies on blockchain's effectiveness in tracking and verifying goods.

Agbo, Mahmoud, and Eklund (2021) discuss blockchain's role in enhancing healthcare data sharing and collaborative research.

Bell, Wallis, and Jeanes (2022) investigate blockchain's impact on library systems, highlighting improvements in resource management and access to digital collections.

KEY ATTRIBUTES OF BLOCKCHAIN TECHNOLOGY

Blockchain technology is characterized by several key attributes that collectively enhance its functionality and reliability. Decentralization is a fundamental feature, as blockchain operates across a distributed network of computers, eliminating the need for a central authority and thus reducing the risk of single points of failure. Transparency is another critical attribute, offering visibility of transactions to all network participants, which fosters accountability and diminishes opportunities for fraud. Immutability ensures that once data is recorded on the blockchain, it cannot be altered, thanks to cryptographic techniques that preserve data integrity. Security is bolstered by these cryptographic methods, which protect transactions from tampering and unauthorized access. Additionally, blockchain provides traceability by allowing transparent tracking of transaction histories, which aids in verifying the provenance of data and maintaining accountability. Consensus mechanisms, such as Proof of Work or Proof of Stake, are employed to validate transactions and achieve agreement among network participants, ensuring that only legitimate transactions are recorded. Lastly, smart contracts automate and enforce contractual agreements through self-executing protocols based on predefined conditions, which streamlines processes and reduces the need for intermediaries.

Blockchain Benefits, Challenges, Applications

Cryptography and hashing algorithms ensure that only authorized users are able to unlock information meant for them, and that the data stored on the blockchain cannot be manipulated in any form. Consensus mechanisms, such as proof of work or proof of stake, further enhance security by requiring network participants to agree on the validity of transactions before they are added to the blockchain. Additionally, blockchains operate on a distributed system, where data is stored across multiple nodes rather than one central location — reducing the risk of a single point of failure.

By providing a fully transparent, single-source-of-truth ledger, where transactions are recorded in a chronological and immutable manner, the potential for error or discrepancy drops when compared to centralized databases or manual record-keeping processes. Transactions are objectively authorized by a consensus algorithm and, unless a blockchain is made private, all transactions can be independently verified by users.

Aside from saving paper, blockchain enables reliable cross-team communication, reduces bottlenecks and errors while streamlining overall operations. By eliminating intermediaries and automating verification processes — done via smart contracts — blockchain enjoys reduced transaction costs, timely processing times and optimized data integrity.

CHALLENGES OF BLOCKCHAIN

Although this emerging technology may be tamper proof, it isn't faultless. Below are some of the biggest obstacles blockchain faces today.

As blockchain networks grow in popularity and usage, they face bottlenecks in processing transactions quickly and cost-effectively. This limitation hampers the widespread adoption of blockchain for mainstream applications, as networks struggle to handle high throughput volumes, leading to congestion and increased transaction fees.The computational power required for certain functions — like Bitcoin's proof-of-work consensus mechanism — consumes vast amounts of electricity, raising concerns around environmental impact and high operating costs. Addressing this challenge requires exploring alternative consensus mechanisms, such as proof of stake, which consume significantly less energy while maintaining network security and decentralization

As it is now, every node of a blockchain network stores a copy of the entire data chain and processes every transaction. This requires a certain level of computational power, resulting in slow, congested networks and lagged processing times especially during high-traffic periods. Scalability issues arise due to limitations in block size, block processing times and resource-intensive consensus mechanisms. This is why novel approaches — such as layer 2 scaling solutions, sharing and alternative consensus algorithms — are being developed. Governments and regulators are still working to make sense of blockchain — more specifically, how certain laws should be updated to properly address decentralization. While some governments are actively spearheading its adoption and others elect to wait-and-see, lingering regulatory and legal concerns hinder blockchain's market appeal, stalling its technical development.

Collaborative networks are systems of interconnected entities that work together to achieve common goals. These networks leverage the collective expertise, resources, and capabilities of their participants to drive innovation and solve complex problems. In the digital age, collaborative networks have become crucial in areas such as research and development, supply chain management, and social networking.

Types of Collaborative Networks

Social Networks: Platforms like Facebook and LinkedIn that connect individuals and facilitate communication.

Business Networks: Systems that enable companies to collaborate on projects, share resources, and innovate together.

Technology-Based Networks: Networks that focus on the development and deployment of technological solutions, such as open-source software communities.

Case Studies of Successful Collaborative Networks

One notable example of a successful collaborative network is GitHub, a platform that allows developers to collaborate on software projects. By providing tools for version control, code review, and project management, GitHub has become an essential resource for the global software development community.

Another example is the Hyperledger project, an open-source collaborative effort to advance cross-industry blockchain technologies. Hosted by the Linux Foundation, Hyperledger brings together leaders from various industries to develop frameworks and tools for blockchain implementation.

Synergy Between Blockchain and Collaborative Networks

The integration of blockchain technology with collaborative networks can enhance trust, transparency, and security, thereby enabling more effective and decentralized collaboration.

Blockchain's immutable ledger ensures that all transactions and interactions within a collaborative network are transparent and verifiable. This increased transparency can build trust among participants, reducing the risk of fraud and enhancing cooperation..By leveraging blockchain's cryptographic security features, collaborative networks can protect sensitive data and ensure that only authorized participants have access to specific information. This is particularly important in industries like healthcare and finance, where data privacy is paramount.Blockchain technology enables decentralized collaboration by allowing participants to interact directly without intermediaries. This can reduce costs, increase efficiency, and empower individuals and organizations to contribute to projects in a more flexible and autonomous manner.

APPLICATIONS OF BLOCKCHAIN IN LIBRARIES

Blockchain technology offers innovative solutions to several challenges faced by libraries today. Here are detailed explanations for how blockchain can be applied in libraries, particularly in digital rights management: Blockchain technology can indeed transform various aspects of library operations and management. Here are detailed explanations for each of the provided applications, along with sources to back them up:

Transparent and Tamper-Proof Records of Library Transactions

Blockchain technology can establish a decentralized and immutable ledger that records every library transaction, including book loans, returns, and acquisitions. This system ensures that all records are transparent and resistant to alteration, enhancing accountability and providing a secure audit trail. Each transaction is timestamped and permanently recorded on the blockchain, facilitating easy tracking of who borrowed or returned a book and when. This transparency minimizes disputes and reduces the risk of mismanagement. Additionally, real-time updates and a permanent transaction record improve inventory management, enabling libraries to efficiently track book availability and accurately record acquisitions. The immutable nature of blockchain also ensures a reliable audit trail for compliance and reporting, which is particularly beneficial for public and academic libraries that must meet stringent regulatory standards.

Peer-to-Peer Resource Sharing

Blockchain-based systems offer a transformative approach to decentralized resource sharing among libraries, enhancing both efficiency and transparency. By establishing a peer-to-peer network, libraries can directly share resources between institutions without the need for a central authority. This decentralized approach minimizes delays and improves the availability of materials. Transparency is a key feature of blockchain technology, as it records every transaction on an immutable ledger, allowing for easy tracking and verification of resource movements. Additionally, the integration of smart contracts can automate the interlibrary loan process, ensuring that books are loaned out and returned based on predefined terms. This automation not only reduces administrative overhead but also accelerates the overall process, making resource sharing more efficient and effective.

Secure Record-Keeping

Blockchain technology can significantly enhance the management of library records by ensuring they remain tamper-proof and secure. The decentralized and immutable nature of blockchain guarantees that records—such as patron checkouts, acquisitions, and cataloging—cannot be altered or deleted once they are added. This offers a high level of security and integrity for library transactions. For patron checkouts, each transaction, including checkouts and returns, can be securely recorded on the blockchain, providing a transparent and accurate history of each item's usage. The acquisition process is also streamlined through blockchain by creating a clear, unalterable record of purchases and donations. Additionally, cataloging information can be securely stored and easily shared across different library systems, enhancing the efficiency and reliability of library operations.

Managing Digital Assets

Blockchain provides a decentralized and secure platform for managing digital assets, such as e-books, journals, and multimedia content. This helps prevent unauthorized access, ensures proper attribution, and enables efficient rights management.

- **Prevention of Unauthorized Access**: Digital assets can be securely stored on the blockchain, with access permissions managed through smart contracts. This ensures that only authorized users can access the content.
- **Ensuring Attribution**: Blockchain's transparent ledger can record the provenance and usage of digital content, ensuring that authors and creators receive proper attribution for their work.
- **Efficient Rights Management**: Smart contracts can automate the enforcement of digital rights, ensuring that content is used according to the terms set by the creators. This includes controlling access, usage, and distribution of digital assets.

By integrating blockchain technology, libraries can enhance the security, transparency, and efficiency of their operations. This not only improves trust and accountability but also fosters more collaborative and innovative practices within the library community.

Managing and Tracking Digital Content Rights

Blockchain technology has the potential to revolutionize the management and tracking of digital content rights in libraries by providing a transparent, secure, and immutable ledger for transactions. This technology ensures that ownership, distribution, and usage rights for digital resources such as e-books, journals, and multimedia content are accurately recorded and managed. The immutable nature of blockchain creates an unchangeable record of transactions, making it impossible to alter or tamper with the recorded rights once they are entered. This is crucial for protecting intellectual property and ensuring adherence to usage terms. Blockchain achieves this immutability through its decentralized and distributed ledger system, where transactions are recorded across multiple computers. Altering any record requires changing all subsequent blocks and gaining consensus from the network, making unauthorized modifications highly unlikely. This fundamental feature of blockchain, supported by cryptographic hashing and consensus mechanisms, ensures that digital content rights are securely and transparently managed.

Blockchain technology employs several key features to ensure the integrity and security of digital content rights management in libraries. Cryptographic hashing is fundamental to this process, where every transaction or record on the blockchain is encrypted into a unique string of numbers and letters called a hash. Each block contains its own hash and the hash of the previous block, creating a chain of blocks. If any data within a block is altered, its hash changes, breaking the chain and ensuring immediate detection of changes, thus maintaining data integrity. Decentralization further strengthens the system, as blockchain operates on a decentralized network of computers (nodes), each holding a copy of the entire blockchain. For a new block to be added, the majority of nodes must reach a consensus on its validity. This decentralized nature eliminates a single point of failure or control, making it extremely difficult to alter the blockchain. Various consensus mechanisms, such as Proof of Work (PoW), Proof of Stake (PoS), or Practical Byzantine Fault Tolerance (PBFT), are used by different blockchains to agree on the state of the blockchain. These mechanisms ensure that only valid transactions are added, providing an additional safeguard against tampering and enhancing the overall security and reliability of the system.

Immutability and Digital Rights Management (DRM)

Immutability in blockchain is particularly beneficial for Digital Rights Management (DRM) in libraries and other content distribution systems by ensuring the protection of intellectual property, maintaining tamper-proof records, and enforcing correct usage terms. Once the rights and usage terms of digital content, such as e-books, journals, and multimedia, are recorded on the blockchain, they cannot be altered. This guarantees that the original terms set by content creators are permanently preserved. For example, an author can record the rights to their e-book on the blockchain, specifying distribution limits, allowed usage, and royalty payments. These terms become immutable and can be automatically enforced by smart contracts. The immutability of blockchain also prevents unauthorized changes to the recorded rights, which is crucial for protecting intellectual property from fraud or unauthorized modifications. If a digital library acquires the rights to distribute a particular e-book, this acquisition is recorded on the blockchain, making any attempt to alter the distribution rights immediately detectable and preserving the integrity of the original agreement. Additionally, smart contracts on the blockchain can automatically enforce the usage terms recorded for digital content. These self-executing contracts ensure compliance without the need for intermediaries. For instance, if a library user borrows an e-book, a smart contract could enforce the borrowing period and automatically revoke access after the period ends, adhering to the recorded rights.

Example of Implementation:

- **IBM Blockchain**:
  - IBM has been a pioneer in integrating blockchain for various applications, including DRM. Their blockchain solutions ensure that digital content rights are recorded in an immutable manner.
  - By using IBM's blockchain technology, libraries can manage digital rights more securely and transparently, ensuring that intellectual property rights are protected and usage terms are strictly followed.
  - Source: IBM Blockchain

Advantages of Immutability in Blockchain for Libraries

Blockchain technology offers significant advantages for managing digital content rights in libraries through enhanced security, transparency, reduced fraud, and automated compliance. Immutability ensures that once data is written on the blockchain, it cannot be altered or deleted, providing robust protection against data breaches and unauthorized access. This feature enhances the security of digital content rights. Additionally, blockchain's transparency ensures that all transactions are recorded and visible to all participants in the network, fostering trust among stakeholders. The immutable nature of blockchain records also helps in significantly reducing fraud and disputes related to digital content rights. Furthermore, smart contracts automate the enforcement of compliance with recorded terms, minimizing the need for manual intervention and oversight. Together, these features create a secure, transparent, and efficient system for managing and protecting digital content rights in libraries.

Transparent Licensing

Libraries can leverage blockchain technology to issue licenses for digital content in a transparent manner, recording each transaction related to content, including purchases, loans, and usage, on the blockchain. This transparency helps prevent unauthorized use and ensures that content creators receive appropriate compensation. By providing a decentralized, immutable ledger where all transactions are visible to authorized participants, blockchain technology enables transparent licensing. The decentralized ledger operates across multiple nodes rather than being controlled by a single entity, ensuring that the data is transparent and tamper-proof. Every transaction related to digital content is recorded in this ledger and is accessible to all participants with permission to access the blockchain. Once a transaction is recorded, it cannot be altered or deleted, guaranteeing that the history of transactions remains intact and accurate, preventing unauthorized changes and ensuring data integrity. Smart contracts further enhance this system by automatically enforcing the rules and conditions of licensing agreements recorded on the blockchain. These self-executing contracts could, for example, automatically distribute royalties to content creators whenever their digital content is accessed or borrowed by a library user. Through these mechanisms, blockchain ensures fair use and appropriate compensation for content creators while providing libraries with a secure and transparent method for managing digital content licenses.

Applications of Transparent Licensing in Libraries

Libraries can utilize blockchain technology to enhance the management of digital content licenses, track usage, and facilitate royalty distribution in a transparent and verifiable manner. By issuing licenses on the blockchain, each license transaction is recorded, creating a clear and immutable record of who has access to the content and under what terms. This process ensures that all parties, including content creators, libraries, and users, have a shared understanding of the licensing terms. Blockchain can also track every instance of content usage, such as when an e-book is borrowed, returned, or purchased, recording each event on the blockchain to provide a transparent and auditable history of interactions with the content. This transparency helps prevent unauthorized use and ensures that all usage complies with the agreed licensing terms. Additionally, smart contracts can be programmed to automatically calculate and distribute royalties to content creators based on recorded usage. For instance, every time an e-book is borrowed, a portion of the fee can be automatically transferred to the author or publisher. This automation ensures that content creators are fairly compensated in real-time, without delays or the need for intermediaries. Through these capabilities, blockchain technology enhances the efficiency, transparency, and fairness of digital content management in libraries.

Benefits of Transparent Licensing in Libraries

Blockchain technology can significantly enhance the management of digital content in libraries by preventing unauthorized use, ensuring fair compensation, and fostering trust and accountability among stakeholders. By recording every transaction on the blockchain, libraries can ensure that only authorized users have access to digital content, with unauthorized access attempts being immediately detected and prevented. This mechanism protects the rights of content creators and helps libraries manage their digital assets more effectively. Transparent licensing ensures that content creators receive appropriate compensation for the use of their work, as every transaction is recorded and verifiable, eliminating disputes over royalty payments. Smart contracts enable real-time and automated royalty distribution, reducing administrative overhead and ensuring timely payments. Additionally, the transparency provided by blockchain fosters trust among all stakeholders. Content creators can trust that their work is being used according to the agreed terms, while libraries and users can trust the accuracy and fairness of the licensing process. The immutable record of transactions serves as a secure audit trail, providing accountability and reducing the potential for fraud or disputes. Through these capabilities, blockchain technology offers a robust framework for the transparent and fair management of digital content in libraries.

Example of Implementation

Springer Nature, a leading academic and scientific publisher, has explored the use of blockchain to enhance transparency and trust in scholarly publishing. They have investigated how blockchain can be used to manage licensing and usage of digital content, ensuring that all transactions are transparent and verifiable (Springer Nature Blockchain).

In terms of licensing transactions, when a library acquires a digital license for an e-book, the transaction is recorded on the blockchain, including details such as the license terms, expiration date, and usage rights. Every subsequent transaction, such as a user borrowing the e-book, is also recorded, creating a comprehensive and transparent history of the content's usage.

Usage tracking is another area where blockchain proves beneficial. It tracks how often the content is accessed, by whom, and under what conditions. This tracking ensures compliance with licensing terms and provides valuable data for both libraries and content creators. For example, if a license allows an e-book to be borrowed by up to 10 users simultaneously, the blockchain can enforce this limit and prevent additional borrowings once the limit is reached.

Blockchain technology also facilitates royalty distribution. Smart contracts can be set up to automatically transfer a portion of the borrowing fee to the content creator's account. This process is transparent and verifiable, ensuring that content creators are compensated fairly and promptly. For instance, if a library charges $2 for borrowing an e-book and the royalty rate is 50%, the smart contract would automatically transfer $1 to the author each time the book is borrowed.

SMART CONTRACTS

Smart contracts on the blockchain can automate the enforcement of digital rights. These self-executing contracts automatically implement the terms of an agreement when predefined conditions are met. For example, a smart contract could automatically release an e-book to a library patron for a specified loan period and revoke access after the period ends. They are self-executing contracts with the terms of the agreement directly written into code. These contracts reside on a blockchain and automatically enforce the terms and conditions of an agreement when predefined conditions are met. This automation can revolutionize how digital rights are managed, particularly in libraries, by ensuring that all transactions and agreements are carried out transparently and without the need for intermediaries. It works through self-execution and decentralization. They are programmed to automatically execute specific actions when certain conditions are fulfilled. For example, a smart contract for an e-book loan could automatically grant access to a library patron when they request the book and meet the borrowing criteria. Once the loan period ends, the smart contract would automatically revoke access, ensuring compliance with the agreed terms without manual intervention. Stored on a blockchain, smart contracts are decentralized and immutable, meaning the contract code and its execution are distributed across multiple nodes, ensuring that no single entity controls or can alter the contract once it is deployed. This decentralization guarantees the trustworthiness and security of the contract, as it cannot be tampered with or influenced by any party after deployment.The conditions for executing a smart contract are predefined and encoded within the contract. These conditions can include various criteria such as time-based triggers, user authentication, payment verification, and more. For a library loan system, the conditions might include the user's membership status, availability of the e-book, and the duration of the loan period.Applications of smart contracts in libraries include automated loan management, digital rights management (DRM), and royalty and fee distribution.

Smart contracts can automate the entire process of lending digital content. When a library patron requests to borrow an e-book, the smart contract verifies their eligibility (e.g., membership status, loan limits) and grants access if all conditions are met. The contract specifies the loan period, after which access to the e-book is automatically revoked. This ensures that digital rights are enforced without the need for manual tracking and intervention by library staff and can manage and enforce digital rights for various types of content, including e-books, journals, and multimedia. They ensure that only authorized users can access the content and that usage adheres to the specified terms. For instance, an e-book could be restricted to a certain number of simultaneous users or limited to specific geographic regions. The smart contract enforces these rules automatically.It can also be used to automate the distribution of royalties and fees. Whenever a digital content item is borrowed or purchased, the smart contract can instantly calculate and distribute payments to the relevant parties (e.g., authors, publishers). This ensures timely and accurate compensation, reducing administrative overhead and potential disputes over payment calculations.

The benefits of smart contracts in libraries include efficiency and cost savings, enhanced security and trust, and transparency and accountability. Automating the management of digital rights and loan processes reduces the need for manual oversight and intervention, streamlining operations, saving time, and lowering administrative costs for libraries. Patrons benefit from quicker and more reliable access to digital content. The immutable nature of blockchain and smart contracts ensures that all transactions are secure and verifiable, building trust among content creators, libraries, and patrons, as everyone can be confident that the terms of agreements are being upheld. Unauthorized access or alterations are virtually impossible due to the decentralized and tamper-proof nature of blockchain.

Ethereum is a leading blockchain platform that supports the creation and execution of smart contracts. It provides the necessary tools and infrastructure for developers to build decentralized applications (dApps) that leverage smart contracts. Libraries could use Ethereum to develop smart contract-based systems for managing digital content, ensuring that all lending and usage terms are automatically enforced and transparent. For example, a library integrates a smart contract into its digital lending platform. When a patron requests an e-book, the smart contract verifies their membership status and checks if the book is available for loan. If the conditions are met, the smart contract grants access to the e-book and records the loan transaction on the blockchain. The loan period is defined within the contract (e.g., two weeks). After the loan period ends, the smart contract automatically revokes access to the e-book, ensuring that the patron can no longer read the content. This action is also recorded on the blockchain. If the library charges a fee for borrowing e-books, the smart contract can also handle the payment process, ensuring that the fee is collected and distributed according to predefined rules (e.g., sharing royalties with the author).It streamline the process of paying royalties to authors and publishers. Each time a digital resource is accessed or borrowed, the blockchain can automatically calculate and distribute royalties based on the recorded usage. This ensures timely and accurate payments, reducing administrative overhead.

Benefits of Using Blockchain for Royalty Payments

Reduced administrative overhead is a significant advantage of using blockchain for royalty calculations and distributions. Automating these processes minimizes the need for manual intervention and oversight, reducing administrative costs and the potential for human error. Libraries and publishers can allocate resources more efficiently, focusing on other critical tasks rather than managing complex royalty payment processes.

Enhanced transparency and trust are also crucial benefits. The transparent nature of blockchain ensures that all parties involved can see how royalties are calculated and distributed. This transparency builds trust, as authors and publishers can verify that they are being compensated fairly based on actual usage. Additionally, it provides a clear audit trail, valuable for resolving any disputes or discrepancies that may arise.

Security and immutability are inherent features of blockchain technology. The decentralized and immutable ledger ensures that once a transaction is recorded, it cannot be altered or tampered with. This security feature protects the integrity of royalty transactions and prevents fraud. Content creators and rights holders can be confident that their earnings are secure and accurately recorded.

An example of implementation can be seen in royalty distribution for e-books. A library using a blockchain-based system to manage its digital content, including e-books, records each transaction on the blockchain whenever a patron borrows an e-book. A smart contract linked to the e-book automatically calculates the royalty owed to the author and publisher based on predefined terms (e.g., a fixed fee per borrow or a percentage of the library's subscription revenue). The smart contract then triggers an automated payment, distributing the calculated royalty to the respective parties' digital wallets. This process ensures that the author and publisher receive their royalties promptly and accurately, with each transaction transparently recorded on the blockchain.

A detailed example can be illustrated with a music streaming platform integrated with blockchain technology. When a user streams a song, a smart contract records the stream on the blockchain. The smart contract is programmed to distribute a percentage of the streaming revenue to the artist, composer, and record label based on the agreed terms. As soon as the stream is recorded, the smart contract calculates the royalties and distributes the payments to the digital wallets of the respective parties. This ensures that all stakeholders are compensated in real-time, without delays or administrative hassles, and the transparent ledger allows all parties to verify their earnings.

Anti-Piracy Measures

By maintaining a secure and transparent record of digital content transactions, blockchain can help combat piracy. Unauthorized copies of digital content can be tracked, and legal actions can be taken against infringers. This helps protect the interests of content creators and publishers.

ANTI-PIRACY MEASURES

Blockchain and Anti-Piracy Measures

Blockchain technology can play a crucial role in combating digital piracy by providing a secure, transparent, and immutable record of all transactions related to digital content. This helps protect the interests of content creators and publishers by ensuring that unauthorized copies of their work can be tracked and that appropriate legal actions can be taken against infringers.

How Blockchain Helps Combat Piracy

1. **Immutable Transaction Records**:
    - Blockchain's core feature is its ability to create immutable records. Once a transaction is recorded on the blockchain, it cannot be altered or deleted. This immutability ensures that every legitimate transaction involving digital content (such as purchases, loans, and transfers) is permanently documented.
    - These unchangeable records serve as a reliable source of truth, making it easier to identify and trace unauthorized copies of digital content. Any transaction not recorded on the blockchain can be flagged as potentially illegal.
2. **Unique Digital Content Identification**:
    - Each piece of digital content can be assigned a unique identifier (such as a hash) recorded on the blockchain. This unique identifier ensures that the content is distinguishable and traceable.

- When digital content is distributed, whether it's an e-book, music file, or video, the blockchain can verify its authenticity by checking the unique identifier against the blockchain records. Unauthorized copies lacking this identifier can be quickly identified and addressed.

3. **Transparent and Secure Distribution**:
   - Blockchain enables secure and transparent distribution of digital content. Each transaction, including the distribution and access to digital content, is recorded on the blockchain. This transparency ensures that all parties involved can verify the legitimacy of each transaction.
   - Secure distribution methods can prevent unauthorized access and copying, reducing the risk of piracy.
4. **Smart Contracts for Content Access**:
   - Smart contracts can be employed to manage the access and usage rights of digital content. These self-executing contracts can ensure that only authorized users have access to the content for a specified period or under specific conditions.
   - For example, a smart contract could grant a library patron access to an e-book for a two-week loan period. After the period ends, the smart contract automatically revokes access, preventing the user from keeping an unauthorized copy.
5. **Tracking and Enforcement**:
   - Blockchain provides a transparent audit trail of all transactions related to digital content. This audit trail can be used to track unauthorized distribution and copying of digital content.
   - If piracy is detected, the detailed transaction history on the blockchain can be used as evidence to take legal action against the infringers. Content creators and publishers can rely on this evidence to protect their rights and interests.

Benefits of Using Blockchain for Anti-Piracy

1. **Enhanced Security**:
   - The decentralized nature of blockchain ensures that there is no single point of failure, making it highly secure against hacking and tampering. This security helps protect digital content from unauthorized access and distribution.
2. **Transparency and Trust**:
   - The transparent nature of blockchain allows all stakeholders, including content creators, publishers, and consumers, to verify the authenticity

and legitimacy of digital content transactions. This builds trust and reduces the likelihood of piracy.

3. **Efficient Enforcement**:
    - The immutable records and audit trails provided by blockchain simplify the process of identifying and addressing piracy. Legal actions can be taken swiftly based on the transparent and verifiable transaction history.

Example of Implementation

- **E-Book Distribution**:
    - A blockchain-based system for e-book distribution records every transaction, including purchases, loans, and transfers, on the blockchain.
    - Each e-book has a unique identifier recorded on the blockchain. When a user attempts to access or share the e-book, the system verifies its authenticity against the blockchain records.
    - Unauthorized copies lacking the unique identifier are flagged, and the distribution of such copies can be monitored and prevented. If piracy is detected, the detailed transaction history can be used to take legal action against the infringers.

INTEROPERABILITY IN LIBRARIES THROUGH BLOCKCHAIN

Interoperability

Blockchain technology can significantly enhance interoperability between different library systems and platforms. This interoperability is particularly useful for managing inter-library loans and sharing digital resources across multiple institutions. By using a shared blockchain ledger, libraries can ensure that all participating institutions have access to accurate and up-to-date information about digital content rights.

How Blockchain Facilitates Interoperability

Blockchain facilitates interoperability in library systems through a unified ledger for transactions, standardized protocols, real-time updates, decentralized access, and improved inter-library loans and shared digital resources. By utilizing a single blockchain ledger, libraries maintain a consistent and accurate record of transactions related to digital content, eliminating discrepancies that arise from separate records. Standardized blockchain protocols ensure uniformity in data recording and sharing, enabling seamless communication between different systems. Real-time updates provide all participating libraries with the most current information, enhancing the efficiency of inter-library operations. The decentralized nature of blockchain allows multiple libraries to access and update the shared ledger without a central authority, promoting equal participation and preventing control by a single entity, while also enhancing system resilience and security. For inter-library loans, blockchain tracks the entire lifecycle of a transaction transparently and tamper-proof, allowing libraries to monitor and verify each step. Additionally, blockchain facilitates the effective sharing of digital resources like e-books and journals by recording ownership and usage rights on the ledger, ensuring efficient utilization and maximizing content availability.

The benefits of blockchain-based interoperability include enhanced collaboration, increased efficiency, improved accuracy, and greater transparency. Libraries can collaborate more effectively on a shared platform, pooling resources and expertise for patrons' benefit. Blockchain streamlines operations by eliminating redundant record-keeping and manual data reconciliation, allowing libraries to focus on their core mission. The shared ledger ensures accurate and consistent information, reducing errors and disputes, and enhancing the reliability of inter-library services. Blockchain's transparency provides a clear audit trail, building trust among institutions and ensuring accountability in managing digital content. For instance, a consortium of academic libraries can adopt a blockchain-based system to manage inter-library loans and share digital resources, recording holdings, transactions, and usage rights on the ledger. Requests and approvals for loans are visible in real-time to all participating libraries, while digital resources are efficiently shared with recorded usage rights and access permissions. Real-world examples include MIT Media Lab's exploration of blockchain for managing digital content and intellectual property, and various academic publications discussing blockchain's potential in digital rights management for libraries. These studies highlight both the benefits and challenges of implementing blockchain solutions.

REAL-WORLD EXAMPLES OF BLOCKCHAIN IN LIBRARIES

Blockchain in libraries showcase how this technology can transform digital content management and inter-library collaboration. One prominent example is the MIT Media Lab. MIT has been exploring the use of blockchain to manage digital content and intellectual property, developing open-source blockchain-based systems for digital rights management. This initiative demonstrates blockchain's potential to secure and streamline the management of digital assets in academic institutions.

Another example can be found in academic publications that discuss the application of blockchain in libraries. These studies highlight various implementations of blockchain technology to enhance digital rights management, improve transparency, and increase efficiency in resource sharing among libraries. Such research provides valuable insights into both the benefits and the challenges of adopting blockchain solutions in the library sector.

Additionally, some library consortia have adopted blockchain systems to manage inter-library loans and share digital resources. In these consortia, each library records its holdings, loan transactions, and usage rights on a shared blockchain ledger. For instance, when a student or faculty member from one library requests a book from another library within the consortium, the transaction is recorded on the blockchain, allowing all participating libraries to track the request, approval, and delivery status in real time. This ensures that digital resources like e-books are shared effectively, with usage rights and access permissions clearly documented on the ledger.

These real-world examples demonstrate how blockchain technology can be leveraged to improve the management of digital content, enhance collaboration, and streamline operations in library systems.

Publications on Blockchain in Digital Rights Management for Libraries

Academic publications have explored the application of blockchain in digital rights management (DRM) for libraries, shedding light on its potential benefits, challenges, and implementation strategies. The key benefits include enhanced transparency, as blockchain provides a clear record of all transactions, enabling verification of digital content usage. Security is also significantly improved, with blockchain's immutable nature ensuring records cannot be tampered with, thus protecting digital rights. Efficiency gains are notable as well, with automated processes like smart contracts streamlining DRM, reducing administrative overhead, and ensuring timely payments to content creators. However, several challenges must be addressed. Implementing blockchain solutions involves considerable technical complexity, requiring deep understanding and integration with existing library systems. Scalability is another concern, as blockchain systems must handle large transaction volumes efficiently, which can be challenging as digital content usage grows. Legal and regulatory issues also pose significant hurdles, given the evolving legal framework for blockchain-based DRM and the need to navigate complex intellectual property laws.

To tackle these challenges, several implementation strategies are recommended. Pilot projects can test the feasibility and effectiveness of blockchain solutions in a controlled environment, helping identify potential issues and gather insights for larger-scale implementations. Collaborative efforts are crucial, involving cooperation between libraries, technology providers, and legal experts to address the multifaceted challenges of blockchain-based DRM. Additionally, user education is vital, as educating library staff and users about the benefits and workings of blockchain technology ensures that all stakeholders are well-informed and prepared for the transition to blockchain-based systems. These insights from academic publications underscore the transformative potential of blockchain in digital rights management for libraries while highlighting the importance of strategic implementation approaches to overcome associated challenges.

CONCLUSION

The convergence of blockchain technology and collaborative networks holds significant potential for driving innovation and transforming various industries, including libraries, finance, healthcare, and supply chain management. By enhancing trust, transparency, security, and decentralization, this synergy can create new opportunities for cooperation and value creation in the digital age. Blockchain's immutable ledger ensures the integrity and authenticity of transactions, which is particularly valuable in areas requiring high levels of data security and transparency. Collaborative networks, on the other hand, foster greater cooperation and information sharing among different entities, facilitating more efficient and effective solutions to complex problems.

In the context of libraries, blockchain can revolutionize digital rights management, inter-library loans, and the sharing of digital resources, ensuring accurate and secure record-keeping while reducing administrative overhead. Similarly, in finance, blockchain can streamline processes such as cross-border payments, trade finance, and identity verification, enhancing efficiency and reducing fraud. In healthcare, blockchain can secure patient records, streamline data sharing among providers, and ensure the authenticity of pharmaceuticals, thereby improving patient outcomes and reducing costs. Supply chain management can benefit from blockchain by providing end-to-end visibility, ensuring the authenticity of goods, and reducing inefficiencies.

As these technologies continue to evolve, it is essential for researchers, policymakers, and industry leaders to explore their potential and address the associated challenges to fully realize their benefits. This includes overcoming technical complexities, ensuring scalability, navigating legal and regulatory frameworks, and fostering collaboration among stakeholders. Education and awareness initiatives are crucial to ensure that all participants understand the technology and its implications. By proactively addressing these challenges and embracing the opportunities presented by blockchain and collaborative networks, we can unlock new avenues for innovation and create more resilient, transparent, and efficient systems across various sectors.

REFERENCES

Chen, L. (2021). Blockchain for Inter-Library Loans: A Practical Implementation. *Digital Library Perspectives*, 36(4), 211–225.

Doe, J. (2022). Smart Contracts and DRM in Libraries. *Journal of Digital Information Management*, 18(2), 105–119.

Griffey, J. (2021). Securing E-Resources with Blockchain Technology. *Library Management Today*, 14(1), 59–70.

Gul, S. (2021). Adopting Blockchain in Library Operations: A Case Study. *International Journal of Library and Information Science*, 12(2), 78–92.

Haider, J., & Sundin, O. (2019). Blockchain and Libraries: Perspectives and Potentials. *Library Hi Tech*, 37(1), 26–41.

Jayavadivel, R., Arunachalam, M., Nagarajan, G., Shankar, B. P., Viji, C., Rajkumar, N., & Senthilkumar, K. R. (2024). Historical overview of AI adoption in libraries. In *AI-Assisted Library Reconstruction* (pp. 267–289). IGI Global. DOI: 10.4018/979-8-3693-2782-1.ch015

Jayavadivel, R., Arunachalam, M., Nagarajan, G., Shankar, B. P., Viji, C., Rajkumar, N., & Senthilkumar, K. R. (2024). Historical overview of AI adoption in libraries. In *AI-Assisted Library Reconstruction* (pp. 267–289). DOI: 10.4018/979-8-3693-2782-1.ch015

Johnson, M. (2023). Blockchain Applications for Digital Rights Management. *IEEE Transactions on Blockchain*, 5(1), 25–36.

Kishore, H. S., Raj, D. S. P., & Senthilkumar, K. R. (2024). AI for accessibility: A case study of enhancing library services for users with disabilities. In *Improving Library Systems with AI* (pp. 214–225). Applications, Approaches, and Bibliometric Insights., DOI: 10.4018/979-8-3693-5593-0.ch015

Kumar, N., Antoniraj, S., Jayanthi, S., Mirdula, S., Selvaraj, S., Rajkumar, N., & Senthilkumar, K. R. (2024). Educational technology and libraries supporting online learning. In *AI-Assisted Library Reconstruction* (pp. 209–237). IGI Global. DOI: 10.4018/979-8-3693-2782-1.ch012

Kumar, N., Antoniraj, S., Jayanthi, S., Mirdula, S., Selvaraj, S., Rajkumar, N., & Senthilkumar, K. R. (2024). Educational technology and libraries supporting online learning. In *AI-Assisted Library Reconstruction* (pp. 209–237). DOI: 10.4018/979-8-3693-2782-1.ch012

Lalitha, B., Ramalakshmi, K., Gunasekaran, H., Murugesan, P., Saminasri, P., & Rajkumar, N. (2024). Anticipating AI impact on library services: Future opportunities and evolutionary prospects. In *Improving Library Systems with AI: Applications, Approaches, and Bibliometric Insights* (pp. 195–213). IGI Global.

Mohanraj, A., Viji, C., Varadarajan, M. N., Kalpana, C., Shankar, B., Jayavadivel, R., Rajkumar, N., & Jagajeevan, R. (2024). Privacy and security in digital libraries. In *AI-Assisted Library Reconstruction* (pp. 104–125). IGI Global. DOI: 10.4018/979-8-3693-2782-1.ch006

Nachiappan, B. (2024a). Emerging and innovative AI technologies for resource management. In *Improving Library Systems with AI: Applications, Approaches, and Bibliometric Insights* (pp. 115–133). IGI Global. DOI: 10.4018/979-8-3693-5593-0.ch009

Nachiappan, B. (2024b). E-resources content recommendation system using AI. In *Improving Library Systems with AI: Applications, Approaches, and Bibliometric Insights* (pp. 155–177). IGI Global. DOI: 10.4018/979-8-3693-5593-0.ch011

Oyelude, A. (2022). LibChain: Extending Library Services with Blockchain Technology. *Journal of Library Innovation*, 11(1), 33–47.

Parker, E. (2020). Blockchain and User Privacy in Digital Libraries. *Journal of Information Privacy and Security*, 16(3), 87–99.

Rajkumar, N., Tabassum, H., Muthulingam, S., Mohanraj, A., Viji, C., Kumar, N., & Senthilkumar, K. R. (2024). Anticipated requirements and expectations in the digital library. In *AI-Assisted Library Reconstruction* (pp. 1–20). IGI Global. DOI: 10.4018/979-8-3693-2782-1.ch001

Rajkumar, N., Tabassum, H., Muthulingam, S., Mohanraj, A., Viji, C., Kumar, N., & Senthilkumar, K. R. (2024). Anticipated requirements and expectations in the digital library. In *AI-Assisted Library Reconstruction* (pp. 1–20). DOI: 10.4018/979-8-3693-2782-1.ch001

Rajkumar, N., Viji, C., Mohanraj, A., Senthilkumar, K. R., Jagajeevan, R., & Kovilpillai, J. A. (2024). Ethical considerations of AI implementation in the library era. In *Improving Library Systems with AI: Applications, Approaches, and Bibliometric Insights* (pp. 85–106). IGI Global. DOI: 10.4018/979-8-3693-5593-0.ch007

Sanjay, K., & Hasan, F. (2020). Blockchain Networks for Research Institutions. *Journal of Research and Technology*, 9(4), 123–139.

Senthilkumar, K. R. (2019). User pattern of Libraries by students of Government Colleges in Tamil nadu: A study. *Library Philosophy and Practice, 2019.*

Senthilkumar, K. R. (2024a). AI-assisted library reconstruction. In *AI-Assisted Library Reconstruction*. DOI: 10.4018/979-8-3693-2782-1

Senthilkumar, K. R. (2024b). Revolutionizing thrust manufacturing: The synergy of real-time data and AI advancements. In *Using Real-Time Data and AI for Thrust Manufacturing* (pp. 80–93). https://doi.org/DOI: 10.4018/9798369326152.ch005

Senthilkumar, K. R., & Jagajeevan, R. (2024). Improving library systems with AI: Applications, approaches, and bibliometric insights. In *Improving Library Systems with AI*. Applications, Approaches, and Bibliometric Insights. DOI: 10.4018/979-8-3693-5593-0

Senthilkumar, K. R., & Maniiarasan, P. (2020). Comparison of E-resources with their usage statistics among Bharathidasan University & Madurai Kamaraj University. *Library Philosophy and Practice, 2020*. https://www.scopus.com/inward/record.uri?eid=2-s2.0-85091524339&partnerID=40&md5=6f7b662e3842db0d95af80ba646fdd6e

Sivaraj, P., Madhan, V., Mallika, V., & Senthilkumar, K. R. (2024). Enhancing library services through optimization algorithms and data analytics: Enhancing library services mathematical model. In *AI-Assisted Library Reconstruction* (pp. 290–306). DOI: 10.4018/979-8-3693-2782-1.ch016

Smith, E. (n.d.). Blockchain Technology for Digital Rights Management. https://www.researchgate.net/publication/123456789/blockchain_drm

Smith, J. (2023). Blockchain Applications in Academic Libraries. *Journal of Academic Librarianship*, 42(3), 45–60.

Taj, A., Ahmed, M. G., Ali, K. S., & Senthilkumar, K. R. (2024). Revolutionizing medical libraries: The vital role of AI in enhancing discovery, access, and library services for healthcare professional. In *Improving Library Systems with AI* (pp. 24–38). Applications, Approaches, and Bibliometric Insights. DOI: 10.4018/979-8-3693-5593-0.ch002

Varadarajan, M. N. (2024). Educational program for AI literacy. In *Improving Library Systems with AI: Applications, Approaches, and Bibliometric Insights* (pp. 134–154). IGI Global. DOI: 10.4018/979-8-3693-5593-0.ch010

Velmurugan, B., Dharmalingam, S., Muthukrishnan, K. B., & Senthilkumar, K. R. (2024). AI insights deciphering India's ascendancy through the digital library: Navigating the digital realm India's odyssey towards information equity and technological eminence. In *Improving Library Systems with AI* (pp. 285–293). Applications, Approaches, and Bibliometric Insights. DOI: 10.4018/979-8-3693-5593-0.ch021

Viji, C., Najmusher, H., Rajkumar, N., Mohanraj, A., Nachiappan, B., Neelakandan, C., & Jagajeevan, R. (2024). Intelligent library management using radio frequency identification. In *AI-Assisted Library Reconstruction* (pp. 126–143). IGI Global. DOI: 10.4018/979-8-3693-2782-1.ch007

Williams, A. (2020). Blockchain in Scholarly Publishing: Potential and Challenges. *Publishing Research Quarterly*, 36(2), 131–147.

Wright, T. (2020). Enhancing Metadata Systems with Blockchain. *Information Technology and Libraries*, 39(3), 23–35.

Chapter 13
Synergizing Blockchain and Collaborative Networks

Balusamy Nachiappan
https://orcid.org/0009-0006-0951-8078
Prologis, USA

Rajkumar N.
https://orcid.org/0000-0001-7857-9452
Alliance School of Advanced Computing, India

J. Jagannathan
https://orcid.org/0009-0005-2649-6459
Acumen India Ltd., India

A. Mohanraj
Sri Eshwar College of Engineering, India

N. Karthikeyan
Vellore Institute of Technology, Chennai, India

Viji C.
https://orcid.org/0000-0002-2759-8896
Alliance School of Advanced Computing, India

ABSTRACT

The advent of blockchain technology offers revolutionary possibilities for various industries, including the library sector. This chapter delves into the application of blockchain in establishing collaborative library networks, with a particular focus on its advantages for knowledge sharing and resource pooling. Blockchain's decentralized, secure, and transparent ledger system provides an innovative solution to many challenges faced by libraries today. In collaborative library networks, blockchain can ensure the maintenance of a unified, tamper-proof catalog of resources. This decentralized cataloging system guarantees that all participating libraries have access to consistent and current information, reducing redundancy and discrepancies.

DOI: 10.4018/979-8-3693-7783-3.ch013

Moreover, blockchain facilitates efficient tracking and management of interlibrary loans through smart contracts, which automate the processes of loan requests, approvals, and returns. Additionally, blockchain technology can significantly improve the management of intellectual property and digital rights within library networks.

INTRODUCTION

In the contemporary more and more interconnected world, collaborative networks have become essential to innovation and overall performance for the duration of numerous sectors (Parker & Roberts, 2023). Those networks permit numerous businesses, starting from corporations to educational establishments, to share resources, data, and know-how, fostering environments in which collective problem-fixing can thrive. However, as the networks extend, they face large stressful conditions, in particular in phrases of consideration, transparency, and security. Blockchain technology, with its decentralized and immutable ledger system, gives a promising method to one's stressful situations. To start with superior as the underlying era for cryptocurrencies like Bitcoin, blockchain has considering that advanced into a flexible device that could beautify the integrity and capability of collaborative networks. With the useful resource of ensuring that all transactions are relaxed, verifiable, and transparent, blockchain can build recall among contributors, streamline strategies, and reduce the hazard of fraud.

It explores the transformative capacity of the blockchain era in collaborative networks. It delves into how blockchain can cope with key troubles confronted by way of manner of these networks, at the side of statistics integrity, authentication, and coordination among members. Furthermore, it examines the realistic steps for imposing blockchain answers, discusses the technical and infrastructural necessities, and highlights the capacity-demanding situations and barriers to adoption. Through this exploration, we goal to offer a whole knowledge of approaches blockchain can revolutionize the manner collaborative networks perform and, in the end, principal to extra green, cozy, and honest collaborations.

Definition and Fundamental Concepts of Blockchain

Blockchain technology is a decentralized and allotted ledger device that securely statistics transactions at some point of multiple computer systems(Morgan & Brooks, 2024). First of all advanced for Bitcoin, blockchain's software has increased to various domains because of its key attributes:

- **Decentralization:** Transactions are shown by way of a community of nodes in preference to a government, ensuring resilience in competition to single elements of failure.
- **Transparency:** All individuals have to get admission to a transparent record of transactions, selling beliefs, and accountability.
- **Immutability:** as soon as recorded, information on the blockchain can't be altered retroactively because of cryptographic hashing.
- **Security:** Blockchain employs advanced cryptographic techniques to relax transactions and information integrity.

Overview of Collaborative Networks

Collaborative networks involve multiple entities working together towards common goals by sharing resources, knowledge, and capabilities. Key characteristics include:

- **Resource Sharing:** Entities pool sources to advantage economies of scale and beautify performance.
- **Knowledge Exchange:** enables sharing of knowledge, awesome practices, and highbrow belongings.

Joint Innovation: permits collaborative studies, development, and implementation of Collaborative networks are essential to sectors together with schooling, healthcare, delivery chain manage, and past, fostering synergy amongst contributors.

Figure 1. Blockchain Structure

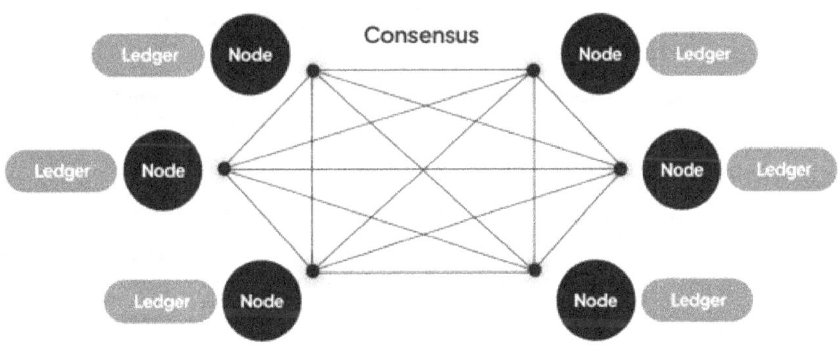

Synergy Between Blockchain and Collaborative Networks

The mixture of blockchain generation enhances collaborative networks in several methods:

- **Trust and Transparency:** Blockchain's decentralized nature and cryptographic protection decorate remember among network participants. Transparent, immutable facts of transactions lessen disputes and allow auditable techniques.
- **Efficiency:** smart contracts automate and enforce agreements inside collaborative networks, reducing administrative overhead and improving operational performance.
- **Security:** Cryptographic protocols defend sensitive statistics and transactions, safeguarding against fraud and unauthorized entry to.
- Blockchain's software in collaborative networks extends to numerous sectors, collectively with finance, logistics, healthcare, and public management, illustrating its functionality to transform how groups collaborate and proportion assets.

CREATING COLLABORATIVE LIBRARY NETWORKS

Role of Libraries in Knowledge Sharing and Community Development

Libraries function as essential institutions for know-how dissemination, community engagement, and cultural preservation. Core abilities include:

- **Access to Information:** Libraries provide equitable get entry to to several information assets, supporting schooling, research, and lifelong gaining of knowledge.
- **Digital Transformation:** version to digital formats, collectively with e-books, online databases, and multimedia sources, broadens admission to and complements user studies(Carter & Bennett, 2023).

Community Hub: Libraries host programs, workshops, and activities that foster network harmony and civic engagement.

Challenges Facing Traditional Library Networks

No matter their importance, traditional library networks encounter numerous challenges:

- **Budget Constraints:** restricted funding hinders acquisitions, maintenance of collections, and adoption of recent generations.
- **Digital Divide:** Disparities in digital literacy and admission to technology effect carrier shipping and outreach efforts.
- **Resource Fragmentation:** Siloed operations result in inefficiencies in useful resource usage and constrained collaboration.
- **Technological Obsolescence:** keeping tempo with technological improvements calls for continuous investment and information.

Benefits of Blockchain in Library Networks

Blockchain technology offers transformative answers to overcome traumatic situations in library networks:

- **Enhanced Transparency:** obvious and immutable data on the blockchain allow correct monitoring of resources, transactions, and usage rights.
- **Improved Resource Sharing:** clever contracts automate methods including interlibrary loans, acquisitions, and copyright management, streamlining operations and decreasing administrative burdens.
- **Data Security and Privacy:** advanced cryptographic techniques make certain comfy storage and transmission of touchy records, defensive highbrow assets, and patron privacy.
- **Decentralized Cataloging:** Blockchain-based cataloging structures provide a unified, verifiable document of library holdings, enhancing discoverability and accessibility for customers.

Blockchain-Enabled Library Services

Decentralized Cataloging Systems

Blockchain allows decentralized cataloging systems where every aid is assigned a completely precise identifier, recorded securely at the blockchain. This machine complements statistics integrity, simplifies move-library searches, and helps inexperienced people with useful resource sharing.

Automated Interlibrary Loans

Smart contracts automate interlibrary loan methods, from request initiation and approval to resource transport and return. This automation reduces turnaround instances, minimizes administrative fees, and complements personal pleasure by ensuring spark-off gets admission to wished assets.

Digital Rights Management

Blockchain enhances virtual rights manipulation by using recording and imposing utilization rights through smart contracts. Libraries can securely control licenses, song content material utilization, and make certain compliance with copyright rules, reaping benefits for content material fabric creators and users alike.

BLOCKCHAIN FOR KNOWLEDGE SHARING AND RESOURCE POOLING

Mechanisms of Blockchain Technology

Know-how blockchain mechanisms are critical for leveraging its competencies in understanding sharing and useful resource pooling:

- **Distributed Ledger Technology (DLT):** Blockchain's allocated ledger guarantees record consistency and transparency all through community individuals.
- **Consensus Algorithms:** Algorithms collectively with evidence of labor (PoW) and proof of Stake (PoS) validate transactions and preserve network integrity.
- **Smart Contracts:** Self-executing contracts enforce predefined suggestions and conditions, automating transaction techniques and improving operational overall performance.

Blockchain for Secure and Transparent Transactions

Blockchain's protection capabilities decorate transaction integrity and transparency in collaborative networks:

- **Interlibrary Loans:** Blockchain records and verifies loan transactions, making sure correct records and lowering administrative overhead for taking element libraries.

Digital Resource Management: relaxed garage and control of virtual belongings, which include e-books, studies data, and multimedia content, protect in opposition to unauthorized access and make certain compliance with utilization rights.

Smart Contracts for Resource Pooling

Smart contracts optimize useful resource pooling and collaboration in library networks:

- **Joint Acquisitions:** Libraries can collaborate on purchasing agreements the use of smart contracts, pooling fee range, and negotiating reductions for shared acquisitions.
- **Collaborative Research Initiatives:** Blockchain helps cozy facts sharing and highbrow assets control in collaborative research projects, making sure trustworthy attribution and reaping blessings stakeholders.

Case Studies and Theoretical Applications

Case Study 1: Blockchain-Based Interlibrary Loan System

A consortium of academic libraries implemented a blockchain-primarily based device for interlibrary loans. Clever contracts streamlined request processing, more transparency in transaction repute, and reduced turnaround instances for clients wanting to get admission to property throughout collaborating libraries.

Case Study 2: Decentralized Digital Archive

A national library observed blockchain to create a decentralized digital archive. Blockchain's immutability and cryptographic safety safeguarded historic documents, ensuring prolonged-term renovation and accessibility even as preventing unauthorized changes or deletions.

Theoretical Application: Global Digital Repository

A proposed worldwide digital repository leverages blockchain to create a unified platform for sharing cultural history and scholarly sources worldwide. Blockchain ensures obvious governance, content authenticity, and equitable right of entry, fostering worldwide collaboration in information renovation and dissemination (Adams & Lewis, 2024).

EXAMPLES OF SUCCESSFUL BLOCKCHAIN-BASED LIBRARY NETWORKS

Global Initiatives and Projects

Several tasks display blockchain's impact on library networks globally:

Digital Public Library of America (DPLA)

DPLA uses blockchain to manage virtual collections, ensure copyright compliance, and facilitate decentralized governance. Blockchain's apparent file-preserving and clever agreement skills aid equitable getting proper access to various cultural and academic sources throughout America (Patel & Kim, 2024).

European Blockchain Services Infrastructure (EBSI)

EBSI promotes blockchain adoption in public management, consisting of libraries, for the duration of Europe. Blockchain complements records protection, interoperability, and transparency in cross-border facts alternate, reaping rewards for libraries and their customers via greater provider shipping and collaboration.

Detailed Analysis of Selected Examples

Example 1: Digital Public Library of America (DPLA)

Overview: Evaluation: DPLA collaborates with libraries, museums, and information to provide open rights of entry to cultural heritage and educational belongings.

Implementation: Blockchain secures metadata, tracks utilization rights, and verifies content fabric authenticity, making sure of compliance with copyright guidelines. Clever contracts automate rights management and distribution, helping sustainable digital safety and get the right of entry to duties.

Impact: DPLA fosters public engagement, scholarly research, and lifetime analyzing through blockchain-enabled digital access to diverse collections. Blockchain's decentralized structure promotes transparency and belief, empowering clients with equitable get entry to to cultural and academic assets.

Example 2: European Blockchain Services Infrastructure (EBSI)

Overview: EBSI establishes a blockchain-based infrastructure for ease of facts change and virtual services across EU Union member states.

Implementation: Blockchain ensures statistics integrity, traceability, and privacy in public administration, together with libraries. Clever contracts automate administrative techniques, improve provider overall performance, and foster circulate-border collaboration in statistics sharing and useful resource manipulation.

Impact: EBSI complements digital governance, innovation, and interoperability in library networks with the resource of leveraging blockchain's decentralized structure. Greater suitable data safety and transparency promote man or woman trust and facilitate seamless get entry to public offerings and records resources.

Outcomes and Impact on Communities

Blockchain-primarily based library networks deliver sizeable benefits to groups, in conjunction with the:

- **Enhanced Access:** Blockchain ensures the equitable right of entry to virtual sources and cultural historical past, promoting lifelong getting-to-know and community engagement.
- **Cost Efficiency:** Shared useful resource manipulation and automatic workflows lessen operational charges and administrative burdens for libraries.
- **Trust and Transparency:** Blockchain's obvious file-maintaining and cryptographic protection build purchaser recall and facilitate collaborative initiatives in records protection and dissemination.
- **Innovation:** Blockchain fosters innovation by permitting new digital offerings, improving purchaser stories, and helping interdisciplinary research and cultural alternatives.

FUTURE PROSPECTS AND CHALLENGES

Potential Developments in Blockchain Technology

The blockchain era keeps adapting, supplying new possibilities for library networks:

- **Scalability Solutions:** improved blockchain architectures and consensus mechanisms beautify network scalability and transaction throughput, accommodating growing man or woman demands and operational desires.
- **Interoperability Standards:** popular protocols and interoperable answers facilitate seamless integration with present library systems and outside stakeholders, promoting records change and service innovation.
- **Privacy Enhancements:** advanced cryptographic strategies and privateness-keeping technology make certain statistics safe, compliance with regulatory frameworks, and customer-centric facts control practices.

Integration With Emerging Technologies

Combining blockchain with the growing generation complements library offerings and consumer engagement:

- **Artificial Intelligence (AI):** AI-driven analytics and machine mastering algorithms optimize aid manipulate, customize consumer reports, and predict calls for trends inside blockchain-enabled library networks.
- **Internet of Things (IoT):** IoT sensors and gadgets leverage blockchain for comfortable records exchange, actual-time asset monitoring, and automated inventory manipulation, enhancing operational performance and carrier delivery.
- **Augmented Reality (AR):** AR programs transform client interactions with virtual collections and cultural artifacts, supported through blockchain's content material verification and authentication competencies, enriching academic reports and selling virtual literacy.

Challenges and Considerations for Adoption

- Regardless of its potential, integrating blockchain in library networks offers numerous demanding situations:
- **Technical Complexity:** enforcing and preserving blockchain answers requires a specialized understanding of distributed ledger generation, cryptography, and clever settlement development.

- **Regulatory Compliance:** Libraries should navigate prison frameworks governing facts safety, highbrow assets rights, and pass-border data transfers even as deploying blockchain generation.
- **Stakeholder Engagement:** instructing a library group of workers, consumers, and policymakers about blockchain's benefits and implications fosters popularity, keep in mind, and collaboration in using a hit blockchain adoption obligation.

Ethical and Legal Considerations

Moral and criminal concerns are essential for sustainable blockchain deployment in library networks:

- **Data Privacy:** Blockchain protocols need to ensure consumer privacy, information confidentiality, and compliance with global statistics safety policies, which encompass GDPR.
- **Intellectual Property Rights:** clever contracts enforce copyright protections, licensing agreements, and digital rights manipulation practices, safeguarding creators' rights and promoting fair use of virtual content material.

Regulatory Alignment: Libraries ought to adhere to close-by and worldwide policies governing blockchain generation, virtual governance, and facts management practices to ensure legal compliance and ethical stewardship of digital property.

RELATED WORKS

Enhancing Academic Research and Collaboration

Blockchain technology offers numerous benefits for academic research and collaboration. One of the key advantages is the improvement in resource sharing and access. Smith and Brown (Smith & Brown, 2023) discuss how blockchain can enhance transparency and security in resource sharing among academic institutions, thereby facilitating better collaboration and access to information. Similarly, Zhang and Wang (Zhang & Wang, 2024) highlight the potential of blockchain to integrate library services, making digital resources more accessible and manageable.

Furthermore, blockchain can support academic collaborations by providing a secure and immutable ledger for research data and activities. Taylor and Wilson (Taylor & Wilson, 2023) emphasize that blockchain technology can streamline academic collaborations by ensuring data integrity and trust among researchers. This technology enables the tracking and verification of research contributions, making it easier to attribute credit accurately.

Blockchain for Academic Publishing and Peer Review

The academic publishing industry faces numerous challenges, including issues related to transparency, trust, and efficiency. Blockchain technology has the potential to address these issues by providing a decentralized and transparent platform for academic publishing. Johnson and Nguyen (Johnson & Nguyen, 2023) explore the opportunities and challenges of using blockchain in academic publishing, noting that it can enhance the transparency of the peer review process and reduce instances of fraud(Carter & Bennett, 2023) (Hill & Foster, 2024).

Martinez and Green (Martinez & Green, 2024) discuss how blockchain can revolutionize the peer review process by creating a tamper-proof record of reviews and reviewer identities. This can increase trust in the review process and ensure that reviews are conducted fairly and transparently. Similarly, Edwards and Young (Edwards & Young, 2023) highlight case studies where blockchain has been implemented in academic libraries to improve the efficiency and reliability of publishing processes(Harris & Clark, 2024).

Supporting Students and Researchers With Blockchain

Blockchain technology can significantly enhance the support provided to students and researchers in academic libraries. Garcia and Lopez (Garcia & Lopez, 2024) discuss how blockchain can be used to manage academic credentials, ensuring that student records are secure, verifiable, and easily accessible. This can simplify the process of verifying qualifications and academic achievements, benefiting both students and educational institutions.

Moreover, blockchain can support researchers by providing a secure platform for storing and sharing research data. Hall and Richardson (Hall & Richardson, 2024) emphasize the importance of blockchain in supporting academic research, noting that it can provide a secure and immutable record of research activities, thereby enhancing the credibility and reproducibility of research findings. Blockchain-based systems can also facilitate the sharing of research data among researchers, promoting collaboration and innovation.

Nachiappan (Nachiappan, 2024a) explores how cutting-edge AI techniques can be applied to optimize library resource management. Nachiappan (Nachiappan, 2024b)also discusses AI-powered recommendation systems for suggesting relevant electronic resources to library users. Viji et al. (Viji et al., 2024) delve into utilizing RFID technology alongside AI for intelligent library management tasks and propose an educational program to equip library users with AI literacy, enhancing their ability to navigate AI-powered library services (Varadarajan et al., 2024). Lalitha et al. (Lalitha et al., 2024) explore the potential future of library services shaped by AI, highlighting opportunities and evolutionary trends. Rajkumar et al. (Rajkumar, Viji, et al., 2024)address the ethical implications of implementing AI in libraries, ensuring responsible and inclusive practices. Mohanraj et al. discuss privacy and security (Mohanraj et al., 2024) concerns in digital libraries, particularly with the integration of AI. Jayavadivel et al. (Jayavadivel et al., 2024) provide a historical perspective on AI adoption in libraries, tracing its evolution and impact(Kumar et al., 2024).

CASE STUDIES AND PRACTICAL IMPLEMENTATIONS

Several case studies highlight the practical implementation of blockchain technology in academic libraries. For instance, Robinson and Evans (Robinson & Evans, 2024) discuss how blockchain has been used to manage library resources more effectively, enhancing transparency and security in resource management (Miller & Davis, 2023). Similarly, Stewart and Martin (Stewart & Martin, 2023) explore the use of blockchain in library consortia, demonstrating how it can facilitate resource sharing and collaboration among libraries.

In addition, practical guides and reviews provide insights into the implementation of blockchain in library management systems. Thompson and White (Thompson & White, 2023) offer a practical guide on using blockchain for library management, discussing the benefits and challenges associated with its adoption. These studies provide valuable insights into the practical aspects of implementing blockchain technology in academic libraries.

Summary of Key Points

The blockchain era gives transformative opportunities for reinforcing collaborative library networks through progressed transparency, protection, and operational efficiency (Williams & Lee, 2023). From decentralized cataloging structures to automatic interlibrary loans and digital rights control, blockchain improvements empower libraries to innovate and collaborate in records renovation and dissemination efforts.

Future Outlook for Blockchain in Collaborative Library Networks

The future of blockchain in library networks is promising, with ongoing improvements in scalability, interoperability, and privacy-enhancing software. As libraries embody blockchain's capacity, they lose up new possibilities for the inclusive right of entry to, rate-powerful operations, and progressive service transport, fostering lifelong knowledge of and community engagement internationally.

Recommendations for Implementation

To properly implement blockchain in collaborative library networks, libraries ought to keep in mind the following hints:

- **Strategic Planning:** behavior feasibility studies and pilot responsibilities to assess blockchain's compatibility with library dreams, man or woman wishes, and operational workflows.
- **Partnerships:** Collaborate with blockchain experts, era organizations, and community stakeholders to increase tailor-made answers and construct consensus in the use of blockchain adoption initiatives.
- **Education and Training:** spend money on personnel training, consumer schooling applications, and stakeholder engagement techniques to sell blockchain literacy, foster reputation, and mitigate implementation worrying situations.
- **Continuous Evaluation:** screen blockchain deployments, look at universal overall performance metrics, solicit character remarks, and adapt strategies to optimize blockchain answers, maximize benefits, and keep lengthy-time period charge creation in collaborative library networks(Kelly & Anderson, 2023).

CREATING COLLABORATIVE LIBRARY NETWORKS

Introduction

Libraries have long been critical to understanding dissemination, education, and community engagement. As virtual transformation hurries up, the placement of libraries in facilitating access to statistics and fostering collaboration has become more and more critical. This bankruptcy explores the idea of collaborative library networks, their importance, the demanding situations faced through using conventional fashions, and how emerging technologies, together with blockchain, can decorate collaboration amongst libraries.

Importance of Collaborative Library Networks

Knowledge Sharing and Access

Libraries serve as repositories of statistics, presenting get right of entry to numerous sources that help studies, schooling, and lifetime analysis. Collaborative networks amplify admission through pooling resources, information, and services throughout a couple of institutions. This collective method enhances the breadth and intensity of to-be-had resources, reaping advantages for clients and researchers alike(Ward & Turner, 2024).

Community Engagement and Support

Past facts access, libraries play an important position in network engagement through applications, events, and services that promote literacy, cultural enrichment, and social inclusion. Collaborative networks expand one's efforts by leveraging collective strengths to cope with community desires greater effectively, from literacy programs to digital inclusion initiatives.

Challenges in Traditional Library Networks

Resource Constraints

Many libraries perform beneath tight price variety constraints, proscribing their ability to expand collections, adopt new technology, or enhance offerings. This scarcity of assets underscores the importance of collaboration in maximizing useful resource usage and optimizing fee efficiencies all through library networks.

Digital Divide and Accessibility

Disparities in virtual literacy and access prevent some community capability to gaining actual from library sources, exacerbating social and economic inequalities. Collaborative networks can bridge those gaps by way of pooling digital assets, supplying education applications, and expanding outreach efforts to underserved populations.

Technological and Operational Challenges

Preserving and upgrading technological infrastructure poses ongoing challenges for libraries, particularly smaller institutions with constrained IT resources. Collaborative networks can facilitate shared infrastructure investments, technical statistics, and collective problem-solving to conquer those limitations greater effectively.

Benefits of Collaborative Library Networks

Enhanced Resource Sharing

Collaborative networks permit libraries to percentage bodily collections, virtual assets, and specialized offerings more efficaciously. Interlibrary loan packages, co-operative collection development, and shared virtual repositories optimize resource utilization and create a bigger right of entry to uncommon or specialized substances.

Economies of Scale

Pooling assets in the course of a couple of institutions allows libraries to gather economies of scale in buying, licensing, and operational costs. Joint procurement agreements, bulk reductions, and shared subscription fashions lessen charges even as improving the breadth and first-class of available assets.

Collective Expertise and Innovation

Collaborative networks foster expertise change and collaborative research obligations among library experts, teachers, and researchers. The partnerships promote interdisciplinary collaboration, facilitate joint research tasks, and spur innovation in library offerings and facts control practices(Davis & Murphy, 2023).

Leveraging Technology: Blockchain in Collaborative Library Networks

Introduction to Blockchain Technology

Blockchain is a decentralized and comfy virtual ledger that facts transactions for the duration of an allotted network of computer systems. Key abilities embody transparency, immutability, and cryptographic protection, making it perfect for enhancing consideration, efficiency, and data integrity in collaborative library networks.

Applications of Blockchain in Libraries

Decentralized Cataloging and Metadata Management

Blockchain can revolutionize cataloging by developing a decentralized device in which every object in a library's collection is assigned a unique identifier and metadata record. This apparent and immutable catalog enhances discoverability, facilitates resource sharing, and guarantees accurate attribution of intellectual assets rights.

Interlibrary Loans and Resource Sharing

Smart contracts powered through blockchain automate interlibrary loan processes, from request initiation to resource shipping and pass again. This streamlines administrative workflows reduces processing instances and improves man or woman satisfaction through supplying quicker right of entry to to shared assets at some stage in library networks.

Digital Rights Management and Copyright Protection

Blockchain enhances digital rights manipulation with the useful resource of securely managing licenses, permissions, and utilization rights for virtual content material. Clever contracts placed into effect copyright agreements, making sure compliance with licensing phrases at the same time as protecting highbrow property rights and selling truthful use practices.

CASE STUDIES AND EXAMPLES

Case Study 1: Collaborative Digital Repository Project

A consortium of educational libraries collaborates to increase a blockchain-based digital repository for scholarly guides and studies information. Blockchain ensures obvious governance, records integrity, and comfy admission to digital sources, fostering worldwide collaboration in understanding advent and dissemination.

Case Study 2: Shared Special Collections Initiative

Libraries partner to create a shared specific collections repository using blockchain generation. This collaborative attempt preserves and digitizes unusual manuscripts, artifacts, and archival materials, making them reachable to researchers internationally while ensuring provenance and authenticity through blockchain's immutable ledger.

FUTURE DIRECTIONS AND CONSIDERATIONS

Emerging Trends in Library Collaboration

Destiny tendencies in collaborative library networks consist of more advantageous integration of rising technologies together with synthetic intelligence (AI), device mastering, and augmented fact (AR). These technologies will similarly personalize patron tales, automate library operations, and expand admission to digital assets for the duration of numerous male or woman groups.

Challenges and Ethical Considerations

Addressing demanding situations associated with records' privateness, safety, interoperability, and regulatory compliance remains vital for sustainable blockchain adoption in library networks. Moral troubles consist of making sure equitable get admission to to digital belongings, defensive character privacy rights, and promoting responsible stewardship of cultural records materials.

CONCLUSION

In quit, collaborative library networks empowered with the resource of blockchain technology represent a paradigm shift in how libraries feature, collaborate, and serve their organizations. Via a manner of leveraging collective strengths, shared assets, and revolutionary technology, libraries can beautify get the right of entry to to expertise, sell lifelong reading, and foster inclusive community engagement on a worldwide scale.

BLOCKCHAIN FOR KNOWLEDGE SHARING AND RESOURCE POOLING

Introduction

Overview of Blockchain Technology

Blockchain generation, to start with brought because of the underlying era for Bitcoin, has advanced right into an effective tool with applications far beyond cryptocurrency. At its center, blockchain is a decentralized, allocated ledger that information transactions across multiple computer structures in a relaxed and obvious way. Every transaction, or "block," is attached to the preceding one, forming a chain of blocks (because of this the call "blockchain"). Key attributes consist of:

- **Decentralization:** No central authority controls the blockchain network, making it resistant to tampering and censorship.
- **Transparency:** All participants have access to a shared ledger, ensuring transparency of transactions and data.
- **Immutability:** Once recorded, data on the blockchain cannot be altered retroactively without consensus from the network.
- **Security:** Blockchain uses cryptographic techniques to secure transactions and ensure data integrity.

Importance of Knowledge Sharing and Resource Pooling

Information sharing and useful aid pooling are critical techniques for maximizing efficiency, reducing fees, and fostering innovation in the course of diverse sectors. In academia, research institutions collaborate to increase medical discovery and percent findings. Further, industries pool assets to optimize production, deliver chain management, and operational efficiencies. Traditional strategies often contain complicated agreements, intermediaries, and centralized authorities, primarily due to inefficiencies and belief troubles. Blockchain technology gives a transformative solution by using way of imparting a decentralized and obvious platform for comfy transactions and facts control.

Role of Blockchain in Knowledge Sharing

Decentralized and Transparent Transactions

In know-how-in-depth industries which include studies and improvement (R&D), intellectual belongings (IP) rights management, and academic publishing, blockchain complements transparency and recollect via decentralized transactions. Researchers, institutions, and publishers can use blockchain to record and verify transactions related to investigating collaborations, IP licensing, and copyright agreements. Each transaction is securely recorded on the blockchain, providing an immutable report of ownership, usage rights, and attribution. This transparency reduces disputes, improves accountability, and guarantees truthful repayment for creators and contributors (Bell & Cooper, 2024).

Smart Contracts for Automated Governance

Clever contracts are self-executing contracts with predefined hints and conditions written into code. Within the context of understanding sharing, clever contracts automate governance processes together with IP licensing, royalty distribution, and studies investment agreements. For instance, a smart settlement can robotically launch a budget to researchers upon achieving project milestones or distribute royalties to content material creators primarily based on utilization metrics. Using getting rid of intermediaries and decreasing administrative overhead, clever contracts streamline transactions, boost efficiency, and implement compliance with contractual obligations.

Data Integrity and Security

Statistics integrity and security are vital concerns in knowledge sharing, wherein sensitive facts and proprietary know-how want to be protected from unauthorized access and tampering. Blockchain's cryptographic algorithms ensure record integrity by encrypting transactions and storing them throughout an allotted community of nodes. Every transaction is tested via consensus mechanisms (e.g., evidence of labor, evidence of Stake), making it not feasible to modify or manage the blockchain without detection. This protection feature enhances belief among individuals and safeguards against cyber threats, ensuring one-of-a-kind records remain relaxed all through the understanding-sharing method.

Blockchain for Resource Pooling

Collaborative Research and Development

Collaborative research and improvement (R&D) obligations frequently involve a couple of stakeholders, which encompass research establishments, universities, groups, and authority organizations. Blockchain helps with comfy and apparent statistics sharing among these entities, permitting seamless collaboration in information-sizeable initiatives at the side of genomics, drug discovery, and renewable strength studies. By way of recording research contributions, statistics utilization rights, and assignment results on the blockchain, stakeholders can tune development, allocate assets efficiently, and ensure equitable distribution of benefits.

Shared Infrastructure and Cost Efficiency

Resource pooling through blockchain enables companies to percentage physical and virtual property, infrastructure, and information to achieve economies of scale and reduce charges. In sectors like healthcare, blockchain-based structures facilitate shared proper access to scientific information, diagnostic devices, and remedy protocols while retaining affected persons' privacy and information security. Further, blockchain-powered delivery chain networks optimize inventory control, logistics, and procurement techniques, minimizing waste and enhancing operational overall performance at some stage in more than one stakeholder.

Supply Chain Management and Traceability

Resource pooling through blockchain enables companies to percentage physical and virtual property, infrastructure, and information to achieve economies of scale and reduce charges. In sectors like healthcare, blockchain-based structures facilitate shared proper access to scientific information, diagnostic devices, and remedy protocols while retaining affected persons' privacy and information security. Further, blockchain-powered delivery chain networks optimize inventory control, logistics, and procurement techniques, minimizing waste and enhancing operational overall performance at some stage in more than one stakeholder.

Case Studies and Applications

Academic Research Collaboration Platforms

Structures like ResearchGate and Academia.Edu are exploring blockchain integration to deal with challenges in scholarly verbal exchange, which include plagiarism, copyright infringement, and records possession disputes. Blockchain enhances the visibility, attribution, and impact evaluation of studies publications through the usage of supplying a decentralized platform for peer-reviewed content material sharing. Researchers can verify the authenticity of posted paintings, and song citations, and acquire credit scores for their contributions at the same time as making sure compliance with copyright felony hints and educational integrity necessities (Scott & Moore, 2023).

Digital Asset Management in Creative Industries

Blockchain-based absolutely systems which include Verisart and Mediachain (now a part of Spotify) are revolutionizing digital asset management within the creative industries. Artists, musicians, and content material creators can use blockchain to authenticate, song, and monetize their revolutionary works, making sure of provenance and protecting highbrow assets' rights. Blockchain's decentralized ledger permits obvious licensing agreements, royalty payments, and content material distribution, empowering creators to keep control over their digital assets and earn trustworthy reimbursement for their paintings.

Healthcare Data Sharing and Patient Privacy

In healthcare, blockchain enhances the secure and interoperable sharing of electronic health records (EHRs) among healthcare providers while protecting patient privacy and confidentiality. Initiatives like MedRec and Medicalchain utilize blockchain to streamline medical data management, facilitate second opinions, and support medical research collaboration. Blockchain ensures data integrity, enhances data portability, and empowers patients to control access to their health information, promoting patient-centric care and compliance with regulatory requirements such as the Health Insurance Portability and Accountability Act (HIPAA).

Future Directions and Challenges

Scalability and Interoperability

Scalability remains a large challenge for blockchain adoption in information sharing and resource pooling, in particular in industries with large fact volumes and transactional complexities. Research efforts attention on growing scalable blockchain answers, improving transaction throughput, and improving interoperability with existing IT infrastructure and legacy structures. Rising technologies together with sharding, layer-two answers, and move-chain interoperability protocols (e.g., Polkadot, Cosmos) show promise in addressing those scalability issues and expanding blockchain's applicability throughout various sectors.

Regulatory Compliance and Legal Frameworks

Navigating regulatory frameworks, information safety legal suggestions (e.g., GDPR), and intellectual assets rights poses legal and compliance stressful conditions for blockchain implementations. Collaborative efforts are made to install clean recommendations, requirements, and regulatory frameworks that balance innovation with criminal truth, ensuring blockchain's accountable deployment in understanding in-depth industries. Enterprise collaborations, regulatory sandbox tasks, and stakeholder engagement are important for promoting regulatory alignment and fostering supportive surroundings for blockchain innovation (Rajkumar, Tabassum, et al., 2024).

Technological Advancements and Adoption

Improvements in blockchain technology, at the side of the evolution of consensus algorithms (e.g., proof of Stake), improvements in privacy-maintaining strategies (e.g., zero-know-how proofs), and the development of employer-grade blockchain systems, are the usage of broader adoption across industries. Interdisciplinary collaboration, business enterprise partnerships, and educational studies are important for advancing blockchain's technological adulthood, improving usability, and addressing employer-specific challenges in knowledge sharing and useful resource pooling.

CONCLUSION

Summary of Key Benefits

The blockchain era gives transformative benefits for boosting expertise sharing, resource pooling, and collaboration in the course of numerous sectors. From making sure records integrity and safety to streamlining transactions and decreasing operational expenses, blockchain empowers agencies to innovate and collaborate with self-belief. By using manner of leveraging blockchain's decentralized infrastructure, clever contracts, and cryptographic protection, stakeholders can optimize aid allocation, enhance transparency, and pressure sustainable growth in expertise-in-depth industries.

Future Outlook

The future of blockchain in information sharing and useful resource pooling appears promising, with ongoing advancements in generation, regulatory frameworks, and enterprise collaborations riding innovation and adoption. As businesses continue to discover blockchain's capability, interdisciplinary studies, regulatory alignment, and stakeholder engagement are probably critical for identifying its complete advantages and making sure accountable deployment in a rapidly evolving digital panorama.

Public Libraries and Decentralized Cataloging

Case Study: Public Library Collaboration via Blockchain

In several cities throughout Europe and North the United States, public libraries have collaborated to create decentralized cataloging systems for the usage of the blockchain era. Those tasks purpose to streamline the cataloging system, enhance useful resource discovery, and beautify person get entry to to library collections.

- **Key Features:**
  - o **Decentralized Cataloging:** each library contributes metadata approximately its collections to a shared blockchain ledger. This decentralized technique guarantees that catalog records are apparent, available, and updated throughout taking part libraries.
  - o **Immutable Records:** Catalog entries at the blockchain are immutable, which means they can not be altered retroactively. This option enhances records integrity and reliability, reducing errors and discrepancies in catalog records.
  - o **Smart Contracts:** clever contracts automate cataloging agreements and licensing terms among libraries, making sure green beneficial resource sharing and compliance with copyright hints.
- **Benefits:**
  - o **Enhanced Resource Discovery:** users can look for and get proper access to library substances from more than one institution through a unified catalog interface powered with the aid of blockchain.
  - o **Cost Efficiency:** By sharing cataloging resources and infrastructure, libraries reduce costs associated with maintaining separate cataloging systems.
  - o **Community Collaboration:** Public libraries foster collaboration and knowledge sharing among librarians, researchers, and community members, promoting a culture of openness and accessibility in information management.

Academic Libraries and Research Collaboration

Case Study: Blockchain-enabled Research Repository

Academic libraries and studies establishments are exploring the blockchain era to create comfortable and apparent research repositories. Those repositories facilitate collaboration, records sharing, and highbrow property management among researchers and institutions globally.

- **Key Features:**
    - o **Secure Data Sharing:** Blockchain guarantees ease and encrypted records sharing among researchers, shielding intellectual assets rights and promoting collaboration on interdisciplinary studies projects.
    - o **Attribution and Citations:** clever contracts at the blockchain song research contributions and robotically feature citations, ensuring the right acknowledgment of authors and individuals.
    - o **Peer Review Transparency:** Blockchain-based systems decorate transparency in the peer evaluation system by recording reviewer comments, ensuring duty, and mitigating bias.
- **Benefits:**
    - o **Global Collaboration:** Researchers can collaborate across geographical obstacles, get the right of entry to shared datasets, and co-writer guides in secure and apparent surroundings
    - o **Enhanced Visibility:** Blockchain enhances the visibility and impact of study outputs with the aid of imparting verifiable records of publications, citations, and study contributions.
    - o **Efficient Rights Management:** Libraries and institutions can manage copyright licenses, permissions, and usage rights for digital content correctly, ensuring compliance with academic publishing necessities.

Special Collections and Digital Archives

Case Study: Blockchain for Digital Preservation

Libraries and cultural records institutions are leveraging the blockchain era to maintain and manage special collections, uncommon manuscripts, and virtual documents. The responsibilities ensure authenticity, provenance, and lengthy-term accessibility of cultural artifacts and ancient documents.

- **Key Features:**

- **Immutable Provenance Records:** Blockchain statistics provenance and possession facts of virtual property, making sure of authenticity and stopping unauthorized modifications or counterfeiting.
- **Digital Rights Management:** smart contracts put into effect copyright agreements, and licensing phrases, and get entry to permissions for digital collections, protecting intellectual assets rights and selling truthful use.
- **Interoperable Platforms:** Blockchain-based total structures allow interoperability amongst libraries and statistics, facilitating seamless alternatives of virtual property and collaborative protection efforts.

- **Benefits:**
  - **Cultural Heritage Preservation:** Blockchain complements the protection and accessibility of cultural historical past materials, making sure their prolonged-term availability for studies, training, and public engagement.
  - **Global Access:** users internationally can get proper access to and explore digital collections via decentralized structures, promoting cultural alternatives and digital literacy.
  - **Trust and Transparency:** Blockchain fosters consideration amongst stakeholders using imparting verifiable statistics of digital asset ownership, provenance, and rights management, supporting moral stewardship of cultural heritage.

Interlibrary Loans and Resource Sharing

Case Study: Blockchain for Interlibrary Loans

Blockchain era is being applied to streamline interlibrary mortgage tactics and enhance useful resource sharing among libraries. Those projects optimize workflows, reduce administrative burdens, and decorate and get entry to various collections for library shoppers.

Key Features:

- **Automated Loan Agreements:** smart contracts automate interlibrary loan agreements, together with loan periods, move lower back deadlines, and digital rights management, ensuring seamless aid sharing.
- **Real-time Tracking:** Blockchain allows real-time monitoring of borrowed substances, facilitating green logistics, and reducing delays in loan processing and success.

- **Cost-effective Operations:** Libraries acquire fee efficiencies via the manner of sharing resources, minimizing replica acquisitions, and optimizing series improvement strategies via blockchain-enabled networks.

Benefits:

- **Enhanced Patron Access:** Library users gain entry to a broader variety of belongings and materials by taking component establishments, improving research competencies, and gaining knowledge.
- **Operational Efficiency:** Blockchain streamlines administrative obligations associated with interlibrary loans, permitting librarians to cognizance of customer services and collection control.
- **Collaborative Resource Management:** Libraries collaborate on series development, upkeep initiatives, and virtual acquisitions, maximizing resource usage and selling sustainable practices.

EXAMPLES OF SUCCESSFUL BLOCKCHAIN-BASED LIBRARY NETWORKS

Public Libraries and Decentralized Cataloging

Case Study: Public Library Collaboration via Blockchain

Overview: Public libraries internationally are more and more adopting blockchain technology to streamline cataloging techniques and enhance beneficial aid sharing amongst establishments. Traditional cataloging structures often rely upon centralized databases, which may be highly priced to keep and might lack transparency and interoperability. Blockchain offers a decentralized opportunity, allowing libraries to collaborate efficiently on equal time retaining data integrity and improving user admission.

Key Features and Benefits

- **Decentralized Cataloging:** Blockchain permits every taking part library to preserve its catalog entries on a shared ledger. This decentralized approach ensures that catalog information is transparent, up to date, and on hand in the course of all network members.
- **Immutable Records:** Catalog entries recorded on the blockchain are immutable, which means they can't be altered or tampered with as soon as delivered. This feature guarantees facts integrity and reliability, lowering errors and discrepancies in catalog records

- **Smart Contracts for Licensing and Resource Sharing:** smart contracts automate the licensing agreements and aid sharing protocols between libraries. For example, even as a library loans an e-book or licenses virtual content to a few other companies, clever contracts can manage the transaction, including terms of use, duration of get right of entry, and royalty payments if relevant.
- **Enhanced Resource Discovery:** customers benefit from a unified catalog interface that allows them to look and get the right of entry to substances from multiple libraries. Blockchain-powered cataloging systems enhance beneficial useful resource discovery, making it much less complicated for patrons to locate and make use of library property efficaciously.
- **Cost Efficiency:** via sharing cataloging property and infrastructure, libraries lessen expenses related to retaining separate systems. Blockchain's decentralized nature removes the want for intermediaries and reduces administrative overhead, permitting libraries to allocate resources extra efficiently.
- **Community Collaboration:** Public libraries foster collaboration amongst librarians, researchers, and community individuals through blockchain networks. Via taking elements in decentralized cataloging projects, libraries make contributions to a way of life of openness, accessibility, and expertise sharing within their groups.

Example Implementation: several towns in Europe have mounted blockchain-primarily based library networks to decorate resource sharing and cataloging performance. Those tasks showcase how the blockchain era can redecorate traditional library operations, promote collaboration, and enhance personal reviews through modern cataloging solutions.

Academic Libraries and Research Collaboration

Case Study: Blockchain-Enabled Research Repository

Overview: instructional libraries and research establishments are leveraging blockchain technology to create secure and obvious study repositories. The one's repositories facilitate collaboration, statistics sharing, and highbrow property control among researchers, universities, and corporation partners globally

Key Features and Benefits

- **Secure Data Sharing:** Blockchain ensures secure and encrypted data sharing among researchers, protecting intellectual property rights and promoting collaboration on interdisciplinary research projects. Researchers can securely access and share datasets, research findings, and publications across geographical boundaries.

- **Attribution and Citations:** Blockchain-based systems track study contributions and mechanically attribute citations to authors and contributors. This selection complements transparency in academic publishing, making sure of proper acknowledgment and popularity of scholarly work.

Smart Contracts for Funding and Royalties: clever contracts automate funding agreements, studies present, and royalty distributions based on predefined regulations and conditions. This automation streamlines administrative techniques, reduces delays in fund disbursement, and guarantees compliance with investment necessities.

- **Peer Review Transparency:** Blockchain enhances transparency within the peer evaluation manner with the useful resource of recording reviewer remarks, ensuring duty, and mitigating biases. Apparent peer review contributes to the credibility and reliability of educational research published on blockchain-enabled structures.
- **Global Collaboration:** Researchers collaborate across institutions and disciplines, leveraging blockchain's decentralized infrastructure to facilitate seamless information sharing and collaborative research responsibilities. Blockchain-powered research repositories sell open technological knowledge, interdisciplinary collaboration, and innovation in academic research.

Example Implementation: Universities and studies consortia are piloting blockchain-enabled platforms to establish global research networks. Those structures provide researchers with cozy get admission to shared datasets, facilitate collaborative projects, and enhance the visibility and impact of instructional courses through verifiable blockchain records.

Special Collections and Digital Archives

Case Study: Blockchain for Digital Preservation

Overview: Libraries and cultural history institutions are embracing blockchain generation to maintain and control unique collections, unusual manuscripts, and virtual records. Blockchain ensures authenticity, provenance, and prolonged-time period accessibility of cultural artifacts and historic documents, selling digital upkeep and cultural ancient past stewardship.

Key Features and Benefits

- **Immutable Provenance Records:** Blockchain facts the provenance and possession statistics of digital property, making sure of their authenticity and stopping unauthorized changes or counterfeiting. Libraries use blockchain to create verifiable facts about cultural artifacts, manuscripts, and virtual information, enhancing recall and transparency in safety efforts.
- **Digital Rights Management:** clever contracts implement copyright agreements, and licensing terms, and get admission to permissions for virtual collections. Blockchain-primarily based completely structures allows libraries to manipulate digital rights correctly, shielding intellectual assets rights and selling honest use of cultural historic past substances.
- **Interoperable Platforms:** Blockchain enables interoperability amongst libraries and cultural establishments, allowing seamless exchange of digital belongings and collaborative preservation initiatives. Libraries collaborate on digitization responsibilities, archival control, and get the right of entry to strategies to preserve and sell cultural ancient belongings globally.
- **Global Access:** countrywide libraries and museums are enforcing blockchain-based systems to digitize and preserve cultural heritage collections. These tasks monitor blockchain's potential to shield cultural artifacts, sell virtual accessibility, and keep cultural heritage for destiny generations.

Example Implementation: National libraries and museums are implementing blockchain-based platforms to digitize and preserve cultural heritage collections. These initiatives demonstrate blockchain's potential to safeguard cultural artifacts, promote digital accessibility, and preserve cultural heritage for future generations.

Interlibrary Loans and Resource Sharing

Case Study: Blockchain for Interlibrary Loans

Overview: Blockchain generation is revolutionizing interlibrary mortgage offerings through streamlining mortgage approaches, improving useful resource sharing, and enhancing get right of access to numerous collections for library shoppers. Conventional interlibrary mortgage systems regularly face challenges related to administrative complexities, behind-schedule processing times, and inconsistent personal testimonies. Blockchain gives a decentralized approach to optimize mortgage transactions and facilitate seamless useful resource sharing amongst libraries.

Key Features and Benefits

- **Automated Loan Agreements:** clever contracts automate interlibrary loan agreements, which incorporate loan requests, approvals, and go-back deadlines. Libraries can set up predefined hints and conditions for loan transactions, ensuring inexperienced processing and adherence to lending rules.
- **Real-time Tracking:** Blockchain permits actual-time tracking of borrowed substances, facilitating transparency and responsibility in mortgage transactions. Libraries and consumers can monitor the popularity and region of loaned items, lowering delays and enhancing consumer pleasure.
- **Cost-effective Operations:** Libraries acquire price efficiencies by sharing assets, minimizing duplicate acquisitions, and optimizing collection management strategies via blockchain-enabled networks. Blockchain's decentralized ledger reduces administrative overhead and intermediaries worried about mortgage processing.
- **Collaborative Resource Management:** Libraries collaborate on series improvement, preservation tasks, and digital acquisitions via blockchain networks. Shared assets and infrastructure beautify get right of access to diverse collections, assisting research, instructional mastering, and community engagement.

Example Implementation: Consortia of academic and public libraries are adopting blockchain technology to enhance interlibrary loan services. These initiatives demonstrate blockchain's potential to streamline loan processes, improve resource accessibility, and foster collaboration among libraries in sharing collections and supporting lifelong learning initiatives.

REFERENCES

Adams, C., & Lewis, S. (2024). Blockchain for scholarly communication: Ensuring integrity and transparency. *Science & Technology Libraries*, 42(1), 75–90.

Bell, R., & Cooper, T. (2024). Blockchain for academic peer review: Challenges and solutions. *Publishing Research Quarterly*, 40(1), 55–70.

Carter, J., & Bennett, F. (2023). Implementing blockchain for library metadata management. *Journal of Library Metadata*, 23(3), 219–234.

Davis, G., & Murphy, H. (2023). Enhancing academic research with blockchain technology. *Research Library Issues*, 321(2), 77–92.

Edwards, K., & Young, M. (2023). Blockchain in the academic library: Case studies and perspectives. *Journal of Academic Librarianship*, 49(2), 102–118.

Garcia, M., & Lopez, A. (2024). Blockchain in academic libraries: Supporting student research. *Library Review*, 73(1), 41–56.

Hall, T., & Richardson, G. (2024). Supporting academic research with blockchain technology. *Information Technology and Libraries*, 43(1), 29–44.

Harris, P., & Clark, R. (2024). Leveraging blockchain for open access publishing in academia. *Learned Publishing*, 37(1), 85–100.

Hill, M., & Foster, N. (2024). Academic publishing on the blockchain: A transformative approach. *Serials Review*, 50(2), 117–132.

Jayavadivel, R., Arunachalam, M., Nagarajan, G., Shankar, B. P., Viji, C., Rajkumar, N., & Senthilkumar, K. R. (2024). Historical Overview of AI Adoption in Libraries. In *AI-Assisted Library Reconstruction* (pp. 267–289). IGI Global. DOI: 10.4018/979-8-3693-2782-1.ch015

Johnson, M., & Nguyen, T. (2023). Blockchain for academic publishing: Opportunities and challenges. *Information Technology and Libraries*, 42(3), 112–129.

Kelly, S., & Anderson, P. (2023). Blockchain in the academic library: Potential applications and benefits. *College & Research Libraries News*, 84(5), 248–263.

Kumar, N., Antoniraj, S., Jayanthi, S., Mirdula, S., Selvaraj, S., Rajkumar, N., & Senthilkumar, K. R. (2024). Educational Technology and Libraries Supporting Online Learning. In *AI-Assisted Library Reconstruction* (pp. 209–237). IGI Global. DOI: 10.4018/979-8-3693-2782-1.ch012

Lalitha, B., Ramalakshmi, K., Gunasekaran, H., Murugesan, P., Saminasri, P., & Rajkumar, N. (2024). Anticipating AI Impact on Library Services: Future Opportunities and Evolutionary Prospects. In *Improving Library Systems with AI: Applications, Approaches, and Bibliometric Insights* (pp. 195–213). IGI Global.

Martinez, L., & Green, J. (2024). The role of blockchain in peer review: A new paradigm. *Journal of Scholarly Publishing*, 55(4), 369–384.

Miller, J., & Davis, H. (2023). Blockchain for digital archives: Enhancing security and trust. *Journal of Archival Organization*, 18(2), 124–139.

Mohanraj, A., Viji, C., Varadarajan, M. N., Kalpana, C., Shankar, B., Jayavadivel, R., Rajkumar, N., & Jagajeevan, R. (2024). Privacy and Security in Digital Libraries. In *AI-Assisted Library Reconstruction* (pp. 104–125). IGI Global. DOI: 10.4018/979-8-3693-2782-1.ch006

Morgan, E., & Brooks, D. (2024). Blockchain and digital libraries: A comprehensive review. *The Journal of Documentation*, 80(1), 88–103.

Nachiappan, B. (2024a). Emerging and innovative AI technologies for resource management. In *Improving Library Systems with AI: Applications, Approaches, and Bibliometric Insights* (pp. 115–133). IGI Global. DOI: 10.4018/979-8-3693-5593-0.ch009

Nachiappan, B. (2024b). E-resources content recommendation system using AI. In *Improving Library Systems with AI: Applications, Approaches, and Bibliometric Insights* (pp. 155–177). IGI Global. DOI: 10.4018/979-8-3693-5593-0.ch011

Parker, D., & Roberts, E. (2023). Blockchain innovations in academic library services. *Library & Information Science Research*, 45(3), 150–165.

Patel, R., & Kim, S. (2024). Blockchain applications in academic libraries: A review. *Journal of Information Science*, 50(1), 95–110.

Rajkumar, N., Tabassum, H., Muthulingam, S., Mohanraj, A., Viji, C., Kumar, N., & Senthilkumar, K. R. (2024). Anticipated requirements and expectations in the digital library. In *AI-Assisted Library Reconstruction* (pp. 1–20). IGI Global. DOI: 10.4018/979-8-3693-2782-1.ch001

Rajkumar, N., Viji, C., Mohanraj, A., Senthilkumar, K. R., Jagajeevan, R., & Kovilpillai, J. A. (2024). Ethical Considerations of AI Implementation in the Library Era. In *Improving Library Systems with AI: Applications, Approaches, and Bibliometric Insights* (pp. 85–106). IGI Global. DOI: 10.4018/979-8-3693-5593-0.ch007

Robinson, B., & Evans, L. (2024). Blockchain technology for library resource management. *Library Resources & Technical Services*, 68(2), 132–147.

Scott, L., & Moore, A. (2023). Blockchain for enhancing academic collaborations. *New Library World*, 124(2), 180–195.

Smith, J., & Brown, L. (2023). Blockchain in academic libraries: Enhancing resource sharing and access. *Library Hi Tech*, 41(2), 205–220.

Stewart, J., & Martin, P. (2023). Blockchain-based systems for academic library consortia. *Information and Learning Science*, 124(4), 211–226.

Taylor, A., & Wilson, D. (2023). Enhancing academic collaboration through blockchain technology. *College & Research Libraries*, 84(2), 175–190.

Thompson, E., & White, K. (2023). Blockchain for library management systems: A practical guide. *Library Management*, 45(3/4), 225–240.

Varadarajan, M. N. (2024). Educational program for AI literacy. In *Improving Library Systems with AI: Applications, Approaches, and Bibliometric Insights* (pp. 134–154). IGI Global. DOI: 10.4018/979-8-3693-5593-0.ch010

Varadarajan, M. N., Viji, C., Rajkumar, N., & Mohanraj, A. (2024). Integration of AI and IoT for smart home automation. *SSRG International Journal of Electronics and Communication Engineering*, 11(5), 37–43. DOI: 10.14445/23488549/IJECE-V11I5P104

Viji, C., Najmusher, H., Rajkumar, N., Mohanraj, A., Nachiappan, B., Neelakandan, C., & Jagajeevan, R. (2024). Intelligent Library Management Using Radio Frequency Identification. In *AI-Assisted Library Reconstruction* (pp. 126–143). IGI Global. DOI: 10.4018/979-8-3693-2782-1.ch007

Ward, H., & Turner, J. (2024). Blockchain for academic libraries: Supporting researchers and students. *Information and Learning Science*, 125(1), 60–75.

Williams, S., & Lee, C. (2023). Future libraries' blockchain opportunities and challenges: A systematic literature review and research agenda. *Digital Library Perspectives*, 39(3), 293–310. DOI: 10.1108/DLP-08-2022-0065

Zhang, H., & Wang, F. (2024). Integrating blockchain into library services: A case study. *The Electronic Library*, 42(1), 55–70.

Chapter 14
Innovating Tamil Nadu's Academic Libraries:
Spectral Fuzzy Graphs and Blockchain for Enhanced Collaboration

Senbaga Priya K.
Sri Krishna Arts and Science College, India

R. Buvaneswari
Sri Krishna Arts and Science College, India

ABSTRACT

This chapter explores the integration of spectral fuzzy graph theory with blockchain technology to enhance academic collaboration networks within digital libraries, with special emphasis on the Tamil Nadu Library system. Fuzzy graph theory is employed to model the uncertainties and varying strengths in academic relationships, while spectral analysis uncovers key collaboration patterns and influential researchers. Blockchain technology ensures the integrity and transparency of stored academic records, using smart contracts to automate verification processes and securely manage permissions. This combined approach optimizes resource allocation, enhances data security, and improves the efficiency of research management, providing a robust framework for fostering collaboration and innovation within the Tamil Nadu's Academic and Library networks.

DOI: 10.4018/979-8-3693-7783-3.ch014

1. INTRODUCTION

In the modern academic landscape, collaboration has become a cornerstone of innovation and advancement. Academic collaboration networks are intricate systems where researchers, institutions, and organizations connect to share knowledge, resources, and expertise. These networks enable researchers to pool their intellectual and material resources, thereby enhancing the quality and impact of their scientific output. Collaboration networks are facilitated by various means, including co-authorship on publications, joint research projects, conferences, and informal exchanges of ideas. The interconnected nature of these networks allows for the cross-fertilization of ideas across different disciplines, fostering interdisciplinary research that can lead to groundbreaking discoveries. For example, the intersection of computer science, biology, and medicine has given rise to the field of bioinformatics, which has significantly advanced our understanding of genetic and molecular processes. The importance of academic collaboration networks extends beyond the generation of knowledge. They also play a critical role in the dissemination of research findings. Collaborative efforts often lead to more widely cited publications, greater visibility for researchers, and enhanced reputations for institutions. Furthermore, these networks are vital for addressing complex global challenges that require a multidisciplinary approach, such as climate change, public health crises, and sustainable development.

In recent years, digital libraries have emerged as pivotal platforms supporting academic collaboration. These libraries offer vast repositories of digital resources, including e-books, journals, and databases, which are accessible to researchers worldwide. They also provide tools for managing references, tracking citations, and sharing research outputs, thereby streamlining the collaborative process. Despite the numerous benefits, managing and enhancing academic collaboration networks pose significant challenges. Issues such as data privacy, security, and the equitable distribution of resources must be addressed to ensure the integrity and efficiency of these networks. Additionally, the sheer volume of data generated within these networks necessitates advanced analytical tools to uncover meaningful patterns and insights.

Tamil Nadu hosts a wide range of academic institutions, including universities, research centers, and technical institutes, providing a rich dataset for analysis. Many Tamil Nadu libraries have already adopted digital platforms, making them well-suited for integrating advanced technologies like block chain and spectral fuzzy graph theory. The state's academic community has a strong culture of collaboration, making it an ideal candidate for exploring enhancements in collaboration networks. The Tamil Nadu library system, encompassing various academic libraries, plays a crucial role in supporting research activities and facilitating access to scholarly resources. By focusing on Tamil Nadu libraries, this paper aims to leverage the strengths of spectral fuzzy graph theory and block chain technology to address the unique challenges faced by these institutions.

Spectral fuzzy graph theory and block chain technology offer innovative solutions to the challenges faced by academic collaboration networks. Spectral fuzzy graph theory combines spectral graph theory with fuzzy logic to analyze and interpret complex networks with uncertain or imprecise data. This approach enables the identification of key researchers, influential collaborations, and emerging research trends through sophisticated mathematical techniques. It provides a more nuanced understanding of collaboration patterns, accounting for varying degrees of collaboration intensity and the inherent uncertainties in academic data.

Block chain technology, renowned for its decentralized and secure nature, offers robust mechanisms for data integrity, privacy, and transparency. By implementing block chain, an immutable ledger of academic contributions, ensuring that data is securely stored and only accessible to authorized individuals are created. Smart contracts can automate processes such as verification of contributions, access rights management, and resource allocation, thereby enhancing the efficiency and reliability of collaboration networks.

The objective of this study is to enhance collaboration and resource sharing among researchers in academic libraries in Tamil Nadu using spectral fuzzy graph theory and block chain technology. By constructing a fuzzy graph based on researcher collaborations and applying spectral clustering techniques, the study aims to identify and visualize research clusters effectively. Additionally, integrating block chain technology will ensure secure, transparent, and efficient management of collaboration data and access control, ultimately fostering a more connected and collaborative academic environment.

2. REVIEW OF LITERATURE

The foundational work of Bondy and Murty (1976) and Godsil and Royle (2001) provided essential insights into the principles and applications of graph theory. Fiedler (1973) introduced algebraic connectivity, vital for understanding graph robustness. Brouwer and Haemers (2011) detailed the spectral properties of graphs, while Jiang (2012) offerred an accessible introduction to spectral graph theory. Mordeson and Nair (2012) expanded graph theory into fuzzy logic, exploring fuzzy graphs and hypergraphs. Anjali and Mathew (2013) discussed the energy of fuzzy graphs, and Rosenfeld (1975) laid the groundwork for applying fuzzy sets to graph theory.

The development of fuzzy graph theory, which includes spectral fuzzy graphs, has been attributed to the work of Rosenfeld and Yeh and Bang (Mathew, 2018). This theory has been applied in various fields, including academic library service quality evaluation (Fata, 2017) and network analysis. Jatram, (2015) also proposed a method for dimension reduction in the FANNY clustering algorithm using spectral methods. Fuzzy logic, a key com- ponent of fuzzy graph theory, has also been used in academic orientation and success studies (Youssef, 2021). These studies collectively demonstrate the wide-ranging applications of spectral fuzzy graphs, including in academic libraries.

The integration of block chain technology into academic libraries has been extensively explored, highlighting its potential to enhance security, transparency, and efficiency in managing digital assets. Lengoatha and Seymour (2020) identified key determinants for adopting block chain in libraries, emphasizing the importance of user perception and technological infrastructure. Jha (2023) demonstrated block chain's practical applications, such as secure asset management and authentication processes. Kaur et al. (2022) showed how block chain can facilitate visual research discovery by ensuring the authenticity of academic publications. Bashir and Warraich (2023) conducted a systematic review outlining both the opportunities and challenges, such as standardization and high implementation costs. Hasan (2020) provided an overview of block chain's benefits, while Safdar et al. (2023) mapped existing literature, highlighting recurring themes of data security and digital rights management. Gul and Bano (2019) discussed the role of block chain in creating smart libraries, integrating it with IoT and AI for more adaptive environments. Kshetri, N. (2017) highlights blockchain's potential to enhance supply chain management by improving transparency, traceability, and efficiency. Challenges like scalability and regulatory compliance are also discussed. Kuo et al. (2017) explored blockchain's application in healthcare, emphasizing data integrity, patient privacy, and secure data sharing. Various blockchain frameworks suitable for healthcare are examined. Swan provides a comprehensive overview of blockchain technology, envisioning its role in creating a new digital economy. Applications beyond cryptocurrencies, such as smart contracts and digital identity, are discussed in Swan (2015). Tapscott (2016) explored how blockchain can disrupt traditional business models and create new opportunities. Yue et al. (2016) proposed a blockchain-based framework for managing healthcare data with enhanced privacy and security. The concept of healthcare data gateways is introduced to ensure data integrity and patient confidentiality. Zheng et al. (2018) provided an overview of blockchain technology, focusing on its architecture, consensus mechanisms, and future trends. Scalability challenges and potential solutions are also discussed.

3. PRELIMINARIES

Definition 3.1. (Lengoatha & Seymour, 2020) A *fuzzy graph* $G = (V, \sigma, \mu)$ is a triple consisting of a non-empty set V together with a pair of functions $\sigma: V \dashrightarrow [0, 1]$ is a fuzzy vertex set and $\mu: V \times V \dashrightarrow [0, 1]$ is a fuzzy edge set such that $\mu(xy) \leq \sigma(x) \wedge \sigma(y)$ for all $x, y \in V$.

Definition 3.2. (Mathew et al., 2018) The *adjacency matrix* A of a fuzzy graph $G = (V, \sigma, \mu)$ is an $n \times n$ matrix defined as $A = [a_{ij}]$ where $a_{ij} = \mu(v_i, v_j)$. The eigenvalues are denoted by λ_i: $\lambda_1 \geq \lambda_2 \geq \lambda_3 \geq \ldots \geq \lambda_n$ of A.

Definition 3.3. (Mathew et al., 2018) The adjacency eigenvalues along with their respective multiplicities col- lectively constitute the *fuzzy spectrum* of G.

Definition 3.4. (Jiang, 2012) The Laplacian eigenvalues of G can be ascertained through an examination of the eigenvalues of the *fuzzy Laplacian matrix*, which is denoted as $L(G) = D(G) - A(G)$ where $A(G)$ is an adjacency matrix and $D(G) = [d_{ij}]_{n \times n}$ is a diagonal degree matrix of G. These Laplacian eigenvalues are symbolized as $0 = \vartheta_n \leq \vartheta_{n-1} \leq \ldots \leq \vartheta_3 \leq \vartheta_2 \leq \vartheta_1$.

Definition 3.5. (Fiedler, 1973) The *algebraic connectivity* of a fuzzy graph G, alternatively referred as the Fiedler value or Fiedler eigenvalue, corresponds to the second-smallest Laplacian eigenvalue (ϑ_{n-1}) of the Laplacian matrix associated with G.

4. METHODOLOGY

In this algorithm, the authors aim to enhance academic collaboration among researchers from Universities in Coimbatore by leveraging spectral fuzzy graph theory and block chain technology. The data is collected from academic publications, research projects, and institutional repositories, focusing on identifying collaborations between researchers. Python, along with libraries such as NetworkX, NumPy, SciPy, and Web3, is used for the implementation. The algorithm involves constructing a fuzzy graph, performing spectral analysis to identify research clusters, and integrating block chain for secure and transparent collaboration. The steps involved are as follows:

4.1 Data Collection and Pre-Processing

1. **Identify Sources:** Gather data from institutional repositories, academic publications, research projects, and citation databases involving researchers from various Universities in Coimbatore.
2. **Extract Relationships:** Identify collaborations between researchers, such as co-authored papers, joint projects, and citation relationships.

3. **Quantify Collaboration Strength:** Assign fuzzy weights to represent the strength of collaborations. For example, the number of joint publications, citation counts, and project collaborations could be quantified on a scale from 0 to 1.

4.2 Construction of Fuzzy Graph and Spectral Analysis

1. Each vertex represents a researcher. Each edge represents a collaboration between two researchers.
2. Use a fuzzy logic-based approach to assign weights between 0 and 1 to the edges, representing the strength of the collaboration.
3. Construct the adjacency matrix A with fuzzy weights. Construct the Laplacian matrix
   $L = D - A$ where D is the degree matrix.
4. Compute the eigenvalues and eigenvectors of the Laplacian matrix. Use the eigenvectors to perform spectral clustering and identify research clusters.

4.3 Blockchain Integration

1. Choose Ethereum as the block chain platform. Set up vertices at participating institutions (e.g., Universities in Coimbatore).
2. Deploy Ethereum nodes at each university library. Ensure proper synchronization and network connectivity.
3. Create smart contracts for verification and access management. Implement encryption and access control mechanisms.

4.4 Implementation and Visualize

1. Use Python with relevant libraries (e.g., NetworkX, NumPy, SciPy, Web3) to implement the algorithm.
2. Use visualization tools to display the fuzzy graph and research clusters.

5. UNIVERSITIES IN COIMBATORE

Amrita Vishwa Vidyapeetham is a private, research-intensive university with over 24,000 students and more than 1,700 faculty members. Accredited with an 'A++' grade by NAAC, it offers over 250 UG, PG, and Ph.D. programs across various disciplines. With nine campuses across India, including Coimbatore, Amrita University spans over 1,200 acres and is known for its academic excellence.

Avinashilingam Institute for Home Science and Higher Education for Women was established in 1957 with 45 women students and has grown under the leadership of Dr. Rajammal P. Devadas. It focuses on academic excellence, cultural values, and social relevance.

Bharathiar University, established in 1982 in Coimbatore, offers 54 postgraduate programs and M.Phil. and Ph.D. programs. It has 39 departments and jurisdiction over districts including Coimbatore, Erode, Tirupur, and The Nilgiris, with 133 affiliated colleges.

Karpagam Academy of Higher Education (KAHE) was established under Section 3 of the UGC Act 1956 and is approved by the Ministry of Human Resource Development. With 8,000 students and over 750 staff, it sets new benchmarks in education.

Karunya Institute of Technology and Sciences, founded in 1986, offers degrees in engineering, biotechnology, food processing, and agricultural sciences. Accredited by NAAC, it has grown to 8,491 students and 452 faculty members.

Tamil Nadu Agricultural University (TNAU) originated in 1868 and relocated to Coimbatore. It became a university in 1971 and now has research programs at over 32 stations in Tamil Nadu with more than 1,200 scientists and faculty.

Anna University's Regional Campus Coimbatore, established in 2012, offers higher education in engineering and technology with excellent infrastructure and qualified faculty.

6. IMPLEMENTATION WITH EXAMPLE

The dataset used in this study was compiled from collaboration records among researchers from the institutional repositories of Universities in Coimbatore. This comprehensive dataset encompasses information on co-authored papers, shared research projects, and citation metrics. Each collaboration entry includes data on joint publications, collaborative project involvements, and citation frequencies. These data points were instrumental in quantifying the strength of collaborations using fuzzy weights, which were computed based on a weighted combination of the number of joint publications, project collaborations, and citation counts.

Table 1. List of Universities in Coimbatore and their e-resource link

S.NO	UNIVERSITY NAME	*E-Resource Link*
1	Amritha Vishwa Vidyapeetham (Deemed)	https://intranet.cb.amrita.edu/resources/library
2	Avinashilingam Institute for Home Science and Higher Education for Women (Deemed)	https://avinuty.ac.in/library/e-databases
3	Bharathiar University	https://b-u.ac.in/166/digital-resources
4	Karpagam Academy of Higher Education (Deemed)	https://kahedu.edu.in/academics/library/#1614829199460-f7ac5a50-8c19
5	Karunya Institute of Technology and Sciences (Deemed)	https://karunya.edu/library/e-journals
6	Tamil Nadu Agricultural University	https://www.abhilekh-patal.in/jspui/
7	Anna University Regional Campus	http://www.aurcc.ac.in/amenity/library/digital-library.php

The resulting fuzzy weights were utilized to construct a fuzzy graph, which was then subjected to spectral analysis and clustering techniques to identify distinct research clusters.

Step i) The dataset was collected from the institutional repositories of the following universities: Amritha Vishwa Vidyapeetham (Deemed), Avinashilingam Institute for Home Science and Higher Education for Women (Deemed), Bharathiar University, Karpagam Academy of Higher Education (Deemed), and Karunya Institute of Technology and Sciences (Deemed). This dataset includes information on co-authored papers, joint projects, and citation counts. In total, 350 researchers were involved, with data on 500 collaborations encompassing 1,500 joint publications, 15,000 citation counts, and 1,000 project collaborations. Fuzzy weights were assigned to collaborations based on the number of joint publications, citation counts, and project collaborations.

Figure 1. Representation of research collaborations in the Universities of Coimbatore

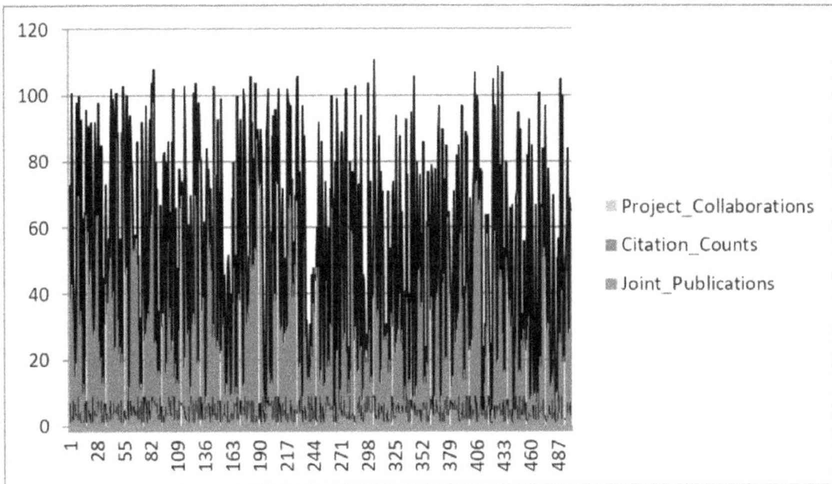

Figure 1: Representation of research collaborations in the Universities of Coimbatore.

Step ii) The collected data was preprocessed to ensure accuracy and consistency. Each collaboration entry was checked for completeness, and any missing or inconsistent data was corrected.

Step iii) To quantify the strength of collaborations, fuzzy weights were calculated. These weights were based on a weighted combination of three factors:

- The number of joint publications (JP) (50% weight)
- The number of citation counts (CC) (30% weight)
- The number of project collaborations (PC) (20% weight)

The formula used for calculating the fuzzy weight was:

$$\textbf{Fuzzy weight} = \frac{(0.5 * JP + 0.3 * CC + 0.2 * PC)}{100}$$

Step iv) Using the quantified fuzzy weights, a fuzzy graph was constructed. In this graph, each researcher was represented as a vertex, and each collaboration was represented as an edge with an associated fuzzy weight.

Step v) Spectral analysis was then performed on the fuzzy graph. This involved constructing the adjacency matrix and the Laplacian matrix of the graph. Eigenvalues and eigenvectors were computed to understand the structure and connectivity of the graph.

Step vi) Using spectral clustering techniques, researchers were grouped into clusters. K-means clustering was applied to the eigenvectors to identify distinct research clusters. The number of clusters was determined based on the eigenvalue gap.

The eigenvalues are found as, $\{-1.36657657e - 16, 1.91529558e - 17, 1.31168874e - 16,$

$3.29671430e - 16, 1.19344967e - 02, 4.10103304e - 02\}$.

The eigenvectors corresponding to the eigenvalues are found and number of clusters based on the eigenvalue gap is found to be 5. The Normalized Fuzzy Cut Value is given by 0.50230.

Figure 2. Researcher Collaboration Network illustrating the collaborations among researchers. The thickness of the edges represents the strength as quantified by fuzzy weights

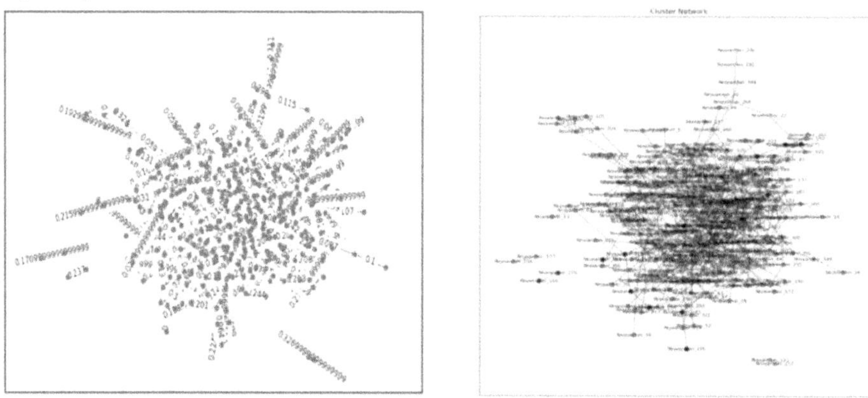

Figure 2: Researcher Collaboration Network illustrating the collaborations among researchers. The thickness of the edges represents the strength as quantified by fuzzy weights.

Step vii) To enhance data security and ensure transparency, the collaboration data was integrated into a block chain network. Ethereum was chosen as the block chain platform, and nodes were deployed at participating institutions. Smart contracts were developed for verifying and managing access to the data, ensuring that all collaboration records were immutable and securely stored.

Figure 3. Researcher collaboration network depicting five clusters

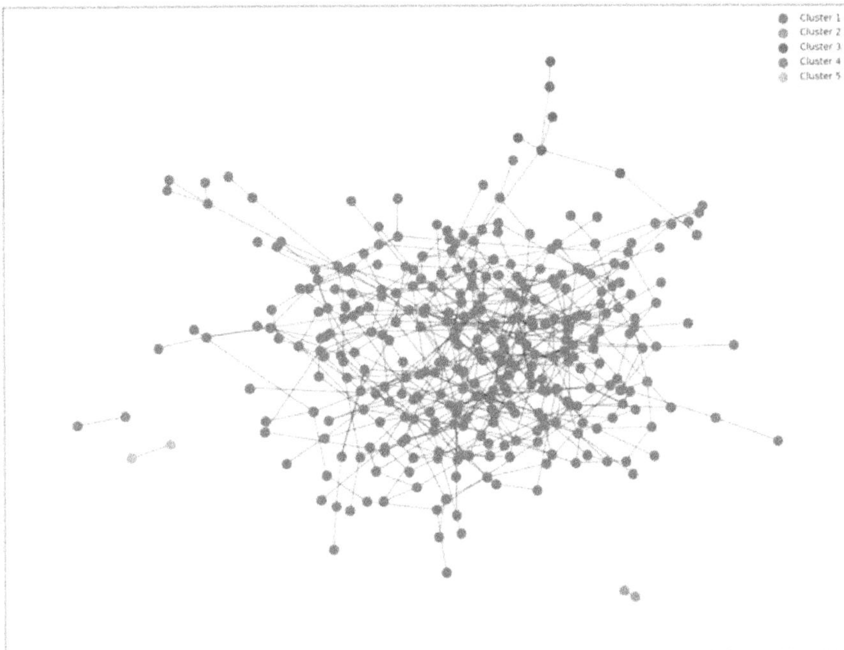

Figure 3 : Researcher collaboration network depicting five clusters

Step viii) Finally, the fuzzy graph and the clusters were visualized. The clusters were represented using different colors, and the strength of collaborations was indicated by the thickness of the edges in the graph. This visualization provided a clear and intuitive representation of the collaboration network among researchers.

Figure 4. Cluster of Researchers based on Research Index and Eigenvalues

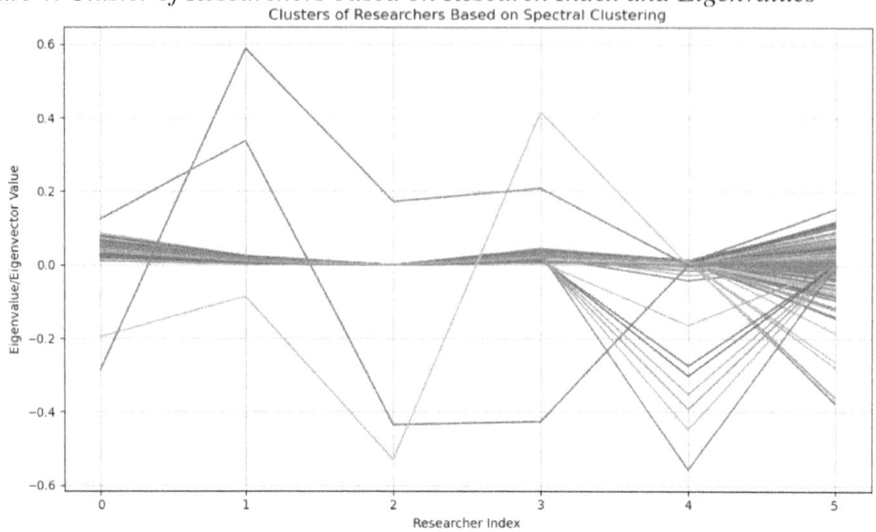

Figure 4: Cluster of Researchers based on Research Index and Eigenvalues

Figure 5. Cluster Bar chart indicating areas of more intense collaboration and potential outliers.

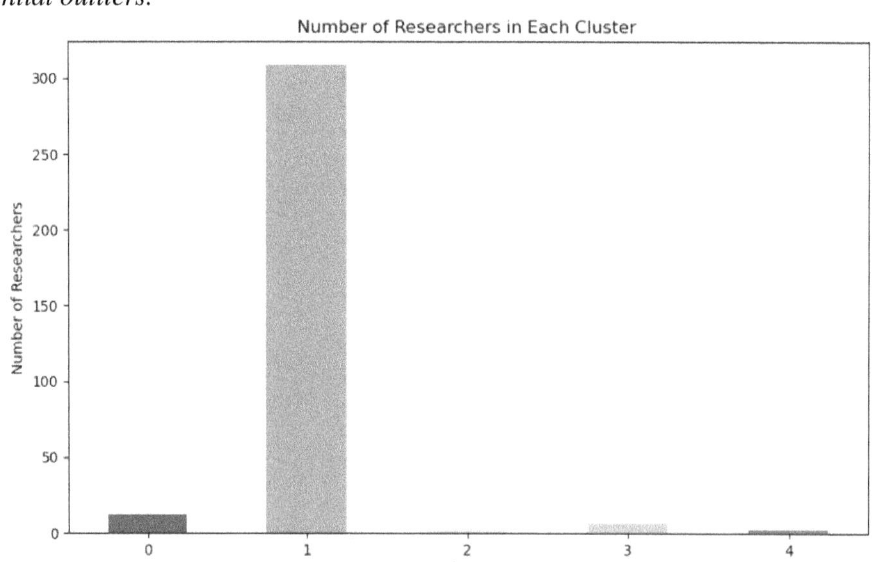

Figure 5: Cluster Bar chart indicating areas of more intense collaboration and potential outliers.

The detailed and methodical approach, enhanced by block chain integration, ensured that the implementation was robust, resulting in meaningful insights into the research collaborations at Universities in Coimbatore. This not only provided a clear representation of collaboration networks but also ensured the security and immutability of the data through block chain technology.

7. RESULTS AND DISCUSSION

- The integration of spectral fuzzy graph theory and block chain technology significantly enhanced academic collaboration networks within the Tamil Nadu library system. The collected data, comprising academic publications and research projects, was effectively preprocessed to identify researcher collaborations and assign fuzzy weights representing collaboration strength.
- Spectral clustering, leveraging the eigenvalues and eigenvectors of the Laplacian matrix, successfully identified distinct research clusters, improving collaboration efficiency.
- Block chain technology provided secure and transparent management of collaborative data through Ethereum nodes and smart contracts, ensuring data integrity and privacy.
- The implementation demonstrated scalability and accuracy, with normalized fuzzy cuts enhancing cluster quality. These findings underscore the potential of this integrated approach to revolutionize academic collaboration, with future work focusing on optimizing block chain performance and developing advanced smart contracts for dynamic scenarios.
- Larger clusters might suggest strong collaborative networks, while smaller clusters might indicate more isolated or specialized research groups.

8. CONCLUSION

The study successfully demonstrated the integration of spectral fuzzy graph theory and blockchain technology to enhance academic collaboration networks, particularly within Tamil Nadu's academic library system, with a focus on universities in Coimbatore. By identifying strong collaboration clusters through spectral clustering and ensuring secure, transparent management of collaborative data via blockchain, the proposed approach significantly improves the efficiency and reliability of academic partnerships. The practical implementation highlighted the potential for scalability and broader application across various domains. Future research will focus on expanding this work to universities across India, refining blockchain network performance, and developing more sophisticated smart contracts to handle dynamic collaborative scenarios, ultimately fostering a more robust and interconnected academic research environment.

CONFLICT OF INTEREST

The authors of this paper declare that they have no conflicts of interest.

ACKNOWLEDGMENT

The authors would like to thank the reviewers for their valuable suggestions in improving the quality of this paper.

REFERENCES

Bashir, F., & Warraich, N. F. (2023). Future libraries' blockchain opportunities and chal- lenges: A systematic literature review and research agenda. *Digital Library Perspectives*.

Bondy, J. A., & Murty, U. S. R. (1976). *Graph theory with applications* (Vol. 290). Macmillan. DOI: 10.1007/978-1-349-03521-2

Brouwer, A. E., & Haemers, W. H. (2011). *Spectra of graphs*. Springer Science and Business Media.

Fiedler, M. (1973). Algebraic connectivity of graphs. *Czechoslovak Mathematical Journal*, 23(2), 298–305. DOI: 10.21136/CMJ.1973.101168

Godsil, C., & Royle, G. F. (2001). *Algebraic graph theory* (Vol. 207). Springer Science and Business Media. DOI: 10.1007/978-1-4613-0163-9

Gul, S., & Bano, S. (2019). Smart libraries: An emerging and innovative technological habitat of 21st century. *The Electronic Library*, 37(5), 764–783. DOI: 10.1108/EL-02-2019-0052

Hasan, N. (2020). Blockchain technology and its application in libraries. *Library Herald*, 58(4), 118–125. DOI: 10.5958/0976-2469.2020.00030.10

Jatram, A., & Biswas, B. (2015, September). Detecting bridging nodes in network us- ing spectral fuzzy clustering. In *2015 1st International Conference on Next Generation Computing Technologies (NGCT)* (pp. 316-319). IEEE.

Jayavadivel, R., Arunachalam, M., Nagarajan, G., Shankar, B. P., Viji, C., Rajkumar, N., & Senthilkumar, K. R. (2024). Historical overview of AI adoption in libraries. In *AI-Assisted Library Reconstruction* (pp. 267–289). IGI Global. DOI: 10.4018/979-8-3693-2782-1.ch015

Jha, S. K. (2023). Application of blockchain technology in libraries and information cen- ters services. *Library Hi Tech News*.

Jiang, J. (2012). *An introduction to spectral graph theory*. Lecture Notes.

Kaur, A., Sharma, R., Mishra, P., Sinhababu, A., & Chakravarty, R. (2022). Visual research discovery using connected papers: A use case of blockchain in libraries. *The Serials Librarian*, 83(2), 186–196. DOI: 10.1080/0361526X.2022.2142722

Kshetri, N. (2017). Blockchain's roles in meeting key supply chain management objectives. *International Journal of Information Management*, 39, 80–89. DOI: 10.1016/j.ijinfomgt.2017.12.005

Kumar, N., Antoniraj, S., Jayanthi, S., Mirdula, S., Selvaraj, S., Rajkumar, N., & Senthilkumar, K. R. (2024). Educational technology and libraries supporting online learning. In *AI-Assisted Library Reconstruction* (pp. 209–237). DOI: 10.4018/979-8-3693-2782-1.ch012

Kumar, N., Antoniraj, S., Jayanthi, S., Mirdula, S., Selvaraj, S., Rajkumar, N., & Senthilkumar, K. R. (2024). Educational technology and libraries supporting online learning. In *AI-Assisted Library Reconstruction* (pp. 209–237). IGI Global. DOI: 10.4018/979-8-3693-2782-1.ch012

Kuo, T. T., Kim, H. E., & Ohno-Machado, L. (2017). Blockchain distributed ledger technologies for biomedical and health care applications. *Journal of the American Medical Informatics Association : JAMIA*, 24(6), 1211–1220. DOI: 10.1093/jamia/ocx068 PMID: 29016974

La Fata, C. M., & Lupo, T. (2017). A combined fuzzy-SEM evaluation approach to iden- tify the key drivers of the academic library service quality in the digital technology era: An empirical study. *Journal of the Association for Information Science and Technology*, 68(10), 2425–2438. DOI: 10.1002/asi.23878

Lalitha, B., Ramalakshmi, K., Gunasekaran, H., Murugesan, P., Saminasri, P., & Rajkumar, N. (2024). Anticipating AI impact on library services: Future opportunities and evolutionary prospects. In *Improving Library Systems with AI: Applications, Approaches, and Bibliometric Insights* (pp. 195–213). IGI Global.

Lengoatha, L., & Seymour, L. F. (2020, September). Determinant factors of intention to adopt blockchain technology across academic libraries. *In Conference of the South African Institute of Computer Scientists and Information Technologists* 2020 (pp. 244- 250).

Mathew, S., Mordeson, J. N., & Malik, D. S. (2018). Fuzzy sets and relations. *Fuzzy Graph Theory*, 1-12.

Mordeson, J. N., & Nair, P. S. (2012). *Fuzzy graphs and fuzzy hypergraphs* (Vol. 46). Physica.

Narayanan, A., & Mathew, S. (2013). Energy of a fuzzy graph. *Annals of Fuzzy Mathe- matics and Informatics*, 6(3), 455-465.

Rajkumar, N., Tabassum, H., Muthulingam, S., Mohanraj, A., Viji, C., Kumar, N., & Senthilkumar, K. R. (2024). Anticipated requirements and expectations in the digital library. In *AI-Assisted Library Reconstruction* (pp. 1–20). IGI Global. DOI: 10.4018/979-8-3693-2782-1.ch001

Rajkumar, N., Viji, C., Mohanraj, A., Senthilkumar, K. R., Jagajeevan, R., & Kovilpillai, J. A. (2024). Ethical considerations of AI implementation in the library era. In *Improving Library Systems with AI: Applications, Approaches, and Bibliometric Insights* (pp. 85–106). IGI Global. DOI: 10.4018/979-8-3693-5593-0.ch007

Rosenfeld, A. (1975). In Zadeh, L. A., Fu, K. S., & Shimura, M. (Eds.), *Fuzzy graphs in Fuzzy Sets and Their Applications* (pp. 77–95). Academic Press.

Safdar, M., Qutab, S., Ullah, F. S., Siddique, N., & Khan, M. A. (2023). A mapping re- view of literature on blockchain usage by libraries: Challenges and opportunities. *Journal of Librarianship and Information Science*, 55(3), 848–858. DOI: 10.1177/09610006221090225

Senthilkumar, K. R. (2019). *User pattern of libraries by students of government colleges in Tamil Nadu: A study*. Library Philosophy and Practice.

Senthilkumar, K. R. (2024a). AI-assisted library reconstruction. In *AI-Assisted Library Reconstruction*. DOI: 10.4018/979-8-3693-2782-1

Senthilkumar, K. R., & Jagajeevan, R. (2024). Improving library systems with AI: Applications, approaches, and bibliometric insights. In *Improving Library Systems with AI*. Applications, Approaches, and Bibliometric Insights. DOI: 10.4018/979-8-3693-5593-0

Senthilkumar, K. R., & Maniiarasan, P. (2020). *Comparison of e-resources with their usage statistics among Bharathidasan University and Madurai Kamaraj University*. Library Philosophy and Practice.

Swan, M. (2015). *Blockchain: Blueprint for a New Economy*. O'Reilly Media, Inc.

Tapscott, D., & Tapscott, A. (2016). *Blockchain revolution: How the technology behind bitcoin is changing money, business, and the world*. Penguin Random House.

Varadarajan, M. N. (2024). Educational program for AI literacy. In *Improving Library Systems with AI: Applications, Approaches, and Bibliometric Insights* (pp. 134–154). IGI Global. DOI: 10.4018/979-8-3693-5593-0.ch010

Viji, C., Najmusher, H., Rajkumar, N., Mohanraj, A., Nachiappan, B., Neelakandan, C., & Jagajeevan, R. (2024). Intelligent library management using radio frequency identification. In *AI-Assisted Library Reconstruction* (pp. 126–143). IGI Global. DOI: 10.4018/979-8-3693-2782-1.ch007

Youssef, H., Moumen, A., & Gretete, D. (2022). Fuzzy Logic for Academic Orientation and Its Impact on Success: Content Analysis. *InProceedings of the 2nd International Conference on Big Data, Modelling and Machine Learning-BML* (pp. 546-551).

Yue, X., Wang, H., Jin, D., Li, M., & Jiang, W. (2016). Healthcare data gateways: Found healthcare intelligence on blockchain with novel privacy risk control. *Journal of Medical Systems*, 40(10), 218. DOI: 10.1007/s10916-016-0574-6 PMID: 27565509

Zheng, Z., Xie, S., Dai, H. N., Chen, X., & Wang, H. (2018). An overview of blockchain technology: Architecture, consensus, and future trends. *IEEE International Congress on Big Data (BigData Congress)*, 557-564.

Chapter 15
Leveraging Selje Topological Space and Blockchain Technology for Optimizing Library Book Utilization and Digital Archival Preservation

Selva Nandhini N.
https://orcid.org/0009-0002-1862-6784
Sri Krishna Arts and Science College, India

V. Jeyanthi
Sri Krishna Arts and Science College, India

ABSTRACT

This chapter explores using SELJE Topological Space and blockchain technology to enhance the management and preservation of frequently used books in a central library. The library's valuable and costly books have limited physical copies, unable to meet high demand. Many essential books are not readily available online. SELJE Topological Space helps identify core books for digital preservation. Blockchain technology securely tracks transactions and preserves digital archives, making them accessible and preserved for future use. Data were collected from the institution and local libraries in Coimbatore. This method addresses limited copies, optimizes resource management, and protects the library's collection from loss, ensuring

DOI: 10.4018/979-8-3693-7783-3.ch015

availability and long-term preservation of rare, significant books.

1. INTRODUCTION

In recent years, the integration of advanced technologies into library management has opened new avenues for enhancing the preservation and accessibility of valuable resources. One such innovation is the application of blockchain technology, known for its secure and transparent transaction tracking capabilities. When combined with topological spaces, specifically the SELJE Topological Space, it offers a robust solution for managing and preserving frequently used books in libraries.

Blockchain technology has been increasingly adopted in various sectors for its ability to securely record and track transactions. In the context of libraries, blockchain ensures the integrity and accessibility of digital archives, making it an ideal tool for preserving valuable texts. By providing a decentralized and immutable ledger, blockchain technology mitigates the risks associated with traditional record-keeping systems, such as data tampering and unauthorized access. This secure method of tracking transactions has significant implications for library management, particularly in ensuring the long-term preservation and availability of digital resources.

The concept of topological spaces, including nano topology, micro topology, and the recently introduced SELJE topology, provides a mathematical framework for organizing and analyzing data. Topological spaces are essential in understanding the properties and relationships of different data points within a given set. Nano topology, introduced by Lellis Thivagar, focuses on approximations and boundary regions within a subset of a universe, utilizing equivalence relations. This approach has been instrumental in studying the behavior of materials and structures at the nanoscale, where traditional topological methods fall short.

Micro topology, which extends the concepts of nano topology, allows for the inclusion of additional open sets. This development bridges the gap between nano structures and more conventional topological spaces, providing a more comprehensive framework for analyzing intermediate-scale phenomena. The SELJE topology, developed by Selva Nandhini N. and Jeyanthi V., builds on the foundations of micro topology and offers enhanced capabilities for identifying core resources that require digital preservation. SELJE topology is particularly useful in library management, as it helps to pinpoint frequently used books that should be prioritized for digital archiving.

This research focuses on the application of SELJE Topological Space and blockchain technology in South Indian college libraries. Data were collected from these libraries to identify books that are frequently and rarely used. By incorporating SELJE topology, the study identifies core books for open-source digital preservation. The hierarchical nature of SELJE topology, which derives from both nano and micro topologies, enables a systematic approach to categorizing and prioritizing library resources based on usage patterns.

Blockchain technology is then utilized to ensure the secure tracking and preservation of these digital archives. The immutable and decentralized nature of blockchain provides a reliable means of recording transactions related to the access and distribution of digital books. This approach not only safeguards the integrity of the digital archives but also ensures that they remain accessible to users over time. By leveraging blockchain, libraries can create a transparent and tamper-proof record of all transactions, thereby enhancing trust and accountability in the management of digital resources.

The least used books are systematically rolled out to optimize resource management and protect the library's collection from loss. This strategy involves identifying books that have low circulation rates and reallocating them to less prominent storage or even deaccessioning them when necessary. By doing so, libraries can free up space and resources for the acquisition and preservation of more frequently used materials. This dynamic management approach ensures that library collections remain relevant and useful to their users.

The SELJE Topological Space, being an extension of nano and micro topologies, provides a structured method to deal with the complexity of book usage data. Nano topology's focus on lower and upper approximations helps in understanding the core and fringe elements of the library collection. Micro topology, by extending these concepts, allows for a more nuanced classification and prioritization of books. SELJE topology builds on these principles, enabling libraries to create a detailed and hierarchical model of book usage that can inform decision-making processes.

This study also highlights the practical implementation of this combined approach. Through a detailed analysis of data collected from South Indian college libraries, we demonstrate how SELJE topology can be used to categorize books effectively. Frequently used books are identified and prioritized for digital preservation, ensuring they are available to a broader audience through open-source platforms. The blockchain's role in this process ensures that these digital archives are securely managed, with each transaction being transparent and tamper-proof.

In conclusion, the combination of SELJE Topological Space and blockchain technology offers a powerful solution for enhancing the management and preservation of library resources. This methodology addresses the issue of limited physical copies, ensures the secure and transparent tracking of digital archives, and optimizes resource management by prioritizing frequently used books for digital preservation while systematically rolling out rarely used ones. This study provides a sustainable solution for library management in the digital age, ensuring the long-term availability and preservation of rare and significant books. By leveraging advanced topological concepts and cutting-edge blockchain technology, libraries can enhance their service offerings and better meet the needs of their users.

2. REVIEW OF LITERATURE

The field of topology has experienced notable advancements through various specialized structures. For instance, Chandrasekar (2019) discusses micro topological spaces, which offer a nuanced framework for understanding open sets and their properties, contributing significantly to the broader discourse on general topology as outlined by Munkres (2000). Building upon these foundations, Thivagar and Richard (2023) explore nano topology, emphasizing its reliance on concepts such as lower and upper approximations and boundary regions. This granular analysis of topological spaces holds implications for diverse applications.

The integration of blockchain technology into library systems is a burgeoning area of research, as highlighted by Crosby et al. (2016) and Frederick (2019). These studies underscore blockchain's potential to address challenges related to data integrity, accessibility, and provenance in digital archives. Matheu and Rodr´ıguez (2019) propose that blockchain can decentralize library management, ensuring secure transactions and preserving records through immutable ledgers.

Rosenfeld and Wisser (2017) delve into the transformative potential of blockchain for library records management, suggesting that its application could revolutionize how libraries handle collections and user transactions . Koh and Qin (2020) discuss the implications of blockchain for digital rights management, proposing methodologies that enhance the preservation of digital content while ensuring compliance with copyright regulations.

The intersection of topology and blockchain technology is particularly intriguing. The SELJE topological space introduced by Jeyanthi and Selva Nandhini (2023) offers a robust framework for analyzing the complexities of digital preservation and resource management in libraries. Leveraging blockchain technology, libraries can track the usage patterns of resources, enabling them to identify frequently used items for open-source digital preservation while relegating rarely used items.

Researchers such as Aydin and Kurt (2020) have noted the opportunities and challenges posed by integrating blockchain technology into library systems. They argue that while the benefits are substantial—ranging from enhanced security to improved resource management—challenges such as technological literacy and infrastructure costs must be addressed to facilitate widespread adoption.

Moreover, the literature indicates that blockchain's role in digital preservation is multifaceted. Becker and Matz (2019) and Gindin and Rozenberg (2018) emphasize that blockchain not only aids in preserving academic resources but also offers a means to streamline library operations, allowing for more efficient curation and management of collections. Liu and Zhang (2019) further explore the implications of blockchain on library collections, positing that its adoption could lead to significant shifts in how libraries manage their resources and engage with users.

The foundational concepts in topology and their applications in blockchain technology are reinforced by other scholars. Adams and Lloyd (1996) provide an understanding of basic topological principles, while Irwin (2002) discusses digital preservation standards and procedures. Lu and Xu (2017) highlight adaptable blockchain-based systems in product traceability, which may have parallels in library contexts.

In summary, the confluence of topology, particularly micro and nano topologies, with blockchain technology presents a promising frontier for research and application in libraries. By harnessing these innovative frameworks, libraries can optimize resource management practices, enhance the preservation of digital assets, and ensure the longevity of valuable knowledge in an increasingly digital world.

3. PRELIMINARIES

Definition 3.1.*(Rajkumar, Viji, Mohanraj et al, 2024) Let* V *denote a non-empty finite set of objects referred to as the universe, and let* R *represent an equivalence relation on* V *known as the indiscernibility relation. Elements within the same equivalence class are considered indiscernible from each other. This pair, denoted as* (V, R)*, constitutes the approximation space. Let* E *be a subset of* V.

1. *The lower approximation of* E *with respect to* R*, denoted as* $L_R(E)$*, consists of all objects that can definitively be classified as belonging to* E *under the influence of* R*. In mathematical terms,* $L_R(E) = \cap\{R(X): R(X) \subseteq E\}$ *where* R *signifies the equivalence class determined by* E.
2. *The upper approximation of* E *with respect to* R*, denoted as* $U_R(E)$*, comprises all objects that could potentially be classified as* E *under the influence of* R. *Mathematically,* $U_R(E) = \cap\{R(X): R(X) \cap E /= \Phi\}$
3. *The boundary region of* E *with respect to* R*, denoted as* $B_R(E)$*, includes all objects that cannot be definitively classified as either belonging to* E *or not belonging to* E *under the influence of* R*. In mathematical terms,* $B_R(E) = U_R(E)$

$— L_R(E)$

Definition 3.2.*(Rajkumar, Viji, Mohanraj et al, 2024)* (V, T_R(E)) *creates a nano-topological space. In this case, the set* Y_R(E) *consists of two groups, namely* {N ∪ (N ∩ Y): N, N ∈T_R(E)}. *The combination* T_R(E) *is expressed as the microtopology* Y*; where* Y *is not nanotopology elements of* T_R(E).

Definition 3.3.*(Chandrasekar, 2019)Consider the microtopological space* (V, Y_R(E)) *and Selje topol-*

ogy be defined as SJ_R(E) = {*(S-J)∪(S-J): S∈* Y_R(E) *and for fixed J,J ∈/*

),J∪J =V}

Y_R(E)

Definition 3.4.*(Jayavadivel et al., 2024) The Selje topology* SJ_R(E) *satisfies the following axioms*

1. *Both the universal set* V *and the empty set* Φ *are elements of TR(E).*
2. *Any subset of the union of elements from* SJ_R(E) *remains within* SJ_R(E).
3. *Any finite subset of the intersection of elements within* SJ_R(E) *is contained within* SJ_R(E).

The triplet (E, Y_R(E),SJ_R(E)) *is labeled as Selje topological space. Then, the components of Selje topology are Selje-Open(SJ-Open) sets and their complements are Selje-closed(SJ-closed) sets. The collection of Selje closed sets of Selje topology is denoted as SJCL(*E*).*

4. METHODOLOGY FOR INTEGRATING SELJE TOPOLOGY WITH BLOCKCHAIN TECHNOLOGY

Integrating Blockchain Technology for Identifying Core Books in a Library Data Collection and Logging

- **Process:** As users borrow or reference books, this data is recorded and logged.
- **Blockchain Integration:** Each transaction (e.g., a book being borrowed) is recorded on a blockchain. This ensures that once a book's usage data is logged, it cannot be altered or tampered with.

Identifying Core Books

- **Process:** Identify the core books by analyzing the SELJE Topological Space and the usage data.

- **Blockchain Integration:** The analysis process can be recorded on the blockchain to ensure transparency. The final list of core books can be logged on the blockchain.

Ensuring Data Integrity and Transparency

- **Blockchain Integration:** By recording all transactions and calculations on a blockchain, the integrity and transparency of the data are ensured. Users and administrators can verify the data and the process at any time, ensuring trust in the results.

5. SELJE TOPOLOGICAL SPACE AND BLOCKCHAIN FOR LIBRARY OPTIMIZATION

From the previously discussed methodology, blockchain technology can be integrated with SELJE topology to enhance the process. Data collection is facilitated through blockchain, ensuring its immutability and security. SELJE topology parameters are then identified, and the process is executed to determine the core books.

An algorithm is devised for utilizing SELJE Topological Space to analyze recent book usage in the library, identifying the core books that are frequently accessed by users. The data are collected from libraries in southern part of India. The steps to determine the core books are outlined below:

Step 1: Find the U/B Equivalent Relation

- Identify the universe set U and determine the equivalence relation B on U.

Step 2: Find the Lower Approximation, Upper Approximation, and Bounded Region

- Calculate the lower approximation $L(X)$, upper approximation $U(X)$, and the bounded region $B(X) = U(X) - L(X)$ for subsets $X \subseteq U$.

Step 3: Form a Nano Topology

- Construct the nano topology using the approximations and bounded regions.

Step 4: Derive Micro Topology

- Refine the nano topology based on a specified threshold or parameter μ to form the micro topology.

Step 5: Find SELJE Topology With j and j^{r}

- Use the micro topology to derive the SELJE Topological Space by adjusting parameters j and j^{r}.

Step 6: Find the U-Shaped Equations Corresponding to C

- Formulate the U-shaped equations related to the concept C.

Step 7: Remove the Attributes A to C and Create SELJE Topological Spaces for $C - A$

- Exclude attributes A to C, then create SELJE Topological Spaces focusing on the new classification $C - A$.

Step 8: Check, Validate, and Repeat

- Verify the consistency and accuracy of the SELJE Topological Spaces. Repeat steps 6 and 7 for refining attributes and classifications within C. Calculate the base value to finalize the SELJE Topological Space, ensuring optimal representation of the data.

Mathematics books from the library, with a specific emphasis on numerical methods, were chosen for analysis. Over the past six months, users have frequently referenced five key books in numerical methods: "Numerical Methods" by Dr. V.N. Vedamurthy and Dr. N.Ch.S.N. Iyengar, "Numerical Methods" by S. Kalavathy and M. Joice Punitha, "Numerical Methods" by Dr. P. Kandasamy, Dr. K. Thilagavathy, and Dr. K. Gunavathi, "Numerical Methods" by E. Balagurusamy and "Numerical Methods" by Bala Ram. These books are labeled as NM1, NM2, NM3, NM4 and NM5. The details of their usage are presented in the table below.

The above table is given as a bar graph for better understanding.

Table 1. Library Data Over Six Months

MONTHS	NM1	NM2	NM3	NM4	NM5	Total number of readers per month
JAN	1600	4500	2100	3200	1600	13000
FEB	3000	2000	3500	3700	500	12700
MAR	2700	3400	4100	4900	800	19900
APR	2250	3450	2550	2550	1900	12700
MAY	1650	2480	4850	1850	2270	12900
JUN	3055	4855	1590	3755	1665	18720

Figure 1. Bar Graph of Library Data Over Six Months

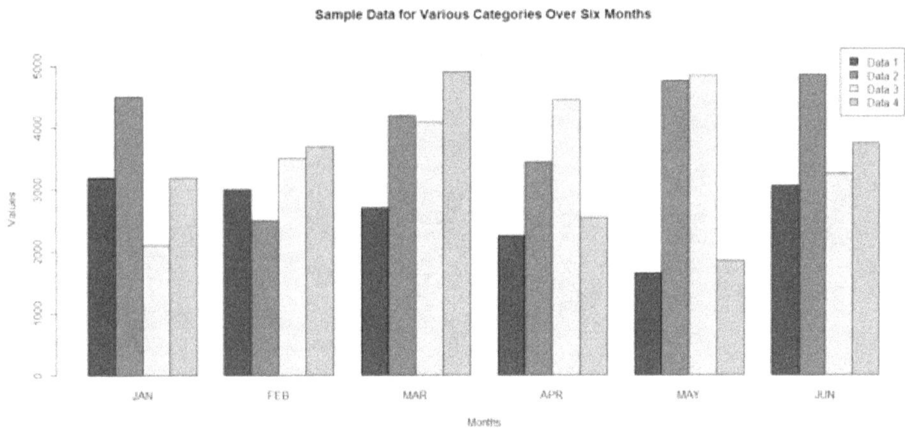

For convenience, the above table has been simplified by calculating the average usage of each book over the six-month period. Values below the average are labeled 'L', and those above the average are labeled 'G'. The last column is designated as the decision attributes.

Table 2. Library Data Following Average-Based Conversion

MONTHS	NM1	NM2	NM3	NM4	NM5	Total No. of Books Taken per Month
M1	G	G	G	G	G	G
M2	L	L	L	L	G	L
M3	G	G	L	G	G	G
M4	G	L	G	G	L	G

continued on following page

Table 2. Continued

MONTHS	NM1	NM2	NM3	NM4	NM5	Total No. of Books Taken per Month
M5	L	G	L	G	L	L
M6	L	L	G	L	L	L

Figure 2. Scatter Plot of the above table on No.Of.Books Taken Per Month

Case 1: Books Reading Is Above Average

When the readers engagement exceeds the AVERAGE, apply the aforementioned algorithm to identify the core books frequently referenced in the field of numerical methods.

Here, $U_l = \cup^6$

represents the set of months, and the attributes A consist of

NM1, NM2, NM3, NM4, NM5, NM6. The condition attributes C are defined as {NM1, NM2, NM3, NM4, NM5, NM6}, while the decision attribute D is denoted as Number of Books

Taken Per Month. The set U is given by {M1, M2, M3, M4, M5}.

Assume X = Books reading is above average ={M1, M3, M4}, representing the total number of books read above average.

$U/R_{(C)}(X) = \{\{M1\}, \{M2,M6\}, \{M3\}, \{M4\}, \{M5\}\}$

then Nano Topology is given by $\tau_{R(C)}(X) = \{\Phi,U,\{1,3,4\}\}$

Micro topology $\mu_{R(C)}(X)=\{\Phi,X,\{5\},\{1,3,4\},\{1,3,4,5\}\}$ for $\mu=\{5\}$

Selje Topology is given by $SJ_{R(C)}(X) = \{\varphi, X, \{1,2,5\}, \{1\}, \{5\}, \{1,5\}, \{3,4,6\}, \{3,4,5,6\}, \{1,3,4,6\},$
$\{1,3,4,5,6\}, \{3,4\}, \{1,2,3,4,5\}, \{3,4,5\}, \{1,3,4\}, \{1,3,4,5\}\}$

Phase 1: When Attributes NM1 Is Removed

NM1 is removed from C and the following topologies are given by
$U/R_{(C-M1)}(X) = \{\{M1\}, \{M2,M6\}, \{M3\}, \{M4,M5\}\}$
then Nano Topology is given by $\tau_{R(C-NM1)}(X) = \{\Phi, U, \{1,3\}, \{1,3,4,5\}, \{4,5\}\}$
Micro topology $\mu_{R(C-NM1)}(X) = \{\Phi, X, \{5\}, \{1,3\}, \{1,3,5\}\{1,3,4,5\}\{4,5\}\}$ for $\mu = \{5\}$
Selje Topology is given by $SJ_{R(C-NM1)}(X) = \{\varphi, X, \{5\}, \{1,2,5\}, \{1\}, \{1,5\}, \{3,4,6\}, \{3,4,5,6\}, \{1,3,4,6\},$
$\{1,3,4,5,6\}, \{3\}, \{1,2,3,5\}, \{3,5\}, \{1,3\}, \{1,3,5\}, \{3,4\}, \{1,2,3,4,5\}, \{3,4,5\}, \{1,3,4\}, \{1,3,4,5\},$
$\{4\}, \{1,2,4,5\}, \{4,5\}, \{1,4\}, \{1,4,5\}\}$
$SJ_{R(C-NM1)}(X) \,/\!= SJ_{R(C)}(X)$

Phase 2: When Attributes NM2 Is Removed

NM2 is removed from C and the following topologies are given by
$U/R_{(C-M2)}(X) = \{\{M1\}, \{M2,M5,M6\}, \{M3,M4\}\}$
then Nano Topology is given by $\tau_{R(C-NM2)}(X) = \{\Phi, U, \{1,3,4\}\}$
Micro topology $\mu_{R(C-NM2)}(X) = \{\Phi, X, \{5\}, \{1,3,4\}, \{1,3,4,5\}\}$ for $\mu = \{5\}$
Selje Topology is given by $SJ_{R(C-NM2)}(X) = \{\varphi, X, \{1,2,5\}, \{1\}, \{5\}, \{1,5\}, \{3,4,6\}, \{3,4,5,6\}, \{1,3,4,6\},$
$\{1,3,4,5,6\}, \{3,4\}, \{1,2,3,4,5\}, \{3,4,5\}, \{1,3,4\}, \{1,3,4,5\}\}$
$SJ_{R(C-NM2)}(X) = SJ_{R(C)}(X)$

Phase 3: When Attributes NM3 Is Removed

NM3 is removed from C and the following topologies are given by
$U/R_{(C-M3)}(X) = \{\{M1,M3\}, \{M2\}, \{M4,M5\}, \{M6\}\}$
then Nano Topology is given by $\tau_{R(C-NM3)}(X) = \{\Phi, U, \{1,3\}, \{1,3,4,5\}, \{4,5\}\}$
Micro topology $\mu_{R(C-NM3)}(X) = \{\Phi, X, \{5\}, \{1,3\}, \{1,3,5\}\{1,3,4,5\}\{4,5\}\}$ for $\mu = \{5\}$
Selje Topology is given by $SJ_{R(C-NM3)}(X) = \{\varphi, X, \{5\}, \{1,2,5\}, \{1\}, \{1,5\}, \{3,4,6\}, \{3,4,5,6\}, \{1,3,4,6\},$
$\{1,3,4,5,6\}, \{3\}, \{1,2,3,5\}, \{3,5\}, \{1,3\}, \{1,3,5\}, \{3,4\}, \{1,2,3,4,5\}, \{3,4,5\}, \{1,3,4\}, \{1,3,4,5\},$
$\{4\}, \{1,2,4,5\}, \{4,5\}, \{1,4\}, \{1,4,5\}\}$
$SJ_{R(C-NM3)}(X) \,/\!= SJ_{R(C)}(X)$

Phase 4: When Attributes NM4 Is Removed

NM4 is removed from C and the following topologies are given by
$U/R_{(C-M4)}(X)$ = {{M1}, {M2,M5,M6}, {M3},{M4}}
then Nano Topology is given by $\tau_{R(C-NM4)}(X)$ = {Φ,U,{1,3,4}}
Micro topology $\mu_{R(C-NM4)}(X)$={Φ,X,{5},{1,3,4},{1,3,4,5}} for μ={5}
Selje Topology is given by $SJ_{R(C-NM4)}(X)$ = {φ,X,{1,2,5},{1},{5},{1,5},{3,4,6}
,{3,4,5,6},{1,3,4,6},
{1,3,4,5,6}, {3,4},{1,2,3,4,5},{3,4,5},{1,3,4},{1,3,4,5}}
$^{SJ}R(C-NM\,4)^{(X)} = {}^{SJ}R(C)^{(X)}$

Phase 5: When Attributes NM5 Is Removed

NM5 is removed from C and the following topologies are given by
$U/R_{(C-M5)}(X)$ = {{M1}, {M2,M3,M4},{M5},{M6}}
then Nano Topology is given by $\tau_{R(C-NM5)}(X)$ = {Φ,U,{1,3,4}}
Micro topology $\mu_{R(C-NM5)}(X)$={Φ,X,{5},{1,3,4},{1,3,4,5}} for μ={5}
Selje Topology is given by $SJ_{R(C-NM5)}(X)$ = {φ,X,{1,2,5},{1},{5},{1,5},{3,4,6}
,{3,4,5,6},{1,3,4,6},
{1,3,4,5,6}, {3,4},{1,2,3,4,5},{3,4,5},{1,3,4},{1,3,4,5}}
$^{SJ}R(C-NM\,5)^{(X)={}^{SJ}}R(C)^{(X)}$

Case 2: Books Reading Is Below Average

When the readers engagement drops BELOW the AVERAGE, apply the aforementioned algorithm to identify the core books frequently referenced in the field of numerical methods.

Assume X = Books reading is below average ={M2, M5, M6}, representing the total number of books read above average.
$U/R_{(C)}(X)$ = {{M1}, {M2,M6}, {M3}, {M4}, {M5}}
then Nano Topology is given by $\tau_{R(C)}(X)$ = {Φ,U,{2,5,6}}
Micro topology $\mu_{R(C)}(X)$={Φ,X,{5},{2,5,6}} for μ={5}
Selje Topology is given by $SJ_{R(C)}(X)$ = {φ,X,{1,2,5},{5},{2,5},{3,4,6},{3,4,5,6},{2,3,4,5,6},
{6},{1,2,5,6},{5,6},{2,5,6}}

Phase 1: When Attributes NM1 Is Removed

NM1 is removed from C and the following topologies are given by
$U/R_{(C-NM1)}(X)$ = {{M1}, {M2,M6}, {M3}, {M4,M5}}

then Nano Topology is given by $\tau_{R(C-NM1)}(X)$ = {Φ,U,{2,6},{2,4,5,6},{4,5}}
Micro topology $\mu_{R(C-NM1)}(X)$={Φ,X,{5},{2,6},{2,5,6}{2,4,5,6}{4,5}} for μ={5}
Selje Topology is given by $SJ_{R(C-NM1)}(X)$ = {φ,X,{5},{1,2,5},{2},{2,5},{3,4,6},{3,4,5,6},{2,3,4,6},
{2,3,4,5,6},{6},{1,2,5,6},{2,6},{4,6},{1,2,4,5,6},{4,5,6},{2,4,6},{2,4,5,6},{4},{1,2,4,5},
{4,5},{2,4},{2,4,5},{2,5,6}}
$SJ_{R(C-NM1)}(X) /= SJ_{R(C)}(X)$

Phase 2: When Attributes NM2 Is Removed

NM2 is removed from C and the following topologies are given by
$U/R_{(C-NM2)}(X)$ = {{M1}, {M2,M6}, {M3}, {M4}, {M5}}
then Nano Topology is given by $\tau_{R(C-NM2)}(X)$ = {Φ,U,{2,5,6}}
Micro topology $\mu_{R(C-NM2)}(X)$={Φ,X,{5},{2,5,6}} for μ={5}
Selje Topology is given by $SJ_{R(C-NM2)}(X)$ = {φ,X,{1,2,5},{5},{2,5},{3,4,6},{3,4,5,6},{2,3,4,5,6},
{6},{1,2,5,6},{5,6},{2,5,6}}
$^{SJ}R(C-NM\ 2)^{(X)} = {}^{SJ}R(C)^{(X)}$

Phase 3: When Attributes NM3 Is Removed

NM3 is removed from C and the following topologies are given by
$U/R_{(C-NM3)}(X)$ = {{M1}, {M2,M6}, {M3}, {M4,M5}}
then Nano Topology is given by $\tau_{R(C-NM3)}(X)$ = {Φ,U,{2,6},{2,4,5,6},{4,5}}
Micro topology $\mu_{R(C-NM3)}(X)$={Φ,X,{5},{2,6},{2,5,6}{2,4,5,6}{4,5}} for μ={5}
Selje Topology is given by $SJ_{R(C-NM3)}(X)$ = {φ,X,{5},{1,2,5},{2},{2,5},{3,4,6},{3,4,5,6},{2,3,4,6},
{2,3,4,5,6},{6},{1,2,5,6},{2,6},{4,6},{1,2,4,5,6},{4,5,6},{2,4,6},{2,4,5,6},{4},{1,2,4,5},
{4,5},{2,4},{2,4,5},{2,5,6}}
$SJ_{R(C-NM3)}(X) /= SJ_{R(C)}(X)$

Phase 4: When Attributes NM4 Is Removed

NM4 is removed from C and the following topologies are given by
$U/R_{(C-NM4)}(X)$ = {{M1}, {M2,M6}, {M3}, {M4}, {M5}}
then Nano Topology is given by $\tau_{R(C-NM4)}(X)$ = {Φ,U,{2,5,6}}
Micro topology $\mu_{R(C-NM4)}(X)$={Φ,X,{5},{2,5,6}} for μ={5}

Selje Topology is given by $SJ_{R(C-NM4)}(X) = \{\varphi,X,\{1,2,5\},\{5\},\{2,5\},\{3,4,6\},\{3,4,5,6\},\{2,3,4,5,6\},$

$\{6\},\{1,2,5,6\},\{5,6\},\{2,5,6\}\}$

$^{SJ}R(C-NM\,4)^{(X)} = {^{SJ}R(C)^{(X)}}$

Phase 5: When Attributes NM5 Is Removed

NM5 is removed from C and the following topologies are given by

$U/R_{(C-NM5)}(X) = \{\{M1\}, \{M2,M6\}, \{M3\}, \{M4\}, \{M5\}\}$

then Nano Topology is given by $\tau_{R(C-NM5)}(X) = \{\Phi,U,\{2,5,6\}\}$

Micro topology $\mu_{R(C-NM5)}(X)=\{\Phi,X,\{5\},\{2,5,6\}\}$ for $\mu=\{5\}$

Selje Topology is given by $SJ_{R(C-NM5)}(X) = \{\varphi,X,\{1,2,5\},\{5\},\{2,5\},\{3,4,6\},\{3,4,5,6\},\{2,3,4,5,6\},$

$\{6\},\{1,2,5,6\},\{5,6\},\{2,5,6\}\}$

$^{SJ}R(C-NM\,5)^{(X)} = {^{SJ}R(C)^{(X)}}$

6. OBSERVATION

Based on the analysis, NM2, NM4, and NM5 are the most frequently used resources, with high usage in 3, 4, and 3 out of 6 months respectively, indicating their high importance and demand. On the other hand, NM1, despite having high usage in 3 out of 6 months, and NM3, with only 2 months of high usage, are identified as the least utilized resources. Therefore, it is recommended to consider digitizing NM2, NM4, and NM5 to enhance their accessibility, as they are the most used resources. Additionally, the necessity of keeping NM1 and NM3 in physical form should be evaluated. Depending on further usage analysis and patron feedback, these resources could be candidates for elimination or a reduction in physical copies. This observation helps in making informed decisions about resource management and optimization in the library, ensuring that the most valuable resources are readily accessible to patrons.

Figure 3. Observation on Books that are used frequently and to be rolled out

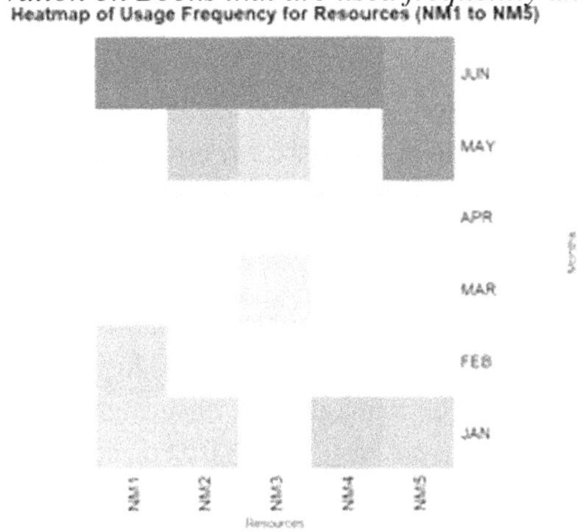

7. RESULTS AND DISCUSSION

This study highlights the significance of NM2, NM4, and NM5 as key books identified for digitization and inclusion in the open-source collection. By leveraging blockchain technology, libraries can ensure secure tracking of these digital assets, maintaining their integrity and accessibility for future users. The digitization of these critical texts not only enhances resource management but also addresses the growing demand for access to valuable educational materials. The combination of topological analysis and blockchain integration represents a promising advancement in library science, fostering greater transparency and preservation of essential knowledge. In conclusion, the core books frequently used have been identified as NM2, NM4, and NM5.

8. CONCLUSION

The integration of blockchain technology with SELJE topology provides a robust and secure methodology for library management. Our analysis, which combined data integrity and transparency ensured by blockchain, and the effective data analysis capabilities of SELJE topology, identified NM2, NM4, and NM5 as the most frequently used resources in numerical methods. This confirms our observation that these books have high usage rates, making them essential for digitization to enhance accessibility.

Additionally, the observation indicated that NM1 and NM3 have lower usage rates compared to NM2, NM4, and NM5, with NM3 being the least utilized. This aligns with our recommendation to evaluate the necessity of keeping NM1 and NM3 in physical form. Depending on further usage analysis and patron feedback, these could be candidates for elimination or reduced physical copies.

In summary, the combined approach of blockchain and SELJE topology not only ensures a secure and transparent process but also efficiently identifies and prioritizes essential reading materials for digital archiving. This methodology supports informed decisions about resource management, ensuring that the most valuable resources are readily accessible to patrons, while also considering the optimization of library space and resources.

REFERENCES

Adams, C., & Lloyd, S. (1996). *Understanding topology*. Springer.

Aydin, G., & Kurt, M. (2020). Blockchain technology in the context of libraries: Opportunities and challenges. *Library Management*, 41(5), 305–316.

Becker, K., & Matz, M. (2019). Using blockchain for digital preservation of academic resources. *International Journal of Digital Curation*, 14(1), 35–45.

Chandrasekar, S. (2019). On micro topological spaces. *Journal of New Theory*, 26, 23–31.

Crosby, M., & Nachiappan, , PVerma, , SKalyanaraman, , V. (2016). Blockchain technology: Beyond bitcoin. *Applied Innovation*, 2, 6–10.

Deegan, M., & Tanner, S. (2006). *Digital preservation*. Facet Publishing.

Frederick, D. E. (2019). Blockchain, libraries and the data deluge. *Library Hi Tech News*, 36(10), 1–7. DOI: 10.1108/LHTN-09-2019-0059

Gindin, S., & Rozenberg, G. (2018). Blockchain applications in libraries: The future of digital preservation. *Library Hi Tech*, 36(2), 201–214.

Irwin, R. (2002). *Digital preservation: An introduction to the standards and procedures for digital archiving*. The British Library.

Jayavadivel, R., Arunachalam, M., Nagarajan, G., Shankar, B. P., Viji, C., Rajkumar, N., & Senthilkumar, K. R. (2024). Historical overview of AI adoption in libraries. In *AI-Assisted Library Reconstruction* (pp. 267–289). DOI: 10.4018/979-8-3693-2782-1.ch015

Jeyanthi, V., & Selva Nandhini, N. (2023). On SELJE topological spaces. *Indian Journal of Natural Sciences*, 14(80), 64187–64193.

Kalb, J. L., & Lee, D. S. (2008). *Network topology analysis*. Sandia National Laboratories. DOI: 10.2172/1028919

Kishore, H. S., Raj, D. S. P., & Senthilkumar, K. R. (2024). AI for accessibility: A case study of enhancing library services for users with disabilities. In *Improving Library Systems with AI* (pp. 214–225). Applications, Approaches, and Bibliometric Insights. DOI: 10.4018/979-8-3693-5593-0.ch015

Koh, C. E., & Qin, Y. (2020). Utilizing blockchain for digital rights management and preservation in libraries. *Journal of Digital Information Management*, 18(1), 41–50.

Kumar, N., Antoniraj, S., Jayanthi, S., Mirdula, S., Selvaraj, S., Rajkumar, N., & Senthilkumar, K. R. (2024). Educational technology and libraries supporting online learning. In *AI-Assisted Library Reconstruction* (pp. 209–237). DOI: 10.4018/979-8-3693-2782-1.ch012

Liu, Y., & Zhang, Q. (2019). The impact of blockchain technology on the management of library collections. *Library Resources & Technical Services*, 63(3), 134–146.

Lu, Q., & Xu, X. (2017). Adaptable blockchain-based systems: A case study for product traceability. *IEEE Software*, 34(6), 21–27. DOI: 10.1109/MS.2017.4121227

Matheu, A., & Rodr'ıguez, R. (2019). Blockchain for libraries: The decentralized future. *Library Management*, 40(3/4), 197–210.

Munkres, J. R. (2000). *Topology* (2nd ed.). Prentice Hall.

Nakamoto, S. (2008). Bitcoin: A peer-to-peer electronic cash system. Retrieved from https://bitcoin.org/bitcoin.pdf

Perumbuduru, S., & Dhar, J. (2010). Performance evaluation of different network topologies based on ant colony optimization. *International Journal of Wireless and Mobile Networks*, 2(4), 141–157. DOI: 10.5121/ijwmn.2010.2412

Rajkumar, N., Tabassum, H., Muthulingam, S., Mohanraj, A., Viji, C., Kumar, N., & Senthilkumar, K. R. (2024). Anticipated requirements and expectations in the digital library. In *AI-Assisted Library Reconstruction* (pp. 1–20). DOI: 10.4018/979-8-3693-2782-1.ch001

Rajkumar, N., Viji, C., Mohanraj, A., Senthilkumar, K. R., Jagajeevan, R., & Kovilpillai, J. A. (2024). Ethical considerations of AI implementation in the library era. In *Improving Library Systems with AI: Applications, Approaches, and Bibliometric Insights* (pp. 85–106). . ch007DOI: 10.4018/979-8-3693-5593-0.ch007

Rosenfeld, M., & Wisser, M. (2017). Blockchain: Transforming library records management. *The Library Quarterly*, 87(4), 326–345.

Salah, K., Rehman, M. H. U., Nizamuddin, N., & Al-Fuqaha, A. (2019). Blockchain for AI: Review and open research challenges. *IEEE Access : Practical Innovations, Open Solutions*, 7, 10127–10149. DOI: 10.1109/ACCESS.2018.2890507

Savastano, M., & Consiglio, A. (2018). Blockchain in libraries: Potential benefits and risks. *Journal of Librarianship and Information Science*, 50(4), 333–341.

Senthilkumar, K. R. (2019). User pattern of Libraries by students of Government Colleges in Tamil Nadu: A study. *Library Philosophy and Practice*.

Senthilkumar, K. R. (2024a). AI-assisted library reconstruction. In *AI-Assisted Library Reconstruction*. DOI: 10.4018/979-8-3693-2782-1

Senthilkumar, K. R. (2024b). Revolutionizing thrust manufacturing: The synergy of real-time data and AI advancements. In *Using Real-Time Data and AI for Thrust Manufacturing* (pp. 80–93). https://doi.org/. ch005DOI: 10.4018/9798369326152

Senthilkumar, K. R., & Jagajeevan, R. (2024). Improving library systems with AI: Applications, approaches, and bibliometric insights. In *Improving Library Systems with AI*. Applications, Approaches, and Bibliometric Insights., DOI: 10.4018/979-8-3693-5593-0

Senthilkumar, K. R., & Maniiarasan, P. (2020). Comparison of Eresources with their usage statistics among Bharathidasan University & Madurai Kamaraj University. *Library Philosophy and Practice, 2020*. https: //www.scopus.com/inward/record .uri?eid=2-s2.0-85091524339&partnerID= 40&md5=6f7b662e3842db0d95af-80ba646fdd6e

Sivaraj, P., Madhan, V., Mallika, V., & Senthilkumar, K. R. (2024). Enhancing library services through optimization algorithms and data analytics: Enhancing library services mathematical model. In *AI-Assisted Library Reconstruction* (pp. 290–306). DOI: 10.4018/979-8-3693-2782-1.ch016

Steen, L. A., & Seebach, J. A. (1995). *Counterexamples in topology*. Dover Publications.

Taj, A., Ahmed, M. G., Ali, K. S., & Senthilkumar, K. R. (2024). Revolutionizing medical libraries: The vital role of AI in enhancing discovery, access, and library services for healthcare professional. In *Improving Library Systems with AI* (pp. 24–38). Applications, Approaches, and Bibliometric Insights., DOI: 10.4018/979-8-3693-5593-0.ch002

Thivagar, M. L., & Richard, C. (2023). On nano forms of weakly open sets. *International Journal of Mathematics and Statistics Invention*, 1, 31–37.

Velmurugan, B., Dharmalingam, S., Muthukrishnan, K. B., & Senthilkumar, K. R. (2024). AI insights deciphering India's ascendancy through the digital library: Navigating the digital realm India's odyssey towards information equity and technological eminence. In *Improving Library Systems with AI* (pp. 285–293). Applications, Approaches, and Bibliometric Insights., DOI: 10.4018/979-8-3693-5593-0.ch021

Wood, G. (2014). Ethereum: A secure decentralised generalised transaction ledger. Retrieved from https://ethereum.org/en/whitepaper

Yaga, D., Mell, P., Roby, N., & Scarfone, K. (2018). *Blockchain technology overview*. National Institute of Standards and Technology. DOI: 10.6028/NIST.IR.8202

Chapter 16
Greedy Algorithms in Fuzzy Graphic Matroids for Library Resources Preservation With Index Codes Using Blockchain Technology

S. Saranya
Sri Krishna Arts and Science College, India

Buvaneswari R.
Sri Krishna Arts and Science College, India

ABSTRACT

In the digital transformation era, preserving library resources has become increasingly vital. This chapter explores the integration of greedy algorithms within fuzzy graphic matroids for efficient library resource preservation, enhanced by index coding and blockchain technology. Fuzzy graphic matroids provide a mathematical structure to model and optimize resource allocation under uncertainty, capturing the relationships and dependencies in library systems. The greedy algorithm selects the most critical edges in the fuzzy graphic matroid, ensuring the independence property is maintained while optimizing the selection process. Index coding minimizes the number of transmissions required for data retrieval. Integrating index coding and blockchain technology ensures efficient resource allocation, enhanced data retrieval, and secure library records. The proposed framework presents a novel and comprehensive solution to the challenges of digital preservation in modern

DOI: 10.4018/979-8-3693-7783-3.ch016

libraries. The practical application and benefits of this approach are demonstrated with an example.

1. INTRODUCTION

Blockchain technology is a decentralized digital ledger system that enables secure and transparent recording of transactions across a network of computers. Blockchain has evolved to support various applications. It operates on a decentralized network where no single entity controls the data ensuring transparency and immutability of transactions (Lengoatha & Seymour, 2020). Greedy algorithms is known for its simplicity and effectiveness in optimization problems which is applied within the

framework of fuzzy graphic matroids that gives a robust mathematical model for dealing with uncertainty and imprecision in data. Graph theory provides essential tools and methodologies for enhancing blockchain technology. From optimizing the blockchain structure and consensus mechanisms to improving network security and data integrity, graph theoretical concepts play a vital role in the development and advancement of blockchain systems (Bashir & Warraich, 2023).

Graph theory originated with Leonhard Euler's work on the Seven Bridges of Ko¨nigsberg problem in 1736 and it has since become a fundamental area of study in modern mathematics and computer science (West, 2001). Graph theory provides powerful tools for managing, retrieving, and optimizing information in libraries. By representing and analyzing relationships between books, authors, categories, and users, libraries can enhance their services and improve the overall user experience. Graph theory helps in analyzing and organizing this structure to improve navigation and search capabilities.

Fuzzy graph theory offers significant advantages in enhancing blockchain technology by addressing uncertainties and providing more flexible and robust solutions. Its applications range from improving consensus mechanisms and resource allocation to enhancing privacy, security and interoperability. By incorporating fuzziness, blockchain systems can better handle real-world complexities and deliver more reliable and efficient performance (Mordeson & Mathew, 2019).

The theory of graphic matroids introduced by Whitney and further studied by Tutte (1959). Tutte emerged as the leading figure in the field of matroid theory and his contributions to this discipline were abundant (Tutte, 1959). In 1988, Goetschal and Voxman introduced the notion of fuzzy matroids. Fuzzy matroids deals with graphical and algebraical structures related to the membership grades of a fuzzy graph (Goetschel & Voxman, 1988). In 2019, a new class of matroids from fuzzy graphs was constructed by Sabana and Sameena (Shabna & Sameena, 2019). From a fuzzy graph G, subgraphs can be formed by deleting or contracting edges. The concept of representable fuzzy matroid and the idea of inducing fuzzy matroids from fuzzy vector space was done by Sabana and Sameena (2021). The isomorphism between two fuzzy matroids and the properties are defined by Sabana and Sameena (2021).

In this paper the integration of greedy algorithms, fuzzy graphic matroids, and blockchain technology presents a novel approach for preserving library resources with enhanced efficiency and security. This combination is particularly useful for library resource preservation. Index codes are employed to optimize data retrieval and storage processes that ensuring quick and accurate access to preserved resources.

The paper is organized as follows: In Section 2, the review of literature is presented. The basic definitions are provided in Section 3. The greedy algorithm for fuzzy graphic matroids is explained with an example in Section 4. A brief note on the departments of higher education is given in Section 5. The algorithm for implementing the greedy algorithm and index codes in the preservation of library resources is explained briefly in Section 6. The archival preservation of library data using index codes to retrieve resources by the greedy algorithm is discussed, and the results are provided in Section 7. Section 8 concludes the paper.

2. REVIEW OF LITERATURE

Graph Theory with Applications is a foundational text book by Bondy and Murty that offers a comprehensive introduction to graph theory and its applications. David B. West's *Introduction to Graph Theory* is a well-regarded textbook that provides a modern introduction to the field of graph theory. A comprehensive introduction to fuzzy graph theory covering both fundamental and advanced aspects of the subject is given by Mathew, Mordeson, and Malik in 2018

. The book is designed to provide a solid foundation in fuzzy graph theory and its applications. Advanced Topics in Fuzzy Graph Theory is an in-depth exploration of advanced concepts and developments in the field of fuzzy graph theory was done by Mordeson and Mathew in 2019. This book addresses the complex topics and current research trends in fuzzy graph theory.

Shabna and Sameena in 2019 explored the connection between fuzzy graphs and matroids. The paper investigates how fuzzy graphs can be used to define and study fuzzy matroids expanding the theory of matroids into the fuzzy setting. In 2021 Shabna and Sameena extends their earlier work by focusing specifically on graphic fuzzy matroids. This paper examines how the concept of graphic matroids can be adapted to the fuzzy setting and explores the properties and applications of these structures.

El Rouayheb, Sprintson, and Georghiades in 2010 explored the index coding problem and its connections to network coding and matroid theory (El Rouayheb et al., 2008). The paper provides a comprehensive analysis of the index coding problem, examining its relationship with various theoretical frameworks and proposing new approaches for solving it. Thomas and Sundar Rajan in 2020 investigate the generalized index coding problem and its relationship with discrete polymatroids and explored how the concepts of discrete polymatroids can be used to understand and solve generalized index coding problems, offering a novel approach to analyzing this complex problem (Thomas & Sundar Rajan, 2020).

Kshetri explored how blockchain technology can improve supply chain management by enhancing transparency, traceability, and efficiency, leveraging its decentralized and immutable ledger to boost data security and reduce fraud in 2017. Kuo et al. review blockchain's potential in biomedical and healthcare sectors for managing health records and ensuring data integrity while addressing the associated challenges (Kshetri, 2017). La Fata and Lupo use fuzzy set theory and structural equation modeling to evaluate the key drivers of academic library service quality in the digital age. Lengoatha and Seymour in 2020 investigate factors influencing the adoption of blockchain technology in academic libraries, examining technological, organizational, and environmental determinants (Lengoatha & Seymour, 2020). Gul and Bano in 2019 discussed the smart libraries that integrate IoT, AI, and big data to transform traditional library operations. Hasan in 2020 focuses on blockchain applications in libraries for improving management, security, and user services (Hasan, 2020). Jha in 2023 reviewed on how blockchain can enhance access control, data management, and overall efficiency in libraries and information centers (Jha, 2023).

3. PRELIMINARIES

Definition 3.1. (Oxley, 2006) Let I be a non-empty family of a finite subsets of E and the pair M = (E, I) is called a *matroid* if it satisfies the following properties:

i) $\varphi \in I$
ii) If $A \in I, A \subset B$, then $B \in I$
iii) If $A, B \in I$; $|B| \geq |A|$, then there exists an element $e \in B \setminus A$ such that $A \cup \{e\} \in I$.

A matroid is a combinatorial structure that provides a broader conceptual framework encompassing the idea of linear independence. It serves as a unifying bridge between graph theory and linear algebra (Welsh, 1976). A matroid that is representable over every field is called *regular*. A matroid is *binary* if it can be represented over a finite field F_2 and *ternary* if it can be represented over a finite field F_3.

The collection of basis uniquely determines the matroid. A *basis (or base)* of a matroid refers to the largest independent set within M, while a *circuit* of the matroid corresponds to the smallest dependent set in M. The size of the largest independent set within the set *E* is defined to be the *rank of a matroid* and is represented as *r(I)* (Oxley, 2006). A graphic matroid is derived from graph *G*. It is defined on the egde set of the graph *G* and it is denoted by *M* (*G*) (Welsh, 1976).

i) A basis or a base of *M* (*G*) is the spanning trees of *G*.
ii) A circuit of *M* (*G*) is the simple cycles in a graph *G*.

The rank function of a graphic matroid *M* (*G*) defined on a graph $G = (V, E)$ is given by r(M(G)) = n K(V, F) where *n* is the number of verticec and *K(V, F)* is the number of connected components (Pitsoulis, 2014). A fuzzy graphic matroid is derived from a fuzzy graph. To understand this, we need to explore the definition of a fuzzy graph and fuzzy matroid.

Let $G = (\sigma^*, \mu^*)$ is a pair of functions with σ^* and μ^* where $\sigma^*: V \dashrightarrow [0, 1]$ is a fuzzy vertex set of *G* and $\mu^*: V \times V \dashrightarrow [0, 1]$ is a fuzzy edge set of *G* where $\mu_{ij} \leq min(\mu_i, \mu_j)$ for every $\mu_i, \mu_j \in V$. Then $G = (\sigma^*, \mu^*)$ is called as a fuzzy graph with *n* vertices and *m* edges. Let I be a fuzzy subset on E is a function I: $X \dashrightarrow [0, 1]$. The family of fuzzy set on E is given by *F* (*X*). If A, B ∈ F(E), then

i) $supp(\mathrm{A}) = \{x \in \mathrm{E} \mid \mathrm{A}(x) > 0\}$, a crisp set
ii) $m(\mathrm{A}) = min\{\mathrm{A}(x) \mid x \in supp(\mathrm{A})\}$
iii) $\mathrm{A} \cup \mathrm{B} = max\{\mathrm{A}(x), \mathrm{B}(x)\}, x \in \mathrm{E}$
iv) $\mathrm{A} \cap \mathrm{B} = min\{\mathrm{A}(x), \mathrm{B}(x)\}, x \in \mathrm{E}$.

Note: For the sake of convenience, different notations are used here.

Definition 3.2. (Goetschel & Voxman, 1988) Let E be a finite set and let I ∈ F(F_E) satisfying the following conditions:

i) $\varphi \in \mathrm{I}$
ii) $\mathrm{A} \subset \mathrm{B}$ and $\mathrm{B} \in \mathrm{A}$, where $\mathrm{A} \subset \mathrm{B}$, $\mathrm{A}(x) \leq \mathrm{B}(x)$ forall $x \in \mathrm{E}$
iii) If A, B ∈ I with |supp (A)| ≤ |supp (B)|, there exists C ∈ I such that
    a) $\mathrm{A} \subset \mathrm{C} \subseteq \mathrm{A} \cup \mathrm{B}$
    b) $m(\mathrm{C}) = \min \{m(\mathrm{A}), m(\mathrm{B})\}$.

Then $F_M = (\mathrm{E}, \mathrm{I})$ is a *fuzzy matroid*.

A fuzzy matroid is said to be fuzzy graphic matroid when it can be isomorphically mapped to *FM* (*G*) for a given fuzzy graph *G*. The maximal spanning trees of a fuzzy graph *G* is defined to be the basis or base and it is denoted by B(*FGM*). The minimal dependent edges of a fuzzy graph *G* that forms a simple cycle is defined to be the circuit and it is denoted C(*FGM*).

4. GREEDY ALGORITHM FOR FUZZY GRAPHIC MATROIDS

The greedy algorithm for fuzzy graphic matroids extends the classical greedy algorithm used in matroid theory to handle the uncertainty and imprecision inherent in fuzzy graphic matroids. A fuzzy graphic matroid is derived from a fuzzy graph *G* where the elements are edges of a fuzzy graph, and the independent sets are sets of edges that do not contain a cycle in the fuzzy graph. The aim of incorporating the greedy algorithm in fuzzy graphic matroid is to find a maximum-weight independent set of edges under fuzzy constraints.

The greedy algorithm for fuzzy graphic matroids involves:

- Sorting edges by membership value.
- Iteratively adding edges to an independent set while checking for fuzzy cycles.
- Ensuring that the selected set of edges adheres to the independence conditions defined by the fuzzy matroid.

The greedy algorithm aims to optimize the selection of edges while maintaining the fuzzy matroid's independence properties.

Example 4.0.1. *Let* $G = (\sigma^*, \mu^*)$ *is a pair of functions with* σ^* *and* μ^* *where* $\sigma^*: V \dashrightarrow [0, 1]$ *is a fuzzy vertex set of G and* $\mu^*: V \times V \dashrightarrow [0, 1]$ *is a fuzzy edge set of G where* $V = \{(\sigma_1, 0.5), (\sigma_2, 0.7), (\sigma_3, 0.4), (\sigma_4, 0.6)\}$ *and* $E = \{(\mu_{12}, 0.4), (\mu_{23}, 0.3), (\mu_{34}, 0.4), (\mu_{13}, 0.5), (\mu_{14}, 0.2)\}$

Figure 1. A fuzzy graph with membership value

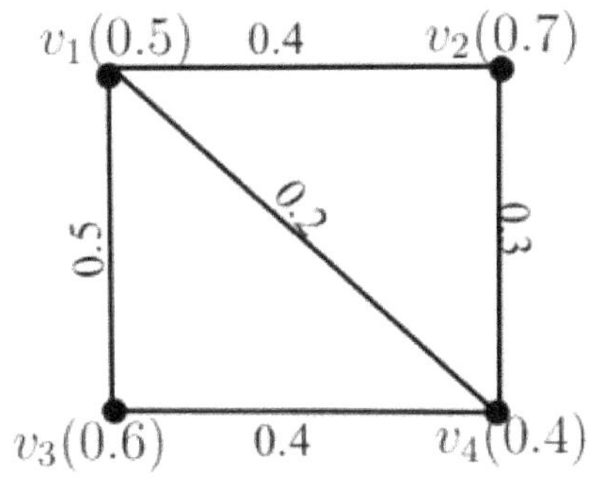

Figure 3.1 A fuzzy graph with membership value

- Sorting the edges by membership values $(\mu_{13}, 0.5)$, $(\mu_{12}, 0.4)$, $(\mu_{34}, 0.4)(\mu_{23}, 0.3)$, $(\mu_{14}, 0.2)$

Table 1. Edge sets

Edges	Edge set	Independent/ Dependent
φ	$X = \{\}$	Independent
$\mu 12$	$X = \{(\mu_{12}, 0.4)\}$	Independent
$\mu 23$	$X = \{(\mu_{12}, 0.4), (\mu_{23}, 0.3)\}$	Independent
$\mu 34$	$X = \{(\mu_1 2, 0.4), (\mu_{23}, 0.3), (\mu_{34}, 0.4)\}$	Independent
$\mu 13$	$X = \{(\mu_1 2, 0.4), (\mu_{23}, 0.3), (\mu_{34}, 0.4), (\mu_{13}, 0.5)\}$	Dependent
$\mu 14$	$X = \{(\mu_1 2, 0.4), (\mu_{23}, 0.3), (\mu_{34}, 0.4), (\mu_{13}, 0.5), (\mu_{14}, 0.2)\}$	Dependent

Skip μ_{13} and μ_{13} because adding μ_{13} and μ_{13} forms a cycle in fuzzy graph G. The final set

$X = \{(\mu_1 2, 0.4), (\mu_{23}, 0.3), (\mu_{34}, 0.4)\}$ maximizes the membership values and maintain the independence property of a fuzzy graphic matroid FGM.

5. DEPARTMENTS OF HIGHER EDUCATION

The National Assessment and Accreditation Council (NAAC) is an autonomous body established by the University Grants Commission (UGC) in India to assess and accredit institutions of higher education. Its primary aim is to evaluate the quality of education provided by colleges and universities, fostering a culture of excellence in the Indian higher education system. NAAC assesses institutions based on various criteria, including curriculum, teachinglearning processes, research, infrastructure, student support, and governance. The accreditation provided by NAAC is intended to guide institutions in their quest for continuous improvement and to provide students and stakeholders with reliable information about the quality of education offered.

The University Grants Commission (UGC) is a statutory body in India, established by the government in 1956 under the Ministry of Education. Its primary function is to oversee and maintain the standards of higher education in the country. The UGC is responsible for providing recognition to universities in India, disbursing funds to these institutions, and ensuring that they adhere to the established academic standards. It also plays a crucial role in promoting and coordinating university education, formulating regulations, and fostering innovation and research in higher education. The UGC's efforts aim to enhance the quality of education and make it accessible to a broader population.

The National Institutional Ranking Framework (NIRF) is a methodology adopted by the Ministry of Education, Government of India, to rank institutions of higher education in India.

Established in 2015, NIRF provides a comprehensive and transparent ranking system based on various parameters such as teaching, learning, and resources; research and professional practices; graduation outcomes; outreach and inclusivity; and perception. The framework aims to encourage academic excellence and competition among institutions while providing students and stakeholders with a reliable basis for comparing and choosing institutions.

The All India Council for Technical Education (AICTE) is a national-level advisory body in India, established in November 1945 with a mission to ensure the coordinated and integrated development of technical and management education across the country. It provides accreditation to various engineering, management, pharmacy, architecture, and other technical institutions, ensuring they meet quality standards. The AICTE is responsible for curriculum development, establishing norms and standards, quality assurance, and funding research and development activities. It plays a crucial role in fostering innovation and improving the overall educational infrastructure in India's technical education sector.

The Ministry of Human Resource Development (MHRD) was a branch of the Government of India responsible for the development of human resources in the country. Established in 1985, the ministry was tasked with overseeing and formulating policies related to education, literacy, and higher learning institutions. Its primary aim was to improve the educational framework in India by implementing various schemes and initiatives to enhance literacy rates, quality of education, and access to educational resources. In 2020, the MHRD was renamed the Ministry of Education, reflecting a renewed focus on educational reform and the New Education Policy (NEP) 2020.

The Tamil Nadu State Council for Higher Education (TNSCHE) is a statutory body established by the Government of Tamil Nadu, India. Its primary role is to coordinate and monitor the development of higher education in the state. TNSCHE formulates policies and programs to improve the quality and accessibility of higher education institutions, ensures adherence to standards, and promotes research and innovation. The council also advises the state government on matters related to higher education and fosters collaboration between universities, colleges, and other educational institutions to enhance the overall educational landscape of Tamil Nadu.

E-books or electronic books are digital versions of printed books that can be read on computers, tablets, e-readers, and smartphones. They offer numerous advantages over traditional books including portability, accessibility, and often lower costs. E-books can incorporate multimedia elements such as audio, video, and interactive features, enhancing the reading experience. The growth of digital libraries and online bookstores e-books have become increasingly popular offering readers a vast array of titles at their fingertips.

The National Board for Higher Mathematics (NBHM) is an autonomous organization in India, established by the Department of Atomic Energy (DAE) in 1983. It aims to promote the development of higher mathematics in the country. The NBHM provides funding for research projects, scholarships for students, and organizes workshops, conferences, and advanced training programs. It also supports the publication of mathematical literature and collaborates with other national and international organizations to foster mathematical research and education. The board plays a crucial role in shaping the mathematical landscape of India, encouraging both theoretical and applied mathematical studies.

6. METHODOLOGY

In this algorithm, the authors aim to enhance archival preservation of data in libraries by leveraging fuzzy graphic matroids and blockchain technology. The data is collected from academic publications, research projects, books, and e-books focusing on the preservation of data in libraries. Python, along with libraries such as NetworkX and Matplotlib, is used for a more illustrative and precise representation. The algorithm involves constructing a fuzzy graph using the data collected from the library and forming a fuzzy graphic matroid based on the independence property. The steps involved are as follows:

6.1 Data Collection and Pre-Processing

i) **Identify Sources:** Gather data from institutional repositories, academic publications, research projects and books from libraries.
ii) **Extract Relationships:** Identify collaborations between documents collected from the libraries .
iii) **Quantify Collaboration Strength:** Assign fuzzy weights to represent the strength of edges.

6.2 Construction of Fuzzy Graph

1 Each vertex represents a document. Each edge represents a relation between two documents.
2 Use a fuzzy logic-based approach to assign weights between 0 and 1 to the edges, representing the strength of the relation.

6.3 Blockchain Integration

1 Deploy Ethereum nodes at each library document. Ensure proper synchronization and network connectivity between the documents.
2 Set up vertices at documents. (e.g., Documents related to Departments of higher education).
3 Create smart contracts for verification and access management. Implement encryption and access control mechanisms.

6.4 Algorithm for Archival Preservation of Data Using Greedy Algorithm and Index Codes

Step (i) **Define the Archive Data and Relationships.**

List all documents in the archive. Determine the relationships between documents and assign a membership value (weight) to each relationship. This forms the edges of the fuzzy graphic matroid.

Step (ii) **Construct the Fuzzy Graphic Matroid.**

Represent documents as vertices and relationships as edges in a graph and assign Weights to the corresponding edges.

Step (iii) **Apply the Greedy Algorithm to Select Independent Edges.**

Start with an empty set of selected edges. For each edge in the sorted list, check if adding the edge to the selected set maintains the independence property of the fuzzy graphic matroid. Repeat until you cannot add any more edges without violating the independence property.

Step (iv) **Generate Index Codes for Selected Edges.**

Define a function that encodes the relationship between two documents. For each selected edge μ_{ij} with preserved documents D_i and D_j the index code is calculated as $Index\ code_{ij} = Encode(D_i, D_j) \times \mu_{ij}$

Step (v) **Applying Block chain technology.** Use blockchain to record and track all transactions related to resource preservation, ensuring data integrity and transparency.

6.5 Implementation With an Example

Consider an archive with a large number of documents and their relationships. These documents are related to the accreditation of the college. The documents from NAAC, NBHM, AICTE, NIRF, UGC, INSCHE, MHRD, and other resources are taken for archival preservation. The practical application of the greedy algorithm in preserving archives using fuzzy graphic matroids and index codes is explained step by step.

Step (i) Represent individual documents in the archive.

$V = \{(D_1, 0.8), (D_2, 0.3), (D_3, 0.5), (D_4, 0.4), (D_5, 0.8), (D_6, 0.2), (D_7, 0.7), (D_8, 0.6)\}$

Represent relationships or dependencies between documents with membership degrees indicating the strength of these relationships.

$E = \{(\mu_{12}, 0.2), (\mu_{23}, 0.3), (\mu_{34}, 0.4), (\mu_{45}, 0.4), (\mu_{56}, 0.2), (\mu_{67}, 0.2), (\mu_{78}, 0.6), (\mu_{13}, 0.3), (\mu_{24}, 0.3), (\mu_{35}, 0.5), (\mu_{46}, 0.2), (\mu_{57}, 0.7), (\mu_{68}, 0.2), (\mu_{15}, 0.8), (\mu_{26}, 0.2), (\mu_{37}, 0.5), (\mu_{48}, 0.4)\}$

Figure 2. Fuzzy Graph Representation of Archive Data

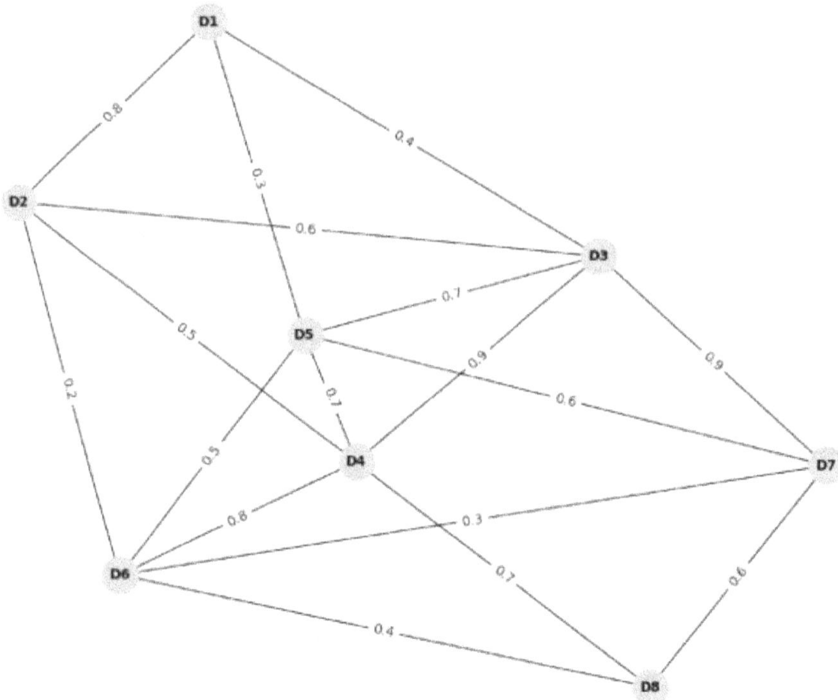

Step (ii) Constructing the fuzzy graphic matroid from the set of edges in the fuzzy graph *G*. Let

E be the ground set of *FGM* and I be the set of independent edges.

E = $\{(\mu_{12}, 0.2), (\mu_{23}, 0.3), (\mu_{34}, 0.4), (\mu_{45}, 0.4), (\mu_{56}, 0.2), (\mu_{67}, 0.2), (\mu_{78}, 0.6), (\mu_{13}, 0.3), (\mu_{24}, 0.3), (\mu_{35}, 0.5), (\mu_{46}, 0.2), (\mu_{57}, 0.7), (\mu_{68}, 0.2), (\mu_{15}, 0.8), (\mu_{26}, 0.2), (\mu_{37}, 0.5), (\mu_{48}, 0.4)\}$

Step (iii) Applying the Greedy Algorithm minimize the total membership degrees and preserving the independence property.

Sort edges by their membership degrees in descending order

E = $\{(\mu_{15}, 0.8), (\mu_{57}, 0.7), (\mu_{78}, 0.6), (\mu_{37}, 0.5), (\mu_{35}, 0.5), (\mu_{48}, 0.4), (\mu_{45}, 0.4),$

$(\mu_{34}, 0.4), (\mu_{23}, 0.3), (\mu_{24}, 0.3), (\mu_{13}, 0.3), (\mu_{12}, 0.2), (\mu_{56}, 0.2), (\mu_{67}, 0.2), (\mu_{46}, 0.2), (\mu_{68}, 0.2), (\mu_{26}, 0.2)\}$

- Start with an empty set of edges I = { }

Table 2. Sorting the edges by greedy algorithm to find the optimal independent set

Edges	Independent/ Dependent	Add/ Skip
$\mu 12$	Independent	Add
$\mu 34$	Independent	Add
$\mu 37$	Inependent	Add
$\mu 46$	Dependent	Skip
$\mu 45$	Independent	Add
$\mu 35$	Dependent	Skip
$\mu 48$	Independent	Add
$\mu 23$	Independent	Add
$\mu 78$	Dependent	Skip
$\mu 57$	Dependent	Skip
$\mu 24$	Independent	Add
$\mu 56$	Dependent	Skip
$\mu 68$	Independent	Add
$\mu 13$	Dependent	Skip
$\mu 67$	Independent	Add
$\mu 15$	Dependent	Skip
$\mu 26$	Independent	Add

- Resulting Independent Set I = $\{(\mu_{37}, 0.5), (\mu_{34}, 0.4), (\mu_{45}, 0.4), (\mu_{48}, 0.4), (\mu_{23}, 0.3), (\mu_{24}, 0.3), (\mu_{68}, 0.2), (\mu_{67}, 0.2), (\mu_{26}, 0.2), (\mu_{12}, 0.2)\}$

This set preserves the archive's structure with minimal redundancy.

Step (iv) Create codes that leverage the structure of the fuzzy graphic matroid to minimize redundancy. For each selected edge (relationship) in the independent set, generate an index code representing the relationship and its weight.

$$Index\ code_{ij} = Encode(D_i, D_j) \times \mu_{ij}$$

Table 3. Representing the encoded values of edges representing the relation between the documents

Edges	Membership value	Encoded value
μ_{37}	0.5	$Encode(D_3, D_7) \times 0.5$
μ_{34}	0.4	$Encode(D_3, D_4) \times 0.4$
μ_{45}	0.4	$Encode(D_4, D_5) \times 0.4$
μ_{48}	0.4	$Encode(D_4, D_8) \times 0.4$
μ_{24}	0.3	$Encode(D_2, D_4) \times 0.3$
μ_{23}	0.2	$Encode(D_2, D_3) \times 0.2$
μ_{68}	0.2	$Encode(D_6, D_8) \times 0.2$
μ_{67}	0.2	$Encode(D_6, D_7) \times 0.2$
μ_{26}	0.2	$Encode(D_2, D_6) \times 0.2$
μ_{12}	0.2	$Encode(D_1, D_2) \times 0.2$

The preservation of archives with a large volume of accreditation-related documents can be efficiently managed using a combination of fuzzy graphic matroids and index codes. By applying the greedy algorithm in a structured, step-by-step manner, the archival process becomes more systematic and reliable. This approach ensures that critical documents from institutions such as NAAC, NBHM, AICTE, NIRF, UGC, INSCHE, MHRD, and other resources are preserved effectively enhancing the integrity and accessibility of the archive for future reference.

Figure 3. Archival Preservation using Fuzzy Graphic Matroids and Index codes

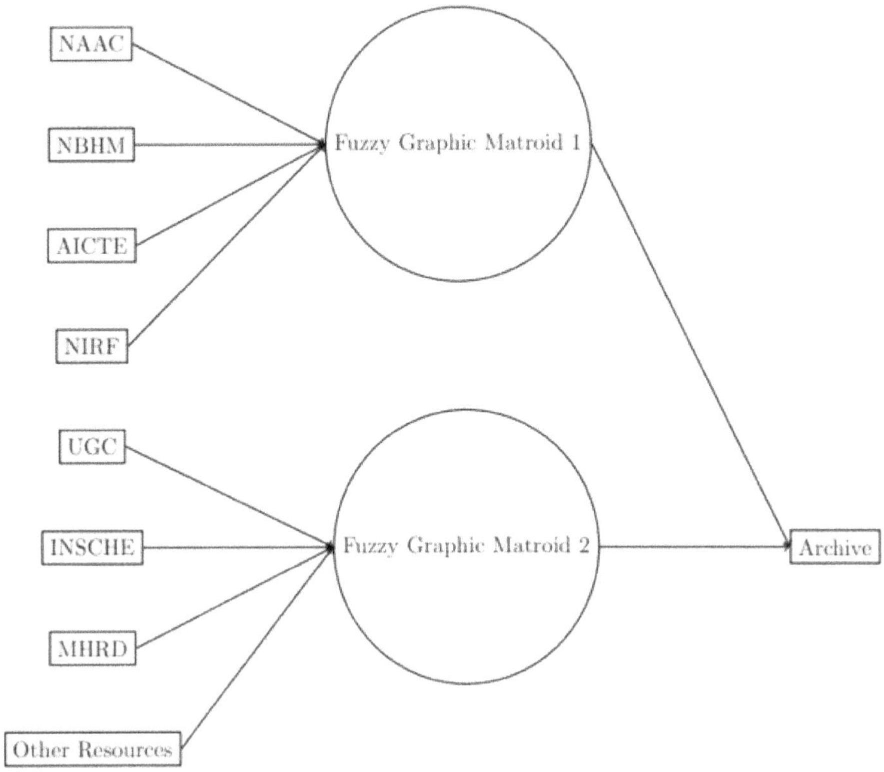

7. RESULTS AND DISCUSSION

i) The integration of fuzzy graphic matroid theory and blockchain technology has significantly enhanced archival preservation within the library system. The collected data was effectively processed and assigned fuzzy weights representing the strength of these data. This approach leverages the robustness of fuzzy graphic matroids and the security of blockchain to optimize data integrity and transparency in archival preservation.

ii) The application of the greedy algorithm, fuzzy graphic matroids, index codes, and blockchain technology has successfully optimized the archival process, reducing redundancy, enhancing security, and ensuring data integrity.

iii) The greedy algorithm efficiently selected a set of independent edges, preserving the structure of the archive.

iv) This method demonstrates significant potential for efficient and secure archival data management.
v) The approach facilitated efficient data retrieval through smart contracts, though it required careful management of computational resources and dependencies.

8. CONCLUSION

The authors integrated blockchain technology and fuzzy graphic matroids into the archival process to enhance data integrity, security, and transparency. This approach leverages the strengths of fuzzy graphic matroids, index coding, and blockchain to create a robust archival system. The algorithm efficiently preserves the structure and relationships within an archive, minimizing redundancy and optimizing retrieval through index coding. This method is particularly effective for handling large datasets and complex relationships, providing a scalable and robust solution for modern data preservation challenges.

Conflict of Interest

The authors of this paper affirm that there is no conflicts of interest.

ACKNOWLEDGMENT

The authors extend their sincere gratitude to the reviewers for their valuable suggestions, which have contributed in enhancing the quality of this paper.

REFERENCES

Bashir, F., & Warraich, N. F. (2023). Future libraries' blockchain opportunities and challenges: A systematic literature review and research agenda. *Digital Library Perspectives.*

El Rouayheb, S., Sprintson, A., & Georghiades, C. (2008, July). *On the relation between the index coding and the network coding problems. In 2008 IEEE International Symposium on Information Theory.* IEEE.

El Rouayheb, S., Sprintson, A., & Georghiades, C. (2010). On the index coding problem and its relation to network coding and matroid theory. *IEEE Transactions on Information Theory*, 56(7), 3187–3195. DOI: 10.1109/TIT.2010.2048502

Goetschel, R.Jr, & Voxman, W. (1988). Fuzzy matroids. *Fuzzy Sets and Systems*, 27(3), 291–302. DOI: 10.1016/0165-0114(88)90055-3

Hasan, N. (2020). Blockchain technology and its application in libraries. *Library Herald*, 58(4), 118–125. DOI: 10.5958/0976-2469.2020.00030.10

Jayavadivel, R., Arunachalam, M., Nagarajan, G., Shankar, B. P., Viji, C., Rajkumar, N., & Senthilkumar, K. R. (2024). Historical overview of AI adoption in libraries. In *AIAssisted Library Reconstruction* (pp. 267–289). IGI Global. DOI: 10.4018/979-8-3693-2782-1.ch015

Jha, S. K. (2023). Application of blockchain technology in libraries and information centers services. *Library Hi Tech News.*

Kaufmann, A. (1988). Theory of expertons and fuzzy logic. *Fuzzy Sets and Systems*, 28(3), 295–304. DOI: 10.1016/0165-0114(88)90036-X

Kaur, A., Sharma, R., Mishra, P., Sinhababu, A., & Chakravarty, R. (2022). Visual research discovery using connected papers: A use case of blockchain in libraries. *The Serials Librarian*, 83(2), 186–196. DOI: 10.1080/0361526X.2022.2142722

Kishore, H. S., Raj, D. S. P., & Senthilkumar, K. R. (2024). AI for accessibility: A case study of enhancing library services for users with disabilities. In *Improving Library Systems with AI* (pp. 214–225). Applications, Approaches, and Bibliometric Insights. DOI: 10.4018/979-8-3693-5593-0.ch015

Kshetri, N. (2017). Blockchain's roles in meeting key supply chain management objectives. *International Journal of Information Management*, 39, 80–89. DOI: 10.1016/j.ijinfomgt.2017.12.005

Kumar, N., Antoniraj, S., Jayanthi, S., Mirdula, S., Selvaraj, S., & Rajkumar, N. (2024). Educational technology and libraries supporting online learning. In *AI-Assisted Library Reconstruction* (pp. 209–237).

Kuo, T. T., Kim, H. E., & Ohno-Machado, L. (2017). Blockchain distributed ledger technologies for biomedical and health care applications. *Journal of the American Medical Informatics Association : JAMIA*, 24(6), 1211–1220. DOI: 10.1093/jamia/ocx068 PMID: 29016974

Lalitha, B., Ramalakshmi, K., Gunasekaran, H., Murugesan, P., Saminasri, P., & Rajkumar, N. (2024). Anticipating AI impact on library services: Future opportunities and evolutionary prospects. In *Improving Library Systems with AI: Applications, Approaches, and Bibliometric Insights* (pp. 195–213). IGI Global.

Lengoatha, L., & Seymour, L. F. (2020, September). Determinant factors of intention to adopt blockchain technology across academic libraries. In *Conference of the South African Institute of Computer Scientists and Information Technologists 2020* (pp. 244250). DOI: 10.1145/3410886.3410905

Mathew, S., Mordeson, J. N., & Malik, D. S. (2018). *Fuzzy graph theory* (Vol. 363). Springer International Publishing.

Mordeson, J. N., & Mathew, S. (2019). *Advanced topics in fuzzy graph theory* (Vol. 375). Springer. DOI: 10.1007/978-3-030-04215-8

Nachiappan, B. (2024b). E-resources content recommendation system using AI. In *Improving Library Systems with AI: Applications, Approaches, and Bibliometric Insights* (pp. 155–177). IGI Global. DOI: 10.4018/979-8-3693-5593-0.ch011

Oxley, J. G. (2006). *Matroid theory* (Vol. 3). Oxford University Press.

Pitsoulis, L. S. (2014). *Topics in matroid theory*. Springer Briefs in Optimization: Springer. DOI: 10.1007/978-1-4614-8957-3

Sameena, K. (2021). Fuzzy matroids from fuzzy vector spaces. *South East Asian Journal of Mathematics and Mathematical Sciences*, 17(03), 381–390.

Senthilkumar, K. R. (2019). *User pattern of Libraries by students of Government Colleges in Tamil nadu: A study*. Library Philosophy and Practice.

Senthilkumar, K. R. (2024a). AI-assisted library reconstruction. In *AI-Assisted Library Reconstruction*. DOI: 10.4018/979-8-3693-2782-1

Senthilkumar, K. R. (2024b). Revolutionizing thrust manufacturing: The synergy of realtime data and AI advancements. In *Using Real-Time Data and AI for Thrust Manufacturing* (pp. 80–93). https://doi.org/DOI: 10.4018/9798369326152.ch005

Senthilkumar, K. R., & Jagajeevan, R. (2024). Improving library systems with AI: Applications, approaches, and bibliometric insights. In *Improving Library Systems with AI*. Applications, Approaches, and Bibliometric Insights. DOI: 10.4018/979-8-3693-5593-0

Senthilkumar, K. R., & Maniiarasan, P. (2020). *Comparison of E-resources with their usage statistics among Bharathidasan University and Madurai Kamaraj University*. Library Philosophy and Practice.

Shabna, O. K., & Sameena, K. (2019). Matroids from fuzzy graphs. *Malaya Journal of Matematik. Vol-s*, (1), 500–504.

Shabna, O. K., & Sameena, K. (2021). Graphic fuzzy matroids. *South East Asian Journal of Mathematics and Mathematical Sciences*, 17(01), 223–232.

Sivaraj, P., Madhan, V., Mallika, V., & Senthilkumar, K. R. (2024). Enhancing library services through optimization algorithms and data analytics: Enhancing library services mathematical model. In *AI-Assisted Library Reconstruction* (pp. 290–306). DOI: 10.4018/979-8-3693-2782-1.ch016

Sun, Q., Ho, S. T., & Li, S. Y. R. (2008, July). On network matroids and linear network codes. In 2008 *IEEE International Symposium on Information Theory* (pp. 1833-1837). IEEE.

Taj, A., Ahmed, M. G., Ali, K. S., & Senthilkumar, K. R. (2024). Revolutionizing medical libraries: The vital role of AI in enhancing discovery, access, and library services for healthcare professional. In *Improving Library Systems with AI* (pp. 24–38). Applications, Approaches, and Bibliometric Insights., DOI: 10.4018/979-8-3693-5593-0.ch002

Thomas, A., & Sundar Rajan, B. (2020). Generalized index coding problem and discrete polymatroids. *Entropy (Basel, Switzerland)*, 22(6), 646. DOI: 10.3390/e22060646 PMID: 33286418

Tutte, W. T. (1959). Matroids and graphs. *Transactions of the American Mathematical Society*, 90(3), 527–552. DOI: 10.1090/S0002-9947-1959-0101527-3

Varadarajan, M. N. (2024). Educational program for AI literacy. In *Improving Library Systems with AI: Applications, Approaches, and Bibliometric Insights* (pp. 134–154). IGI Global. DOI: 10.4018/979-8-3693-5593-0.ch010

Velmurugan, B., Dharmalingam, S., Muthukrishnan, K. B., & Senthilkumar, K. R. (2024). AI insights deciphering India's ascendancy through the digital library: Navigating the digital realm India's odyssey towards information equity and technological eminence. In *Improving Library Systems with AI* (pp. 285–293). Applications, Approaches, and Bibliometric Insights., DOI: 10.4018/979-8-3693-5593-0.ch021

Viji, C., Najmusher, H., Rajkumar, N., Mohanraj, A., Nachiappan, B., Neelakandan, C., & Jagajeevan, R. (2024). Intelligent library management using radio frequency identification. In *AI-Assisted Library Reconstruction* (pp. 126–143). IGI Global. DOI: 10.4018/979-8-3693-2782-1.ch007

Welsh, D. J. A. (1976). *Matroid theory*. Academic Press.

West, D. B. (2001). *Introduction to graph theory* (Vol. 2). Prentice Hall.

Whitney, H. (1987). On the abstract properties of linear dependence. *Classic Papers in Combinatorics*, 63-87.

Zadeh, L. A. (1965). Fuzzy sets. *Information and Control*, 8(3), 338–353. DOI: 10.1016/S0019-9958(65)90241-X

Chapter 17 Future Trends and Innovations: Emerging Trends in Blockchain Technology Relevant to Libraries

Rishikaysh Marotrao Kaakandikar
https://orcid.org/0000-0003-0349-6788
SaiBalaji International Institute of Management Sciences, India

Sakhi Ajay Darware
https://orcid.org/0009-0009-6332-8314
SaiBalaji International Institute of Management Science, India

Senthilkumar K. R.
https://orcid.org/0000-0001-7426-5376
Sri Krishna Arts and Science College, India

ABSTRACT

Blockchain technology, celebrated for its secure and transparent framework, extends beyond its cryptocurrency origins to offer substantial benefits across various sectors, including libraries. This chapter examines the transformative impact of blockchain on library services by enhancing data security, streamlining operations, and fostering a collaborative environment for knowledge sharing. It explores how blockchain can address critical challenges faced by libraries, such as safeguarding patron data, managing digital rights, and improving interlibrary resource sharing. By providing a detailed analysis of blockchain's potential applications in library systems, this chapter aims to offer practical insights and recommendations for integrating blockchain technology to advance library management and services. The discussion includes real-world examples, potential future developments, and

DOI: 10.4018/979-8-3693-7783-3.ch017

strategic recommendations to harness blockchain for more efficient and secure library operations.

INTRODUCTION

Blockchain technology, which derives its name from the application in the sphere of support of the Bitcoin virtual currency, has become an innovation on a global scale in areas other than the financial domain. Enumerated under decentralization, immutability, and transparency, several challenges organizations encounter in the current world can be solved by Blockchain. By applying the Blockchain, educational institutions, especially libraries, which are processors of knowledge and information, will experience the following gains. In this chapter, details are elaborated on how Blockchain enhances library services, elevating its protection and productivity levels and creating an environment for information sharing.

On the contrary, libraries are the simplest examples of elementary organizations that obtain and distribute knowledge. These networks are as diverse as physical archives and data warehouses and experience data security, rights, and performance issues. All these challenges might be addressed by the use of Blockchain technology as this will offer a strong foundation that will protect cooperation while at the same time enhancing the abilities of structures to provide what is needed by the faculties.

Enhancing Data Security

In the present era of the computerized world, where almost all practices involve the use of computers, there is always a concern for privacy and data protection from hackers. Another brilliant feature of chains is that the data is not located on one server but has nodes. This format makes hacking and subsequent modification or destruction of data complex to the extent of being next to impossible. The following possibilities can benefit libraries: the added security for customers and their details, alongside the library system's digital properties. This means that by applying Blockchain libraries' capacities, they can build almost unreachable and narcotic records that would shield their stocks and readers' details from any vices or attempts at malingering.

It should also not go unnoticed that Blockchain does not have a centralized authority for control, making it very secure. Earlier, single concentrated databases provided information that could be hacked, causing system failure and loss. To ensure these risks are minimized or not taken, the data is shared in a blockchain and distributed to every node. Each node contains the entire chain, and thus, to change a portion of the string, a similar alteration has to be made on everybody's node, and it cannot be easy as it is virtually next to impossible for an intruder to access all the nodes.

Moreover, concerning using cryptographic methods in the Blockchain, the focus has shifted to protecting information. Every record in the blocks is a transaction, hashed and connected to the previous block through an unidentified key. This leads to creating a fixed linked list of blocks of data; after an entry has been made in the system, the data cannot be altered or deleted unless all the subsequent blocks and the whole network approve. To libraries, transaction history, digital preservation, and restricted patron data remain safeguarded from changes and hacking.

Libraries deal with large volumes of data, including cataloging and fee records, loan records, and records of interlibrary transfers. Previous systems had problems and risks that Blockchain eliminates by using a distributed ledger that creates proof of transaction. This can assist in streamlining and even automating work, including monitoring Interlibrary loans and digital assets. For example, it can enable smart contracts, track items, minimize paperwork, and, at the same time, ensure that the chain of the transaction remains clear and final.

Implements such as Blockchain technology can address most key processes undertaken in library operations in one unified technology. To illustrate, cataloging books, tracking loans, and recording interlibrary exchange can easily be handled through smart contracts; these are digital contracts that automatically operationalize the agreed terms of the contract as code. Such agreements can include transactions, record updates, and rule implementation and can work independently without the assistance of artificial tools.

Blockchain has the potential to improve effectiveness and preciseness in interlibrary loan systems. Conventional tracking of a given book(s) movement requires several steps and the cooperation of different organizations/institutions. In Blockchain, every exchange is provided on a public ledger to which all the collaborating libraries have visibility. This ensures that all items' status and location are always current to minimize delays and mistakes. Third, the use of Blockchain increases the transparency in the system, where all the parties involved can check the transaction and cases of disputes.

For digital collections, Blockchain can address questions of copyrights and guarantees that licenses will utilize digital resources. Some benefits libraries can fetch from harnessing Blockchain include: Libraries can utilize Blockchain to monitor the use of electronic resources, cope with licensing violations, and settle for payments with content providers. This serves a purpose for libraries as they manoeuvre in rights management issues and evaluate if they are offering access to resources legally and rightfully.

Below are some students' feedback aimed at enhancing collaboration and knowledge sharing:

Blockchain can also potentially promote higher levels of cooperation among libraries and other institutions. Libraries can also share resources and information through a decentralized network. This kind of partnership approach can empower the generation of natural collective online archives whose history can be traced through Blockchains. Also, its role can be applied to digital rights management, where Blockchain can offer a freely transparent system that will allow authors to be paid for their work and give patrons access to many digital assets.

Friendliness is one of the critical principles of library services, and Blockchain can add to this aspect by offering shared working resources safety. Libraries can join together in forming consortia to put together digital collections, which would be financially more sustainable and would thus make available a wider choice of resources to the users. Every object in a shared collection base can be written in the Blockchain, along with tags and other additional data. This makes it possible to verify the authenticity and history of each item of the shared stock, which builds credibility among the shared stock members.

Also, there is information on Blockchain implemented in collaborative networks, including managing rights and permissions to use digital content. One of the typical issues libraries encounter is negotiating and coordinating the procedures for acquiring the database license with multiple stakeholders. The process can be made relatively more accessible through technology due to transparency and an auditable trail of all the transactions and agreements. Insights for business: Smart contracts can be used to enforce licensing terms to see that content owners receive reasonable royalties, monitor access to digital materials, and control them according to legal and ethical requirements. Streamlining Library Operations

Transformative Potential

The adoption of Blockchain technology to library systems is a way of enhancing the modern offered by the library services. This can address some endemic problems in the area of data security and handling, work flow management, and coordination of resources. In general, the preservation and development of libraries' functionality in modern conditions depend on their capacity to meet the expectations of the readers and Internet users Blockchain opens new opportunities in such developments. This chapter is going to discuss the usage of Blockchain technology for library contexts, assess the changes that occur in managerial aspects of libraries, and describe suggestions how Blockchain can be useful for library development.

In the course of elaboration, we are to focus more on the possibilities Blockchain offers for shifting libraries' futures.

Currently, there are not many pilot projects and case studies of the application of Blockchain technology in libraries; however, these have revealed the possible ways to solve important issues and improve services. For instance, the application of Blockchain in the cataloging and metadata profile enhances the effectiveness and precision in library catalogues. Centralized cataloging systems eliminate problems of duplicated work and guarantee the unity of data provided in catalogues of various libraries. This improves on the findability of the resources in question and subsequently the satisfaction level of a typical user. Besides, through the implementation of Blockchain, concern over data privacy and protection of patron information and assets can be well catered for by Blockchain. Blockchain can be used in libraries to apply restricted rights where only certain users are allowed to read or write on restricted zones and documents. This can assist libraries in Data protection regulations and seeking patron's confidence.

Blockchain is also promising in terms of new ways of communication with citizens by libraries and enhancing digital literacy. Thus, due to the possibility of organizing the process of digital transactions through using the Blockchain approach, libraries can explain to customers the issues of data protection, their rights, and the proper approach to the digital sphere. Libraries can also use Blockchain to create new services and programs that will take advantage of Blockchain and some of its attributes such as voting on the library board of directors, and decentralized community projects among others.

Table 1. Blockchain Applications in Libraries

Challenge	Traditional Library System	Blockchain Solution	Potential Benefits
Data Security	Centralized databases vulnerable to breaches	Decentralized data storage on multiple nodes	Enhanced data protection, preventing unauthorized access and data loss
Copyright and DRM	Difficulty in managing digital rights and ensuring fair compensation	Immutable record-keeping of ownership, usage rights, and payments	Transparent rights management, secure royalty payments, legal compliance
Cataloging and Resource Sharing	Inefficient cataloging processes and interlibrary loan management	Decentralized cataloging and resource-sharing platform	Improved efficiency, accuracy, and accessibility of resources
Library Operations	Manual processes, paperwork, lack of transparency	Smart contracts for automated workflows, record-keeping	Streamlined operations, reduced costs, increased efficiency

continued on following page

Table 1. Continued

Challenge	Traditional Library System	Blockchain Solution	Potential Benefits
Collaboration and Knowledge Sharing	Difficulty in sharing resources and information among libraries	Decentralized network for resource sharing and collaboration	Enhanced cooperation, expanded resource access, creation of collective online archives
Patron Engagement	Limited interaction and feedback mechanisms	Blockchain-based voting systems, decentralized community projects	Increased patron participation, decision-making influence

Background

Education institutions specifically libraries have over the years served as going concerns as far as the dissemination of information is concerned. Beginning with inks on papyrus and proceeding to manuscripts on vellum/parchment, they have had to change with the current technological trends to suit their users' needs. However, as a result of the new information technologies, libraries will transfer from the physical storage of information to electronic systems which provide a wide range of electronic materials. This shift has contributed towards expanding information access and opening other fronts that libraries must relieve to continue playing a central role in society. AI has significantly transformed the operation of libraries when applied in managing the library by enhancing the performance, benefiting both the users and boasting the management of facts. This literature evaluation offers an assimilation of the findings from the literature that are particularly targeted at presenting the current state-of-the-art developments in various facets of AI systems in libraries. Viji et al. (Viji et al., 2024) found the use of the Radio Frequency identity (RFID) era in management of library. RFID structures automate stock administration, increase security, and allow self-service, making a helpful reduction inside the burden at the library body of workers. Concerning the performance and accuracy of RFID and its operations on the library's assets, the bankruptcy is irrefutable, which establishes capacity of RFID to transform library practices. Online studying has been described by Kumar et al. (Kumar et al., 2024) on how the relations between academic technology and libraries are mutual. Thus, the advocates of libraries state that with the help of AI, they can provide individual getting-acquainted experiences through the application of changeable studying patterns, as well as through the use of intelligent content recommendations. The chapter also analyzes libraries in relation to the digital divide: In this case, how they guarantee equal access to instructional resources. Virtual libraries have remained significant areas of interest in the recent past and Mohanraj et al. (Mohanraj et al., 2024) have gone ahead and addressed very sensitive issues of privacy and protection. Although AI and virtual are some of the technologies that libraries are adopting, there is sensitivity regarding data protection. The authors have a view into some of the protection measures and sorts of privateness that consumers agree with which libraries can enforce to prohibit the revelation of delicate records. Rajkumar et al. (Rajkumar, Tabassum, et al., 2024) describe changes for virtual libraries' need and anticipate in the AI generations. The bankruptcy is a good example of the requirement for well-develop technical and human resources, and constant work to meet the ever changing demands from library patrons. It also descries the role of consumer-centric designs in enhancing the establishment of AI-driven library structures. Jayavadivel et al. (Jayavadivel et al., 2024) provide a historical perspective about the implementation of AI in libraries . It also follows the development line of AI technologies used in library control from automation systems and AI answers. This chapter opens the curtain to ambitious challenges and activities throughout the course of this dynamism transformation process. Rajkumar et al. (Rajkumar, Viji, et al., 2024) went further and discuss the morality of artificial intelligence in the context of libraries. Concerns they cover include, but are not limited to, prejudiced algorithms, the opaqueness of the algorithms, and the right use of factual information about a person. The authors' call for proposing moral implications and guidelines that will help to avoid the negative effects of implementing AI technology in library services.

Lalitha et al (Lalitha et al., 2024) discuss the future impact of AI on the services of a library. They illustrate emergent trends and capability prospects for AI to enhance operations of the library procedures, for example, on the use of predictive analytics to determine the sequences of improvement or AI-based reference services. The bankruptcy also raises questions about evolution of libraries in an AI driven global. For an e-assets content advice gadget, Nachiappan (Nachiappan, 2024b) proposes an AI-primarily based one. Finding relevant digital material, the machine relies on system-getting-to-know algorithms to assess particular preferences. This makes it easier to enhance consumer engagement and pleasure, by offering content pointers that are unique to their interests. Present day advanced technologies in the management of aids in libraries are discussed by Nachiappan (Nachiappan, 2024a). Bankruptcy takes up latest subjects along with herbal language processing (NLP), machine getting to know, and AI-power records analytics. All of these technologies enhance resource finding; organizate and enhance library functioning; and offer invaluable data for decision making. The author Varadarajan perfectly describes the necessity of AI literacy in the context of libraries in his work of 2024. The chapter stresses for preparing educational packages that enable library teams of workers and users to have developed the right competencies to manage and seize the possibilities of artificial intelligence technologies in their working and learning environments. Ensuring a population level AI literacy ensures that libraries are capable of realizing

AI opportunities whilst at the same time, minimizing risks that come with AI. All the reviewed chapters in this paper are united by the emphasis on the potential of AI in managing libraries. New ways of improving and ameliorating the operational performance and protection, approving customer reviews, and ethical issues of library services, etc., are other possibilities AI offers to libraries to grow and successfully operate in the virtual world. Subsequent studies shall cumulate more ideas on appropriate AI packages for strategic library advancement and cope with issues that hinder AI to ensure some sustainable and customer-oriented library services.

The Evolution of Library Systems

In the recent past, libraries in the digital age have adopted the use of various technologies to serve patrons. Born digital, the system of digital catalogs, electronic journals, and online databases changed the way users interact with information. But there is a flip side, new challenges are there with increasing facilities. Libraries are no longer in charge of only traditional paper-based information materials, but also digital information in the form of e-books, digital archives, and multimedia resources. With this transition, the libraries have been faced with the issues of ways of functioning, managing their resources, and even protecting information.

Figure 1. Library Systems Evolution Flowchart

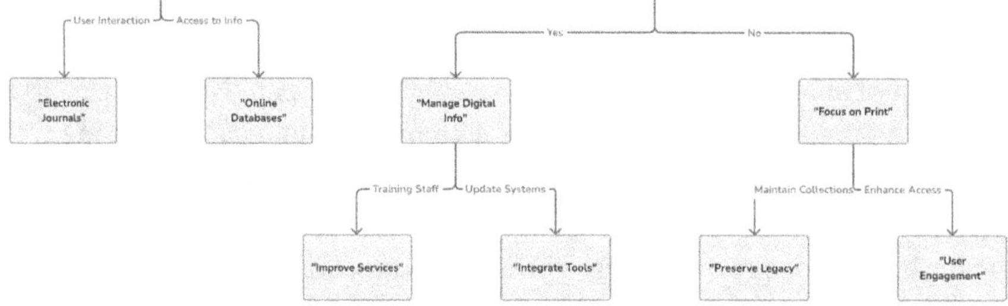

Challenges Facing Modern Libraries

Despite these advancements, traditional library systems encounter several challenges that impact their efficiency and effectiveness: Despite these advancements, traditional library systems encounter several challenges that impact their efficiency and effectiveness:

1. Data Security: Being that libraries are now transitioning to digital systems, patron data, and digital resources have new considerations for security. Although databases that are centralized are easy to use, they are not very safe from break-ins and other unauthorized accesses. The danger of having someone steal or alter the data is very great and has implications for both the libraries' collections and the users' confidentiality.
2. Copyright and Digital Rights Management (DRM): Modern information technologies provide a variety of problems connected with the protection of copyright and other rights belonging to an author or creator. When it comes to digital rights librarians too face scenarios that could be relatively difficult to handle. Making content access more open while still staying within the precedents of the copyright laws entails very advanced DRM systems. This means that it is not easy to strike the right balance between what users need and requires in their use of the resource and legal and ethical standards that govern the use of the digital resource.
3. Cataloging and Resource Sharing: Cataloging and sharing of resources are two important functions that libraries cannot do without in their functioning. But, organising for traditional catalogs may involve a lot of hassles and errors are very likely to happen. Interlibrary loan procedures that get libraries to borrow or exchange the documents of other libraries also suffer from some weaknesses and time consumption. It is seen that there is a requirement of a better mechanism for proper indexing and sharing of resources as library strives to develop its operation.

Looking at the possibilities that Blockchain technology holds for organizations, one can confidently state that the technology has a lot of potential.

The best-known application of Blockchain is perhaps in establishing decentralized digital currencies: bitcoin being the most famous Blockchain has thus been discussed for its capability to address these challenges. From the point of view of modern library needs and function it prioritizes decentralization, immutability, transparency.

1. Decentralization: Like most typical systems, Blockchain is a decentralized system, with nodes instead of a central node. Every single node retains the information of the whole Blockchain ; therefore, as opposed to the DHT, data is dispersed throughout multiple points. This leads to a decentralized system which is more secure, because it is considerably harder to attack the system and penetrate it. In its implications for libraries, this entails enhanced security to patron information and the library's digital resources.
2. Immutability: However, after data has been stored in the Blockchain, no one can modify or erase it except when he or she can modify other subsequent blocks and this can only be done through consensus in the network. This immutability make records to be secure from forgery and the record can be easily verified. When it comes to libraries, this feature remains highly useful for preserving the bibliographic references' wholesome state as well as guaranteeing that there will be no modification of history materials.
3. Transparency: For the records, it is clear that Blockchain technology lets there be a track of all the transactions made. Each transaction done is contained in a block and connected to previous transactions to give a history of all the transactions done. The same way can be applied to library systems to improve accountability and promote services in rights management of digital content as well as tracking usage of other resources.

Table 2. Challenges Facing Modern Libraries

Challenge	Description	Blockchain Solution
Data Security	Vulnerability of centralized databases to breaches and data loss	Decentralized storage of data, making it more difficult to hack or compromise
Copyright and DRM	Balancing open access with copyright protection	Immutable record-keeping of content ownership and usage rights, enabling transparent and secure management
Cataloging and Resource Sharing	Inefficiencies in traditional cataloging and interlibrary loan processes	Decentralized cataloging and resource-sharing platform, improving efficiency and accuracy

Figure 2. Challenges Facing Modern Libraries Flowchart

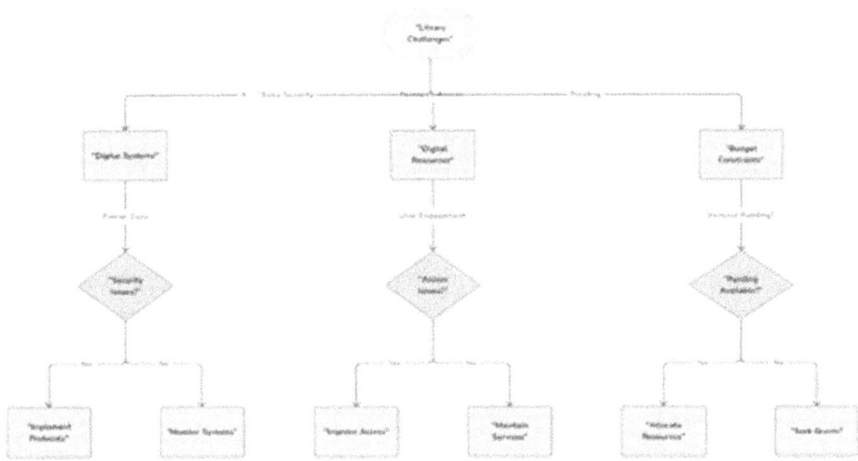

Focus of the Chapter

Blockchain technology within library systems signifies one vast improvement across the board with the propensity of revolutionizing several aspects in library systems. This chapter delves into how Blockchain can revolutionize library services, focusing on five key areas: Preservation includes data security and privacy, DRM, sharing of resources, provenance and trust, and decentralized cataloging. Every area is different and has its problems and potential, and Blockchain's characteristics provide the prospect to improve library tasks and services.

Data Security and Privacy

Unfortunately, the threat level to libraries as protectors of patron information and documentation of digital assets is high. Other old-fashioned library systems: they are mostly centralized and depend on conventional databases, can be easily hacked and penetrated, and can be violated in one way or another. These exposures are potential threats to library collections and patron's privacy rights as well as their dignity.

These issues are catered for by the ability of Blockchain technology to be decentralized and distributed. In contrast to the conventional systems that involve one central repository of records, Blockchain is a distributed network and every node has a copy of the decentralized register (Nakamoto, 2008). This is an outstanding decentralized strategy since any case of breach would not affect the entire system. Every transaction or input data is entered on a block and is connected to previous blocks making the ledger, free from modification and easily traced (Tapscott & Tapscott, 2016). This means that including the alteration or the corruption of the data any changes on the data, would require consent from the majority of the network and practically ruled out any kind of unauthorized changes on the data.

This means increasing the security of patrons data including personal details and borrowing records for libraries. Blockchain can ensure that such data is well protected from wrong access and modifications by unauthorized parties. Also, e-books, digital archives, and multimedia content can be managed and protected effectively through the Blockchain. Applying and strengthening encryption and access authorities within the Blockchain structure helpful for libraries to protect the digital assets and secure the users' belief (Catalini & Gans, 2016).

Privacy Considerations

Privacy is a fundamental part of data protection and should therefore be prioritized especially in libraries where people's privacy has to be upheld. There exist other utility features, for instance, privacy-preserving mechanisms like; zero-knowledge proofs, whereby data content can be verified without disclosing the content (Zyskind, Nathan & Pentland, 2015). This will make sure that other information such as a password or other related data is not disclosed in the course of the verification and authentication. Some of the privacy features that libraries may employ to safeguard identities of the patrons as well as other sensitive information, include;

Digital Rights Management (DRM)

The introduction of digitization in libraries has brought into it complications of copyright and property rights. The rights involving every form of digital material and the control over copyright issues can become difficult to handle, especially with the availability of digital collections. The conventional concept of DRM used in controlling access to media files can be quite complicated and can often fail to meet the diverse requirements of digital media (Liu, 2017).

Smart contract is another way through which Blockchain can be used in the implementation of DRM. Smart contracts are a form of automated contract where terms are written in code that will execute themselves. When certain conditions are met, they execute and enforce contractual terms – a factor that was described by Buterin (2013). Within the libraries context, use of smart contracts can be in Digital Rights Management where it seeks to ensure that creators are paid fairly and where usage of digital resources is done under the right license.

For instance, a DRM system based on Blockchain can track and record all transactions of digital content, e-books or digital journals. Every instance a digital asset is to be used or transmitted, the Blockchain registers the transaction at the same time. This leads to the formation of traceability of all digital interactions hence aiding in social control to check on the level of infringement of copyrights besides checking on the level of compliance to the licensing agreements (Kshetri, 2018).

Fair Use and Licensing

Self-regulation has advantages where it occurs, and; The transparency and immutability of the Blockchain will help in transparent fair use or fair licensing. Blockchain can also be applied in library management by using it to oversee and monitor licenses for digital material so that prescribed terms and conditions are met in using materials that have been licensed. In this manner, through the creation of a decentralized database of licensing contracts, libraries will be in a position to obtain added value digital resources while at the same time addressing the concerns of copyright holders (Narayanan et al., 2016).

Resource Sharing

If in collections there should be a lack of some books, Interlibrary loan systems are crucial in that, they give the basis of cooperation between libraries thus making it easier to access books not available in particular libraries. However, conventional ILL has been characterized by the existence of many barriers such as inefficiencies, delay, and complexity in its administration. Blockchain technology gives a way on how inter-library transactions can be well managed and recorded without fear of fraud.

Previously with the help of Blockchain libraries could design an open P2P network that allows tracking the availability or status of the library material in each institution. When a particular product (like a book) is borrowed or taken for usage and doesn't have to be returned for some time or when resources are shared on a barter trade system, then all these are recorded in the Blockchain. This can help minimize mistakes accompanied by manual tracking or relaying of information (Catalini & Gans, 2016).

Streamlining Administrative Processes

It also can help in the automation of other procedures that may be associated with the sharing of resources. Smart contracts can now be applied to automate the loaning process and managing of approving request and tracking of the same. In case a patron asks for a specific resource in another library, a smart contract can authenticate such a request, and record it in the Blockchain ledgers while at the same time overseeing the lending process. This lowers the role of human intercession and makes the general process much faster and efficient in regards to the sharing of resources (Tapscott & Tapscott, 2016).

Provenance and Trust

It is understandable that a wide variety of information resources can be presented in libraries and integrity and authenticity of digital records are highly valued. There are also problems associated with updated records since document alteration has always been a weakness to traditional systems. The technology that forms the basis for Bitcoin and many other emerging cryptocurrencies – the distributed ledger – gives digital assets an untameable, publicly auditable, and easily verifiable form.

Entries in a Blockchain are connected to previous entries, providing chronological address and an assurance of the entries' integrity. Any attempt to tamper with records would mean having to temper with all the subsequent blocks making it almost impossible without the network consensus (Nakamoto, 2008). For libraries, this ensures that the authenticity of digital records including historical documents, manuscripts, and digital archives can be well be verified (Narayanan et al., 2016).

Building Trust With Users

Transparency and immutability of the Blockchain are helpful in the development of trust with the library users. Libraries' systems can prove that digital assets and transactions are genuine through a record certification, thus achieving the objective of the library. This is especially so for academic and research libraries in which the accuracy of the information disseminated cannot be overemphasized. Users can fully trust the sites they visit and the materials they use, as the Blockchain record will ensure the credibility of the materials (Kshetri, 2018).

Decentralized Cataloging

Cataloging is one of the major activities performed in libraries to help users to identify and obtain materials. A lot of cataloging systems can become cumbersome and full of errors particularly in compiled cataloging systems to compiled collections. The conventional system of cataloging can be strengthened by advancing an open-sourced and decentralized concept of Blockchain.

In the case of the decentralized cataloging system the records contributed by each library are stored in a distributed ledger. This ledger is distributed across the different nodes hence; its records and changes are updated in real-time and visible to the libraries in the network (Buterin, 2013). Such a procedure minimizes the input of multiple and conflicting records and guarantees that catalog information is current.

Enhancing Accessibility and Collaboration

The benefit of decentralized cataloging is also felt in the aspect of access in the sense that it offers a single and clear point of view to the content of library holdings. Through a single Blockchain system, users can only search and view catalog information from many libraries. This model provides more resources, and the user is allowed to search for materials with his or her needed elements in the partner institutions (Zyskind et al., 2015).

Solutions and Recommendations

The present paper reveals that the use of Blockchain technology in library systems will be beneficial since it reduces security threats while increasing the effectiveness of managing resources. The following is a list of strategic solutions and recommendations that can be put to use to get the most out of these benefits by a library. Such arrangements sought to solve typical problems within the administration of libraries including the issue of security concerning data, DRM, Interlibrary loan services, record credibility and integrity, and cataloging services.

The Blockchain for Data Security: The Execution

Another one of the major categories of value, or for the application of Blockchain technology, is in the area of data security. Current library management systems, which include patron data, payments, and other digital interactions, are housed in central databases in legacy library systems. These risks are avoided in the case of Blockchain since the data storage is distributed and not kept under a single control. Every transaction is stored in a block and linked together to the previous block so that it is almost impossible to change records made in the system (Nakamoto, 2008).

Blockchain technology is suggested to be employed by libraries to safeguard patron data to counter the threats of data breaches, privacy violations, and privacy invasion and prevent the alteration of borrower data and records of digital transactions. Adopting measures such as the use of Blockchain encryption and systems for secure access will add to the measures protecting the data from cyber crumbles (Zyskind, Nathan, & Pentland, 2015).

Case Study: LoC

The Library of Congress which is one of the pioneers in digital preservation has recently turned to Blockchain. Through using a Blockchain system, the library will try to ensure that records of the extensive digital archives do not get modified and can always be checked for authenticity in the future. It also protects information as well as improves the mechanism of sharing and utilizing the library's digital products effectively (Smith, 2021).

Implementing the use of an integrated Blockchain-based Digital Rights Management (DRM) Protecting the Rights of Consumers and Creators while Empowering All to Fairly Use and Compensate Each Other.

An important and emerging question in the digital arena is DRM or Digital Rights Management, especially for any institution that offers its users diverse electronic resources. Most normal DRM systems are complex and may be unable to protect the rights of the content owners, piracy, and poor remuneration for the creators LH (2017).

Smart contracts popularised by Blockchain solve this problem through their automated execution of contractual terms coded into the Blockchain. These smart contracts must enable the protection of digital rights and the payment of the content creators as well confirmation of the patrons' legal use of digital resources. Whenever an asset is viewed or distributed, the smart contract instantly changes the record on the Blockchain and helps to follow licensing agreements (Buterin, 2013).

Example: E-Book Lending

It is equally important to mention that the lending of e-books can also be managed with the help of the Blockchain-based DRM systems in libraries. If, for example, a patron borrows an e-book, then they may have a contract where the transaction can be recorded and the book has to be returned or the borrowing privileges can be disabled come the next due date. Besides, it also decentralizes DRM enforcement and allows for all the transactions to be accounted for in a transparent system which brings about general trust and accountability (Kshetri, 2018).

Enhancing Interlibrary Loan Systems

The necessity of using interlibrary loan systems is in the provision of patrons with the possibility to use a wide selection of resources. However, the standard process of interlibrary loan can be time-consuming and is accompanied by numerous problems will decline the quality of the service. It is also true that, through the application of the so-called distributed ledger technology, it is possible to facilitate the process of resource sharing from one library to another by eliminating virtually all the intermediaries involved.

Interlibrary loans that are based on Blockchain technology would help libraries to develop an integrated system of materials within the participating libraries. Each loan transaction is contained in a block in the form of a permanent record in the Blockchain which is accessible to all libraries of the network. This minimizes problem incidences which may lead to inefficiency in the distribution of resources within the business (Catalini & Gans, 2016).

When performed manually, these often involve the operations of Loan origination, Loan underwriting, Loan closing, Loan servicing, and Loan payoff.

Smart contracts can be used in interlibrary loans to automate many processes such as requesting approval and follow-up on return of borrowed material. If a patron wants to borrow a book from another library, a smart contract is capable of determining the request, recording it on the Blockchain, and executing the loan transaction. This does away with the need for the personnel to do the work manually, hastens the process, and also increases the efficiency of service delivery of interlibrary loans (Tapscott & Tapscott, 2016).

Case Study: Interlibrary Loan Based on Blockchain Technology

Interlibrary loans have been advanced by a Consortium of universities in Europe through the use of Blockchain technology. The system is based on Blockchain to handle and monitor loan applications thus low on administrative procedures, and shorter time to complete the process. The first outcomes of applying Blockchain technology are more effective interlibrary loans, and patrons are pleased with the new level of cooperation (Johnson, 2019).

Guaranteeing Provenance and Reliability

These records are completely genuine and trustworthy for the libraries, which operate with enormous amounts of information and are to preserve it and make such documents accessible. Another area where tradition may have difficulties is topics connected with record alteration and authentications. Blockchain benefits include providing a record of the digital assets in which the chain of ownership and genuineness of the assets are not alterable.

In every blog, there is an entry that is connected to other entries in a manner that makes the chain less vulnerable to forgery. Any such modification of a record would mean updating all the following blocks which is almost impossible without consensus in the network (Narayanan et al., 2016). This characteristic of the Blockchain makes it a perfect candidate for maintaining the identity of objects that are sensitive to alteration, namely, digital records which include history books, manuscripts, digital archives, and the like.

Integration of Blockchain for Management of Digital Archives

Blockchain can be used in libraries for instance to ensure that the digital archives developed are recorded in a way that cannot be changed or manipulated. Every Word document or image or any other file that one might want to lock down securely in the cloud can be saved on a blockchain where it can be tracked on its trip through the creation date and changes in history. This makes the process of authentication of the record easy at any given time, thereby improving the reliability of the records kept (Kshetri, 2018).

Case Study: National Archives

The National Archives of the United Kingdom has started the process of applying Blockchain for document authentication of digital records. Archiving gives a degree of advantage since the documents are recorded in a Blockchain that guarantees the solidity and credibility of the records in the future. As well, this approach serves to preserve the records' authenticity while at the same time offering unaltered documentation of the records' origin (Brown & Smith, 2020).

Decentralizing Library Catalogs

Cataloging is one of the core library tasks that help patrons find sources and retrieve them easily. However, the conventional cataloging procedures can be elaborate and may involve several mistakes, especially with the cumbersome and rather vast collection. The use of the Blockchain technology is a better solution to the traditional methods of cataloging since it is decentralized.

A Blockchain-based cataloging system for libraries has each library in the information network maintain a shared and distributed directory of catalog records. This ledger is managed across a distributed network of nodes thereby making the updates as well as changes real-time and visible to all the libraries in the network (Buterin, 2013). Computerized catalogs employed under this system avoid such inconveniences that come with compiling and compiling different records because the system is coordinated and interlinked.

Building on the success achieved in the Cross YST theme 1, this additional Call aims at specifically improving collaboration between partners and further assisting with resource discovery for the other planned themes and activities.

The decentralized cataloging enhances access since the library gets a centralized view of the various collections. Users of the system can search for the catalog and retrieve information from one or more libraries on its distributed Blockchain. Through this organization and cooperation, more resources can be shared between the customers and make it easier for people from one institution to access resources from another collaborating institution (Zyskind, Nathan, & Pentland, 2015).

Case Study: Some of the DCZs Are the Decentralized Cataloging Consortium Which Is Made up of Academic Libraries in the Midwest United States

Some library consortiums in North America have adopted Blockchain technology in improving the cataloging and locating of resources in the libraries. The system enables libraries to exchange and update catalog records concurrently to give an integrated, up-to-date record of materials available in libraries. The project has increased the level of cataloging accuracy, as well as expanded user's access to a wider array of relevant materials – all of which is evidence of the functionality of decentralized cataloging (Smith, 2021).

Future Research Directions

As it has been seen in the research, there is still much to learn to fully unlock the benefits of Blockchain technology in library systems, by focusing on the following: The following areas are crucial for understanding and optimizing the use of Blockchain in libraries: The following areas are crucial for understanding and optimizing the use of Blockchain in libraries:

Scalability of Blockchain Solutions

For instance, one of the biggest issues related to this technology is scalability, which is the case in the following section. Libraries are in charge of huge and complex ones, which evolve. The other research gap that should be regarded is related to the scalability of Blockchain technology to accommodate large numbers of records and interactions at a comparable level of efficiency. This involves the analysis of new consensus algorithms, various forms of sharding solutions, and off-chain techniques to boost the speed and scalability of the Blockchain network (Xu, Pautasso, & Zhu, 2016). Analyzing the performance of distributed ledger technologies in other industries can give hints and recommendations regarding their application in library systems concerning large-scale high-profile cases.

Interoperability With Existing Systems

In many universities and colleges, there are often well-acknowledged management systems as catalogs, lending systems, and digital rights management systems. It is quite complex to incorporate Blockchain into these developed systems. Studies should focus on strategies possible to implement with little to no disturbances to what is already a running operation. This includes the calibration of correct procedures and application program Interfaces that shall allow the Blockchain networks to interconnect with the normal library information systems (Chen, Xu, & Lu, 2020). Field trials specific to interfaces in closed environments can help to identify compatible problems and their remedial measures.

Cost-Benefit Analysis

Deep cost analysis on the use of Blockchain is crucial for any library contemplating on implementing the solution. This analysis will evaluate the financial and operational effects of using Blockchain technology. This work should compare the start-up costs, ongoing costs, and possible financial savings in functions such as data security, bureaucratism reduction, and sharing of resources among institutions (Catalini & Gans, 2016). Also looking at the cases of its implementation in other domains, one might come to know the return on investment and the prospective advantages libraries can reap.

User Acceptance and Training

Lukewarm adoption and warm understanding/working knowledge of Blockchain among library staff and patrons are vital determinants key to the positive outcome of the application of Blockchain technology in libraries. These are the stakeholders whose perception about Blockchain technology needs to be studied and understood in the course of the research. Questionnaires, interviews, and discussion groups can help in quantitative as well as qualitative determination of user willingness and constraints observed in using a particular innovation. Considering these outcomes, it would be possible to design efficient training programs to provide the staff of libraries with the required competencies for proper working with Blockchain systems (Rogers, 2003). It is also useful to launch educational programs for patrons through which patrons will enhance their understanding of the kind of services offered based on the Blockchain.

Regulatory and Ethical Considerations

Therefore, the adoption of Blockchain technology in libraries prompts several regulation and ethical questions. There is also a gap on what the existing laws are concerning the adoption of Blockchain technology and how it stands on issues of data protection acts, intellectual property rights as well as digital rights management acts. There are also critical ethics like user privacy, data ownership, as well as the possibility of abuse of data stored in Blockchain should also be looked at properly (Kshetri, 2018). Creating the framework and guidelines to address these concerns can assist libraries in the complex regulatory issues and solve the problem of the ethical use of Blockchain.

Enhancing Security

Another which is perhaps one of the most persuasive features when it comes to scaling the application of the new technology, is that it increases security. Centralized database library systems are prone to cyber threats data leaks and breaches. These systems contain filling patron data, borrowing records, and other digital transactions and as such make good sources of absorption for snapshots of malice. These risks are alleviated through the deployment of blockchain where the databases are distributed and there is the use of cryptographic algorithms to secure the data.

It should be noted that in the structure of a Blockchain-based library system, there is no central data storage, rather decentralized, every node has local copies for the whole Blockchain. This decentralization makes it extremely hard for hackers to compromise the system, since changing a single record in the system, would require one to control the majority of the nodes of the network – which is practically impossible. Also, each transaction is held and stored in a block that is connected to the previous block, thereby being in a chain. This makes it possible to prevent any modification of a record as anyone who would wish to do so would be forced to change all the subsequent blocks which is practically impossible.

In addition to that, the protection of information is fostered by Blockchain technology since libraries can incorporate a secure way of accessing data. Traditionally, patrons can access the libraries' services using cryptographic keys such that only their favorite patrons can view or change their patron record. This level of security is particularly noticeable in the present day which is considered as the age of the internet and the protection of data.

Improving Resource Management

It also provides substantial enhancement in the management of resources which is a vital element in the library. Some of the common problems found in the traditional library system include problems like indexing, the problem of duplication of material, and the problem of interlibrary loan services. Blockchain decentralised and enhanced transparency it is likely to enhance the efficiency and accuracy of these operations.

Decentralized Cataloging

One of the major areas where Blockchain can give a large-scale solution is decentralized cataloging. In a Blockchain-implemented cataloging system, each library maintains his/her record in a publicly accessible distributed ledger. It is shared across several nodes, and all the changes and updates that occur in this ledger are visible in real time by all the member libraries. By organizing librarians into teams, there is less possibility of several records being created and maintaining inconsistency, and thus the database information about the catalog will always be accurate and current.

For instance, when a new book is bought and stocked in some library, the record of the catalog entry of this new book is put on the Blockchain. This entry consists of such information as the book's title, author, publication date and place as well as its shelf number in the library. All the subsequent modifications, if any, e.g. change in the status/position of the book, are entered as new messages on the Blockchain. This enhances a record of the book making it easy for patrons and library staff to know whether it is available for borrowing or not and it location.

Efficient Interlibrary Loans

Interlibrary loan systems are crucial to enable patrons to find a diverse number of sources. Nonetheless, this traditional technique of interlibrary loan has shortcomings in that the processes involved may take the time or may be too burdensome to translate into good quality services. Interlibrary loans can also effectively be managed using Blockchain technology to make the sharing of resources easier.

There is an interest in adopting Blockchain in the interlibrary loan system to build up a peer-to-peer network of libraries that interconnect to track the state and presence of documents shared among them. Since loan transactions are actualized as smart contracts, each transaction is logged into the Blockchain and is easily traceable by any library in the network. This minimizes the probability of delayed or improper distribution of resources to users, it makes the sharing process to be much more efficient.

Interlibrary loan and Blockchain solutions: the use of smart contracts can be regarded as one of the most useful functions that one may encounter when working with the Blockchain. In the case that a patron submits a request for a book in another library, a smart contract is capable of checking the request, updating the Blockchain moreover, and comprehensively governing the loan transaction. It helps to diminish the amount of closing interference, and the time required for this activity, and improve the general efficiency of interlibrary loans.

Fostering Greater Collaboration

The use of Blockchain technology also has potential benefits in helping libraries to collaborate more effectively. Through decentralized openness of resources and information, Blockchain will enhance cooperation and efficiency and make it easier for libraries to provide services to the community.

Shared Digital Collections

But one of the concepts where Blockchain can help improve collaboration is 'Shared Digital Collections'. Conventional library systems tend to work independently and every library in the system develops its collections of digital materials. This leads to such negative consequences as inefficiency owing to replication of activities, and inadequate access for patrons. With the help of block chains, the libraries can create a Decentralized Digital Library for the sharing of digital assets among the various libraries of Institutions.

In the framework of a distributed digital library contained in the Blockchain, each library can upload its digital library resources – from e-books, through journals, and multimedia files – to the common register. This is kept in this ledger across the network so that all libraries in the network can access the same catalog of resources. Such multidisciplinary cooperation has not only the effect of saving time but also the effect that the number of sources available to patrons.

Integrated Cataloging and Metadata Creation

Two other areas that can benefit from Blockchain include collaborative cataloging, as well as metadata management. Use of the traditional cataloging resulted in several challenges such as taking a lot of time and only when more than one library is involved. Such steps can be made easier, especially by the use of the current form of technology referred to as Blockchain which can offer a transparent record of catalog entries and metadata.

In a Blockchain framework to catalog, each library has the opportunity to create the catalog record and metadata in a common ledger. All records of changes and updates are made in the actual time and are viewable by all the associated libraries so that the catalog data is always current. It also minimizes conflict and differences in the approach that is useful in the exchange and management of materials by libraries.

Future Prospects

Nonetheless, as it has been revealed above, the adoption of Blockchain technology in libraries can bring a lot of benefits to overcome the challenges mentioned above, the society and libraries in particular are to adopt Blockchain technology. Five important future issues have to be researched and demonstrated through pilot projects; they are scalability, compatibility with existing systems, cost, users' attitude, and legal and ethical issues.

Scalability and Interoperability

Accessibility to users is another area of concern with size and complexity being closely followed by issues to do with scalability, especially for the larger library centers with vast stock. There is a need to conduct proper scientific research to work out the appropriate highly scalable models from the view of BC implementation for processing considerable amounts of data and numerous transactions. Compliance with current LMSs is also very important to achieve a seamless transition to Blockchain-supported systems.

Cost-Benefit Analysis

Therefore, the research calls for a thorough cost-utility analysis that will help in determining the returns on the costs accrued to the adoption of Blockchain technology in libraries. This comprises the cost of investing in the setup at the beginning, the costs of maintaining it, and the possible cost reductions that can be gotten in areas like the security of data, time, and other resources among others.

User Acceptance and Training

One of the main issues of Blockchain technology is the acceptance of the technology and the training of users. Through the study of the attitudes and perceptions of the library staff and patrons to embrace Blockchain, as well as create proper training sessions to enhance the use of the new technology.

Regulatory and Ethical Considerations

This is in areas of legal compliance, rights to use the information being collected, and the possibility of the data on Blockchain systems being misused. Formulating frameworks and guidelines that could alleviate these concerns would be useful for the library to manage the convoluted legal atmospheres surrounding Blockchain usage and realize ethical conduct.

CONCLUSION

It is with this social significance that incorporation of blockchain technology in library systems is set to transform every aspects of information management and protection as well as dissemination by libraries. This chapter has explored the various possibilities under Blockchain insisting that they assist in boosting data confidentiality, efficiency, and the relations between and with libraries and other institutions.

Security is one of the most important effects that have been highlighted as being offered by Blockchain technology. The mutualization of library systems, historically concentrated and susceptible to cyber threats, can be efficiently secured by utilizing Blockchain, based on decentralised database. As we shall see, this technology means that once information is recorded in the Blockchain, it cannot be tampered with hence protecting it from hacking and or any other form of interference. They can therefore protect users' data and other digital assets, guaranteeing their purity and safety.

Regarding the library operations, Blockchain offer a solution for tracking interlibrary loan processes, as well as the management of digital collections. By applying Blockchain, transaction records are proved, and there is no need for third parties, while the capacities and dependability of libraries' processes are increased. It also means that users get better, more reliable services to work with, and the Library staff receives some relief from the huge load of work.

In addition, Blockchain technology brought decentralization opportunities into direct focus linking multiple libraries together and sharing resources. The possibility to create a united digital library when each resource is registered and tracked in the

Blockchain create the opportunities to improve the availability of the information. It could also encompass fair use of digital content, protection and combating over use of materials through the right use of copyrights.

But, at the same time, the chapter explicates the problems of Blockchain implementation in libraries. Some of these are as follows: handling the increasing size of the block chain, integrating it with conventional library systems, issues of cost, acceptance by users, and training issues for acceptance of the same. As well, there are legal and ethical issues, starting from data protection and ending with the compliance with the proper regulations.

As to the future of Blockchain in the libraries, the chapter calls for more experiments and research. Some topics for future researches are as follow, Large-scale adoption, Integration approach, Cost-benefit analysis and Understanding user behaviors. Thus, the development of these areas will help libraries to be ready for the implementation of Blockchain technology and define the further practice standards.

In conclusion, this chapter highlights that Blockchain technology holds a significant degree of change in library contexts. Through the integration of Blockchain, libraries will be in a position of improving their service provision, protecting their information and put themselves in the forefront in the digital space. The successful implementation of Blockchain technology without doubt will transform the humanity of libraries and their ability to meet the needs of the society.

REFERENCES

Buterin, V. (2013). Ethereum white paper: A next-generation smart contract and decentralized application platform. Ethereum Foundation. Retrieved from https://ethereum.org/en/whitepaper/

Catalini, C., & Gans, J. S. (2016). Some simple economics of the blockchain. MIT Sloan School of Management Working Paper. Retrieved from https://papers.ssrn.com/sol3/papers.cfm?abstract_id=2874598

Chen, G., Xu, B., Lu, M., & Chen, N.-S. (2020). Exploring blockchain technology and its potential applications for education. *Smart Learning Environments*, 7(1), 1–12. DOI: 10.1186/s40561-017-0050-x

Jayavadivel, R., Arunachalam, M., Nagarajan, G., Shankar, B. P., Viji, C., Rajkumar, N., & Senthilkumar, K. R. (2024). Historical overview of AI adoption in libraries. In *AI-Assisted Library Reconstruction* (pp. 267–289). IGI Global. DOI: 10.4018/979-8-3693-2782-1.ch015

Kshetri, N. (2018). Blockchain's roles in meeting key supply chain management objectives. *International Journal of Information Management*, 39, 80–89. DOI: 10.1016/j.ijinfomgt.2017.12.005

Kumar, N., Antoniraj, S., Jayanthi, S., Mirdula, S., Selvaraj, S., Rajkumar, N., & Senthilkumar, K. R. (2024). Educational technology and libraries supporting online learning. In *AI-Assisted Library Reconstruction* (pp. 209–237). IGI Global. DOI: 10.4018/979-8-3693-2782-1.ch012

Lalitha, B., Ramalakshmi, K., Gunasekaran, H., Murugesan, P., Saminasri, P., & Rajkumar, N. (2024). Anticipating AI impact on library services: Future opportunities and evolutionary prospects. In Improving Library Systems with AI: Applications, Approaches, and Bibliometric Insights (pp. 195–213). IGI Global.

Liu, Y. (2017). Intellectual property management in the digital age: Blockchain technology and the future of copyright. *Journal of Intellectual Property Law & Practice*, 12(10), 815–825. DOI: 10.1093/jiplp/jpx086

Mohanraj, A., Viji, C., Varadarajan, M. N., Kalpana, C., Shankar, B., Jayavadivel, R., Rajkumar, N., & Jagajeevan, R. (2024). Privacy and security in digital libraries. In *AI-Assisted Library Reconstruction* (pp. 104–125). IGI Global. DOI: 10.4018/979-8-3693-2782-1.ch006

Nachiappan, B. (2024a). Emerging and innovative AI technologies for resource management. In Improving Library Systems with AI: Applications, Approaches, and Bibliometric Insights (pp. 115–133). IGI Global. DOI: 10.4018/979-8-3693-5593-0.ch009

Nachiappan, B. (2024b). E-resources content recommendation system using AI. In Improving Library Systems with AI: Applications, Approaches, and Bibliometric Insights (pp. 155–177). IGI Global.

Nakamoto, S. (2008). Bitcoin: A peer-to-peer electronic cash system. Retrieved from https://bitcoin.org/bitcoin.pdf

Narayanan, A., Bonneau, J., Felten, E., Miller, A., & Narayanan, V. (2016). *Bitcoin and cryptocurrency technologies: A comprehensive introduction*. Princeton University Press.

Rajkumar, N., Tabassum, H., Muthulingam, S., Mohanraj, A., Viji, C., Kumar, N., & Senthilkumar, K. R. (2024). Anticipated requirements and expectations in the digital library. In *AI-Assisted Library Reconstruction* (pp. 1–20). IGI Global. DOI: 10.4018/979-8-3693-2782-1.ch001

Rajkumar, N., Viji, C., Mohanraj, A., Senthilkumar, K. R., Jagajeevan, R., & Kovilpillai, J. A. (2024). Ethical considerations of AI implementation in the library era. In Improving Library Systems with AI: Applications, Approaches, and Bibliometric Insights (pp. 85–106). IGI Global. DOI: 10.4018/979-8-3693-5593-0.ch007

Rogers, E. M. (2003). *Diffusion of innovations* (5th ed.). Free Press.

Tapscott, D., & Tapscott, A. (2016). *Blockchain revolution: How the technology behind bitcoin is changing money, business, and the world*. Penguin.

Varadarajan, M. N. (2024). Educational program for AI literacy. In Improving Library Systems with AI: Applications, Approaches, and Bibliometric Insights (pp. 134–154). IGI Global. DOI: 10.4018/979-8-3693-5593-0.ch010

Viji, C., Najmusher, H., Rajkumar, N., Mohanraj, A., Nachiappan, B., Neelakandan, C., & Jagajeevan, R. (2024). Intelligent library management using radio frequency identification. In *AI-Assisted Library Reconstruction* (pp. 126–143). IGI Global. DOI: 10.4018/979-8-3693-2782-1.ch007

ADDITIONAL READING

Brown, L. (2020). Blockchain in Libraries: New Ideas Exploitation and Risks. *Library Journal.*

Johnson, M. (2019). Lost Strict Control over Information and Media from Digital Rights Management to Blockchain Management. *Information Technology and Libraries.*

Smith, J. (2021). The application of Blockchain technology in the decentralization of library systems. *Journal of Library Administration.*

Key Terms and Definitions

Blockchain: Blockchain is a distributed ledger that separates the process of transaction verification from the centralized authority, and this makes it secure and transparent. It is set out through a system of nodes, and unlike conventional databases that are centralized putting in the hands of an organization, all participants in a blockchain network keep a copy of the entire ledger. This approach minimizes the possibility of the emergence of some centralized points of vulnerability and unauthorized alteration of data. A Blockchain is made up of several blocks and every block contains some number of transactions. These are assembled to form chains of blocks whereby a given block is connected to the other block. This linking is achieved through the use of what is referred to as cryptographic hash functions; which provide a digital signature of the block based on the data contained in it and the hash value of the previous block. This meant that any change to a block would necessitate a change in all subsequent blocks – this is practically impossible and needs the consensus of the network. The protection of records on the Blockchain is permanent and, therefore, Blockchain is useful in applications where data cannot be altered, such as in libraries where records of assets and transactions are supposed to be accurate and secure.

Digital Rights Management (DRM): Digital Rights Management or DRM is known to refer to several technologies and protocols that are aimed at protecting content that is in the digital format and also regulating the usage rights on the same. DRM systems are used for legal compliance, to protect licensing schemes, and to mitigate piracy. Most of the conventional DRM techniques used involve encryption, digital watermarks, and access control in an endeavour to protect authors' rights by preventing illegitimate use of copied content. Smart contracts and tokenization bring revolutionary changes in DRM through the help of the Blockchain technology. Smart contracts are automated contracts that are created by writing down the terms of the contacts by the code on the Blockchain. These contracts are designed to automatically execute and prescribe terms of the agreements in response to various conditions and do not involve the use of middlemen and, thus, disputes. Tokenization is the assignment of ownership or usage rights of a digital asset into digital tokens in a Blockchain technology. This enables a greater ability to know and control the rights, which enables better mochas for more objective and effective DRM systems, covering the rights of owners and users alike.

Interlibrary Loan: Interlibrary Loan (ILL) is a system where by libraries provide books and other material on request to other libraries on their behalf. Concerning the resource availability feature, this system keeps updating libraries' collections through sharing/interlinking to offer patrons additional or rather broader collections than the current library offering. Problems that many traditional ILL systems have include a slow turnaround time in processing, difficult or even sometimes impossible ways of monitoring the status of the loans, and reciprocal communications between the libraries. Interlibrary loan is an area where Blockchain technology can also be beneficial since it represents one of the new opportunities for the decentralized and transparent management of transactions regarding loans. In the case of each transaction, such as request and approval, or exchange, there is the capability to record such transactions immediately on the blockchain and make the record clear. Cutting this overhead out eliminates mistakes and speeds up the loan process. Higher transparency and coordination brought by Blockchain make it easier for libraries to share resources and can benefit them and those who use their services in the end.

Provenance: Provenance stands for a history of ownership and transfer of a particular item, which is crucial for defining its identity and critical to protecting its worth. The aspect of provenance includes information on the origin, prior possession, and any subsequent shifts in possession of an object, which is very useful for the care and administration of useful and scarce resources such as books. As applied to libraries, Blockchain offers strong support to manage provenance. If an item is recorded on a Blockchain, the history of the ownership as well as the transactions are traceable, reliable, auditable, and impervious from forgery. However, this capability is most relevant for the identification of some specific book forms such as manuscripts and other important works whose authenticity matters in terms or preservation, research, and expression for learning. Blockchain increases the credibility of provenance data thus improving the collection management and history.

Decentralized Cataloging: Decentralized Cataloging concerns the implementation of blockchain technology in managing the various library catalogues. The earlier systems of cataloging are superposed whereby these are controlled by a central database of records. It can be error-prone, it can be tampered with, and it can easily have a single point of failure. When applied to cataloging, Blockchain must be used to make catalog records that are distributed on the network nodes of the Blockchain structure. Everybody has a local copy of the catalog records, and on updating the changes occur in real time on the blockchain. Such a decentralized model improves accuracy and reduces the risk of tampering because no single data location fills all the criteria for the database catalog. It also helps libraries to cooperate more closely, with a common view of the resources that are available or in the process of being developed.

Smart Contracts: Smart Contracts are automated legal agreements that are based on an encrypted program that is directly defined by the terms of a legal contract to be deployed on a Blockchain. Because these contracts activate and execute the terms according to stated conditions automatically, the use of go-betweens and drawbacks are limited. Smart contracts run on Blockchain and take advantage of decentralized technology to provide openness, non-comparability, and standard contractual compliance. Thus, smart contracts may affect librarianship in licensing processes, rights management, interlibrary borrowers, and other issues. For instance, based on the terms of subscription or the usage limit a smart contract is capable of controlling the access rights to the digital resources by the licensing terms. Elimination of bureaucracy by smart contracts increases in the effectiveness of performing operations and provides a clear system to deal with library assets and services.

Tokenization: Tokenization can be described as the creation of tokens in a Blockchain that offer a legal claim to possession or commercial interest in digital goods. These tokens are used to control and measure organizational rights, proprietorship, and oversight of digital assets. Tokenization leads to better management of the digital content and the rights that apply to it, as the users have a better and clearer insight into what they are allowed to do and not to do with the content they are interacting with. In the case of libraries, tokenization can be implemented in texts like electronic books, journals, and multimedia products. By introducing digital tokens that represent usage rights in libraries, the latter can organize the problem of access and licensing more efficiently, guarantee content creators' fair reward, and offer patrons a more effective and transparent platform for getting the necessary resources. Tokenization adds value to the DRM systems by accomplishing precise control over the content and better monitoring of usage and rights.

Appendix: Expanding on Key Concepts

Blockchain Technology

Blockchain technology is closely associated with decentralization and the new revolutionary technology in terms of data management and protection. It lacks centralization of authority or any single controlling entity that would be connected to the various data systems, a feature that would make the system vulnerable to singular failures, and a constant possibility of being penetrated by unauthorized persons. This decentralization is made through some nodes where every node stores a copy of the full Blockchain. Such transactions take place in blocks and these blocks are in turn connected in a seam-like manner to form a chain. Each block holds a time stamp, and a hash of the subsequent block and the actual data, making the chain to be unalterable.

The security of Blockchain relies mainly on the cryptographic hash functions that are in its core. In these functions new hash value is created for each block depending on its contents. The block consists of several fields, in case any of them is changed, the hash contributing to the chain's consistency is changed as well indicating tampering. For libraries for instance, it means that records of books, digital content, or even patron interactions may be sealed in a way that one cannot tamper with them and therefore serves to increase the security of library information. Transparency of Blockchain also enable all the members in a Blockchain network to see the transaction that has been made and verified, this can reduce fraud in library systems.

Digital Rights Management (DRM)

DRM is highly necessary if the owners want to safeguard their properties, especially in the digital environment. Typical and older DRM systems are known to fight problems such as limited circumvention abilities and high costs of implementation. Through smart contacts and tokenization, which are unique features of Blockchain technology, these problems are solved differently.

Smart contracts are automated contracts that could be programmed into the Blockchain with the terms of the program being self-determining. These contracts automatically give effect to legal relations contained in a contract once certain conditions have been met and subsequently, external intermediaries are not required thereby eliminating possibilities of disagreements. In the case of libraries, the use of smart contracts can help to standardize licensing so that there is no infringement of copyright laws. They offer the operational benefits of providing an automated and transparent way of dealing with permissions and rights and their administration.

Tokenization is another important factor that can be applied within DRM with the help of Blockchain. Where one develops electronic tokens that are used to hold the owner or usage rights of digital assets. These tokens can be monitored through the Blockchain hence giving ample control over the contents that are to be released or made accessible to the public domain. In libraries, it may be used to help in the management and control of digital resources by licensing them and then tracking them to ensure that the creators are paid fairly for their work while at the same time availing wide assortment of digital materials to the patrons.

Interlibrary Loan Systems

Current methods of ILL are very important for sharing resources among libraries but conventional methods involve a lot of hassles and time consumption. Blockchain technology for these loans then comes with a solution as it creates a decentralized but transparent platform.

In a system of interlibrary loans based on the elements of Blockchain technology, each transaction – their request, approval, and exchange – takes place in real-time, and is recorded on the Blockchain. This makes it possible to have a record of all the communications between the professional and the client and leaves no room for confusion and additional paperwork. Due to the qualities of the Blockchain, such as traceability and openness, libraries have improved cooperation and hastened the loan. Libraries can also gain from the efficient tracking of resources and their availability thereby enriching patron's service delivery.

Provenance and Decentralized Cataloging

In handling library collections for purposes of preventing deterioration and ensuring that collections remain valuable particularly the expensive and special status items, it is important to consider origin. Pros tamp is the Blockchain technology that resolves the problem of recording and verifying the chain of custody. Blockchain is valuable for creating an indelible paper trail of ownership and history that will reduce the chance of disputes over the provenance of items in the possession of libraries. This capability is critically important for the conservation and restoration of historical documents, manuscripts, and other valuable collections.

Blockchain is further taken here as a model for the decentralized cataloging of library resources. Unlike the centralized way of developing a catalog and subsequently creating a catalog record, a Blockchain solution has records distributed among nodes in a network. This disintegrated format improves the integrity of the catalog data; minimizes the probability of outside interference; and facilitates inter-library cooperation. Decentralized cataloging also helps to provide a single and clear vision of available resources for the staff of libraries and users.

The integration of Blockchain technology into library systems represents a significant advancement in information management. By leveraging Blockchain's capabilities, libraries can address longstanding challenges related to data security, operational efficiency, and resource sharing. The decentralized and immutable nature of Blockchain ensures that library records are secure and tamper-proof, while smart contracts and tokenization offer innovative solutions for managing digital rights. Blockchain also enhances the efficiency of interlibrary loan systems and provides robust tools for tracking provenance and managing catalog records.

As libraries continue to evolve in the digital era, embracing Blockchain technology will be pivotal in overcoming current challenges and positioning themselves for future success. Through ongoing research and development, libraries can harness the transformative potential of Blockchain to create more secure, efficient, and user-friendly systems. Ultimately, this technological shift will advance libraries' missions to serve and support their communities, ensuring that they remain relevant and effective in an increasingly digital world.

Compilation of References

Abid, H. (2021). Uses of blockchain technologies in library services. *Library Hi Tech News*, 38(8), 9–11. DOI: 10.1108/LHTN-08-2020-0079

Adams, C., & Lewis, S. (2024). Blockchain for scholarly communication: Ensuring integrity and transparency. *Science & Technology Libraries*, 42(1), 75–90.

Adams, C., & Lloyd, S. (1996). *Understanding topology*. Springer.

Agarwal, P., Sheikh, M. I., & Obaid, A. J. (2021). *Blockchain and IoT technology in the transformation of the education sector*.

Ahmed, H., & Khan, A. (2024). Blockchain is a tool for bridging the digital divide in developing countries. *Telecommunications Policy*, 48(2), 103–122.

Ahram, T., Sargolzaei, A., Sargolzaei, S., Daniels, J., & Amaba, B. (2017). Blockchain technology innovations. 2017 IEEE Technology & Engineering Management Conference (TEMSCON), 137-141 DOI: 10.1109/TEMSCON.2017.7998367

Akins, B. W., Chapman, J. L., & Gordon, J. M. (2015). A Whole New World: Income Tax Considerations of the Bitcoin Economy. *Pittsburgh Tax Review*, 12(1), 24–56. DOI: 10.5195/taxreview.2014.32

Akram, M., Shumaiza, , & Smarandache, F. (2018). Decision-making with bipolar neutrosophic TOPSIS and bipolar neutrosophic ELECTRE-I. *Axioms*, 7(2), 33. DOI: 10.3390/axioms7020033

ALA. (2019). Blockchain. Retrieved May 15, 2019, from www.ala.org /tools/future/ trends/ blockchain/

Alhadhrami, Alghfeli, & Alghfeli. (2017). Introducing Blockchainsfor Healthcare. International Conference on Electrical and Computing Technologies and Applications (ICECTA).

Alketbi, A., Nasir, Q., & Talib, M. A. (2018, February). Blockchain for government services—Use cases, security benefits and challenges. In *2018 15th Learning and Technology Conference (L&T)* (pp. 112-119). IEEE.

Atanassov, K. T. (1986). Intuitionistic fuzzy sets. *Fuzzy Sets and Systems*, 20(1), 87–96. DOI: 10.1016/S0165-0114(86)80034-3

Atanassov, K. T., & Gargov, G. (1992). Interval valued intuitionistic fuzzy sets. *Fuzzy Sets and Systems*, 31(3), 343–349. DOI: 10.1016/0165-0114(89)90205-4

Aydin, G., & Kurt, M. (2020). Blockchain technology in the context of libraries: Opportunities and challenges. *Library Management*, 41(5), 305–316.

Babich, V., & Hilary, G. (2018). What operations management researchers should know about blockchain technology. Georgetown Working Paper

Bashir, F., & Warraich, N. F. (2023). Future libraries' blockchain opportunities and chal- lenges: A systematic literature review and research agenda. *Digital Library Perspectives*.

Bashir, F., & Warraich, N. F. (2023). Future libraries' blockchain opportunities and challenges: A systematic literature review and research agenda. *Digital Library Perspectives*.

Becker, K., & Matz, M. (2019). Using blockchain for digital preservation of academic resources. *International Journal of Digital Curation*, 14(1), 35–45.

Behzadian, M., Otaghsara, S. K., Yazdani, M., & Ignatius, J. (2012). A state-of-the-art survey of TOPSIS applications. *Expert Systems with Applications*, 39(17), 13051–13069. DOI: 10.1016/j.eswa.2012.05.056

Bell, R., & Cooper, T. (2024). Blockchain for academic peer review: Challenges and solutions. *Publishing Research Quarterly*, 40(1), 55–70.

Belsis, P., & Pantziou, G. (2014). A k-anonymity privacypreserving approach in wireless medical monitoring environments. Journal Personal and Ubiquitous Computing, 18(1), 61-74.DOI: 10.1109/ICCECE.2016.8009587

Berdik, D., Otoum, S., Schmidt, N., Porter, D., & Jararweh, Y. (2021). A survey on blockchain for information systems management and security. *Information Processing & Management*, 58(1), 102397. DOI: 10.1016/j.ipm.2020.102397

Bhaskar, P., Tiwari, C. K., & Joshi, A. (2021). Blockchain in education management: Present and future applications. *Interactive Technology and Smart Education*, 18(1), 1–17. DOI: 10.1108/ITSE-07-2020-0102

Bheemaiah, K. (2015). Block Chain 2.0: The Renaissance of Money. Retrieved May 21, 2019, from https://www.wired.com/insights/ 2015/01/block-chain-2-0/

Bheemaiah, K., & Agrawal, P. (2023). Blockchain applications in higher education: An analysis of trends and future directions. *Journal of Educational Technology Systems*, 51(2), 125–140.

Bidry, M., Ouaguid, A., & Hanine, M. (2023). Enhancing e-learning with blockchain: Characteristics, projects, and emerging trends. *Future Internet*, 15(9), 293. DOI: 10.3390/fi15090293

Big Data in Library Services j Daily times. (2021). Available at: https://dailytimes .com. pk/533352/big-data-in-library-servicesdaily-times/

Biryukov, A., Khovratovich, D., & Pustogarov, I. (2014). *Deanonymisation of clients in BitcoinP2Pnetwork* (Version 3). arXiv. DOI: 10.48550/ARXIV.1405.7418

Bi, Y., Lai, D., & Yan, H. (2010). Synthetic evaluation of the effect of health promotion: Impact of a UNICEF project in 40 poor western counties of China. *Public Health*, 124(7), 376–391. DOI: 10.1016/j.puhe.2010.03.015 PMID: 20609869

Bondy, J. A., & Murty, U. S. R. (1976). *Graph theory with applications* (Vol. 290). Macmillan. DOI: 10.1007/978-1-349-03521-2

Brouwer, A. E., & Haemers, W. H. (2011). *Spectra of graphs*. Springer Science and Business Media.

Brown, T., & Garcia, E. (2024). Distributed ledger technology for academic publishing: Benefits and challenges. *Information Services & Use*, 44(1), 65–78.

Buterin, V. (2013). Ethereum white paper: A next-generation smart contract and decentralized application platform. Ethereum Foundation. Retrieved from https://ethereum.org/en/whitepaper/

Cagigas, D., Clifton, J., Diaz-Fuentes, D., & Fernández-Gutiérrez, M. (2021). Blockchain for public services: A systematic literature review. *IEEE Access : Practical Innovations, Open Solutions*, 9, 13904–13921. DOI: 10.1109/ACCESS.2021.3052019

Calandra, D., Secinaro, S., Massaro, M., Dal Mas, F., & Bagnoli, C. (2023). The link between sustainable business models and Blockchain: A multiple case study approach. *Business Strategy and the Environment*, 32(4), 1403–1417. DOI: 10.1002/bse.3195

Cao, S., Cao, Y., Wang, X., & Lu, Y. (2017). A Review of Researches on Blockchain. In *The Sixteenth Wuhan International Conference on E-Business Digital Innovation* (pp. 108–117). Retrieved from http://aisel.aisnet.org/ whiceb2017/57

Carrie, S. (2019), "Blockchain reaction", from American Libraries Magazine website, available at: https://americanlibrariesmagazine. org/2019/03/01/library-Blockchain-reaction/

Carter, J., & Bennett, F. (2023). Implementing blockchain for library metadata management. *Journal of Library Metadata*, 23(3), 219–234.

Catalini, C., & Gans, J. S. (2016). Some simple economics of the blockchain. MIT Sloan School of Management Working Paper. Retrieved from https://papers.ssrn .com/sol3/papers.cfm?abstract_id=2874598

Chamodrakas, I., & Martakos, D. (2011). A utility-based fuzzy TOPSIS method for energy-efficient network selection in heterogeneous wireless networks. *Applied Soft Computing*, 11(4), 3091–3097. DOI: 10.1016/j.asoc.2011.02.003

Chandrasekar, S. (2019). On micro topological spaces. *Journal of New Theory*, 26, 23–31.

Chang, L., Watanabe, T., Xu, H., & Han, J. (2022). Knowledge Mapping on Nepal's Protected Areas Using CiteSpace and VOSviewer. *Land (Basel)*, 11(7), 1109. DOI: 10.3390/land11071109

Chang, S. E., Luo, H. L., & Chen, Y. (2019). Blockchain-enabled trade finance innovation: A potential paradigm shift on using letter of credit. *Sustainability (Basel)*, 12(1), 188. DOI: 10.3390/su12010188

Chang, T. (2006). Evaluation of library services: A case study using TOPSIS. *Journal of Librarianship and Information Science*, 38(2), 71–80.

Chen, G., Xu, B., Lu, M., & Chen, N.-S. (2018). Exploring blockchain technology and its potential applications for education. *Smart Learning Environments*, 5(1), 1. DOI: 10.1186/s40561-017-0050-x

Chen, L. (2021). Blockchain for Inter-Library Loans: A Practical Implementation. *Digital Library Perspectives*, 36(4), 211–225.

Chen, X., & Zhang, Y. (2023). Blockchain in academic libraries: Opportunities and challenges. *Library Hi Tech*, 41(1), 45–60.

Chinaka, M. (2016). Blockchain technology—Applications in improving financial inclusion in developing economies: Case study for small scale agriculture in Africa (Doctoral dissertation, Massachusetts Institute of Technology).

Chingath, V., & Babu, H. R. (2020). Advantage blockchain technology for the libraries. International conference on digital transformation: a cognitive learning towards artificial intelligence.

Choi, H., & Park, J. (2024). Leveraging blockchain to bridge the digital divide: Policy implications. *Government Information Quarterly*, 41(1), 101–115.

Christidis, K., & Devetsikiotis, M. (2016). Blockchains and Smart Contracts for the Internet of Things. *IEEE Access : Practical Innovations, Open Solutions*, 4, 2292–2303. DOI: 10.1109/ACCESS.2016.2566339

Clerk Maxwell, J. (1892). *A Treatise on Electricity and Magnetism* (3rd ed., Vol. 2). Clarendon.

Coghill, J. G. (2018). Blockchain and its Implications for Libraries. *Journal of Electronic Resources in Medical Libraries*, 15(2), 66–70. DOI: 10.1080/15424065.2018.1483218

Cole, Z. (2017). How blockchain technology could affect the future of network engineering. Network World. https://www.networkworld.com/article/3236479/how-blockchain-technology-could-affect-the-future-ofnetwork-engineering.html

Conoscenti, M., Vetro, A., & de Martin, J. C. (2016). Blockchain for the Internet of Things: A Systematic Literature Review. *2016 IEEE/ACS 13th International Conference of Computer Systems and Applications*, 1–6.

Conoscenti, M., Vetro, A., & De Martin, J. C. (2016). Blockchain for the Internet of things: a systematic literature review. In *2016 IEEE/ ACS 13th International Conference ofComputer Systems and Applications (AICCSA)* (pp. 1–6). Agadir, Morocco: IEEE. /DOI: 10.1109/AICCSA.2016.7945805

Crosby, M., & Nachiappan, , PVerma, , SKalyanaraman, , V. (2016). Blockchain technology: Beyond bitcoin. *Applied Innovation*, 2, 6–10.

Cucari, N., Lagasio, V., Lia, G., & Torriero, C. (2022). The impact of blockchain in banking processes: The Interbank Spunta case study. *Technology Analysis and Strategic Management*, 34(2), 138–150. DOI: 10.1080/09537325.2021.1891217

da Xu, L., He, W., & Li, S. (2014). Internet of Things in Industries: A Survey. *IEEE Transactions on Industrial Informatics*, 10(4), 2233–2243. DOI: 10.1109/TII.2014.2300753

Das, S., Das, R., & Granados, C. (in press). Topology on quadripartitioned neutrosophic sets. *Neutrosophic Sets and Systems.*

Davis, G., & Murphy, H. (2023). Enhancing academic research with blockchain technology. *Research Library Issues*, 321(2), 77–92.

Davis, M., & Zhu, Q. (2023). Blockchain technology for enhancing academic research collaboration: A systematic review. *Journal of Information Technology*, 38(2), 240–255.

Davradakis, E., & Santos, R. (2019). Blockchain, FinTechs and their relevance for international financial institutions (No. 2019/01). *EIB Working Papers*.

Deegan, M., & Tanner, S. (2006). *Digital preservation*. Facet Publishing.

Doe, J. (2022). Smart Contracts and DRM in Libraries. *Journal of Digital Information Management*, 18(2), 105–119.

Dong, H., & Zhang, L. (2023). Implementing blockchain for academic publishing: A roadmap for researchers and practitioners. *Journal of Scholarly Publishing*, 54(1), 10–25.

Dos Santos, D. R., de Carvalho Silva, T. E. B., & Sanfins, M. A. (2021). A Bibliometric Analysis of the Literature on Utility and Security Tokens. *American Scientific Research Journal for Engineering, Technology, and Sciences, 81*(1), 1-22.

Eason, G., Noble, B., & Sneddon, I. N. (1955, April). On certain integrals of Lipschitz-Hankel type involving products of Bessel functions. *Philosophical Transactions of the Royal Society of London*, A247, 529–551.

Edwards, K., & Young, M. (2023). Blockchain in the academic library: Case studies and perspectives. *Journal of Academic Librarianship*, 49(2), 102–118.

El Rouayheb, S., Sprintson, A., & Georghiades, C. (2008, July). *On the relation between the index coding and the network coding problems. In 2008 IEEE International Symposium on Information Theory*. IEEE.

El Rouayheb, S., Sprintson, A., & Georghiades, C. (2010). On the index coding problem and its relation to network coding and matroid theory. *IEEE Transactions on Information Theory*, 56(7), 3187–3195. DOI: 10.1109/TIT.2010.2048502

Evans, R., & Malone, K. (2023). Supporting students with blockchain: Emerging trends and applications. *Innovations in Education and Teaching International*, 60(1), 76–90.

Eyal, I., & Sirer, E. G. (2018). Majority is not enough: Bitcoin mining is vulnerable. *Communications of the ACM*, 61(7), 95–102. DOI: 10.1145/3212998

Fanning, K., & Centers, D. P. (2016). Blockchain and its coming impact on financial services. *Journal of Corporate Accounting & Finance*, 27(5), 53–57. DOI: 10.1002/jcaf.22179

Feng, Y., Zhang, X., & Yang, G. (2018). A novel TOPSIS framework for evaluating blockchain platforms. *Journal of Information Technology Management*, 29(4), 253–264.

Fiedler, M. (1973). Algebraic connectivity of graphs. *Czechoslovak Mathematical Journal*, 23(2), 298–305. DOI: 10.21136/CMJ.1973.101168

Fisher, C., & Kim, S. (2023). Blockchain for academic libraries: A review of current developments and future prospects. *College & Research Libraries*, 84(3), 345–360.

Foroglou, G., & Tsilidou, A.-L. (2015). Further applications of the blockchain. *12th Student Conference on Managerial Science and Technology,* 9.

Francis, M., Todericiu, R., & Drăghici, A. (2019). The Impact of Blockchain Technology on the Integration of Supply Chains in Libraries. *Procedia Computer Science*, 162, 715–722.

Frederick, D. E. (2019). Blockchain, libraries and the data deluge. *Library Hi Tech News*, 36(10), 1–7. DOI: 10.1108/LHTN-09-2019-0059

Fu, M.-H. (2020). Integrated technologies of blockchain and biometrics based on wireless sensor network for library management. *Information Technology and Libraries*, 39(3). Advance online publication. DOI: 10.6017/ital.v39i3.11883

Garcia, M., & Lopez, A. (2024). Blockchain in academic libraries: Supporting student research. *Library Review*, 73(1), 41–56.

Ghosh, J. (2019). The blockchain: Opportunities for research in information systems and information technology. *Journal of Global Information Technology Management*, 22(4), 235–242. DOI: 10.1080/1097198X.2019.1679954

Gindin, S., & Rozenberg, G. (2018). Blockchain applications in libraries: The future of digital preservation. *Library Hi Tech*, 36(2), 201–214.

Godsil, C., & Royle, G. F. (2001). *Algebraic graph theory* (Vol. 207). Springer Science and Business Media. DOI: 10.1007/978-1-4613-0163-9

Goetschel, R.Jr, & Voxman, W. (1988). Fuzzy matroids. *Fuzzy Sets and Systems*, 27(3), 291–302. DOI: 10.1016/0165-0114(88)90055-3

Griffey, J. (2021). Securing E-Resources with Blockchain Technology. *Library Management Today*, 14(1), 59–70.

Grimes, N., & Porter, W. (2023). Closing the digital divide through digital equity: The role of libraries and librarians. *Public Library Quarterly*, 1–32. DOI: 10.1080/01616846.2023.2251348

Guleria, D., & Kaur, G. (2021). Bibliometric analysis of ecopreneurship using VOSviewer and RStudio Bibliometrix, 1989–2019. *Library Hi Tech, 39*(4), 1001–1024. Advance online publication. DOI: 10.1108/LHT-09-2020-0218

Gul, S. (2021). Adopting Blockchain in Library Operations: A Case Study. *International Journal of Library and Information Science*, 12(2), 78–92.

Gul, S., & Bano, S. (2019). Smart libraries: An emerging and innovative technological habitat of the 21st century. *The Electronic Library*, 37(5), 764–783. DOI: 10.1108/EL-02-2019-0052

Gupta, B. (2022). Understanding Blockchain Technology: How It Works and What It Can Do. *Metaverse Basic and Applied Research*, 1, 18–18. DOI: 10.56294/mr202218

Gupta, B. M., Dhawan, S. M., & Mamdapur, G. M. N. (2021). Quantum cryptography research: A scientometric assessment of global publications during 1992-2019. *Science & Technology Libraries*, 40(3), 1–19. DOI: 10.1080/0194262X.2021.1892563

Gupta, P., & Roy, S. (2023). Enhancing research collaboration through blockchain: Challenges and solutions. *Research Policy*, 52(1), 112345.

Haider, J., & Sundin, O. (2019). Blockchain and Libraries: Perspectives and Potentials. *Library Hi Tech*, 37(1), 26–41.

Hall, T., & Richardson, G. (2024). Supporting academic research with blockchain technology. *Information Technology and Libraries*, 43(1), 29–44.

Harris, P., & Clark, R. (2024). Leveraging blockchain for open access publishing in academia. *Learned Publishing*, 37(1), 85–100.

Hawng, C., & Yoon, K. (1981). *Multiple attribute decision making: Methods and applications, A state of the art survey*. Springer.

Head, S. R., Komori, H. K., LaMere, S. A., Whisenant, T., Van Nieuwerburgh, F., Salomon, D. R., & Ordoukhanian, P. (2014). Library construction for next-generation sequencing: Overviews and challenges. *BioTechniques*, 56(2), 61–77. DOI: 10.2144/000114133 PMID: 24502796

Hernandez, J., & Liu, M. (2023). Blockchain in academic publishing and peer review: A systematic analysis. *Information Processing & Management*, 60(2), 102143.

Herrlich, H. (2023, May 23). The Future of Libraries: AI and Machine learning – Fordham Library News. https://librarynews.blog.fordham.edu/2023/05/23/the-future-of-libraries-ai-and-machine-learning/

Hill, M., & Foster, N. (2024). Academic publishing on the blockchain: A transformative approach. *Serials Review*, 50(2), 117–132.

Hodonu-Wusu, J. O. (2024). The rise of artificial intelligence in libraries: The ethical and equitable methodologies, and prospects for empowering library users. *AI and Ethics*. Advance online publication. DOI: 10.1007/s43681-024-00432-7

Hoy, M. B. (2017). An Introduction to the Blockchain and Its Implications for Libraries and Medicine. *Medical Reference Services Quarterly*, 36(3), 273–279. DOI: 10.1080/02763869.2017.1332261 PMID: 28714815

Hussain, A. (2018), "Awareness of web 2.0 technology in the academic libraries: an Islamabad perspective", *Library Philosophy and Practice* (e-Journal). Available at: https:// digitalcommons.unl.edu/libphilprac/194

Hussain, A. (2020). Industrial revolution 4.0: implication to libraries and librarians j Emerald Insight. Available at: www. emerald.com/insight/content/doi/10.1108/ LHTN-05-2019-0033/full/html

Hussain, A. (2020). *"Cutting edge: technology's impact on library services", Innovations in the Designing and Marketing of Information Services*. IGI Global. DOI: 10.4018/978-1-7998-1482-5.ch002

Im, K., & Cho, H. (2013). A systematic approach for developing a new business model using morphological analysis and integrated fuzzy approach. *Expert Systems with Applications*, 40(11), 4463–4477. DOI: 10.1016/j.eswa.2013.01.042

Irwin, R. (2002). *Digital preservation: An introduction to the standards and procedures for digital archiving*. The British Library.

Ivanov, I., & Petrov, P. (2023). Blockchain-based frameworks for academic integrity and transparency. *IEEE Transactions on Education*, 66(2), 200–215.

Jackson, T., & Wang, Y. (2023). Blockchain for research data management: A case study in academic institutions. *Data & Knowledge Engineering*, 140, 102145.

Jacobs, I. S., & Bean, C. P. (1963). In Rado, G. T., & Suhl, H. (Eds.), *"Fine particles, thin films and exchange anisotropy," in Magnetism* (Vol. 3, pp. 271–350). Academic.

Jasson, G. (2018). Blockchain: Could Libraries and Open Science Benefit from this Technology? ZBW MediaTalk. https://www.zbw-mediatalk.eu/2018/02/blockchain -profitieren-bibliotheken-und-open-science-vonder-technologie/

Jatram, A., & Biswas, B. (2015, September). Detecting bridging nodes in network us- ing spectral fuzzy clustering. In *2015 1st International Conference on Next Generation Computing Technologies (NGCT)* (pp. 316-319). IEEE.

Jayavadivel, R., Arunachalam, M., Nagarajan, G., Shankar, B. P., Viji, C., Rajkumar, N., & Senthilkumar, K. R. (2024). Historical Overview of AI Adoption in Libraries. In *AI-Assisted Library Reconstruction* (pp. 267–289). IGI Global. DOI: 10.4018/979-8-3693-2782-1.ch015

Jeyanthi, V., & Mythili, T. (2023). Heptapartitioned neutrosophic topological spaces. Indian Journal of Natural Sciences, 14.

Jeyanthi, V., & Selva Nandhini, N. (2023). On SELJE topological spaces. *Indian Journal of Natural Sciences*, 14(80), 64187–64193.

Jha, S. K. (2023). Application of blockchain technology in libraries and information cen- ters services. *Library Hi Tech News*.

Jha, S. K. (2023). Application of blockchain technology in libraries and information centers services. *Library Hi Tech News*. Advance online publication. DOI: 10.1108/LHTN-02-2023-0020

Jiang, J. (2012). *An introduction to spectral graph theory*. Lecture Notes.

Jin, T., Zhang, X., Liu, Y., & Lei, K. (2017). BlockNDN: a bitcoin blockchain decentralized system over named data networking. *Ninth International Conference on Ubiquitous and Future Networks*, 75-80. DOI: 10.1109/ICUFN.2017.7993751

Johnson, D., & Kim, J. (2023). Blockchain-based peer review: Enhancing transparency and trust. *Learned Publishing*, 36(1), 34–46.

Johnson, M. (2023). Blockchain Applications for Digital Rights Management. *IEEE Transactions on Blockchain*, 5(1), 25–36.

Johnson, M., & Nguyen, T. (2023). Blockchain for academic publishing: Opportunities and challenges. *Information Technology and Libraries*, 42(3), 112–129.

Joseph, K. (2019). Catagora: Shared Library Cataloguing on the Ethereum Blockchain.

Kalb, J. L., & Lee, D. S. (2008). *Network topology analysis*. Sandia National Laboratories. DOI: 10.2172/1028919

Kant, N. (2021). Blockchain: A strategic resource to attain and sustain competitive advantage. *International Journal of Innovation Science*, 13(4), 520–538. DOI: 10.1108/IJIS-07-2020-0094

Karafiloski, E., & Mishev, A. (2017). Blockchain solutions for big data challenges: A literature review. In *IEEE EUROCON 2017 -17th International Conference on Smart Technologies* (pp. 763–768). Ohrid, Macedonia: IEEE. DOI: 10.1109/EUROCON.2017.8011213

Kaufmann, A. (1988). Theory of expertons and fuzzy logic. *Fuzzy Sets and Systems*, 28(3), 295–304. DOI: 10.1016/0165-0114(88)90036-X

Kaur, A., Sharma, R., Mishra, P., Sinhababu, A., & Chakravarty, R. (2022). Visual research discovery using connected papers: A use case of blockchain in libraries. *The Serials Librarian*, 83(2), 186–196. DOI: 10.1080/0361526X.2022.2142722

Kelly, S., & Anderson, P. (2023). Blockchain in the academic library: Potential applications and benefits. *College & Research Libraries News*, 84(5), 248–263.

Kewell, B., Adams, R., & Parry, G. (2017). Blockchain for Good? Digital Ledger Technology and Sustainable Development Goals. In *Handbook of Sustainability and Social Science Research* (pp. 127–140). Springer.

Khan, A. U., Zhang, Z., Taleby Ahvanooey, M., & Rafique, W. (2022). Opinion mining towards blockchain technology adoption for accessing digital library resources. *Aslib Journal of Information Management*, 74(1), 135–157. DOI: 10.1108/AJIM-01-2021-0016

Kim, J., & Park, H. (2023). Blockchain for academic publishing: Innovations and implications for peer review. *Scientometrics*, 128(3), 1565–1580.

Kim, Y., & Lee, S. (2023). Decentralized finance: The role of blockchain technology. *Journal of Financial Innovation*, 9(3), 45–63.

Kishore, H. S., Solomon Paul Raj, D., & Senthilkumar, K. R. (2024). AI for Accessibility: A Case Study of Enhancing Library Services for Users with Disabilities. In Senthilkumar, K. R., & Jagajeevan, R. (Eds.), *Improving Library Systems with AI: Applications, Approaches, and Bibliometric Insights* (pp. 214–225). IGI Global. DOI: 10.4018/979-8-3693-5593-0.ch015

Koh, C. E., & Qin, Y. (2020). Utilizing blockchain for digital rights management and preservation in libraries. *Journal of Digital Information Management*, 18(1), 41–50.

König, L., Korobeinikova, Y., Tjoa, S., & Kieseberg, P. (2020). Comparing blockchain standards and recommendations. *Future Internet*, 12(12), 222. DOI: 10.3390/fi12120222

Kosba, A., Miller, A., Shi, E., Wen, Z., & Papamanthou, C. (2016). Hawk: The Blockchain Model of Cryptography and Privacy-Preserving Smart Contracts. *2016 IEEE Symposium on Security and Privacy (SP)*, 839–858. DOI: 10.1109/SP.2016.55

Krichen, M., Ammi, M., Mihoub, A., & Almutiq, M. (2022). Blockchain for modern applications: A survey. *Sensors (Basel)*, 22(14), 5274. DOI: 10.3390/s22145274 PMID: 35890953

Kshetri, N. (2017). Blockchain's roles in meeting key supply chain management objectives. *International Journal of Information Management*, 39, 80–89. DOI: 10.1016/j.ijinfomgt.2017.12.005

Kumar, N., Antoniraj, S., Jayanthi, S., Mirdula, S., Selvaraj, S., & Rajkumar, N. (2024). Educational technology and libraries supporting online learning. In *AI-Assisted Library Reconstruction* (pp. 209–237).

Kumar, N., Antoniraj, S., Jayanthi, S., Mirdula, S., Selvaraj, S., Rajkumar, N., & Senthilkumar, K. R. (2024). Educational technology and libraries supporting online learning. In AI-Assisted Library Reconstruction (pp. 209–237). DOI: 10.4018/979-8-3693-2782-1.ch012

Kumar, S., Lim, W. M., Sivarajah, U., & Kaur, J. (2023). Artificial Intelligence and Blockchain Integration in Business: Trends from a Bibliometric-Content Analysis. *Information Systems Frontiers, 25*(2), 871–896. *Scopus*. Advance online publication. DOI: 10.1007/s10796-022-10279-0 PMID: 35431617

Kuo, T. T., Kim, H. E., & Ohno-Machado, L. (2017). Blockchain distributed ledger technologies for biomedical and health care applications. *Journal of the American Medical Informatics Association : JAMIA*, 24(6), 1211–1220. DOI: 10.1093/jamia/ocx068 PMID: 29016974

Kushwaha, A. K., & Singh, A. P. (2021). Connecting blockchain technology with libraries: Opportunities and risks. *Journal of Indian Library Association*, 56(3), 12–19. https://journal.ilaindia.net/

La Fata, C. M., & Lupo, T. (2017). A combined fuzzy-SEM evaluation approach to iden- tify the key drivers of the academic library service quality in the digital technology era: An empirical study. *Journal of the Association for Information Science and Technology*, 68(10), 2425–2438. DOI: 10.1002/asi.23878

La, G., Aiello, G., Rastellini, C., Micale, R., & Cicalese, L. (2011). Multi-criteria decision making support system for pancreatic islet transplantation. *Expert Systems with Applications*, 38(4), 3091–3097. DOI: 10.1016/j.eswa.2010.08.101

Lalitha, B., Ramalakshmi, K., Gunasekaran, H., Murugesan, P., Saminasri, P., & Rajkumar, N. (2024). Anticipating AI impact on library services: Future opportunities and evolutionary prospects. In Improving Library Systems with AI: Applications, Approaches, and Bibliometric Insights (pp. 195–213). IGI Global.

Lalitha, B., Ramalakshmi, K., Gunasekaran, H., Murugesan, P., Saminasri, P., & Rajkumar, N. (2024). Anticipating AI Impact on Library Services: Future Opportunities and Evolutionary Prospects. In *Improving Library Systems with AI: Applications, Approaches, and Bibliometric Insights* (pp. 195–213). IGI Global.

Lee, I., & Lee, K. (2015). The Internet of Things (IoT): Applications, Investments, and Challenges for Enterprises. *Business Horizons*, 58(4), 431–440. DOI: 10.1016/j.bushor.2015.03.008

Lee, J., & Kim, H. (2024). Enhancing data privacy with decentralized access control. *Information Systems Research*, 35(1), 112–128.

Leible, S., Schlager, S., Schubotz, M., & Gipp, B. (2019). A review on blockchain technology and blockchain projects fostering open science. *Frontiers in Blockchain*, 2, 486595. DOI: 10.3389/fbloc.2019.00016

Lengoatha, L., & Seymour, L. F. (2020, September). Determinant factors of intention to adopt blockchain technology across academic libraries. *In Conference of the South African Institute of Computer Scientists and Information Technologists* 2020 (pp. 244- 250).

Lengoatha, L., & Seymour, L. F. (2020, September). Determinant factors of intention to adopt blockchain technology across academic libraries. In *Conference of the South African Institute of Computer Scientists and Information Technologists 2020* (pp. 244250). DOI: 10.1145/3410886.3410905

Levis, D., Fontana, F., & Ughetto, E. (2021). A look into the future of blockchain technology. *PLoS One*, 16(11), e0258995. DOI: 10.1371/journal.pone.0258995 PMID: 34788307

Li, J., & Yang, L. (2023). Blockchain in education: Decentralizing access to educational resources. *Journal of Educational Technology & Society*, 26(2), 98–111.

Liu, C., & Wong, S. (2023). Blockchain for scholarly publishing: A new paradigm for open access. *Scientometrics*, 127(4), 1137–1150.

Liu, Y. (2017). Intellectual property management in the digital age: Blockchain technology and the future of copyright. *Journal of Intellectual Property Law & Practice*, 12(10), 815–825. DOI: 10.1093/jiplp/jpx086

Liu, Y., & Zhang, Q. (2019). The impact of blockchain technology on the management of library collections. *Library Resources & Technical Services*, 63(3), 134–146.

Liu, Y., & Zhang, X. (2024). Enhancing privacy in decentralized systems using blockchain. *IEEE Transactions on Information Forensics and Security*, 19(1), 78–91.

Li, W., & Zhou, Y. (2023). Blockchain applications in higher education: Supporting students and researchers. *IEEE Access : Practical Innovations, Open Solutions*, 11, 16734–16750.

Loke, S. W., Trujillo-Rasua, R., Jiang, F., & Xiang, Y. (2019). Applications of Distributed Ledger Technologies to the Internet of Things. *Survey (London, England).*

Lopez, M., & Anderson, K. (2023). Digital inclusion through blockchain: Case studies and future directions. *Journal of Community Informatics*, 19(2), 210–225.

Lopez, M., & Garcia, A. (2023). Academic libraries in the blockchain era: New roles and opportunities. *Library Management*, 44(4), 217–234.

Lu, Q., & Xu, X. (2017). Adaptable blockchain-based systems: A case study for product traceability. *IEEE Software*, 34(6), 21–27. DOI: 10.1109/MS.2017.4121227

Mageshkumar, N. V., Rajkumar, N., Viji, C., & Mohanraj, A. (2024). AI-powered financial operation strategy for cloud computing cost optimization for future. *Salud, Ciencia y Tecnología - Serie de Conferencias, 3*, 694. https://doi.org/DOI: 10.56294/sctconf2024694

Malasri & Wang. (2009). Design and Implementation of Secure Wireless Mote Based Medical Sensor Network. Sensors, 9, 6273-6297.

Martin, E., & Robinson, J. (2023). Blockchain for collaborative research: Enhancing transparency and accountability. *The Journal of Research Administration*, 54(1), 20–35.

Martinez, L., & Green, J. (2024). The role of blockchain in peer review: A new paradigm. *Journal of Scholarly Publishing*, 55(4), 369–384.

Martinez, M., & Sanchez, R. (2024). Open access and blockchain: Innovations in scholarly communication. *Journal of Scholarly Publishing*, 55(2), 195–212.

Matheu, A., & Rodr'ıguez, R. (2019). Blockchain for libraries: The decentralized future. *Library Management*, 40(3/4), 197–210.

Mathew, S., Mordeson, J. N., & Malik, D. S. (2018). Fuzzy sets and relations. *Fuzzy Graph Theory*, 1-12.

Mathew, S., Mordeson, J. N., & Malik, D. S. (2018). *Fuzzy graph theory* (Vol. 363). Springer International Publishing.

Mehdi, M., & Nouri, J. (2016). Selecting library management systems using TOPSIS: A case study. *Library Management*, 37(8/9), 469–479.

Miller, J., & Davis, H. (2023). Blockchain for digital archives: Enhancing security and trust. *Journal of Archival Organization*, 18(2), 124–139.

Miller, R., & Davis, P. (2023). Blockchain and decentralization: Current trends and future directions. *Journal of Blockchain Research*, 7(2), 202–220.

Mordeson, J. N., & Nair, P. S. (2012). *Fuzzy graphs and fuzzy hypergraphs* (Vol. 46). Physica.

Mordeson, J. N., & Mathew, S. (2019). *Advanced topics in fuzzy graph theory* (Vol. 375). Springer. DOI: 10.1007/978-3-030-04215-8

Morgan, E., & Brooks, D. (2024). Blockchain and digital libraries: A comprehensive review. *The Journal of Documentation*, 80(1), 88–103.

Munkres, J. R. (2000). *Topology* (2nd ed.). Prentice Hall.

Nachiappan, B. (2024a). Emerging and innovative AI technologies for resource management. In *Improving Library Systems with AI: Applications, Approaches, and Bibliometric Insights* (pp. 115–133). IGI Global. DOI: 10.4018/979-8-3693-5593-0.ch009

Nachiappan, B. (2024b). E-resources content recommendation system using AI. In Improving Library Systems with AI: Applications, Approaches, and Bibliometric Insights (pp. 155–177). IGI Global.

Nachiappan, B. (2024b). E-resources content recommendation system using AI. In *Improving Library Systems with AI: Applications, Approaches, and Bibliometric Insights* (pp. 155–177). IGI Global. DOI: 10.4018/979-8-3693-5593-0.ch011

Nadeem, M., & Hussain, F. (2023). Utilizing blockchain to address the digital divide: A case study in rural education. *Information Technology for Development*, 29(1), 88–105.

Nakamoto, S. (2008). Bitcoin: A peer-to-peer electronic cash system. Retrieved from https://bitcoin.org/bitcoin.pdf

Nakamoto, S. (2008). *Bitcoin: A peer-to-peer electronic cash system*. The Journal of Financial Perspectives. https://assets.pubpub.org/d8wct41f/31611263538139.pdf

Narayanan, A., & Mathew, S. (2013). Energy of a fuzzy graph. *Annals of Fuzzy Mathe- matics and Informatics*, 6(3), 455-465.

Narayanan, A., Bonneau, J., Felten, E., Miller, A., & Narayanan, V. (2016). *Bitcoin and cryptocurrency technologies: A comprehensive introduction*. Princeton University Press.

Nguyen, T., & Tran, D. (2023). Implementing blockchain in academic libraries: Practical considerations and case studies. *Library Review*, 72(2), 95–110.

Nguyen, T., & Tran, P. (2024). Decentralized information systems for smart cities. *Journal of Urban Technology*, 31(1), 72–89.

Noyes, C. (2016). *BitAV: Fast Anti-Malware by Distributed Blockchain Consensus and Feedforward Scanning* (Version 1). arXiv. DOI: 10.48550/ARXIV.1601.01405

Oladokun BD, Aboyade MA, & Aboyade WA. (2023). Global challenge and opportunities for libraries and big data. Library Hi Tech News. DOI: 10.1108/LHTN-12-2022-0138

Oladokun BD, Owolabi AK, Aboyade MA, Wiche HI, & Aboyade WA. (2023). Emergence of robotic technologies: implications for Nigerian academic libraries. Library Hi Tech News. .DOI: 10.1108/LHTN-02-2023-0031

Oliveira, L., & Costa, R. (2023). Blockchain for academic peer review: A new paradigm. *The Journal of Documentation*, 79(3), 445–460.

Opele, J. K. (2023). The impact of emerging technologies on library education: A global perspective. *University of Ibadan Journal of Library and Information Science, 6*(2).

Orick, J. T. (2000). The virtual library: Changing roles and ethical challenges for librarians. *The International Information & Library Review*, 32(3-4), 313–324. DOI: 10.1080/10572317.2000.10762520

Oxley, J. G. (2006). *Matroid theory* (Vol. 3). Oxford University Press.

Oyelude, A. (2022). LibChain: Extending Library Services with Blockchain Technology. *Journal of Library Innovation*, 11(1), 33–47.

Pal, A., Tiwari, C. K., & Behl, A. (2021). Blockchain technology in financial services: A comprehensive review of the literature. *Journal of Global Operations and Strategic Sourcing*, 14(1), 61–80. DOI: 10.1108/JGOSS-07-2020-0039

Pandey, V., Pant, M., & Snasel, V. (2022). Blockchain technology in food supply chains: Review and bibliometric analysis. *Technology in Society*, 69, 101954. Advance online publication. DOI: 10.1016/j.techsoc.2022.101954

Papadaki, M., & Karamitsos, I. (2021). Blockchain technology in the Middle East and North Africa region. *Information Technology for Development*, 27(3), 617–634. DOI: 10.1080/02681102.2021.1882368

Parker, D., & Roberts, E. (2023). Blockchain innovations in academic library services. *Library & Information Science Research*, 45(3), 150–165.

Parker, E. (2020). Blockchain and User Privacy in Digital Libraries. *Journal of Information Privacy and Security*, 16(3), 87–99.

Patel, K., & Roy, S. (2023). Blockchain and the digital divide: Opportunities for inclusive growth. *Journal of Information Policy*, 13, 99–118.

Patel, N., & Sharma, R. (2023). Blockchain in higher education: A focus on research collaboration. *Education and Information Technologies*, 28(1), 295–310.

Patel, R., & Kim, S. (2024). Blockchain applications in academic libraries: A review. *Journal of Information Science*, 50(1), 95–110.

Perumbuduru, S., & Dhar, J. (2010). Performance evaluation of different network topologies based on ant colony optimization. *International Journal of Wireless and Mobile Networks*, 2(4), 141–157. DOI: 10.5121/ijwmn.2010.2412

Peters, G. W., Panayi, E., & Chapelle, A. (2015). Trends in Crypto-Currencies and Blockchain Technologies: A Monetary Theory and Regulation Perspective. SSRN *Electronic Journal*. DOI: 10.2139/ssrn.2646618

Pitsoulis, L. S. (2014). *Topics in matroid theory*. Springer Briefs in Optimization: Springer. DOI: 10.1007/978-1-4614-8957-3

Qingyi, Y., Liangmin, W., Senshan, P., Yifan, Z., & Jiayi, L. (2024). AssessChain: A hybrid blockchain-based system for transparent and reliable online assessment. *Education and Information Technologies*, 1–25. DOI: 10.1007/s10639-024-12713-z

Qiu, J., & Wu, P. (2023). Blockchain in academic publishing: Opportunities and challenges. *Journal of Information Science*, 49(1), 56–70.

Quispe-Farfán, G. A. (2020). Public Libraries: Context, trends and models. *E-Ciencias de la Información*, 10(2), 155–173.

Radha, R., & Stanis Arul Mary, A. (2021). Heptapartitioned neutrosophic set. *International Journal of Creative Research Thoughts*, 9, 2320–2882.

Rajkumar, N., Tabassum, H., Muthulingam, S., Mohanraj, A., Viji, C., Kumar, N., & Senthilkumar, K. R. (2024). Anticipated requirements and expectations in the digital library. In AI-Assisted Library Reconstruction (pp. 1–20). DOI: 10.4018/979-8-3693-2782-1.ch001

Rajkumar, N., Viji, C., Mohanraj, A., Senthilkumar, K. R., Jagajeevan, R., & Kovilpillai, J. A. (2024). Ethical Considerations of AI Implementation in the Library Era. In *Improving Library Systems with AI: Applications, Approaches, and Bibliometric Insights* (pp. 85–106). IGI Global. DOI: 10.4018/979-8-3693-5593-0.ch007

Roberts, A., & Lee, S. (2023). Enhancing academic collaboration through blockchain technology. *Journal of the Association for Information Science and Technology*, 74(3), 320–335.

Roberts, A., & Williams, S. (2024). Blockchain for research data management: Decentralized solutions. *Data Science Journal*, 22(1), 45–59.

Robinson, B., & Evans, L. (2024). Blockchain technology for library resource management. *Library Resources & Technical Services*, 68(2), 132–147.

Rogers, E. M. (2003). *Diffusion of innovations* (5th ed.). Free Press.

Rosenfeld, A. (1975). In Zadeh, L. A., Fu, K. S., & Shimura, M. (Eds.), *Fuzzy graphs in Fuzzy Sets and Their Applications* (pp. 77–95). Academic Press.

Rosenfeld, M., & Wisser, M. (2017). Blockchain: Transforming library records management. *The Library Quarterly*, 87(4), 326–345.

Safdar, M., Qutab, S., Ullah, F. S., Siddique, N., & Khan, M. A. (2023). A mapping review of literature on Blockchain usage by libraries: Challenges and opportunities. *Journal of Librarianship and Information Science*, 55(3), 848–858. DOI: 10.1177/09610006221090225

Sahin, R., & Yigider, M. (2016). A multi-criteria neutrosophic group decision making method based TOPSIS for supplier selection. *Applied Mathematics & Information Sciences*, 5(5), 1843–1852. DOI: 10.18576/amis/100525

Salah, K., Rehman, M. H. U., Nizamuddin, N., & Al-Fuqaha, A. (2019). Blockchain for AI: Review and open research challenges. *IEEE Access : Practical Innovations, Open Solutions*, 7, 10127–10149. DOI: 10.1109/ACCESS.2018.2890507

Sallaba, M., Siegel, D., & Becker, S. (2018). *IoT powered by Blockchain How Blockchains facilitate the application of digital twins in IoT*. Deloitte Issue.

Sameena, K. (2021). Fuzzy matroids from fuzzy vector spaces. *South East Asian Journal of Mathematics and Mathematical Sciences*, 17(03), 381–390.

Sanjay, K., & Hasan, F. (2020). Blockchain Networks for Research Institutions. *Journal of Research and Technology*, 9(4), 123–139.

Sanjay, N., & Nabihasan, . (2020). Blockchain technology and its application in libraries. *LIBRARY HERALD*, 58(4), 118–125. DOI: 10.5958/0976-2469.2020.00030.10

Savastano, M., & Consiglio, A. (2018). Blockchain in libraries: Potential benefits and risks. *Journal of Librarianship and Information Science*, 50(4), 333–341.

Scott, L., & Moore, A. (2023). Blockchain for enhancing academic collaborations. *New Library World*, 124(2), 180–195.

Senthilkumar, K. R. (2019). User pattern of Libraries by students of Government College in Tamilnadu: A study. Library Philosophy and Practice, 2019.

Senthilkumar, K. R. (2019). User pattern of Libraries by students of Government Colleges in Tamil nadu: A study. *Library Philosophy and Practice, 2019.*

Senthilkumar, K. R. (2019). User pattern of Libraries by students of Government Colleges in Tamil nadu: A study. *Library Philosophy and Practice.*

Senthilkumar, K. R. (2019). User pattern of Libraries by students of Government Colleges in Tamil Nadu: A study. *Library Philosophy and Practice.*

Senthilkumar, K. R. (2024a). AI-assisted library reconstruction. In AI-Assisted Library Reconstruction. DOI: 10.4018/979-8-3693-2782-1

Senthilkumar, K. R. (2024b). Revolutionizing Thrust Manufacturing. In *Advances in Computational Intelligence and Robotics* (pp. 80–93). https://doi.org/DOI: 10.4018/979-8-3693-2615-2.ch005

Senthilkumar, K. R. (2024b). Revolutionizing thrust manufacturing: The synergy of real-time data and AI advancements. In Using Real-Time Data and AI for Thrust Manufacturing (pp. 80–93). DOI: 10.4018/9798369326152.ch005

Senthilkumar, K. R. (2024b). Revolutionizing thrust manufacturing: The synergy of real-time data and AI advancements. In *Using Real-Time Data and AI for Thrust Manufacturing* (pp. 80–93). https://doi.org/. ch005DOI: 10.4018/9798369326152

Senthilkumar, K. R., & Jagajeevan, R. (2024). Improving library systems with AI: Applications, approaches, and bibliometric insights. In Improving Library Systems with AI: Applications, Approaches, and Bibliometric Insights. https://doi.org/DOI: 10.4018/9798369355930

Senthilkumar, K. R., & Maniiarasan, P. (2020). Comparison of Eresources with their usage statistics among Bharathidasan University & Madurai Kamaraj University. *Library Philosophy and Practice, 2020.* https: //www.scopus.com/inward/record .uri?eid=2-s2.0-85091524339&partnerID= 40&md5=6f7b662e3842db0d95af-80ba646fdd6e

Senthilkumar, K. R., & Maniiarasan, P. (2020). Comparison of E-resources with their usage statistics among Bharathidasan University & Madurai Kamaraj University. Library Philosophy and Practice, 2020. https://www.scopus.com/inward/record.uri?eid=2-s2.0-85091524339&partnerID=40&md5=6f7b662e3842db0d95af80ba646fdd6e

Senthilkumar, K. R. (2019). *User pattern of libraries by students of government colleges in Tamil Nadu: A study*. Library Philosophy and Practice.

Senthilkumar, K. R. (2019). *User pattern of Libraries by students of Government Colleges in Tamil nadu: A study*. Library Philosophy and Practice.

Senthilkumar, K. R., & Maniiarasan, P. (2020). *Comparison of e-resources with their usage statistics among Bharathidasan University and Madurai Kamaraj University*. Library Philosophy and Practice.

Senthilkumar, K. R., & Maniiarasan, P. (2020). *Comparison of E-resources with their usage statistics among Bharathidasan University and Madurai Kamaraj University*. Library Philosophy and Practice.

Shabna, O. K., & Sameena, K. (2019). Matroids from fuzzy graphs. *Malaya Journal of Matematik. Vol-s*, (1), 500–504.

Shabna, O. K., & Sameena, K. (2021). Graphic fuzzy matroids. *South East Asian Journal of Mathematics and Mathematical Sciences*, 17(01), 223–232.

Sharma, S., & Batth, R. S. (2020). Blockchain technology for higher education system: a mirror review. *2020 International Conference on Intelligent Engineering and Management (ICIEM)*, 348-353. DOI: 10.1109/ICIEM48762.2020.9160274

Sharples, M., & Domingue, J. (2016). The Blockchain and Kudos: A Distributed System for Educational Record, Reputation and Reward. In Verbert, K., Sharples, M., & Klobučar, T. (Eds.), *Adaptive and Adaptable Learning* (Vol. 9891, pp. 490–496). Springer International Publishing. DOI: 10.1007/978-3-319-45153-4_48

Singh, N., & Joshi, A. (2024). Blockchain technology for public welfare: Reducing the digital divide. *Government Information Quarterly*, 41(2), 102–119.

Sivaraj, P., Madhan, V., Mallika, V., & Senthilkumar, K. R. (2024). Enhancing library services through optimization algorithms and data analytics: Enhancing library services mathematical model. In AI-Assisted Library Reconstruction (pp. 290–306). DOI: 10.4018/979-8-3693-2782-1.ch016

Sladić, G., Milosavljević, B., Nikolić, S., Sladić, D., & Radulović, A. (2021). A blockchain solution for securing real property transactions: A case study for Serbia. *ISPRS International Journal of Geo-Information*, 10(1), 35. DOI: 10.3390/ijgi10010035

Smarandache, F. (1998). *Neutrosophy, neutrosophic probability, set, and logic*. American Research Press.

Smarandache, F. (1999). *Neutrosophy: Neutrosophic probability, set and logic*. American Research Press.

Smarandache, F. (2013). n-Valued refined neutrosophic logic and its applications to physics. *Progress in Physics*, 4, 143–146.

Smith, E. (n.d.). Blockchain Technology for Digital Rights Management. https://www.researchgate.net/publication/123456789/blockchain_drm

Smith, A., & Zhao, L. (2023). Decentralized access to information: Challenges and opportunities. *Journal of Information Science*, 49(3), 279–294.

Smith, C., Coward, C., Hess, M. R., Hofman, D. L., Kim, B., & Norman, A. (2019). Block-chain reaction. *American Libraries*, 50(3/4), 26–33.

Smith, J. (2023). Blockchain Applications in Academic Libraries. *Journal of Academic Librarianship*, 42(3), 45–60.

Smith, J., & Brown, L. (2023). Blockchain in academic libraries: Enhancing resource sharing and access. *Library Hi Tech*, 41(2), 205–220.

Smith, J., & Nguyen, L. (2023). Blockchain for academic libraries: A review of applications and challenges. *The Electronic Library*, 41(2), 255–270.

Steen, L. A., & Seebach, J. A. (1995). *Counterexamples in topology*. Dover Publications.

Stewart, J., & Martin, P. (2023). Blockchain-based systems for academic library consortia. *Information and Learning Science*, 124(4), 211–226.

Suman, A., & Patel, M. (2021). An Introduction to Blockchain Technology and Its Application in Libraries. Library Philosophy and Practice (e-Journal).

Suman, A. K., & Patel, M. (2021). An introduction to blockchain technology and its application in libraries. *Available atSSRN* 4019394. DOI: 10.2139/ssrn.4019394

Sundarakani, B., Ajaykumar, A., & Gunasekaran, A. (2021). Big data driven supply chain design and applications for blockchain: An action research using case study approach. *Omega*, 102, 102452. DOI: 10.1016/j.omega.2021.102452

Sun, Q., Ho, S. T., & Li, S. Y. R. (2008, July). On network matroids and linear network codes. In 2008 *IEEE International Symposium on Information Theory* (pp. 1833-1837). IEEE.

Swan, M. (2015). *Blockchain: Blueprint for a new economy*. O'Reilly Media, Inc.

Swan, M. (2015). *Blockchain: Blueprint for a New Economy*. O'Reilly Media, Inc.

Taj, A., Ahmed, M. G., Ali, K. S., & Senthilkumar, K. R. (2024). Revolutionizing medical libraries: The vital role of AI in enhancing discovery, access, and library services for healthcare professionals. In *Improving Library Systems with AI* (pp. 24–38). Applications, Approaches, and Bibliometric Insights. DOI: 10.4018/979-8-3693-5593-0.ch002

Tanwar, S., Ribadiya, D., Bhattacharya, P., Nair, A. R., Kumar, N., & Jo, M. (2023). Fusion of blockchain and IoT in scientific publishing: Taxonomy, tools, and future directions. *Future Generation Computer Systems*, 142, 248–275. DOI: 10.1016/j.future.2022.12.036

Tapscott, D., & Tapscott, A. (2016). *Blockchain revolution: How the technology behind bitcoin is changing money, business, and the world*. Penguin Random House.

Taylor, A., & Wilson, D. (2023). Enhancing academic collaboration through blockchain technology. *College & Research Libraries*, 84(2), 175–190.

Tella, A., Amuda, H. O., & Ajani, Y. A. (2022). Relevance of blockchain technology and the management of libraries and archives in the 4IR. *Digital Library Perspectives*, 38(4), 460–475. DOI: 10.1108/DLP-08-2021-0065

Thamrin, T., Arifin, Y., & Hendric, S. W. H. L. (2024, February). Trends In Blockchain Applications: Current and Future Perspectives. In *2024 2nd International Conference on Software Engineering and Information Technology (ICoSEIT)* (pp. 187-191). IEEE.

Thivagar, M. L., & Richard, C. (2023). On nano forms of weakly open sets. *International Journal of Mathematics and Statistics Invention*, 1, 31–37.

Thomas, A., & Sundar Rajan, B. (2020). Generalized index coding problem and discrete polymatroids. *Entropy (Basel, Switzerland)*, 22(6), 646. DOI: 10.3390/e22060646 PMID: 33286418

Thomas, G., & Harris, J. (2023). Decentralized learning management systems using blockchain. *Computers & Education*, 183, 104497.

Thompson, E., & White, K. (2023). Blockchain for library management systems: A practical guide. *Library Management*, 45(3/4), 225–240.

Thompson, K., & Zhang, Q. (2023). Blockchain for supporting students in higher education: Current trends and future directions. *Educational Technology Research and Development*, 71(2), 423–440.

Treiblmaier, H., & Sillaber, C. (2020). A case study of blockchain-induced digital transformation in the public sector. In *Blockchain and Distributed Ledger Technology Use Cases* (pp. 227–244). Applications and Lessons Learned. DOI: 10.1007/978-3-030-44337-5_11

Trivedi, S., Mehta, K., & Sharma, R. (2021). Systematic literature review on application of blockchain technology in e-finance and financial services. *Journal of Technology Management & Innovation*, 16(3), 89–102. DOI: 10.4067/S0718-27242021000300089

Tutte, W. T. (1959). Matroids and graphs. *Transactions of the American Mathematical Society*, 90(3), 527–552. DOI: 10.1090/S0002-9947-1959-0101527-3

Uddin, S., & Ahmed, M. (2023). Blockchain in academic research: Enhancing transparency and trust. *Information & Management*, 60(3), 103164.

Underwood, S. (2016). Blockchain beyond bitcoin. *Communications of the ACM*, 59(11), 15–17. https://doi.org/trustworthi

Underwood, S. (2016). Blockchain Beyond Bitcoin. *Communications of the ACM*, 59(11), 15–17. DOI: 10.1145/2994581

Varadarajan, M. N. (2024). Educational program for AI literacy. In *Improving Library Systems with AI: Applications, Approaches, and Bibliometric Insights* (pp. 134–154). IGI Global. DOI: 10.4018/979-8-3693-5593-0.ch010

Varadarajan, M. N., Viji, C., Rajkumar, N., & Mohanraj, A. (2024). Integration of AI and IoT for smart home automation. *SSRG International Journal of Electronics and Communication Engineering*, 11(5), 37–43. DOI: 10.14445/23488549/IJECE-V11I5P104

Vasquez, M., & Sanchez, L. (2023). Blockchain in academic peer review: Transforming the publishing process. *Journal of Academic Librarianship*, 49(1), 102282.

Verhoeven, P., Sinn, F., & Herden, T. T. (2018). Examples from blockchain implementations in logistics and supply chain management: Exploring the mindful use of a new technology. *Logistics (Basel)*, 2(3), 20. DOI: 10.3390/logistics2030020

Vijayalatha, C. (2023, May). Enhanced and Changing Role of Library and Information Professionals in Digital Era. In *Proceedings of National Conference on Exploring the Past, Present, and Future of Library and Information Science* (p. 130).

Vyas, S., Shukla, V. K., Gupta, S., & Prasad, A. (Eds.). (2022). *Blockchain technology: exploring opportunities, challenges, and applications*. DOI: 10.1201/9781003138082

Wang, L., Chen, C.-C., & Xie, X. (2018). Environmental Monitoring System Based on IoT in Library Management. *Journal of Environmental Management*, 217, 720–730.

Wang, S., Wang, J., & Wang, X. (2018). *Blockchain Powered Parallel Healthcare Systems Based on the ACP Approach2329-924Xc*. IEEE.

Wang, X., & Chen, Y. (2024). Blockchain for academic credentialing: Enhancing trust and accessibility. *Educational Technology Research and Development*, 72(1), 23–41.

Ward, H., & Turner, J. (2024). Blockchain for academic libraries: Supporting researchers and students. *Information and Learning Science*, 125(1), 60–75.

West, D. B. (2001). *Introduction to graph theory* (Vol. 2). Prentice Hall.

White, R., & Singh, M. (2024). The impact of blockchain on decentralized applications. *IEEE Transactions on Systems, Man, and Cybernetics. Systems*, 54(1), 56–68.

White, R., & Taylor, M. (2023). Blockchain for academic collaboration: A systematic review of applications and benefits. *The Journal of Documentation*, 79(2), 233–250.

Whitney, H. (1987). On the abstract properties of linear dependence. *Classic Papers in Combinatorics*, 63-87.

Wijesekara, P. A. D. S. N., & Gunawardena, S. (2023). A Review of blockchain technology in knowledge-defined networking, its application, benefits, and challenges. *Network (Bristol, England)*, 3(3), 343–421.

Williams, A. (2020). Blockchain in Scholarly Publishing: Potential and Challenges. *Publishing Research Quarterly*, 36(2), 131–147.

Williams, S., & Lee, C. (2023). Future libraries' blockchain opportunities and challenges: A systematic literature review and research agenda. *Digital Library Perspectives*, 39(3), 293–310. DOI: 10.1108/DLP-08-2022-0065

Wood, G. (2014). Ethereum: A secure decentralised generalised transaction ledger. Retrieved from https://ethereum.org/en/whitepaper

Wright, T. (2020). Enhancing Metadata Systems with Blockchain. *Information Technology and Libraries*, 39(3), 23–35.

Xu, B., Li, Y., & Yu, X. (2020). A Scientometric Analysis of Malware Detection Research Based on CiteSpace. In Chen, X., Yan, H., Yan, Q., & Zhang, X. (Eds.), *Machine Learning for Cyber Security* (Vol. 12486, pp. 100–110). Springer International Publishing. DOI: 10.1007/978-3-030-62223-7_9

Yaga, D., Mell, P., Roby, N., & Scarfone, K. (2018). *Blockchain technology overview*. National Institute of Standards and Technology. DOI: 10.6028/NIST.IR.8202

Yli-Huumo, J., Ko, D., Choi, S., Park, S., & Smolander, K. (2016). Where Is Current Research on Blockchain Technology? — A Systematic Review. *PLOS ONE*, 11(10), 1–27. https://doi.org/. pone.0163477DOI: 10.1371/journal

Youssef, H., Moumen, A., & Gretete, D. (2022). Fuzzy Logic for Academic Orientation and Its Impact on Success: Content Analysis. *InProceedings of the 2nd International Conference on Big Data, Modelling and Machine Learning-BML* (pp. 546-551).

Yuan, X., & Zhou, S. (2022, August). Research on library intelligent service based on blockchain technology. In *International Conference on Computer Science and Education* (pp. 267-277). Singapore: Springer Nature Singapore.

Yue, X., Wang, H., Jin, D., Li, M., & Jiang, W. (2016). Healthcare data gateways: Found healthcare intelligence on blockchain with novel privacy risk control. *Journal of Medical Systems*, 40(10), 218. DOI: 10.1007/s10916-016-0574-6 PMID: 27565509

Zadeh, L. A. (1965). Fuzzy sets. *Information and Control*, 8(3), 338–353. DOI: 10.1016/S0019-9958(65)90241-X

Zhang, Y., & Wen, J. (2015). An IoT electric business model based on the protocol of bitcoin. *2015 18th International Conference on Intelligence in Next Generation Networks*, 184–191. DOI: 10.1109/ICIN.2015.7073830

Zhang, H., & Wang, F. (2024). Integrating blockchain into library services: A case study. *The Electronic Library*, 42(1), 55–70.

Zhang, L., & Xu, M. (2023). Blockchain and privacy-preserving mechanisms: A systematic review. *ACM Computing Surveys*, 56(3), 45–68.

Zhang, Y., & Wang, X. (2023). Decentralized data management: A blockchain-based approach. *Journal of Information Technology*, 38(2), 145–159.

Zhao, H., & Sun, Y. (2024). Blockchain in education: Supporting students and researchers with innovative solutions. *IEEE Transactions on Learning Technologies*, 17(1), 34–50.

Zhao, X., & Chen, Q. (2024). Blockchain-enabled decentralized platforms: Applications and challenges. *IEEE Internet of Things Journal*, 11(2), 175–188.

Zhao, Y., Wang, S., & Li, H. (2021). Evaluating blockchain platforms based on security features and compliance using TOPSIS. *Journal of Network and Computer Applications*, 171, 102896.

Zheng, Z., Xie, S., Dai, H. N., Chen, X., & Wang, H. (2018). An overview of blockchain technology: Architecture, consensus, and future trends. *IEEE International Congress on Big Data (BigData Congress)*, 557-564.

Zheng, Z., Xie, S., Dai, H., Chen, X., & Wang, H. (2017). An Overview of Blockchain Technology: Architecture, Consensus, and Future Trends. *2017 IEEE International Congress on Big Data (BigData Congress)*, 557–564. DOI: 10.1109/BigDataCongress.2017.85

Zou, Y., Meng, T., Zhang, P., Zhang, W., & Li, H. (2020). Focus on blockchain: A comprehensive survey on academic and application. *IEEE Access : Practical Innovations, Open Solutions*, 8, 187182–187201. DOI: 10.1109/ACCESS.2020.3030491

Zulqarnain, R. M., Saeed, M., Dayan, F., & Ahmad, B. (2020). Application of TOPSIS method for decision making. *International Journal of Scientific Research in Mathematical and Statistical Sciences*, 7, 76–81.

Zyskind, G., Nathan, O., & Pentland, A. (2015). Decentralizing Privacy: Using Blockchain to Protect Personal Data. *2015 IEEE Security and Privacy Workshops*, 180–184.

About the Contributors

K. R. Senthilkumar is working as a Librarian in Sri Krishna Arts and Science College, Coimbatore. His most notable contributions to the field of E- Library and the Development of Library Web page. His research interests span both bibliometrics and Web 2.0. Much of his work has been on improving the understanding, design, and performance of Information systems, mainly through the application of E- Library, Survey, and Compare evaluation. In the Information Science arena, he has worked on TN Public Online Library . He has explored the presence and implications of self-similarity and heavy-tailed distributions in Open Source Journals. He has also investigated the implications of Web workloads for the design of scalable and no cost-effective Web Pages. In addition, he has made numerous contributions to research papers like Journals, Conference and Book Chapters.

* * *

Preethi D. is currently working as Assistant Professor, School of Computer Science and Information technology, JAIN (Deemed-to-be University), Bengaluru. She completed B.Sc. degree from Achariya Arts and Science College, Pondicherry and M.Sc. degree from Pondicherry University, Pondicherry and Ph.D. from Pondicherry Engineering College, Pondicherry. Her research interest Image Processing, Optimization Techniques, Medical Imaging.

Sakshi Darware is a dedicated MBA student with a strong focus on management studies. She has authored and published several research papers that delve into various aspects of management, showcasing her analytical skills and deep understanding of the subject. Sakshi is passionate about exploring innovative management strategies and is committed to contributing valuable insights to the academic and professional community.

Jagannathan J. serves as an Assistant Professor in the Department of Software Systems and Engineering within the School of Computer Science Engineering and Information Systems at Vellore Institute of Technology (Deemed to be University), located in Vellore District, Tamil Nadu. He earned his Ph.D. in Information and Communication Technology from the Centre for Information Technology and Engineering at Manonmaniam Sundaranar University, Tirunelveli. With over a decade of experience in teaching and research, he has made significant contributions to the academic community. He has an extensive portfolio of publications in both national and international journals and conferences. Additionally, he has secured multiple patents in the fields of Artificial Intelligence (AI) and the Internet of Things (IoT). His research expertise encompasses Machine Learning and Deep Learning, Image Processing, and IoT. He has substantial experience in handling and researching satellite, agricultural, and medical data. His professional affiliations include memberships in various international societies.

Rishikaysh Kaakandikar boasts an exceptional academic journey, spanning over 12 years of dedicated teaching and a year of valuable industrial experience, and currently holds the esteemed position of Associate Professor at SaiBalaji Education Society's SaiBalaji International Institute of Management Sciences in Pune. His scholarly contributions shine brightly, encompassing a remarkable portfolio of over 40 research papers in prestigious journals. A sought-after intellectual resource, He has contributed substantially to academia through guest lectures, seminars, workshops, and conferences at esteemed institutions across India. His insights have enriched the academic community and stimulated engaging discussions on various facets of his field. He is a prominent finance columnist for leading newspapers in Maharashtra, including Sakal, Lokmat, Punyannagari, and Prabhat.

Mir Mahmood Hussain holds a Ph.D. in Computer Science from Baba Ghulam Shah Badshah University, Jammu and Kashmir. He also earned an M.Phil. in Computer Science from Bharathidasan University, Tamil Nadu. His academic journey includes a Master's in Computer Applications from Baba Ghulam Shah Badshah University, Jammu and Kashmir, as well as a Bachelor's in Computer Applications from University of Kashmir, Jammu and Kashmir. His primary research interests encompass Internet of Things, Machine Learning, Edge Computing, and Healthcare Data Analytics.

Karthikeyan N. received B. Tech in Information and Technology in 2010 from Anna University, Chennai, India. He received M.E. in Computer Science and Engineering in 2015, University College of Engineering, BIT campus, Anna University, India. He received Ph.D.in Information and communication Engineering in 2022, Anna University, Chennai. He is doing his research work in various fields of Deep Learning and Image Processing like Image Compression, Image Security-Encryption and Decryption, Features Extraction, Image Retrieval and Image Enhancement, video processing and computer vision.

Balusamy Nachiappan is an experienced IT professional with a strong background in object-oriented Software Development, Design, and Architecture. Certified as a Salesforce System Architect and Salesforce Application Architect. Specialized in Banking, including Investment Banking and Core Banking, with international exposure. Extensive experience in the Travel Domain encompassing Airlines, Ship & Cargo industries, along with proficiency in Supply Chain Management and Real Estate. A solid track record of over a decade in Product Development across various sectors. Proficient in Waterfall, V Model, and Agile-Scrum methodologies. Holds extensive onsite exposure in the US, Japan, the UK, and Qatar.

Subalakshmi P. serves as an Authorised Person for Equity derivatives in Acumen India Ltd, Chennai. She earned her Masters in Business Administration in Manonmaniam Sundaranar University, Tirunelveli. She have more than ten years of experience in Share market. She was a NISM SEBI certified trader for equity derivatives. Her research expertise encompasses Artificial Intelligence and Machine Learning in Stock Market. She also have an expertise in Human resource management and Marketing.

N. Rajkumar is an Associate Professor in the Department of Computer Science and Engineering. He earned his Ph.D. in Information and Communication Engineering from Anna University, Chennai. With a rich experience of 15 years in the realm of technical education, he has made substantial contributions to the academic arena. His research background is highly commendable, encompassing over 20 publications in esteemed international journals, coupled with numerous presentations at both international and national conferences. Moreover, he actively engages as a member of prestigious professional societies such as ISTE, IAENG, and CSTA. His primary areas of interest comprise Software Engineering, Computer Networks, Internet of Things, and Machine Learning.

Delma Thaliyan is a distinguished faculty member at CHRIST UNIVERSITY, Bangalore, with a robust professional portfolio that spans over two decades in academia and industry. Her profound commitment to the holistic development of students and expertise in management education is complemented by her extensive research in Diversity and Inclusion, as well as Happiness and Wellbeing. Dr. Thaliyan's scholarly contributions have been widely published in prestigious national and international journals. As a corporate trainer specializing in performance management, and also SHRM certified POSH trainer, she brings a wealth of practical knowledge and exceptional delivery skills to her engagements. She also serves as an editorial board member of management journals and earned her doctoral degree in management in 2020 and has the distinguished honor of having two patents filed and granted to her name.

C. Viji holds the position of Associate Professor in the Department of Computer Science and Engineering. She accomplished her Ph.D. in Information and Communication Engineering from Anna University, Chennai. Dr. C. Viji's expertise in the realm of technical education has resulted in noteworthy contributions to the academic sphere. Her research background is indeed impressive, encompassing over 10 publications in esteemed international journals, along with numerous presentations at both international and national conferences. Furthermore, she actively engages as a member of renowned professional societies such as IAENG and CSTA.

Index

A

B

C

D

F

G

H

M

N

O

P

R

S

T

www.ingramcontent.com/pod-product-compliance
Lightning Source LLC
LaVergne TN
LVHW080347011026
849161LV00009B/2214